LIVING IN THE BLESSING

A 365-DAY DEVOTIONAL

CHARLES "CHIC" SHAVER

THE FOUNDRY
PUBLISHING®

Interior designer: Sharon Page

Library of Congress Cataloging-in-Publication Data
Names: Shaver, Charles, 1935- author.
Title: Living in the blessing : a 365-day devotional / Charles "Chic" Shaver.
Description: Kansas, MO : The Foundry Publishing, 2022. | Includes bibliographical references and index. | Summary:
    "Living in the Blessing is a 365-day devotional book inspired by the faith journey of Dr. Charles "Chic" Shaver, who
    has traveled the world winning people to Jesus Christ. The devotions are ordered to move readers from the basic
    tenets of the Christian life to the reflections of a mature and seasoned faith"— Provided by publisher.
Identifiers: LCCN 2021038156 (print) | LCCN 2021038157 (ebook) | ISBN 9780834140844 |
    ISBN 9780834140851 (ebook)
Subjects: LCSH: Devotional calendars.
Classification: LCC BV4811 .S3763 2022 (print) | LCC BV4811 (ebook) | DDC 242/.2—dc23
LC record available at https://lccn.loc.gov/2021038156
LC ebook record available at https://lccn.loc.gov/2021038157

The internet addresses, email addresses, and phone numbers in this book are accurate at the time of publication. They are provided as a resource. The Foundry Publishing does not endorse them or vouch for their content or permanence.

10 9 8 7 6 5 4 3 2 1

To Nancy

You have been, besides Jesus Christ, the most important person and greatest impact in my life. Through years of pastoring, evangelistic ministry, teaching, and writing, you have been my encourager, advisor, supporter, and pray-er. Your investment in our three children is powerful. Ever since you sang and glowed as a twenty-year-old nursing student in that St. Joseph, Missouri, revival, my heart has been smitten. Still is. What adventures we have had following Jesus together across the country and around the world. You have been part of all the experiences and truths in this book. Thank you for being my sweetheart!

To our dear friends *who have spanned our lifetime and showered us with so much love.*

Contents

Acknowledgment

Thank you to Joy Parke—woman of God, dear Christian friend, former managing director of the Chic Shaver Center for Evangelism, and the typist and stylist of the first draft of these devotionals. Joy, I can never thank you enough for your careful reproduction, grammar and style corrections, loving work, dedication, and more. You have a part in all the blessings that flow from this book.

About the Author

Charles F. Shaver, Jr., was born in Manchester, Connecticut, on January 5, 1935. To distinguish from his dad's name, he was given the nickname "Chic" from an early age. He was raised in a comfortable, middle-class home with his sister, Joanne. His father was a salesman for Yale and Towne Hardware and, later in life, owned and operated a resort motel on Treasure Island, Florida. Chic's mother, Vera, was a homemaker.

Chic attended Dartmouth College with a pre-law emphasis and a heavy interest in politics. Through the witness of his friend Peter Gunas, Chic experienced a dramatic conversion to Christ on November 20, 1955. Sensing a need for a more victorious Christian life, on September 2, 1956, he was sanctified entirely by the infilling of the Holy Spirit. By the time of his graduation from Dartmouth, he sensed a call to ministry.

While Chic was preaching at a youth revival in St. Joseph, Missouri, a young lady in training to become a nurse was called upon to sing a special. When Nancy Doro sang, Chic said "she glowed." They were married on June 1, 1959. Their children are Rachel, Paul, and Miriam.

Chic has a BA from Dartmouth College, an MDiv from Nazarene Theological Seminary, and a DMin from Fuller Seminary. His first pastorate was in a remodeled horse shed. In 1967, he began in ministry as a full-time itinerant evangelist; in 1969, he preached on forty-six Sundays during revival services. In 1970, he was called to teach evangelism at Nazarene Theological Seminary. He continued to serve in that position, and was eventually appointed to be the Frank and Gladys Cooper Professor of Evangelism. He retired in 2000. From 1974 to 2003, he also served as minister of outreach at First Church of the Nazarene in Kansas City, Missouri. He continued his revival and evangelistic ministry through 2020, leading close to nine hundred revivals. He has preached and/or taught evangelism in South Africa, the Philippines, Korea, Russia, and at Billy Graham's headquarters.

His concern for new converts led him to write *Basic Bible Studies for New and Growing Christians*, which has surpassed more than 750,000 copies sold in English and has been published in more than fifty-five languages. His other writings are used across a number of denominations and include *Witnessing without Fear, Living in the Power of the Spirit, The Bible Speaks to Me about My*

Witness, and *Basic Bible Studies for the Spirit-Filled and Sanctified Life.* Since 1992, he has served as executive director of the Chic Shaver Center for Evangelism.

In 2019, at the Church of the Nazarene's M19 Conference, Dr. Shaver and Nancy were presented the Lifetime Achievement Award. As a husband, father, grandfather, preacher, teacher, author, pastor, and evangelist, Chic's heart glows with the presence of God and a concern for people everywhere to know Christ personally.

Chic and Nancy on their fifty-fifth wedding anniversary

Also by the Author

I have had a long, encouraging, and warm relationship with The Foundry Publishing. Listed are my other books, CDs, and DVDs that this fine company has published over the years. To order, you may contact The Foundry at:

The Foundry Publishing
PO Box 419527
Kansas City, MO 64141-6527

1-800-877-0700

orders@thefoundrypublishing.com

978-0-8341-2502-5	*Who Is This Jesus? The Gospel of John Chapters 1–15* (2009)
978-0-8341-2503-2	*The Mission of Jesus: The Gospel of John Chapters 12–21* (2009)
978-0-8341-0411-2	*Conserve the Converts: A Manual to Help Conserve the Results of Personal and Mass Evangelism* (1976)
S-250	*Living in the Power of the Spirit* (1986)
S-250LG	*Living in the Power of the Spirit, Leader Guide w/ DVD* (2004)
CDR-1	*People, Sex, & God: A Biblical Approach (CD)* (2007)
CDR-2	*A New Creation: My Personal Testimony (CD)* (2006)
DVD-1701	*A Personal Evangelism Call (DVD)*
VE-80	*Basic Bible Studies for New and Growing Christians* (1972)
VE-91	*Basic Bible Studies for the Spirit-filled and Sanctified Life* (1991)
978-0-8341-2058-7	*Basic Bible Studies in Everyday English* (2003)
U-4040	*Witnessing Without Fear* (2001)
CDR-1695	*Sermons on the Spirit-filled and Sanctified Life* (2008)
CDR-1595	*Lord, Teach Us to Pray (CD)* (2008)

Introduction

As I was growing up, though I was raised in a Protestant church, God was never real to me. While I was a pre-law student at Dartmouth College, I crossed paths with Peter, a student body leader who had dropped out of school because of alcohol but had now returned. Right after a chapel service, Peter shook my hand and said, "Chic, I'm different than I used to be because I've found the Lord."

Peter's words impacted me. I had never heard anyone talk that way—God was real to him. A few weeks later, Peter came to my dormitory and shared in detail how he had met and received Christ. He invited me to his church. In a Sunday night service on November 20, 1955, Christ entered my heart and life. I knew I was forgiven, and God became real to me and present in me. I knew exceeding joy.

Over the next few months, I grew spiritually. The Bible came to life, and I experienced a close connection to God in prayer. I regularly shared my faith with others, never missed a church service, and experienced profound changes in my daily life.

About sixth months into this new life, I began to notice ugly tempers arising from the basement of my soul—resentment, jealousy, pride, a critical spirit, and a lack of spiritual power in my attempts to influence others. My willpower was not enough to resolve these problems.

In the midst of my growing concern, I began to hear and read promises of a deeper spiritual life—a life of victory. This deeper life was referred to by terms such as: "sanctified through and through;" "filled with the Holy Spirit;" "the rest of faith;" "to be crucified with Christ;" "holiness;" "life more abundantly." I began to seek God for his answer.

On September 2, 1956, God dramatically answered my prayers for this new life with a fiery cleansing of my heart. I died to the old Chic Shaver, and God's Holy Spirit filled and sanctified me through and through. Immediately, my whole Christian life moved to a new, higher level.

I had many lessons to learn. Beyond the moment of being filled with the Spirit, there lay a whole life of living and walking in the Spirit. Galatians 5:25

became my key verse: "Since we live by the Spirit, let us keep in step with the Spirit."

By this time, I had received a call to ministry, and I began to preach and teach this life to others. Over time, I discovered that many Christians were confused or uncertain about this deeper life. As I came to the latter part of my life and ministry, a strong conviction grew within me to write a daily devotional book about this life of holiness in language that would be understandable to ordinary people. I've included several reflections written by my daughters, Rachel and Miriam, and my wife, Nancy.

You now hold that book in your hands. A scripture and a truth flows from each day. I have tried to show how these truths work in everyday life. In doing so, I have drawn from other books and writers; testimonies of Christians from the past; interviews with present-day Christians; and my own life experience.

You may use this devotional book along with your personal Bible reading; you may even keep a journal of your thoughts, insights, and prayers as you go. You may use this book according to day-by-day calendar dates. It may be that you are a newer Christian and have started your life with Christ in the middle of the calendar year. You will note an alternate system, which is simply a number system of 1 to 365. You can start at 1 even in the middle of the year. Perhaps you have been in a Bible study with a friend in your new faith. Some of you may have been going through *Basic Bible Studies for New and Growing Christians*. These devotionals will correspond with and support what you have been learning.

So let us adventure together, "that you may be filled to the measure of all the fullness of God" (Ephesians 3:19). Don't be scared off by such a tall order; the next verses from Ephesians 3 say, "Now to him who is able to do immeasurably more than all we ask or imagine, according to his power that is at work within us, to him be glory" (vv. 20–21).

Between ages thirty-three and fifty-eight, my son, Paul, had five major cancer surgeries, the most severe of which involved the removal of his voice box. Still, he is remarkably joyous and happy in life. Many people have asked him, "How come?"

With his new, raspy voice Paul replies, "I was living under the blessing before cancer, I was under the blessing after they removed my voice box, and I'm living under the blessing today." For this reason, when I was concerned about what to call this book, Paul suggested *Living in the Blessing*.

Many early Holiness preachers called sanctification "the second blessing." The sanctification song "I Surrender All" includes the following verse:

All to Jesus I surrender,
Lord, I give myself to thee;
Fill me with thy love and power,
Let thy blessing fall on me.[1]

Some believe that Paul's words in Romans 15:29—"I know that when I come to you, I will come in the full measure of the blessing of Christ"—describe his own sanctified, Spirit-filled life. Whatever the case, we are eager to see everyone experience Spirit-filled entire sanctification. When we "keep in step with the Spirit" (Galatians 5:25) on a daily basis, we can truly say, "We are living in the blessing!"

These devotionals are filled with the stories of real people. In some cases I have changed names to protect privacy, but the stories are true.

This book includes a number of devotionals written by others; in each of these cases, the author's name is listed. Additionally, for years, my wife, Nancy, and I have written devotionals for various publications. With permission, we have included a number of those devotionals within this book.

---

1. Judson W. Van DeVenter (words), Winfield S. Weeden (music), 1896, "I Surrender All," *Sing to the Lord: Hymnal* (Kansas City, MO: Lillenas Publishing Company, 1993), #486.

Into Your Future

The apostle Paul took his ministry deeply to heart. He said, "[God] gave me the priestly duty of proclaiming the gospel of God, so that the Gentiles might become an offering acceptable to God, *sanctified by the Holy Spirit*" (Romans 15:16). In the same chapter he said, "I know that when I come to you, I will come in the *full measure of the blessing of Christ*" (v. 29).

In the Psalms, David asks, "Who may ascend the mountain of the LORD? Who may stand in his holy place? The one who has clean hands and a pure heart, who does not trust in an idol or swear by a false god. They will *receive blessing from the LORD* and vindication from God their Savior" (Psalm 24:3–5).

To the Ephesians, Paul rejoiced, "Praise be to the God and Father of our Lord Jesus Christ, who has blessed us in the heavenly realms with *every spiritual blessing in Christ*" (1:3).

To each one who reads this book, may you live in its lessons and continue *living in the blessing*.

He Is Greater Than . . .

You, dear children, are from God and have overcome them,
because the one who is in you is greater than the one who is in the world.
1 John 4:4

An amazing thing happened to you when you came to Jesus Christ. Revelation 3:20 contains these words: "Here I am! I stand at the door and knock. If anyone hears my voice and opens the door, I will come in and eat with that person, and they with me."

We understand that when a person opens the door of their heart to Christ, Christ enters. He says he will eat with that person, which is his way of expressing deep fellowship. Because of these truths, you may honestly say, "Christ lives in me."

Prior to today's scripture in 1 John 4:4, John warns his readers about evil spirits and false prophets in the world. Then John assures all true Christians that the *Christ living in them is greater* than any evil force in the world. By his presence and power, we may be victorious over any evil.

Think of all the benefits that are now part of your life because Christ lives in you:

- All your sins have been *forgiven.* "I am writing to you, dear children, because your sins have been forgiven on account of his name" (1 John 2:12).
- You are now *alive* spiritually. "But because of his great love for us, God, who is rich in mercy, made us alive with Christ even when we were dead in transgressions—it is by grace you have been saved" (Ephesians 2:4–5).
- We can now be *comforted* in every hard place in life. "Praise be to the God and Father of our Lord Jesus Christ, the Father of compassion and the God of all comfort, who comforts us in all our troubles, so that we can comfort those in any trouble with the comfort we ourselves receive from God" (2 Corinthians 1:3–4).
- You are now under God's *keeping* power. "He will also keep you firm to the end, so that you will be blameless on the day of our Lord Jesus Christ" (1 Corinthians 1:8).
- God will carry you and your new life to *completion.* "Being confident of this, that he who began a good work in you will carry it on to completion until the day of Christ Jesus" (Philippians 1:6).

Peter's life was filled with alcohol and immorality. In today's terms, he was spending a thousand dollars a month on alcohol. It got so bad that he resigned his position on the college varsity soccer team and resigned as the president of his fraternity. He dropped out of college. He began living up and down the east coast of the United States. He slept in the back of his car and got in trouble with the police in six different states. His life became a disaster.

Peter crossed paths with some Christians whose lives were entirely different from his. One of these Christians told him that Jesus was the difference. Peter thought, *Maybe that's what I need.*

He began searching. One Sunday, as he listened to a sermon, his sins flashed in front of him, and God became real to him. Peter left the church as soon as possible and drove to a quiet spot in the country. He got on his knees and confessed his sins. Later, when describing that moment, Peter would say, "God changed me." He admitted it sounded strange but said, "I crawled up on the car seats and went to sleep—it was the first peaceful sleep I'd had since I was four years old." Peter was delivered.

Peter grew spiritually and began telling others what Jesus had done. He was soon readmitted to the college he had left. In the years that followed, he lived a happy, joyous Christian life and became a man of prayer and a teacher of the Bible.

Peter was the man who brought me to Christ.

All the benefits of being a Christian listed above became true in Peter's life; they can be true in your life too. Christ in you is greater than any evil force in the world. You can overcome.

New Year, New Start

Therefore, if anyone is in Christ, the new creation has come:
The old has gone, the new is here!
2 Corinthians 5:17

Every January, many people make New Year's resolutions. These resolutions are the expressed hope of replacing old, negative things with new, positive things. Often, people are unsuccessful in keeping their pledges.

God's way of making a new start is helping you have a personal relationship with Christ. Being "in Christ," as the verse puts it, results in a new way, a new life, a new creation.

Spontaneous testimonies after a week of revival services at a Michigan church reveal just how new Christ can make a person. Here are a few of those testimonies:

- A middle-aged mother found new light-heartedness: "I got instant heart surgery—God removed my bitterness."
- An usher received: cleansing from "a critical spirit."
- Another mother said: "The Spirit gave me peace and power."
- A high school student expressed thanks to be "back on track."
- A grandmother said: "It's not about me; it's about Jesus."
- A school counselor testified: "One word comes to mind—surrender."
- A skilled machinist was struck by Scripture's promise of "no condemnation!"
- Another congregant recalled the ongoing source of spiritual power: "I forgot how simple we really are . . . and how much I needed to get back into his presence."

What new thing has Christ done for you in the past year? What new thing will you ask Christ to do for you this year?

Don't Stop God's Chosen

Joshua son of Nun, who had been Moses' aide since youth,
spoke up and said, "Moses, my lord, stop them!" But Moses replied,
"Are you jealous for my sake? I wish that all the LORD's people were
prophets and that the LORD would put his Spirit on them!"
Numbers 11:28–29

Is it not good that our heavenly Father is in control? I say let us rejoice and give thanks wherever, whenever, and however God chooses to work. Let us give, encourage, support, cheer, and be there for one another as we go about our Father's business.

Let no one rain on our parades. Let no one say our dreams can't come true. Let no one drop their negativity onto our visions from God, because he chooses the most unlikely, he uses those who are available, he selects the cream of the crop, he convicts those I don't think are ready, he calls those who are already too busy. He convinces me that "I can" in his strength, he scares me out of my comfort zone because he cares so much, and he always gives me another chance.

So, let's keep on when we're struggling. Let's keep on when we can't see clearly. Let's keep on when doubts arise and fears dismay. Let's keep on until we get home—because we have been chosen.

Nancy Shaver[2]

Is There a God?

*The heavens declare the glory of God; the skies proclaim
the work of his hands. Day after day they pour forth speech;
night after night they reveal knowledge.*
Psalm 19:1–2

An atheist says there is no God. An agnostic doubts and says, "I'm not sure if there is a God." I was agnostic as a young adult, though I had been raised with a church background.

In college, I was troubled. I thought, *If there is a God, I'd better get this settled.* I felt I was a very logical person and determined to think it through. I eventually established six basic ideas:

1. I possess a highly accurate and perfectly functioning watch. As it is hard to believe there is a watch without a watchmaker behind it, so it is hard to believe there is a perfectly functioning world without a world-maker behind it.
2. If this whole world could be destroyed by atomic power in one year (as my chemistry professor taught), then ultimately life doesn't make much sense unless there is a God and an afterlife.
3. If this is true and there is a God, the most important thing in the world would be to get to know him.

---

2. Previously published in *Come Ye Apart* September-October-November 1998 (Kansas City, MO: Nazarene Publishing House), 91. Used by permission. (This publication became *Reflecting God*.)

4. If God isn't real to me (and he wasn't), there must be a barrier between us. Chances are the barrier is caused by my neglect of him or my sin against him.
5. If he is the offended party and there is a barrier between us, then he has the right to tell me how to cross the barrier and come to him.
6. That is the very thing he did in sending Jesus Christ into this world—he is the bridge over the barrier to God.

Paul highlights this final truth so clearly when he writes, "God was reconciling the world to himself in Christ, not counting people's sins against them" (2 Corinthians 5:19). And moreover, "God made him who had no sin to be sin for us, so that in him we might become the righteousness of God" (v. 21).

From these conclusions, I stepped out into a search for God. And within months, by God's kindness to me, I found him. Where are you? Have you stepped out in that search yet?

Conversion—What's Next?

But Barnabas took him and brought him to the apostles.
He told them how Saul on his journey had seen the Lord and
that the Lord had spoken to him, and how in Damascus
he had preached fearlessly in the name of Jesus.
Acts 9:27

Then Barnabas went to Tarsus to look for Saul, and when
he found him, he brought him to Antioch. So for a whole year
Barnabas and Saul met with the church.
Acts 11:25–26

Conversion is also called being "born again" (John 3:3). It is compared to physical birth. Imagine if, after you were born, all your parents did was talk about the moment you were born. They never held you, bathed you, fed you, or cared for you. What would your condition be after three weeks? You would get sick and die.

So in the spiritual life, after you have been converted—or born again—you must be nurtured, spiritually fed, guided. Barnabas, who is also called "son of encouragement," is one of the best disciples, or follow-up workers, in the Bible. He is the one who reached out to Saul (later Paul), made a bridge that brought him into the life of the church, and repeatedly worked with him until Saul became a great spiritual leader. Together, Barnabas and Saul served in Antioch (Acts 11:26) and were sent by the whole church on a missionary journey (13:2–3).

The same pattern is happening today. Dave, a young adult, was new in the city. When he saw a teen church car wash, he stopped. The teens who washed his car were so friendly that he decided to visit their church on Sunday. After his visit, a pastor phoned him and asked if they could stop by and visit. Dave gladly agreed.

The pastor brought with him a seminary student named Dan, whom he had been training in pastoral skills. During a warm visit at Dave's apartment, they discovered that Dan had accepted Christ in college and was now in the city for an engineering job. The pastor suggested Dave begin *Basic Bible Studies for New and Growing Christians*, and Dan agreed to meet with Dave weekly to review his studies. Dave grew spiritually through Dan's love and guidance and later joined the church by profession of faith. He eventually married Linda, a godly young woman he met through a church activity.

Dan finished seminary and began his first pastorate. David and Linda moved to a new state, where they got fully involved in their local church. David became the church treasurer and eventually published a book of considerable spiritual power.

Barnabas and Saul. David and Dan. The pattern is the same: after conversion come growth, strength, and service because of faithful discipleship. Where do you fit in this story?

Johnny and the Penny Jar

Repent, then, and turn to God.
Acts 3:19

To open their eyes and turn them from darkness to light, and from the
power of Satan to God, so that they may receive forgiveness of sins and
a place among those who are sanctified by faith in me.
Acts 26:18

His dad regularly came home and dumped all his pocket change, from quarters to pennies, into the "penny jar." It was a big jar with a fairly small opening. This money was always reserved for a special family project. The family rule was that no one was to get into the penny jar until Dad felt it was time for the family project.

One day, Mom and Dad left the house for a short time to pick up a surprise gift for Johnny. They left him at home, trusting him to be on his best behavior.

As soon as they left, Johnny decided he could get some money out of the jar, buy candy at the store next door, eat it, and make sure the jar was back in place before his parents returned—no one would be the wiser. He could barely get his hand through the opening at the top of the jar, but he jammed his hand deep into the stash of coins and got his fistful. But there was a problem—his fistful of coins was too big to come up through the opening of the jar. Just then, he heard the car door slam, and he realized his parents would enter the house in moments.

In his childish mind, he thought, "I can hold onto the precious coins with my hand trapped in the jar, or I can let go of all the coins and make my hand small enough to pull out of the jar. I can have my freedom, or I can keep grasping the coins and be trapped and caught."

Johnny chose freedom, let go of the coins, and put the jar back in place. Mom and Dad were excited as they came in and placed the surprise gift in his hands. Because he'd let go of the coins, his hands were now completely free to receive the gift.

Repentance is letting go of our sins. Salvation is receiving the gift of forgiveness of sins. You can't keep holding onto your sin and still receive God's forgiveness. Turn from sin and turn to God so that you may receive.

No Condemnation

Therefore, there is now no condemnation for those who are in Christ Jesus.
Romans 8:1

Two sins when I was six, four sins when I was eight, eight sins when I was ten . . . and the closer I got to the present, the more sins and selfishness I saw. I felt guilty, condemned, and sorry. Hold that scene for a few moments.

Why do we feel condemned? Some of us feel condemned because we confuse sins and mistakes. To sin is to break a known law of God. A mistake may fall short of God's perfect will, but because it is done in ignorance, or with good motives, it is a mistake. Even James recognizes this when he writes, "If anyone, then, knows the good they ought to do and doesn't do it, it is sin for them" (James 4:17). You must *know* about it for it to be sin. If you lump sins and mistakes together, you will condemn yourself needlessly for mistakes.

Some feel condemned because they have low self-image. Their thoughts about themselves, perhaps stemming from childhood, are, "I'm not worth very much," or "I'm not very talented." But that is not what God thinks about them—God values them so much that he actually gave his one and only Son to secure their forgiveness and salvation: "For God so loved the world that he gave his one and only Son, that whoever believes in him shall not perish but have eternal life" (John 3:16). God teaches that each Christian has at least one gift, but because our God-given gifts are different, we are different from each other. Even Jesus taught, "Love your neighbor as *yourself*" (Matthew 19:19).

But the main reason people feel condemned is not because they confuse sins and mistakes; not because of low self-image—but because they have been sinning. They are guilty; they feel condemned; they are condemned.

For years, I thought I would have to wait until death and the final judgment—then, and only then, would I know if God accepted me. But that is not what the Word teaches: "There is now no condemnation for those who are in Christ Jesus." It says *now*—there is no condemnation here and now. You can *know now* that you are not condemned, that your sins are forgiven, and that you are right with God.

Do you not realize "that God's kindness is intended to lead you to repentance?" (Romans 2:4). "Therefore, since we have been justified by faith, we have peace with God through our Lord Jesus Christ" (5:1). We are no longer condemned. This reality is for only one group of people. See today's scripture again: "Now no condemnation for those *who are in Christ Jesus.*"

That night, I reviewed my sins from age six, told God I was sorry for disobeying and neglecting him, and that, with his help, I was turning from my sins. I then accepted Jesus Christ and received him into my heart and life as my Savior and Lord. Immediately, I sensed total forgiveness from God—I was no longer condemned. There is now no condemnation for anyone who comes to this place—they are "in Christ Jesus."

To the One Who Is Victorious

To the one who is victorious, I will give the right to sit with me on my throne, just as I was victorious and sat down with my Father on his throne.
Revelation 3:21

The overcomers are celebrated in the book of Revelation. But to hear some Christians talk today, the default pattern for the Christian life seems to be the defeated.

Note how strongly victory is stressed in Christ's letters to the seven churches in Revelation:

- "To the one who is victorious, I will give the right to eat from the tree of life, which is in the paradise of God" (2:7).
- "The one who is victorious will not be hurt at all by the second death" (v. 11).
- "To the one who is victorious, I will give some of the hidden manna. I will also give that person a white stone with a new name written on it, known only to the one who receives it" (v. 17).
- "To the one who is victorious and does my will to the end, I will give authority over the nations" (v. 26).
- "The one who is victorious will, like them, be dressed in white. I will never blot out the name of that person from the book of life, but will acknowledge that name before my Father and his angels" (3:5).
- "The one who is victorious I will make a pillar in the temple of my God. Never again will they leave it. I will write on them the name of my God and the name of the city of my God, the new Jerusalem, which is coming down out of heaven from my God; and I will also write on them my new name" (v. 12).
- "To the one who is victorious, I will give the right to sit with me on my throne, just as I was victorious and sat down with my Father on his throne" (v. 21).

Overcoming, or "victory," is defined in Revelation 12 as victory over "the accuser of our brothers and sisters" (v. 10), "the devil" (v. 12): "They triumphed over him by the blood of the Lamb and by the word of their testimony" (v. 11). There are victors today, overcoming sin and the devil by the blood and testimony. For example, let me tell you about Chuck.

A friend urged me to call on Chuck at the county jail—he said Chuck had recently accepted Christ. When Chuck discovered I was a minister, he greeted me warmly and told me his story: He'd been involved in drugs, committed robbery to buy drugs, and dramatically accepted Christ as Savior and Lord. Instantly, he was delivered from his desire for drugs. He went to the police, reported his crimes, and was now in jail. He was radiant in his faith. He started *Basic Bible Studies for New and Growing Christians*, and we agreed to have a weekly discipleship meeting to review his studies.

During our third meeting, Chuck was troubled. He told me his old desire for drugs was coming back. I reminded him of 1 Corinthians 10:13, a verse he had previously memorized: "No temptation has overtaken you except what is common to mankind. And God is faithful; he will not let you be tempted beyond what you can bear. But when you are tempted, he will also provide a way out so that you can endure it."

"Chuck," I said, "God won't let you be tempted beyond what you can bear. He knows that with his help, you can overcome it. I had sins in my life, and they controlled me; I didn't control them. But when Christ came into my life, he gave me power I never had before. Not once have I returned to those sins. He can do it for you!"

"Yeah!" Chuck said. "I can make it!" And Chuck went on from there in victory. He completed each week's Bible study successfully. He led several other prisoners to Christ. He was filled with joy and devotion. He never went back to drugs.

Finally, Chuck was released from jail. The judge required him to live under the roof and influence of his family's Baptist minister. The last time I talked to him on the phone, I asked, "Chuck, how are you doing?"

He answered, "I'm doing great. I'm planning to go to Bible school. I think God has called me into ministry."[3]

"Yeah! I can make it!" An overcomer!

3. Reported in *The Good News: The Chic Shaver Center for Evangelism Newsletter* (September 2012).

I Dare Not Face People or Problems

But I cry to you for help, Lord; in the morning my prayer comes before you.
Psalm 88:13

What do you face in the first three hours of your day? What do you do to prepare for those hours?

A few days ago, I was listening to a person I had invested in deeply as he taught a class in church. He said, "As Pastor Shaver so emphasized, 'I dare not face people or problems until I first face the Lord.'" He had incorporated this practice in his own life. I was reminded by his words how truly important this issue was and is to me.

I had come to Christ my junior year in a secular college. I sensed I would be living in a spiritually unfriendly atmosphere. Out of three thousand students, about thirty would show up in daily chapel, and six to eight gathered daily for prayer. It would be important for me to get up early and spend time in the Bible and prayer before I faced people or problems. I considered it my time to "put on the full armor of God, so that [I could] take [my] stand against the devil's schemes" (Ephesians 6:11).

Of course, if you work the night shift, your day may begin in the late afternoon. If you cannot give God the beginning of the day, give him a time when your mind is alert. Give him the best part of your day; don't give him the leftovers.

Now, sixty-five years after my conversion, I still follow this practice: "I dare not face people or problems until I first face the Lord." The fruit of this practice has been amazingly rich.

Join me in this practice. The Bible says of Jesus, "Very early in the morning, while it was still dark, Jesus got up, left the house and went off to a solitary place, where he prayed" (Mark 1:35). You will be in good company.

Repentance Is Such a Good Thing

Peter replied, "Repent and be baptized, every one of you, in the name of
Jesus Christ for the forgiveness of your sins. And you will receive the gift
of the Holy Spirit. The promise is for you and your children and for all
who are far off—for all whom the Lord our God will call."
Acts 2:38–39

If God is holy—and he is—then it is logical to assert that people holding onto their sins will not be able to be in his presence in eternity. This is so clear that Peter quotes the Lord: "Be holy, because I am holy" (1 Peter 1:16).

So, what will you and I do about the sins we've committed? Peter says, "repent." Repentance means to be so sorry for your sins that you ask God to forgive you and turn from sin in the future. It is also at that moment that you turn to Jesus Christ. By coming to Christ, you now are empowered to live a new life—to be righteous. Romans 3:22 says, "This righteousness is given through faith in Jesus Christ to all who believe." Second Corinthians 5:17 says, "Therefore if anyone is in Christ, the new creation has come." Christ makes you new; you may now live a different and righteous life.

God loves you so much that he sent Christ to forgive your past and the Holy Spirit to empower you for your future. Brennan Manning says, "How much does God love you? So much that he'd rather die than live without you—and so he did."[4]

This is how Michael Henderson defines a Christian: "A Christian is one who is currently following Jesus and doing what he said to do."[5] E. Stanley Jones says that to obey God because he might hurt us is characteristic of an immature Christian; to obey God because we might hurt him is characteristic of the mature Christian.[6]

My son, Paul, developed melanoma on his shoulder, and surgery was required. The surgeon went in deep and cut out a lot of his shoulder. Do you think I got angry with that doctor? Did I fume, "What right did he have to invade my son's body and take so much of his shoulder?" No—I rejoiced that the doctor went deep, got all the cancer, and gave Paul an extended life. I rejoiced.

Repentance is like that—God is going deep to deal with your sins. And just think, all your sins can be forgiven, and you can be a new person. That's why Romans 2:4 says, "Do you show contempt for the riches of his kindness,

---

4. Quotation from sermon notes. Original source unknown.
5. D. Michael Henderson, *Making Disciples—One Conversation at a Time* (Kansas City, MO: Beacon Hill Press of Kansas City, 2006), 28.
6. Quotation from sermon notes. Original source unknown.

forbearance and patience, not realizing that God's kindness is intended to lead you to repentance?" Repentance is such a good thing.

Lord, How Could You?

The eternal God is your refuge, and underneath are the everlasting arms.
Deuteronomy 33:27

When our son called to tell us he would have a cancer surgery on his neck that would probably remove his voice box, his mom responded. Here is her written description:

> I was standing in the kitchen when I first heard Paul telling us about his throat cancer, and I just fell in a little heap. "Lord, how could you let this happen? Please, Lord, not our only son!" and he said, "Yes, Nancy, I want to use him." So, I surrendered right then, and in a few moments, he poured a bucket of peace over me. It stayed with me all through the thirteen-hour surgery; and when it was over, they had removed the cancer, performed a tracheotomy, and rebuilt his esophagus. He was up and walking the next day, and you know the rest. You can trust God all the way home. I know this because God picked me up and held me in his arms that day, and he loved me and cared for me and filled me with strength to face the future with whatever happens because he knows Paul's name and yours and mine. You can take it to the bank and deposit it—the one in heaven, I mean. He is making us stronger and braver because there is no fear in love.[7]

Paul's victorious life story after his voice box removal has been told in twenty-eight churches, and Paul gave his testimony to 2,200 in a South Carolina Baptist church.

And for Nancy, "underneath are the everlasting arms."

---

7. Shaver Christmas letter, 2015.

A Scientist and God

Lift up your eyes and look to the heavens.
Isaiah 40:26

For some, science and faith are enemies. Yet, for others, science and faith embrace each other.

An anti-church attitude was built into Joe—his father's negative church experience was behind it. But, when Joe met Doris during college, his attitude began to change. Doris was raised in a Christian family, made a commitment to God at the age of fourteen during a revival service, and enjoyed living in relationship with Christ. When Doris explained Christ and church to Joe, his mind opened, and he took Christ and the church into his heart.

They married just prior to graduation. Joe knew that because of the war in Korea, he would be drafted into military service. During his time in the army, he completed his basic training as a tank commander, went on to officer training, and eventually was assigned to work in the army's chemical laboratory.

After being released from the army, Joe worked for Standard Oil of California for nine years. He then obtained a position at the Bayer lab in Kansas City, where he worked as a senior chemist for twenty-five years. For Joe and the fourteen chemists working under him, the objective was to develop, redevelop, and improve the various pesticide recipes that Bayer was selling.

After retiring, Joe started his own laboratory. One of his clients called from Europe, explaining that their chemists had worked on a special recipe for three years, but were having a problem: their containers kept exploding. Joe assumed responsibility for solving their problem. That evening, he went to God and asked for help. God told him he already knew the answer, and to apply his chemistry knowledge to the problem. Within three days, Joe had the answer from his earlier medical training.

Incredulous, the client company's president and staff came to Joe's lab to see for themselves. They could hardly believe that none of the bottles were exploding, regardless of the temperature at which they were stored or for how long they were stored.

Joe now owns fifteen basic patents and 253 total patents, counting all those associated with various companies throughout the world.

What a blend—a chemical scientist and faith in a living, prayer-answering God. No wonder Isaiah said, "Lift up your eyes and look to the heavens: Who created all these? He who brings out the starry host one by one and calls forth each of them by name" (40:26).

What Does "Believe" Mean?

Abram believed the LORD, and he credited it to him as righteousness.
Genesis 15:6

"Only believe in Jesus and you will be saved" is a commonly repeated idea in much of Christianity. Yet there is something hollow, something lacking in that statement. The answer is in a right understanding of the word "believe."

"Believe" means more than intellectually accepting that Jesus exists. Even James says that is not enough when he writes, "You believe that there is one God. Good! Even the demons believe that—and shudder" (James 2:19). Obviously, the demons "believe" God exists, but they definitely are not saved. Victor Hamilton says, "To believe in the Lord is to trust in the Lord. Understanding belief as trust moves belief from something you accept in your head to something you are willing to do with your life."[8]

The Bible repeatedly ties the idea of belief or trust in the Lord to lived-out service, sacrifice, commitment, and heroic life. James 2:22–24 elaborates: "You see that his [Abraham's] faith and his actions were working together, and his faith was made complete by what he did. And the scripture was fulfilled that says, 'Abraham believed God, and it was credited to him as righteousness,' and he was called God's friend. You see that a person is considered righteous by what they do and not by faith alone."

I have a simple way to understand the concept of belief or faith. If I tell you, "I really believe in my wife, Nancy," do I simply mean that she exists? Or does my belief mean I trust her, depend on her, seek to please her, take her into account in my decisions, care for her, and commit to her?

What kind of belief do you believe in?

---

8. Victor Hamilton, "Commentary Genesis 14:17–15:6," *Illustrated Bible Life*, September–November 2015 (Kansas City, MO: WordAction Publishing Co.), 7.

An Amazing Thing, an Awesome Thing

❖

"Which is easier: to say, 'Your sins are forgiven,' or to say,
'Get up and walk'? But I want you to know that the Son of Man has
authority on earth to forgive sins." So he said to the paralyzed man,
"Get up, take your mat and go home." Then the man got up and
went home. When the crowd saw this, they were filled with awe;
and they praised God, who had given such authority to man.
Matthew 9:5–8

My own daughter challenged me, "Dad, at least once a week, write down at least one amazing thing, one awesome thing, that happened that week." I decided to accept the challenge. When the people of Jesus's day saw that Christ could forgive sin and heal the paralyzed, they were filled with awe and *praised God*. I felt the exercise would cause me to be more alert to God's work in my life, to be more thankful, and to give God more praise. It would keep me from highlighting the negative and remembering the positive. So I began to list the awesome things. Here are some of them:

- I shared the warm spirit of Christmas Day with my family.
- After I asked the Lord to send funds for the Evangelism Center's end-of-year needs, we received financial gifts totaling six thousand dollars.
- One hundred people showed up to honor both my retirement from forty-five years of teaching a discipleship class and my eighty-fifth birthday. My family and I felt loved, supported, appreciated, and encouraged.
- I wrote eight devotionals in seven days.
- I saw *Charlie and the Chocolate Factory* at the Kauffman Center. (For years, I had wanted to attend the Kauffman at least once.)
- I received the sweetest love note from Nancy I could ask for.
- One Saturday, I met with some fellow Christians, one of whom affirmed his faith in Christ and agreed to do the *Basic Bible Study*, and the others who agreed to be his follow-up partners.
- One Sunday, I preached a sermon titled "My Heart—Christ's Home" to a crowd of 186. Afterward, 33 people sought Christ.
- I got to experience the beauty of the Naples Botanical Gardens.

- Our GPS failed, but Rachel had trained me to use Siri on my smartphone. Siri was able to give me directions.

Some of these were awesome answers to prayer; some were my delight in the beauty of nature; others were practical, like Siri guiding me safely home. And how my spirit is lifted as I review—it is amazing, awesome. So I join the descendants of Jacob: "They will acknowledge the holiness of the Holy One of Jacob, and will stand in awe of the God of Israel" (Isaiah 29:23).

Would you like to try it—one awesome thing each week?

God's Promises for You

Even though I walk through the darkest valley,
I will fear no evil, for you are with me.
Psalm 23:4

It's a love letter from God to you. That's one way to describe the Bible.

One good way to read the Bible is to start with one specific book, like the Gospel of John. A way to read through the Bible in a year is to procure and read the *One Year Bible*, which gives you a reading for each day of the year. These readings have roughly two Old Testament chapters, one New Testament chapter, half a Psalm, and three verses from Proverbs. By following your calendar, you cover the whole Bible in a year.

To read with the greatest meaning, follow the advice of Earl Lee, who taught "SMU." This does not stand for Southern Methodist University, but for "What does it *say*? What does it *mean*? How can I *use* it?" By finding personal applications of the Bible, you will experience the greatest growth.

The Bible gives commands, advice, and promises. The promises give us great help in times of challenge. Of course, particular promises were made in specific past situations to a specific person or group—but often, these promises are also enduring principles that continue to apply to people today.

Dorothy Hamilton has a list of promises that may especially help us. Here are some—apply them to yourself:
- "So do not fear, for I am with you; do not be dismayed, for I am your God. I will strengthen you and help you; I will uphold you with my righteous right hand" (Isaiah 41:10).

- "And we know that in all things God works for the good of those who love him, who have been called according to his purpose" (Romans 8:28).
- "For now we see only a reflection as in a mirror; then we shall see face to face. Now I know in part; then I shall know fully" (1 Corinthians 13:12).
- "Husbands, in the same way be considerate as you live with your wives, and treat them with respect . . . , so that nothing will hinder your prayers" (1 Peter 3:7).
- "Cast all your anxiety on him because he cares for you" (1 Peter 5:7).
- "My grace is sufficient for you, for my power is made perfect in weakness" (2 Corinthians 12:9).

The pressure of a deadline was on me. It was my final project for my doctor of ministry degree at Fuller Seminary. I was writing a twelve-lesson discipleship study, and it had to be done by the end of December.

The pressure wasn't just from this project. I was serving as a professor of evangelism and as an outreach pastor, in addition to being involved in numerous speaking responsibilities. I felt very stressed. I put my head down on my desk and felt like I was having a nervous breakdown. I had just written a question for the discipleship study: "What is the biblical expectation of power to overcome difficulty for the sake of Christ?" With the question I included a reference to Philippians 4:13: "I can do all this through him who gives me strength." I think my head was still on the desk when I heard the Holy Spirit say, "Why don't you put your project in there?"

I read the verse again with the word "project" added: "I can do this project through him [Christ] who gives me strength." As I did so, strength flowed into me—I knew I could do it. The Spirit spoke again, saying, "It will be done on time, and it will be published." The project arrived at Fuller early, and it was published as *Living in the Power of the Spirit*. I knew God's promise had worked in my life—I expect the same will be true for you.

When We Do Not Understand

*"Why were you searching for me?" [Jesus] asked. "Didn't you know I
had to be in my Father's house?" But they did not understand what he
was saying to them. Then he went down to Nazareth with them and was
obedient to them. But his mother treasured all these things in her heart.
And Jesus grew in wisdom and stature, and in favor with God and man.*
Luke 2:49–52

One of the godliest women in the history of the world was Mary, mother of
Jesus. As Luke 1:28 says, "[An] angel went to her and said, 'Greetings, you
who are highly favored! The Lord is with you.'"

Seeing Mary's troubled heart, the angel continued, "Do not be afraid,
Mary. You have found favor with God. You will conceive and give birth to
a son, and you are to call him Jesus. He will be great and will be called the
Son of the Most High. The Lord God will give him the throne of his father
David, . . . his kingdom will never end" (vv. 30–33). The angel then added,
"The Holy Spirit will come on you, and the power of the Most High will over-
shadow you. So the holy one to be born will be called the Son of God" (v. 35).

Later, when Jesus was twelve, he, Mary, and Joseph journeyed to Jerusalem for the Passover festival. As extended family members headed home,
Jesus's parents realized that Jesus was not among them. They returned to
Jerusalem, found Jesus, and questioned his actions. He replied that he had to
be in his Father's house, but *they did not understand.*

Though God's angel had spoken so clearly to Mary, at this stage of Jesus's
growth, they still did not understand. Yes, it is possible that there are issues
the godly do not understand.

For example, in 2020 I was asking, "Why COVID-19?" Is it simply because, throughout world history, we face periodic major diseases? Is it a judgment from God on disobedient people? The grumbling, disobedient Israelites
in the wilderness angered the Lord, "and he struck them with a severe plague"
(Numbers 11:33). Is it simply because we live in a damaged, off-balance world
ever since sin entered humanity? Even so, we live in the hope "that the creation
itself will be liberated from its bondage to decay and brought into the freedom
and glory of the children of God." Moreover, "we wait eagerly for our adoption
to sonship, the redemption of our bodies" (Romans 8:21 and 23). I don't know,
I don't understand, but I have been praying that God will use this tragic series
of events to draw people to himself—Savior, forgiver, healer, the Lord.

Millions of people pulled away from others in self-imposed quarantines
to stop human transmission of the disease. What do people who are normally busy with work, school, sporting events, entertainment, and shopping do
when most everything stops? When they sit at home day after day, what is

going through their minds? What are they thinking about? Is it possible that God might be getting their attention?

Living for Two Worlds

We are confident, I say, and would prefer to be away from the body and at home with the Lord. So we make it our goal to please him, whether we are at home in the body or away from it. For we must all appear before the judgment seat of Christ, so that each of us may receive what is due us for the things done while in the body, whether good or bad.
2 Corinthians 5:8–10

On April 1, 2020, Dr. Anthony Fauci predicted that hundreds of thousands of Americans would die in the coronavirus pandemic. In light of this, wouldn't it be wise for everyone to be sure they are living for two worlds—both this one and the next? The apostle Paul spoke of being "away from the body and at home with the Lord." As a result, "we make it our goal to please him." This issue is so monumental that we must all appear before the judgment seat of Christ.

Jesus defined eternal life in John 17:3: "Now this is eternal life: that they know you, the only true God, and Jesus Christ, whom you have sent." It is a present, vital relationship with the true God and Jesus Christ. But the end result of it also takes us into life after death. Jesus explains this further in John 10:27: "My sheep listen to my voice; I know them, and they follow me." Here, the tense of this verb "follow" means "are now following me." Jesus states, 'I give them eternal life, and they shall never perish; no one will snatch them out of my hand" (v. 28).

The present life is to be one of faithfulness and service. Matthew 25:34–36 says, "Then the King will say to those on his right, 'Come, you who are blessed by my Father; take your inheritance, the kingdom prepared for you since the creation of the world. For I was hungry and you gave me something to eat, I was thirsty and you gave me something to drink, I was a stranger and you invited me in, I needed clothes and you clothed me, I was sick and you looked after me, I was in prison and you came to visit me.'"

Beyond that, this present life with Christ is filled with great satisfaction. In John 10:10, Jesus says, "I have come that they may have life, and have it to the full." Paul says in Romans 14:17, "For the kingdom of God is not a matter of eating and drinking, but of righteousness, peace and joy in the Holy Spirit."

But there is also the next life. Christ tells of a rich man whose farm yielded an abundant harvest. His reaction was, "I will tear down my barns and build bigger ones, and there I will store my surplus grain. And I'll say to myself, 'You have plenty of grain laid up for many years. Take life easy; eat, drink and be merry'" (Luke 12:18–19). But the flaw in his philosophy was that he lived only for this world. God speaks, "You fool! This very night your life will be demanded from you. Then who will get what you have prepared for yourself?" (v. 20).

There is the next life. The apostle Paul writes from prison, "For to me, to live is Christ and to die is gain. If I am to go on living in the body, this will mean fruitful labor for me. Yet what shall I choose? I do not know! I am torn between the two: I desire to depart and be with Christ, which is better by far" (Philippians 1:21–23). Paul is so satisfied with his earthly life that he says, "I have fought the good fight, I have finished the race, I have kept the faith. Now there is in store for me the crown of righteousness, which the Lord, the righteous Judge, will award to me on that day—and not only to me, but also to all who have longed for his appearing" (2 Timothy 4:7–8).

And we have a larger glimpse of the next life—a loud voice speaks, "God's dwelling is now among the people, and he will dwell with them. They will be his people, and God himself will be with them and be their God. 'He will wipe every tear from their eyes. There will be no more death' or mourning or crying or pain, for the old order of things has passed away" (Revelation 21:3–4).

Now, let's be sensible. Prepare to live for both worlds.

My Soul Pants for You, My God

As the deer pants for streams of water, so my soul pants for you, my God.
Psalm 42:1

The crackle of breaking underbrush is the first signal. And then you see him—a beautiful specimen at the brook's edge. The deer is wet with sweat, but his throat craves moisture. The brook slakes his thirst; he is refreshed with new life. But then the far-off bay of hounds tenses his muscles again, and into the stream he goes. The brook is his safety—dogs cannot follow his scent in water.

We too need refreshing, life, and safety. Too long have the howling hounds chased us. We thirst! Ah, but here is God—he satisfies our thirst, gives us new life, and in the safety of his countenance, the hounds lose the trail. Brother, sister, may you ever drink at God's fountain. All other water supplies are either polluted or insufficient, but Jesus said, "Whoever drinks the water I give them will never thirst" (John 4:14).[9]

It's Happening

About midnight Paul and Silas were praying and singing hymns to God, and the other prisoners were listening to them. Suddenly there was such a violent earthquake that the foundations of the prison were shaken. The jailer called for lights, rushed in and fell trembling before Paul and Silas. He then brought them out and asked, "Sirs, what must I do to be saved?"
Acts 16:25–26a, 29–30

Praying and singing hymns—that's what they were doing as they sat in jail for preaching Jesus in the city of Philippi. They had been severely beaten and their feet were fastened in stocks—still, they sang and prayed. Then, an earthquake shook the prison.

The prisoners' attitude, their praying and singing, and the earthquake all got the guard's attention. God got his attention! Before dawn, the guard and his whole family had come to the Lord. And after the jailer washed the prisoners' wounds, he and his family were baptized. The family then treated Paul and Silas to a late supper.

Two weeks before I wrote these pages, I wrote the devotional #16 for January 16, "When We Do Not Understand." In it, I asked, "Why COVID-19?" The final paragraph of that devotional said this: *Millions of people pulled away from others in self-imposed quarantines to stop human transmission of the disease. What do people who are normally busy with work, school, sporting events, enter-*

---

9. Previously published in *Come Ye Apart* January–February–March 1964 (Kansas City, MO: Nazarene Publishing House), 39. Used by permission. (This publication became *Reflecting God*.)

tainment, and shopping do when most everything stops? When they sit at home day after day, what is going through their minds? What are they thinking about? Is it possible that God might be getting their attention?

In the sports section of *The Kansas City Star* in April 2020, I read a story about Rex Hudler, who broadcasts for the Kansas City Royals. In 1978, Hudler signed with the Yankees right out of high school. He began playing in the majors in 1984, and he retired in 1998. Soon afterward, he began broadcasting for the Los Angeles Angels, and in 2009 he joined the Royals broadcasting team. The coronavirus pandemic was difficult for Hudler—COVID-19 shut down baseball, and like many of us, Hudler faced extra hours at home and an unrelenting stream of bad news. During lockdown, Hudler said he made a conscious effort to skip the morning news, describing how his routine changed:

> I've been able to get closer to God during this time and, you know, I am not a religious guy, I'm a spiritual guy. And so when I wake up in the morning, I open my eyes and thank God for life . . . You know how we have alerts on our phones? Fox, CNN, all the publications are on your phone, waiting for you to restart your day here. Uh-uh. I'm starting with God. I'm gonna go find some Scripture and read some Scripture and start my day with him, not with the world.[10]

Is it possible that God is getting people's attention? It's happening!

Paul Shaver—Before and After Cancer, Part 1

*Do not be anxious about anything, but in every situation, by prayer
and petition, with thanksgiving, present your requests to God.
And the peace of God, which transcends all understanding,
will guard your hearts and your minds in Christ Jesus.
Philippians 4:6–7*

Allow me to tell you a story of what happened to my family in 2014.

Our son, Paul, lives in Muncie, Indiana, with his wife, Lori. He is fifty-two years old and drives trucks in a six-state territory, delivering food to

---

10. Pete Grathoff, "Rex Hudler Is Missing More Than Baseball These Days," *For Pete's Sake* (column), *The Kansas City Star*, April 2, 2020, https://www.kansascity.com/sports/spt-columns-blogs/for-petes-sake/article241714041.html.

Kroger grocery stores. Paul and Lori have two children at home, two married daughters, and three grandchildren living nearby. Paul and his family are active in their local church.

In late September 2014, Paul phoned me to say he had developed a hole in his neck and his voice had become raspy. He wondered if he should wait a few months to visit the doctor—his new insurance would take effect in January. Because he had had cancer surgery before, I told him he must go to the doctor immediately.

A biopsy revealed aggressive basal cell cancer in his neck. Surgery was set for the end of October. The doctor predicted that surgery would take ten to twelve hours; that they may need to remove Paul's voice box; that Paul would be hospitalized twelve to fourteen days.

When I heard how serious my son's condition was, I went to prayer in a more specific way. I hadn't been praying two minutes when the most wonderful, comforting *peace* settled upon me—a sense of well-being. The Lord did not tell me that Paul would be healed, or even that his voice box would be saved. Instead, he said this: "I will walk with you through this whole ordeal." As I prayed this in a revival service in another state, my wife, Nancy, prayed at home, and *peace* descended on her too. This peace has never left us.

Meanwhile, Paul began experiencing God's work in amazing ways. Once, he met a construction worker and asked, "How are you doing?"

The worker replied, "Great! I have Jesus!"

Yes, thought Paul, *that's the secret.*

In one of his deliveries, as Paul was handing paperwork to a client, she looked at him and asked, "Are you okay?" He said yes but apparently did not convince her because she asked him the same question twice more. Then the client asked, "May I pray for you?" and prayed a long, fervent prayer on his behalf. Paul was amazed.

Paul asked his pastor for permission to sing and testify in the Sunday morning service on October 19. He sang "Nothing between My Soul and the Savior," "Learning to Lean," and "Jesus Loves Me." Before the congregation, he testified, "I'm the right person for this challenge; I can handle this best; and I believe this will bring glory to God."

Paul wept as he testified, and so did the congregation. Then he knelt at the altar and prayed, "If there are any sins in my heart, forgive me." He also prayed for his family. As the pastor anointed and prayed for Paul, nearly the whole congregation gathered to support him.

Other congregants began asking the pastor to anoint and pray for them—as the pastor later said, "God was all over the place." A woman visiting from

Wisconsin said, "This is the most amazing church I've ever been to. If you will tell me of a church like this in Wisconsin, I will go to it."

A few days later, Nancy and I drove to Muncie. That night, we video-taped Paul because we thought it might be the last time we would ever hear his natural voice. But Paul told us he was not afraid: "I'm ready," he said. He sang and shared his testimony of God's closeness. Then he sang a trio with his daughters. It seemed a remarkable *peace* had permeated Paul's life. He was so courageous.

At 5:30 the next morning, we arrived at Indiana University Hospital in Indianapolis. The cancer surgeon and the plastic surgeon described in detail what they would do, and at 7:30, Paul was wheeled into surgery. Every ninety minutes, a nurse came out to update us. The cancer surgeon reported to us at 3:00 p.m.; at 8:40 p.m., the plastic surgeon. All told, Paul was in surgery for thirteen hours.

The surgeons removed cancer and flesh from his chin to lower neck; they also removed his voice box. They took grafts from his chest muscle and tissues. The doctors told us, "We will get him walking and teach him to breathe, to swallow, to eat—and eventually, to talk." The doctor said he had never seen a case like Paul's.

Paul Shaver—Before and After Cancer, Part 2

Do not be anxious about anything, but in every situation, by prayer
and petition, with thanksgiving, present your requests to God.
And the peace of God, which transcends all understanding,
will guard your hearts and your minds in Christ Jesus.
Philippians 4:6–7

The next day, we visited Paul in intensive care. He was covered with tubes, and his neck was very swollen. But his face was so handsome as he smiled. He could not speak, but he gave us hand signals and wrote messages on a tablet. The nurse reported that he had been walking with help and had been sitting in a chair for three hours—he was doing great. By the time we left, they were moving him to progressive care.

Meanwhile, Lori was posting updates about Paul on Facebook. In almost all of them, she noted that we expected that God would be glorified in this experience. More than two hundred people commented, from high school and college classmates; to members of his church; to athletic friends from his years of refereeing. Nearly all of them said, "We're praying for you."

As I continued to lift up Paul's situation before God, I felt prompted to pray for someone to lead a fundraising effort for the family's living and medical expenses while Paul was unable to work. Within hours, a friend approached me and said he wanted to raise money for them. Paul's church established a fund and bought him a special reclining chair and an iPad Mini to help him communicate.

Our daughter Rachel was in the stairwell at her workplace when she heard the following words in her spirit: "My God shall supply all your needs." Ten minutes later, she received a phone call informing her of an unexpected, generous gift to the fund at Paul's church. When the church gave them the money they had raised, Paul and Lori wept.

Paul came home after eight days in the hospital—far fewer than the fourteen days the doctor had predicted. By the first week of December, he was speaking with his new, deep voice, and had returned to full-time work.

I wonder how God will use all this. I'm reminded that Joni Eareckson Tada was never known in health, but after her paralysis and disability, she began a worldwide ministry showing God's sufficient grace. Could it be the same for Paul? He is living the closest to God I've ever seen him, and through everything, the *peace* has never left.

Patterns for Praying

*Yet the news about him spread all the more, so that crowds of
people came to hear him and to be healed of their sicknesses.
But Jesus often withdrew to lonely places and prayed.*
Luke 5:15–16

Though he was God in the flesh, Jesus Christ still felt it extremely important to pray consistently to his heavenly Father. As you develop your prayer life, draw encouragement from Jesus's pattern of prayer.

Luke 11:1 says, "One day Jesus was praying in a certain place. When he finished, one of his disciples said to him, 'Lord, teach us to pray, just as John taught his disciples.'" Note the phrase "a certain place"—this could mean Jesus had a regular spot where he went to pray. We know when he was in Jerusalem, "Jesus went out *as usual* to the Mount of Olives" (Luke 22:39), and in verse 41, he "knelt down and prayed."

You will do well to find a regular spot to pray. I have a favorite chair where I sit with a cup of coffee, read the Bible, then write key thoughts in a notebook, including a key verse I've read, praises, and requests. Then, I go to a quiet office in the basement of my home to pray specifically.

According to Luke 3:21–22, "When all the people were being baptized, Jesus was baptized too. And as he was praying, heaven was opened and the Holy Spirit descended on him in bodily form like a dove. And a voice came from heaven: 'You are my Son, whom I love; with you I am well pleased.'"

Here is Jesus at the beginning of his adult life, the beginning of his ministry. What does he do? He doesn't heal. He doesn't preach. He prays. This speaks to me: we must begin our days with prayer. In my early Christian life, I felt I must, before the people or problems of the day, first go to God. I would get up early in the morning to spend the prime part of my day with him. If for some reason you can't spend your mornings with God, then give him the best part of your day—don't give him the leftovers.

As you read Luke 5:15–16, notice that Jesus was having great success with the crowds, preaching, and healing. But Jesus regularly withdrew from it all to find privacy and pray. This tells us that prayer was more important than anything else. Prayer was his priority, and he disciplined himself to do it. Likewise, we all need to *decide* to *make time* to pray.

Luke 9:18 says, "Once when Jesus was praying in private and his disciples were with him, he asked them, 'Who do the crowds say I am?'" Notice the oxymoron here: Jesus was both "in private" and had his disciples "with him." There are several ways to explain this, but the bigger lesson is that the disciples learned to pray by hearing Jesus pray—he was training by example. Who do you meet with to pray so that you learn by their example?

Luke 6:12–13 says, "One of those days Jesus went out to a mountainside to pray, and spent the night praying to God. When morning came, he called his disciples to him and chose twelve of them, whom he also designated apostles." What do you suppose Jesus was asking God throughout that night? I believe it was, "O God, out of many disciples, whom should I choose to be my twelve apostles?" In other words, Jesus prayed and sought God's leadership for his important choices in life—and so should we.

Will you let Jesus's pattern of prayer guide your own? Take it a step at a time. It's okay to start small—maybe ten minutes each morning. As you grow in prayer, you will begin to sense that God is speaking back to you when you ask for his guidance.

What an adventure! Note that when Jesus prayed in Luke 3:21, "heaven was opened." If you want to live with an opened heaven, take time to pray.

Moses and the Lord—Very Personal

Then Moses climbed Mount Nebo . . . to the top of Pisgah, across from
Jericho. There the LORD showed him the whole land. . . . Then the LORD
said to him, ". . . I have let you see it with your eyes, but you will not cross
over into it." And Moses the servant of the LORD died there in Moab, as the
LORD had said. He buried him in Moab. . . . Moses was a hundred and
twenty years old when he died, yet his eyes were not weak nor his strength
gone. . . . Since then, no prophet has risen in Israel like Moses, whom the
LORD knew face to face, who did all those signs and wonders the LORD sent
him to do in Egypt—to Pharaoh and to all his officials and to his whole
land. For no one has ever shown the mighty power or performed
the awesome deeds that Moses did in the sight of all Israel.
Deuteronomy 34:1, 4–6a, 7, 10–12

How personal can you get? The personal relationship between Moses and God is overwhelmingly powerful—and heartwarming. From Pisgah's peak, "the LORD showed him the whole land" (v. 1). *The Lord showed him.* This is what Moses had worked and led toward for forty daunting years. Now, the dream was realized before his eyes.

Deuteronomy says, "Then the LORD said to him, 'This is the land I promised.'" *The Lord said*—oh, so many times he had spoken to Moses. Then, God further says, "I have let you see it . . . but you will not cross over into it." *You will not cross over into it.*

The obstacle to Moses's crossing came earlier at Kadesh over the water supply. When there was no water for Moses's hundreds of thousands of people in the desert, the Lord told Moses to speak to a rock, and water would pour out. Moses gathered the people, rebuked them, and said, "Must we bring you water out of this rock?" (Numbers 20:10). He struck the rock twice with his staff, and water gushed out.

Immediately the Lord spoke, saying that because Moses and Aaron did not honor the Lord as holy, they would not be allowed to bring Israel into the land. It is unclear what exactly their offense was—was it Moses's anger at his complaining people? His failure to follow the Lord's clear directions? Or perhaps his claim that *"we* bring you water," thus taking credit for the *Lord's* miracle? (See Numbers 20:1–12.)

Moses had pleaded with the Lord to allow him to "go over and see the good land beyond the Jordan—that fine hill country and Lebanon," though the Lord had already said he would not enter the land (Deuteronomy 3:25). In response, the Lord said, "That is enough" (v. 26). He told Moses that he would get to see the land, but he would not "cross this Jordan" (v. 27). God also instructed Moses to commission Joshua to lead the people in (v. 28). This spirited conversation between Moses and the Lord indicated their intimate speaking terms—this was not the first time Moses had pleaded.

The Lord was very specific in describing Moses's future: "There on the mountain that you have climbed you will die and be gathered to your people" (32:50). How often are we told the circumstance and time of our death? But Moses indicates no sign of distress over this announcement. He commissions Joshua and encourages him and the people: "Be strong and courageous, for you must go . . . into the land that the Lord swore. . . . The Lord himself goes before you" (31:7b, 8a). His words show no self-pity—only concern for the success for the mission.

After Moses's death, Deuteronomy gives us this conclusion: "Since then, *no prophet* has risen in Israel *like Moses*, whom the Lord *knew face to face*, who did all those *signs and wonders* the Lord *sent* him to do in Egypt—to Pharaoh and to all his officials and to his whole land. For *no one* has ever shown the mighty power or performed the *awesome deeds* that Moses did in the sight of all Israel" (34:10–12).

Moses saw the promised land but did not enter it. Moses, "servant of the Lord" (34:5); Moses, "prophet" (v. 10); Moses, "whom the Lord knew face to face" (v. 10); Moses, "man of God" (33:1). Moses did not make it into the promised land, but when he died on Mount Nebo, he was promoted upward to the presence of the Lord, the greater promise.

How close are our personal relationships with the Lord?

Was Prayer Answered?

Pray that I may be kept safe from the unbelievers in Judea and that
the contribution I take to Jerusalem may be favorably received by
the Lord's people there, so that I may come to you with joy,
by God's will, and in your company be refreshed.
Romans 15:31–32

Have you ever prayed and not been answered? Paul asked the Romans to pray for three things: (1) that he would be rescued from unbelievers in Judea; (2) that his service to the Jerusalem saints would be accepted; (3) that by God's will, he could come to them with joy.

The first part of Paul's prayer was not answered—as a matter of fact, the Jewish unbelievers were responsible for his beating, trial, and military escort to Rome. But Paul's unanswered first prayer became the means to the answering of his third prayer.

Gordon Wetmore said, "Prayer is not so much how we speak, but how we listen." And Paul said, "The Spirit helps us in our weakness. We do not know what we ought to pray for, but the Spirit himself intercedes for us" (Romans 8:26). In trials, God said to Paul, "Take courage! As you have testified about me in Jerusalem, so you must also testify in Rome" (Acts 23:11).

Under house arrest, he spoke to the many who came to hear him (28:23). In prison, Paul couldn't get away from his guards, but his guards also couldn't get away from him, and eventually, all the palace guards came to know about Christ (Philippians 1:13).

God spoke to Paul, and his mission was fulfilled. His third prayer was answered![11]

It's Not Fair

---

11. *Reflecting God* June–July–August 2010 (Kansas City, MO: WordAction Publishing Co.), 18. Used by permission.

For receiving instruction in prudent behavior,
doing what is right and just and fair.
Proverbs 1:3

I have learned the secret of being content in any and every situation,
whether well fed or hungry, whether living in plenty or in want.
I can do all this through him who gives me strength.
Philippians 4:12–13

"It's not fair!" she screamed. The four-year-old girl submitted her complaint to parents while her eight-year-old brother looked on.

A couple wrote in to the newspaper columnist Miss Manners about a dinner they were hosting for a small number of friends of a man recently deceased. A few people who were not invited to the dinner were upset because they thought they deserved to be there. "It's not fair," they said.

I called my phone company—whose specialty is effective communication by phone—to correct an error on my phone bill. After talking to one person (not the right person) for two minutes and being on hold for fifty-three minutes, I had to hang up to get to work: "It's not fair."

The wise King Solomon wrote that the purpose of his proverbs was to give "instruction in prudent behavior, doing what is right and just and fair" (Proverbs 1:3). It would be fair to say that this is God's goal for humanity. We want fair; we expect fair; but in our world damaged by sin, that is often not the case.

Jesus tells a parable of a landowner hiring laborers throughout the day. He paid them each a denarius, which was the usual daily wage. The ten-hour workers complained that the one-hour workers received the same pay as they did: "It's not fair." If the number of hours worked were the only issue, they would be correct. The landowner answered that he paid the ten-hour laborers exactly the amount they had agreed upon. There had been no deceit; it was honest action based on an agreement. The landowner felt that if he wanted to be generous to someone, that was his right. While the ten-hour workers were upset because of their assumptions and expectations, the landowner was operating on their honest agreement. When we always expect fairness, we set ourselves up for frustration.

The apostle Paul had an answer to this: "I have learned the secret of being content in any and every situation" (Philippians 4:12). He had been beaten, stoned, and imprisoned for preaching Christ, and his income was inconsistent. It wasn't fair! But he was content. He had found the secret to contentedness: "I can do all this through him who gives me strength" (v. 13).

The indwelling Christ gave him an indwelling strength to handle all the unfairness of life—and this strength is available to all of us.

All Kinds

"I am Jesus, whom you are persecuting," he replied. "Now get up and go into the city, and you will be told what you must do."
Acts 9:5

One of those listening was a woman from the city of Thyatira named Lydia, a dealer in purple cloth. She was a worshiper of God. The Lord opened her heart to respond to Paul's message.
Acts 16:14

At fifteen years old, Bekah had her writing published in *Holiness Today*. Part of her article read: "My dad has been my challenger while my mom has been my encourager. He has been the one to teach me how to face the world while she has been the one to prepare me to do just that. He has challenged me to dream, to try new things, and to trust God even in the unknown. . . . The gift of being shaped by Christian parents will never lose its effect on my life."[12]

Pretty powerful, wouldn't you say?

Saul, later known as Paul, had a dramatic conversion on the Damascus road. As light from heaven flashed around him, he fell to the ground and actually heard Jesus Christ speak to him, saying, "I am Jesus, whom you are persecuting."

Later, after Paul had been serving as God's missionary, he arrived in Philippi, visited a river site, and found a group of women there, including Lydia. As Paul spoke, "the Lord opened her heart to respond to Paul's message" (16:14). Lydia's conversion was sweet and subdued, but real. She invited Paul and his companions to stay at her house, and they agreed. And later, after Paul and Silas's imprisonment for teaching and healing, they went to Lydia's house. There was a gathering at Lydia's home (maybe a house church), and there, Paul and Silas encouraged the brothers and sisters (v. 40).

---

12. Bekah Rainey, "Kingdom Shapers," *Holiness Today* May–June 2020 (Lenexa, KS: Church of the Nazarene), 38.

Here's the point: conversion to Christ can be dramatic and spectacular or sweet and subdued. Both can be equally real.

In Paul's Philippian ministry, the Lord delivered a demon-possessed slave girl. The Lord saved Lydia, a wealthy businesswoman. The Philippian jailer was converted after a violent earthquake. And after the jailer brought Paul home for supper, his wife and his children accepted the Lord. Here in this city three classes of people are saved—and in the jailer's case, we have both adult and child conversions.

We find another pattern of family response when Paul writes to young pastor Timothy in 2 Timothy 1:5: "I am reminded of your sincere faith, which first lived in your grandmother Lois and in your mother Eunice and, I am persuaded, now lives in you also." There's a good chance that Timothy had a childhood conversion because of the godly influence of his grandmother and mother. It may even have been a home where the husband/father was not a believer.

Whatever your conversion experience, the most important thing is that you can say, "Christ is in my heart and life right now, and I am following him."

There are biblical truths that speak of assurance and certainty:

- 1 John 5:11–12—"And this is the testimony: God has given us eternal life, and this life is in his Son. Whoever has the Son has life; whoever does not have the Son of God does not have life."
- 2 Timothy 4:7–8 (Paul's end-of-life testimony)—"I have fought the good fight, I have finished the race, I have kept the faith. Now there is in store for me the crown of righteousness."
- Romans 8:16—"The Spirit himself testifies with our spirit that we are God's children."

When I talked to fifteen-year-old Bekah, who wrote the amazing article quoted above, I asked her how she came to Christ. She said, "When I was four years old, my mom had been telling me a story. I asked her questions about what it meant to accept Christ. Then I said I wanted to accept Jesus in my heart. My mom pulled our truck into a gas station, and we prayed right there. I felt I accepted Jesus then. As I got older, some questions arose. Those were all cared for when I was sanctified, which made me much stronger."

So, *all kinds* of people are finding Jesus. And they experience conversion in *all kinds* of ways. But thank God, each one *may know Jesus* personally.

Fixing the Flat Tire

My dear children, I write this to you so that you will not sin. But if anybody does sin, we have an advocate with the Father—Jesus Christ, the Righteous One. He is the atoning sacrifice for our sins, and not only for ours but also for the sins of the whole world.
1 John 2:1

God's plan, intention, expectation for you is "that you will not sin." But what if I should sin, even as a sanctified Christian? What should I do?

For the conscientious Christian, there are great temptations to despair. But the message is plain: Stop right there. Do not wait until the next church service or even the next morning. No, right there, take the matter immediately to Christ. He is your Advocate who speaks to the Father in your defense. Confess the sin, turn from it, and ask for the restoration of your relationship with God. Christ's "atoning sacrifice for our sins" (1 John 2:2) will cleanse you afresh.

Imagine you are driving from Columbus to Dayton, Ohio. Suddenly, you have a flat tire. What do you do? Three possibilities:

1. You can get out of the car, look at the flat, and say, "That tire's flat. I give up. I won't make it to Dayton. As a matter of fact, I'm going to quit driving altogether."
2. You can say, "The tire's flat. I'm going to drive on it until I can find a service station." By the time you drive that far, you'll need a new tire, maybe a new wheel, and who knows what damage you will have done to the underside of your car as you've clunked along.
3. You can stop the moment the flat happens, hop out, get out the spare, change the tire, and continue with only a slight interruption in your trip.

Christians tripped up in sin should not decide to quit the Christian life. Nor should we wait until the next Sunday service, or even the next day—if we do, we'll end up needing a major spiritual overhaul. Rather, we should take the sin immediately to the Lord and repent, trusting Christ for forgiveness, cleansing, and restoration. This way, we can continue on our way with hardly a break in fellowship with God. This is one truth of 1 John 1:7: "If we walk in the light, as he is in the light, we have fellowship with one another, and the blood of Jesus, his Son, purifies us from all sin." So remember the "if" clause of 1 John 2:1.

He Knows My Need

Your Father knows what you need before you ask him.
Matthew 6:8

Nancy and I had been meeting regularly with two young Christians, Myra and Christopher, to disciple them. They were engaged and planning a wedding. One Tuesday, Christopher was working late and only Myra could come see us. I prayed that the Lord would guide our conversation. Often in our meetings, I had a pretty specific agenda, but that night, I didn't.

"So, Lord," I prayed, "what should we share with Myra?" I had been impacted by my Scripture reading of Numbers 1 that day, so it seemed an appropriate thing to share. Specifically, I wanted to talk about the incredible truth revealed by God's instructions in Numbers 1—God knows my name! Before our meeting, Nancy also handed me a book I had not seen before, in which a Christian woman writes to other women about self-image and value.

As we shared the idea that "God knows my name" and the book about self-image and value, Myra's face lit up and began to shine. She told us that she had been struggling with her sense of worth. "You've given me exactly what I needed," she said.

"Myra," I said, "God did. Myra, he knows *your* name. Even more, he knows *your* need."

And you, reading these words—he knows *your name*. He knows *your need*. As today's scripture states, "Your Father knows what you need before you ask him."

They Shared

Anyone who loves their life will lose it, while anyone who hates their life
in this world will keep it for eternal life. Whoever serves me must
follow me; and where I am, my servant also will be.
My Father will honor the one who serves me.
John 12:25–26

As he faced the cross, ready to lay down his life for the salvation of the world, Christ challenged his followers. He called them to give their whole lives to Christ, to follow him, to share themselves with God (John 12:23–26).

I have read about people who do just this—I also know some personally.

Bob and Bessie Black, farmers from the midwestern United States, gave themselves to Jesus and shared with God by moving to Papua New Guinea, where Bessie worked as a teacher and Bob repaired and maintained the mission station.

Keith Fitzsimmons, an accountant, began following Jesus and felt God's call to give up part of his time to serve as a church custodian.

Bev Burgess experienced the saving grace of Jesus and his healing power. Afterward, she decided to spend her life telling others how to come to know Jesus.

Rees Howells was a Welsh coal miner. After he met Christ, he felt called to intercession, and he spent hours in prayer every day. Eventually, he prayed the Bible College of Wales into existence.

Hobby, a newspaper printer, accepted Jesus at age sixty. He then learned the truth of Malachi 3:10: "'Bring the whole tithe into the storehouse, that there may be food in my house. Test me in this,' says the LORD Almighty, 'and see if I will not throw open the floodgates of heaven and pour out so much blessing that there will not be room enough to store it.'" Joyously, Hobby began tithing, exclaiming, "In the light of what Jesus has done for me, that's the least I can do for him." Hobby shared with God.

Charles Colson, an attorney and one of President Richard Nixon's closest advisors, was convicted of and imprisoned for Watergate-related crimes. Shortly before his imprisonment, he accepted Christ. Colson reported the following about an especially trying time in his sentence:

It was that night in the quiet of my room that I made the total surrender, completing what had begun in Tom Phillips's driveway eighteen long months before: "Lord, if this is what it is all about," I said, "then I thank You. I praise You for leaving me in prison, for letting them take away my license to practice law, yes—even for my son being arrested. I praise You for giving me your love through these men, for being God, for just letting me walk with Jesus."

With those words came the greatest joy of all—the final release, turning it all over to God as my brother Harold had told me to do. And in the hours that followed I discovered more strength than I'd ever known before. This was the real mountaintop experience. Above and around me the world was filled with joy and love and beauty. For the first time I felt truly free, even as the fortunes of my life seemed at their lowest ebb.[13]

Forty-eight hours later, Judge Gerhard Gesell announced Colson's release from prison. Colson shared his surrendered life with God by founding the Prison Fellowship organization, which he led for the rest of his life. The organization has been the greatest force for prison reform in the United States of America.

All these stories occurred because people shared with God.

Lord, You Did It Again!

For the Lord your God dried up the Jordan before you until you had crossed over. The Lord your God did to the Jordan what he had done to the Red Sea when he dried it up before us until we had crossed over. He did this so that all the peoples of the earth might know that the hand of the Lord is powerful and so that you might always fear the Lord your God.
Joshua 4:23–24

"Trust your high moments with God." I think V. Raymond Edman said that, but regardless of who said it, it's wise and true. Probably the greatest high moment for Israel was the miraculous parting of the Red Sea that opened their escape route from Egyptian slavery. Now, after forty years of travel, they had just crossed the Jordan into their promised land.

Their travel had been tedious. Their problems were often self-imposed. They had grumbled, disobeyed, and rebelled, and in turn, God had rebuked and judged them. Though there had been miracles like manna, quail, and water from a rock, the Israelites' overall mood had been negative and defeatist.

---

13. Charles W. Colson, *Born Again* (Old Tappan, NJ: Fleming H. Revell, 1977), 339–40.

But God was striving to lead, empower, and encourage them. And then he did it again—he dried up the Jordan River as he had done to the Red Sea. Israel was reminded that God had done it! He had made a way for them through the Red Sea, and now he had made a way through the Jordan. Joshua called it an "amazing thing" (3:5). He told Israel, "This is how you will know that the living God is among you" (v. 10).

If you think that crossing a river is not as impressive as crossing a sea, wait a minute—listen before you diminish God's work here. The text tells us that the Jordan was at flood levels (v. 15), and the water was "piled up in a heap a great distance away" at the town of Adam (v. 16). In the middle of the Jordan, the priest "stood on dry ground" until the whole nation crossed on "dry ground" (v. 17).

After they had successfully crossed, Joshua reminded Israel—God did it again! Three times in 4:23–24, he uses the phrase, "the LORD your God." So personal, so near, so close, so real. Israel's courage must have soared. For Israel, this would be a reminder to fear the Lord; it would also be a testimony to the peoples of the earth.

Surely this is a message for you and me today: Whatever you are now facing, even if it seems very dark, the God who worked in your life before will work again. Lean on him hard. Be open to his voice and guidance and be watching. What next? If you've had a Red Sea moment, you may just be on the edge of a Jordan River moment. Never doubt in the dark what God has told you in the light.

A Flat Day

Elijah was afraid and ran for his life. . . . He came to a broom bush, sat down under it and prayed that he might die. "I have had enough, LORD,"
he said. "Take my life; I am no better than my ancestors."
Then he lay down under the bush and fell asleep.
1 Kings 19:3a, 4b–5

Once in a while, I have a flat day. So did Elijah—he had a very flat day.

He was a mighty man of God. He had confronted the evil King Ahab and set up a contest among the 450 false prophets of Baal, all of whom were supported by the king's wife, Jezebel. The wood was prepared; the false prophets slaughtered a bull and called on Baal to set fire to their sacrifice. They called from morning to midday, but Baal said nothing. Meanwhile, Elijah rebuilt the Lord's altar, put the wood and his sacrificed bull on it, and poured water over all of it. The god who answered by fire would be the true God. Elijah prayed a short prayer, and the fire of the Lord fell. The people seized the prophets of Baal and killed them.

Next, Elijah told Ahab to get something to eat because a miraculous, heavy rain was coming to break the drought. Elijah went to Carmel, assumed a posture of prayer, and sent his servant to check the clouds seven times. Finally, a cloud—Ahab rode in his chariot off to Jezreel. The rain poured, and Elijah ran ahead of Ahab. Ahab told Jezebel what had happened, and she threatened Elijah with death. This is why Elijah was afraid (I Kings 18:1–19:3).

Elijah's words show that he was depressed. The reasons for the depression might have included fear of his own death; physical exhaustion; and mental and emotional exhaustion after expending so much spiritual energy.

So what does Elijah do? He takes a nap. The angel of God visits him, and he takes something to eat. He takes another nap, the angel visits him again, and he obeys the angel's instructions by traveling to a private place. There, he and God meet and have a good conversation. There is an earthquake and fire, but God is not in those events; rather, he is in a gentle whisper. God gives Elijah an assignment, and he obeys—the depression was past (I Kings 19:3–21).

When I have a flat day, I maintain the following practices:

1. I still read the Word. All its promises are still true. I take courage in the angel's word to Joshua: "Be strong and courageous. Do not be afraid or terrified because of them, for the LORD your God goes with you; he will never leave you nor forsake you" (Deuteronomy 31:6).
2. I still pray. I recognize that though my receptivity to God's voice—my spiritual hearing—may be diminished for any number of reasons, God is still there and still speaking even when my hearing is not acute.
3. I still journal. In my journal entry, I note my flatness.
4. I search my heart to see if any sin is blocking my communication with God.
5. I check my recent activities. Have I had proper sleep and food?
6. I check my recent service for the Lord. If it has been very intense, emotional retraction may be normal. Rest is very helpful.
7. I do what Hazel Lee did when she received word that her son Gary had been captured and imprisoned in the takeover of the American Embassy in Iran. She was emotionally numb. She prayed, "Lord, what

should I do?" God responded, "Just take the next step." So Hazel went about her regular duties—she went to Sunday school, taught her class, and went to church. I, too, will go about my regular duties.

As I maintain these practices, I will not be surprised if, a little ways down the road, I receive a divine visit or hear a word from the Lord. And when it comes, I will have a joyous day.

God Offers Help in Trouble

God is our refuge and strength, an ever-present help in trouble. Therefore we will not fear, though the earth give way and the mountains fall into the heart of the sea, though its waters roar. The LORD Almighty is with us; the God of Jacob is our fortress.
Psalm 46:1–3, 11

For me, there was no question about it—once I became a Christian, I had to break away from my college fraternity and its problems with prejudice, liquor, and secrecy. But there came a critical letter from my dad that cut deeply—it seemed the earth would "give way." My girlfriend wrote a letter calling me demented, and she broke off our relationship—"mountains fall into the . . . sea." My fraternity put pressure on me—"its waters roar."

But hold on, my soul. These are circumstances; then there is the Lord, "our refuge and strength, an ever-present help in trouble." Within twenty-four hours, on three separate occasions, God gave me a verse I had not previously known: "When my father and my mother forsake me, then the LORD will take me up" (Psalm 27:10, KJV). Within six months, my mother was converted. Within fifteen months, my old fraternity invited me back to speak to them on how to become a Christian. Within four years, the Lord led me to a gracious Christian girl who became my wife. Within five years, my dad accepted Jesus Christ and is now in heaven waiting for me: "The LORD Almighty is with us."[14]

---

14. Previously published in *Come Ye Apart* January–February–March 1964 (Kansas City, MO: Nazarene Publishing House), 38. Used by permission. (This publication became *Reflecting God*.)

What about the Person Who's Never Heard of Christ?

*You, therefore, have no excuse, you who pass judgment on someone else,
for at whatever point you judge another, you are condemning yourself,
because you who pass judgment do the same things.*
Romans 2:1

If the Bible teaches that a person can come to the Father and find salvation only through Christ (John 14:6), what about the person who's never heard of Christ? It doesn't seem fair. What does Scripture say about this question?

1. "Since the creation of the world God's invisible qualities—his eternal power and divine nature—have been clearly seen, being understood from what has been made, so that people are without excuse" (Romans 1:20). Creation gives a powerful witness to *all* of God's power and nature, and all humanity can experience the created world.

2. "You, therefore, have no excuse, you who pass judgment on someone else, for at whatever point you judge another, you are condemning yourself" (2:1). How does this happen? Imagine a man who lives in an isolated tribe. He has never heard of Christ and lives in a culture that permits multiple wives. As this man is gathered with other men around a campfire, he lectures them, "It's not right for you to beat your wives!" The next night, his second wife puts too much salt on his roast beef, and he becomes incensed and beats her. He stands condemned and under God's judgment because he has violated the very standard he set for others—he has condemned himself. Even though the man has never heard of Christ, there is a fair standard by which he is judged.

3. No wonder Romans further says, "God's kindness is intended to lead you to repentance" (2:4).

4. And more: "They show that the requirements of the law are written on their hearts" (2:15). People's thoughts may accuse or defend them. "This will take place on the day when God judges people's secrets through Jesus Christ" (2:16). This is still a fair standard!

5. However, if you despair that, despite the fair standard, "all have sinned and fall short of the glory of God" (3:23), is there a way to somehow

obtain righteousness in the place of sin? "This righteousness is given through faith in Jesus Christ to all who believe" (Romans 3:22).

6. No wonder it is so important to give the message of Christ to everyone I know, and to do my part to send the message around the world.

Planning the Route

"Good teacher," he asked, "what must I do to inherit eternal life?"
Mark 10:17

Three thousand five hundred miles with ten stops lasting from one night to one week, all by car—that was my project today. It took careful planning, including locating and reserving a motel for the end of each day. It also included visiting a nephew, spending several days with a longtime friend, leading a week of revival services, and having a week of vacation. I was planning the route, but always with the goal of locating and safely arriving at specific destinations.

Planning routes and attaining goals are common patterns in life. You may choose a college or technical school to achieve the goal of a certain job or career. You may put some of your weekly earnings into a tax-sheltered annuity to save for your retirement. You may buy life insurance to provide for loved ones you leave behind.

A man ran up to Jesus and asked, "What must I do to inherit eternal life?" In this man's mind, "must I do" was the route, and "eternal life" was the goal. Jesus told him he must keep the Ten Commandments; the man said he had. Jesus, by his miraculous power, saw into the man's heart and located the key issue, the one area in which the man was lacking. He told him to cash in his physical resources and give the money to the poor—then he would have treasure in heaven. Additionally, he told the man, "Come, follow me" (Mark 10:21).

Other passages of Scripture flesh out our understanding of this goal of eternal life:

- Jesus, in John 17:3—"Now this is eternal life: that they know you, the only true God, and Jesus Christ, whom you have sent."
- John 3:16—"For God so loved the world that he gave his one and only Son, that whoever believes in him shall not perish but have eternal life."

- Paul, in Romans 6:23—"For the wages of sin is death, but the gift of God is eternal life in Christ Jesus our Lord."
- John again, in 1 John 5:11–12—"And this is the testimony: God has given us eternal life, and this life is in his Son. Whoever has the Son has life; whoever does not have the Son of God does not have life."

We all carefully plan routes toward goals that are limited to this life. How many of us have planned a route that leads to eternal life—a goal that will shape both this life and the next?

God First Loved Us

There is no fear in love. But perfect love drives out fear, because fear has to do with punishment. The one who fears is not made perfect in love.
1 John 4:18

"She'll have to apologize first. I'm willing to forgive and forget. But after the way she talked to me, I figure she owes me an apology." Have you ever heard anyone talk like that?

I wonder what would have happened to the Samaritan woman at Jacob's well if Jesus had taken that attitude toward her. There's no doubt the woman owed God an apology—more than that, she needed to repent. But she didn't seem to be in much of a "confessing" mood until the Savior first went to her. That is a mark of love—it will seek out the one who needs help.

But before love can be complete, there must be someone to receive and reciprocate it. Love is the only level on which people and God can perfectly communicate. Because we are human, we are limited by our varied abilities. However, our purpose and intent, if steadfastly motivated by the love of God, can be blessed with perfection. This is possible "because he first loved us" (v. 19).[15]

---

15. Previously published in *Come Ye Apart* January–February–March 1964 (Kansas City, MO: Nazarene Publishing House), 37. Used by permission. (This publication became *Reflecting God.*)

Telling Others

*Jesus . . . said, "Go home to your own people and tell them how much
the Lord has done for you, and how he has had mercy on you."*
Mark 5:19

When the wild man who lived in the graveyard met Jesus face to face, Jesus
recognized that he was demon-possessed. Once Jesus set him free from the
demons, the man changed—soon, he was "sitting there, dressed and in his
right mind" (Mark 5:15). He so appreciated what Jesus had done for him that
he asked Jesus if he could travel with him as Jesus went from town to town
preaching and healing. Jesus said no and gave him an assignment. Let's break
down Jesus's instructions to him phrase by phrase:

- "Go home to your own people"—Go to the ones you already know, the
  ones you understand, the ones who know you, including your past.
- "Tell them how much"—Describe the powerful, positive difference
  Christ has made in your life.
- "The Lord has done"—It's all about what Christ has done for you, not
  what you have done for Christ.
- "For you"—It's your personal story, not what someone else has said or
  experienced.

A year and a half after becoming the campus alcoholic and flunking out
of school, my friend Peter showed up in a chapel service. When we ran into
each other there, he gave me a one-sentence testimony: "Chic, I'm different
than I used to be because I found the Lord." Peter's words opened the door
to another complete testimony: within twenty-four hours of hearing Peter's
story, I received Christ.

My friend Jolene explained her acceptance of Christ like this: "My life
was like all the pieces of a puzzle, but God was the puzzle master."

Tom Phillips, president of Raytheon Corporation, testified to former
White House counsel Charles Colson:

> I didn't seem to have anything that mattered. It was all on the sur-
> face. All the material things in life are meaningless if a man hasn't discov-
> ered what's underneath them. . . .
>
> One night I was in New York on business and noticed that Billy Gra-
> ham was having a Crusade in Madison Square Garden . . . I went—cu-
> rious, I guess—hoping maybe I'd find some answers. What Graham said

that night put it all into place for me. I saw what was missing, the personal relationship with Jesus Christ, the fact that I hadn't ever asked him into my life, hadn't turned my life over to him. So I did it—that very night at the Crusade.

. . . I asked Christ to come into my life and I could feel his presence with me. His peace within me. I could sense his Spirit there with me. Then I went out for a walk alone on the streets of New York. I never liked New York before, but this night was beautiful. I walked for blocks and blocks. Everything seemed different to me. It was raining softly and the city lights created a golden glow. Something had happened to me and I knew it.[16]

Notice Phillips stressed a delineation between his life before Christ and after Christ.

One Wednesday night, I shared my faith and the way to eternal life with Lyle, a vice superintendent of schools. Lyle told me he was a careful and thoughtful person and couldn't accept Christ that night—he had to think about it. On Friday, he went to a hardware store to buy hinges for the new kitchen cabinets he was building. As he leaned over the displays, he heard a voice saying, "You are buying something that will rust. I want to give something that will last forever." So Lyle went out to his car, prayed, and received Jesus Christ and his eternal life. Within a year, Lyle had joined his church by profession of his faith and been elected Sunday school superintendent of his local church.

Do you know who spoke to Lyle in the hardware store? It was the Holy Spirit. Jesus said, "When the Advocate comes—the Spirit of truth—he will testify about me. And you also must testify" (John 15:26–27). The Holy Spirit is the great evangelist of the Trinity. He will back up and reinforce your witness and testimony, even if you are afraid.

Your Spiritual Story

---

16. Charles W. Colson, *Born Again* (Old Tappan, NJ: Fleming H. Revell, 1977), 110.

Jesus . . . said, "Go home to your own people and tell them how much the
Lord has done for you, and how he has had mercy on you."
Mark 5:19

As we apply Mark 5:19 to our lives today, we see that Jesus's words also describe our own testimonies.

Your spiritual story:
- Is positive—"how much"
- Glorifies the Lord—"the Lord"
- Is personal—"has done for you"
- Is verbal—"tell them"

It includes Before, How, and Since:
- What I was *before* I met Christ
- *How* I came to accept Christ
- What Jesus Christ has meant in my life *since*

And now I urge you—in one-on-one conversation and in public services, please tell "how much the Lord has done for you."[17]

Make Disciples Who Will Make Disciples

Go and make disciples of all nations.
Matthew 28:19

Still other seed fell on good soil, where it produced a crop—
a hundred, sixty or thirty times what was sown.
Matthew 13:8

He who wins souls is wise.
Proverbs 11:30, NKJV

The mission of the church is to make disciples who will make disciples who will make disciples—this was repeatedly exclaimed by godly pastor and seminary president Gordon Wetmore. And we have seen it demonstrated!

---

17. *The Good News: The Chic Shaver Center for Evangelism Newsletter* (March 2014).

A 1968 movement of the Holy Spirit made impact on young adults at a Shawnee, Kansas, church. Public school teacher Kathy told teacher Mike about Christ. Mike and his wife, Linda, visited the church. Pastor Melvin and his wife, Jeannie, went to their apartment. They shared the gospel, and both accepted Christ. After attending church several times and reading the Bible, Mike poured his liquor down the drain and proclaimed, "I don't think a Christian should be drinking." The next Palm Sunday, twenty-eight people were baptized, mostly young adults. Soon Mike was telling his pastor, "I believe God's leading me into the ministry."

Before long, Mike was enrolled in theological seminary to prepare. When, in his evangelism class, he was given an assignment to make contact with an unchurched person or family, Mike went across the street and talked to Jan on the front step of her home. Curt and Jan had moved from Indiana only ten days earlier. For them, April 1972 meant not only a new location but also an attempt to rebuild their life. Their boys, Scott and Chip, were only one and three.

That Sunday morning, they were at the Shawnee church, and a revival was in progress. As the evangelist preached, Curt felt conviction, wept, went forward to pray, repented, and received Jesus Christ as his Savior and Lord. Jan had prayed to receive Christ a few weeks earlier back in Indiana but had not known what to do next. Now Curt and Jan were on the same page. That night, Curt publicly told the Sunday evening crowd of nearly three hundred people what Christ had done for him that morning.

Five days later, the pastor went to Curt and Jan's home and started them on *Basic Bible Studies for New and Growing Christians.* Curt and Jan grew spiritually. Curt was delivered from tobacco and alcohol right away. Soon they began tithing. Whatever the Bible study said, they did. As a Kmart manager, Curt was given a different store nearly every year, and every year they moved. Everywhere they found great churches, great children's leaders, great teen leaders, and great pastors. Curt and Jan discipled their kids, and the churches discipled the whole family. With every move, the church was always their loving friendship base.

At age three and a half, Scott was led to Christ by his mom and dad in the home. In the sixth grade, Scott had a strong experience of the Spirit sanctifying him completely. After college, Scott felt God calling him away from a medical career and into the ministry. After he graduated in 1993, he married Jenni, and they began ministry assignments in Fort Wayne, Indiana. I called Scott, invited him to attend seminary, offered him an evangelism scholarship, and asked him to work on staff with me at a Kansas City church. Under his evangelism training, we saw many come to Christ.

After seminary, Scott returned to Fort Wayne as evangelism pastor. Soon, he was called to be lead pastor at a Houston church that flourished under his leadership. In eight and a half years, there was an attendance increase from four hundred to seven hundred, a new building, a church plant, and more. In the midst of the church's success, God interrupted and called Scott's family into missions. In 2012, Scott, Jenni, and their daughters, Bekah and Sarah, arrived in Kiev, Ukraine, and in 2015, Scott was commissioned by the denomination as field strategy coordinator for the Commonwealth of Independent States. Scott became responsible for pastoral training, discipleship, and evangelism for twelve nations in Europe and Asia. In 2018, Scott was elected to be an international director of Sunday school and discipleship. Now, his influence extends to all churches of his denomination across the world.

From 1968 to 2020. From Kathy, to Mike, to Linda, assisted by Rev. McCullough. To Curt and Jan. To Scott and Chip (who are now both in ministry). To pastors and new believers in Ukraine, Russia, Armenia, and the world: "Other seed fell on good soil, where it produced a crop—a hundred, sixty or thirty times what was sown" (Matthew 13:8). Make disciples who will make disciples who will make disciples.

Sowing to Please the Spirit

Whoever sows to please the Spirit, from the Spirit will reap eternal life. Let us not become weary in doing good, for at the proper time we will reap a harvest if we do not give up.
Galatians 6:8–9

"Hi, sir," the email began. The message continued: "My name is Joe Kumor. I participated in my ordination board today in Hastings, Nebraska. I hope to become a military chaplain. The pastor, Rev. John Whitsett, asked if I knew Frank and Peggy Kumor. They are my parents, although my mother passed away a number of years ago. He thought it amazing that he remembered an evangelism class taught by you around thirty-five years ago that mentioned my parents and now he was grilling their kid in an ordination board."

Do I ever remember Frank and Peggy Kumor! In 1975, they visited the local church where I served as minister of outreach. They were so open and friendly that I asked if we could visit with them further about their lives and the beliefs of our church. They said yes, that's what they wanted!

That Thursday night, two laypeople went with me to visit the Kumors at their home. The Holy Spirit opened doors and their hearts, and at 11:00 p.m. on February 13, 1975, both Frank and Peggy received Jesus into their hearts and lives as Savior and Lord (Revelation 3:20). By the next night, they had both completed the first lesson of *Basic Bible Studies for New and Growing Christians*. It was amazing—they had never studied the Bible like this before. Eight weeks after accepting Christ, they completed all the studies successfully. Their spiritual growth was rapid and strong—they attained victory over tobacco, began joyously tithing, and joined the church by profession of faith. Peggy also began writing some awesome spiritual truths. Three weeks after her conversion, she wrote, "February 13, at 11:00 p.m., I was happier than I've ever been. I believe what amplified the initial happiness was knowing this particular happiness is enduring. Knowing that Jesus has given me a place in heaven gives me daily happiness."

Frank soon completed his watch-making training in Kansas City. Afterward, they moved back to their native Nebraska. Frank began working in a jewelry store, and they became leaders in a local church. Frank eventually became owner of the store, and they became parents to seven children.

I had contact with the Kumors in 1996 while preaching at an Omaha church. Peggy had been through a battle with cancer, and soon after, she faced another. She told me she was so glad she could teach her children about eternal life. Soon, Peggy herself would be standing in the Lord's presence.

Time passed, and in 2015, when I received Joe Kumor's email, I had to call him and catch up on the family. I discovered several wonderful things. Joe is an associate pastor at a church. Frank, now married to Pat and still owner of the jewelry store, is active in the church. One of Joe's brothers, a medical doctor in the Air Force, served a short-term assignment at a mission hospital in Papua New Guinea. Six of the children are active in the church.

Upon hearing all this, I could only praise God. It was obvious the grace of God was all over this family, and they were walking in it. How encouraging that what was sown in 1975 reaped such a harvest forty years later. Let us sow—and, in the proper time, reap.

Snowball!

Jesus replied, "Very truly I tell you, everyone who sins is a slave to sin."
John 8:34

For little Jacob, the mountainside snow was simply an invitation to come out and play. He determined to build the biggest snowball he'd ever built. He packed snow together with his hands, and when his snowball was the right size, he placed it on the ground and began to roll it. The farther he rolled, the bigger it got. Soon, the snowball was heavy enough that pushing it was too hard. It occurred to Jacob that, instead of pushing it *around* the mountainside, pushing it *down* the mountain would be easy. As he pushed it down, the snowball started to roll on its own and began gathering speed. He had to run to keep up. Then he stumbled and his little body fell flat against the rolling snowball. In one revolution, fresh snow caked over him. Before he could break free, the snowball rotated again, and he was enveloped in another layer of snow. Faster and faster, layer after layer. Jacob was totally trapped. The snowball imprisoning Jacob plummeted down the mountain to rocks below. It smashed, and Jacob was killed. His play started out so innocently. But one commitment to roll a snowball *down* the mountain took Jacob beyond the point he intended to go.

Sin is like that—it will take you beyond the point you intended to go. Think about what happens when you lie and you're questioned about it: you need to tell another lie to cover the first one. That's why Jesus said sin will make you its *slave*. When I thought of my own past, I had to admit, "Sin controlled me; I didn't control it."

And what is the end result of this slavery to sin? Romans 6:23 tells us, "The wages of sin is death"—like Jacob at the bottom of the mountain. If sin is that powerful, what can we do? A greater power is required. The only answer is to come to Jesus Christ, the Son of God, who said, "If the Son sets you free, you will be free indeed" (John 8:36).

Thy Kingdom Come

And do not grieve the Holy Spirit of God, with whom you
were sealed for the day of redemption.
Ephesians 4:30

The kingdom of the world has become the kingdom of our Lord
and of his Messiah, and he will reign for ever and ever.
Revelation 11:15

Your kingdom come.
Luke 11:2b

The year 2020 was a troubling one for the United States. The coronavirus pandemic ravaged the country (as it did many other countries), but on top of that, the lockdowns and quarantines exacerbated the struggles of those battling addictions and mental health issues. Many Americans were restless and rebelled against the suggested restrictions. Racial tensions also escalated with the unjust police killing of a black man in Minneapolis. Americans of all backgrounds united in calling for justice, but the unity and peaceful protests were soon drowned out by riots and looting all over the country.

I was troubled, sad, and I prayed. The teachings of Christianity used to be influential in the United States. Over the years, the erosion of these values has been evident. Personal morals and behaviors became increasingly immoral. People have grieved the Holy Spirit, who has so greatly exerted his influence in our nation. It's been said that the word "grieve" is a love word. When we grieve the Spirit, he leaves. As a grieved God takes his hands off us, the decay and deterioration of our society sets in. It's as if God says, "Okay, try it your way, and see how life works with me left out."

Eventually, we will realize our only solution is the Lord. No wonder the voices of heaven were loud: "The kingdom of the world has become the kingdom of our Lord and his Messiah, and he will reign for ever and ever." And the twenty-four heavenly elders reply, "You have taken your great power and have begun to reign. The nations were angry, and your wrath has come" (Revelation 11:17–18). Christians are still praying, "Thy kingdom come."

She Was a Witness

But you will receive power when the Holy Spirit comes on you;
and you will be my witnesses in Jerusalem, and in all Judea
and Samaria, and to the ends of the earth.
Acts 1:8

She had hardly finished the sixth grade. Poverty and the demands on her as an older child in the family forced her to get a job as soon as possible. Her strong, early church training was neglected once she was out in the world, married, and raising children.

In her late forties, Jesus came to visit Vera again. In a revival service, she knelt, prayed, confessed, and received the Savior. After the service, Vera admitted she had been considering ending her own life. Now her burden of guilt was lifted. Jesus had not only saved her soul, but he had also saved her life.

She grew spiritually, attained victory over her tobacco and alcohol addictions, and became active in the church. She discovered she could have an even deeper relationship with God. Soon, in full surrender, Vera experienced the sanctifying and empowering work of the Holy Spirit.

My family needs to hear about this, she thought. So Vera drove from her Florida home to upstate New York. She made the rounds to as many of her siblings, nieces, and nephews as she could.

Her sister Mary was not a regular churchgoer, but Vera shared her faith and convinced Mary to go with her to services in Watertown. And Mary accepted Christ! She began attending the church regularly and growing spiritually.

Mary and her new church friends who lived in LaFargeville found the twenty-five-mile drive to the Watertown church to be especially difficult in three-feet-deep winter snows. They thought, *What about planting a Holiness church in little LaFargeville?* So they did!

Over the years, Mary kept up a steady witness to her nieces and nephews. At age eighty-seven, her heart was failing, and she was nearing the end. Relatives gathered around her.

Her nephew heard about her condition and phoned from a thousand miles away. He spoke to Mary briefly—she was so weak. She said, "It's sunshiny here, but it's better over there."

The next morning, the nephew called again, and family reported she had died early that morning. "Did she say anything else?" he asked.

"Yes," they said, "all night long she lay back on the pillow so weak. All of a sudden this morning, she sat up, raised her hands above her head and said, 'Oh, oh, they're all around me. The angels, they're all around me.' Then she lay back on her pillow and died."

By the power of the Spirit, Vera was a witness. By the power of the Spirit, Mary was a witness. I know the story well. Vera was my mom; Mary was my aunt.

Three or Four Filled with the Spirit

*When all the people were being baptized, Jesus was baptized too.
And as he was praying, heaven was opened and the Holy Spirit descended
on him in bodily form like a dove. And a voice came from heaven:
"You are my Son, whom I love; with you I am well pleased."*
Luke 3:21–22

He was Jesus, God in the flesh, and yet the Holy Spirit descended on him. And Scripture tells us more about the Spirit in Jesus's life:

- Luke 4:1—"Jesus, *full of the Holy Spirit*, left the Jordan."
- Luke 4:1—"was *led by the Spirit* into the wilderness."
- Luke 4:13—"Jesus returned to Galilee *in the power of the Spirit*."
- Luke 4:18—"The *Spirit of the Lord is on me*, because he has *anointed* me to proclaim good news to the poor."

If Jesus needed to be filled with the Spirit, what about his followers? On the day of Pentecost, the Holy Spirit fell on 120 praying followers of Jesus. Acts 2:4 tells us, "All of them were filled with the Holy Spirit," and a resulting great spiritual movement spread through Jerusalem.

Five years later, a problem arises in the church over distribution of food to widows. The apostles, needing help with this problem, call for the church to appoint lay leaders to take over this project. Note their requirements for these leaders: "Brothers and sisters, choose seven men from among you who are *known to be full of the Spirit* and wisdom" (6:3). Only Christians born of the Spirit, who were *known to be full of the Spirit*, could be chosen.

What happens next? Acts 6:5 tells us, "They chose Stephen, a man *full of faith and of the Holy Spirit.*" When Stephen stands and speaks boldly for Christ, a mob attacks him and eventually kills him. Yet Stephen is able to face this violence with amazing power and love. How come? Acts 7:55 tells us, "But Stephen, *full of the Holy Spirit,* looked up to heaven and saw the glory of God, and Jesus standing at the right hand of God." Stephen is so filled with love and forgiveness that just before he dies, he prays, "Lord, do not hold this sin against them" (v. 60).

Many Christians today realize the need for a deeper relationship with God beyond their present relationship with Christ. They wish to do more for God, but do not have the power to do it on their own. They know they have been born of the Spirit (John 3:5), but now need to be filled with the Spirit.

Sherwood Wirt, former editor of *Decision* magazine for the Billy Graham organization, realized that his Christian life was filled with inner struggles—especially feelings of bitterness and resentment and lack of love. In Isaiah 61:1, 3, he read, "The Spirit of the Lord God is upon me . . . to give unto them beauty for ashes, the oil of joy for mourning, the garment of praise for the spirit of heaviness" (KJV). He waited on the Lord, and later testified:

> I was abdicating the throne of my life (my Christian life, that is) . . . When I asked him to crucify me, he accepted my statement and fulfilled my request. In his own time and at his own pleasure, he sent a divine solvent into this troubled heart . . . I don't know just how the Love came in, but I know that all the bitterness I held against others—including those near me—disappeared. Resentment—hostility—hurt feelings—you name it. They all dissolved. Evaporated. Went.[18]

Love became Sherwood Wirt's theme. And no wonder! Romans 5:5 says, "And hope does not put us to shame, because God's love has been poured out into our hearts through the Holy Spirit, who has been given to us."

Jesus, Stephen, Sherwood Wirt—all three filled with the Holy Spirit. Should your name be added to that list?

---

18. Sherwood Eliot Wirt, *Afterglow: The Excitement of Being Filled with the Spirit* (Grand Rapids: Zondervan, 1976), 17–19.

A Love Relationship

Whoever has my commands and keeps them is the one who loves me.
The one who loves me will be loved by my Father, and I too
will love them and show myself to them.
John 14:21

Jared and I met in Maryland during a local church revival and had a great conversation. There, he told me the story of his spiritual journey:

I was raised in church. I was living what looked like a good Christian life to outsiders, but inside, I was lukewarm. I had a relationship with Christ, but not a love relationship. I never saw my dad read the Bible, and he showed no emotion in his faith. Then, four years ago, he was sanctified. He put both hands in the air and began to sing. I can't get over the change in him. Now, every morning he is studying his Bible and writing in his notebook. His relationship with his wife and children rose to a whole new level. He became a spiritual leader.

A short time later, Jared was mowing along the roadside. Jared continues his testimony:

God said clearly, "Is this all you're going to give me?" I had been selfish with time, and God wasn't top priority. It hit me so hard.

I said back to God, "I'm yours. Do what you want with me." It's the scariest thing I've ever said.

I sensed a call to ministry. I went home to tell my wife. I was bawling the whole time. She asked, "What's wrong?"

I said, "Babe, I'm scared to death. I'm afraid God is going to move us out of here."

She said, "Jared, I married you, and I serve the same God you do. I'm in. I trust him, and I trust you."

I was sanctified in revival a year ago. God began to prune stuff out of me. Hebrews 12:1 tells us to "throw off everything that hinders." He took away certain TV shows and whatever was keeping me from closeness to the Lord. He became all I needed.

Jared became involved in youth ministry. His testimony continues:

The youth program grew to more than thirty teens. Some of the teens caught fire. God put peace in my heart. It's thriving when God is leading.

When I speak, I can tell when God is talking through me. This is what it means to be filled with the Spirit.

It has been fulfilling. I can't tell you the amount of prayers answered this week since Sunday. I know it's because I've given authority over to God.

As you can see, Jared has moved into a love relationship with Jesus. Jesus's words in John 14:21 are part of his promise to send the Holy Spirit to his disciples (vv. 15–21). What a privilege that this same love relationship is available to us all.

Sanctified by the Holy Spirit

He gave me the priestly duty of proclaiming the gospel of God,
so that the Gentiles might become an offering acceptable to God,
sanctified by the Holy Spirit.
Romans 15:16

Some people laughed at Jeff and Melissa for attending a Bible study on the Holy Spirit on Friday nights. People said that they were too young, that they should be out on the town doing more fun things.

However, Melissa reports, "I cannot tell you how much fun Jeff and I have had with *Living in the Power of the Spirit*." Further, she says:

I have learned what it means to be completely sanctified and filled with the Spirit . . . I have learned how my selfish nature controls my life and how to die to self and let the Spirit guide and control me . . . I have been able to completely forgive friends that have hurt me in the past and mend those broken relationships. I have been able to establish a daily practice of spending time in the Word and in prayer . . . I have seen the Spirit's guidance in making some important school and career decisions. And I have seen how living in the power of the Spirit can enrich one's life . . . because that is what has happened to me.

Even today, how true this is to Paul's ministry—Jeff and Melissa are "an offering acceptable to God, sanctified by the Holy Spirit."[19]

---

19. Taken from *Reflecting God* June–July–August 2010 (Kansas City, MO: WordAction Publishing Co.), 12. Used by permission.

Without Grumbling

❖

Do everything without grumbling or arguing, so that you may become blameless and pure, "children of God without fault in a warped and crooked generation." Then you will shine among them like stars in the sky as you hold firmly to the word of life.
Philippians 2:14–16

"I complain all the time at my job," he blurted out. Elgin was part of an intense discipleship group that was spending twelve weeks studying the work of the Holy Spirit. He had worked for years at a Christian publishing company. He was shocked and embarrassed when he realized how much he complained.

For the most part, Elgin lived a devoted Christian life, and he read his Bible. But maybe for the first time, this verse caught his attention. He was in this discipleship group for the sake of his spiritual growth, so he was determined to change his habit of complaining. By the twelfth week of the study, he was reporting and rejoicing that he could go a whole day without complaining.

A friend of mine had to go to her basement greenhouse to get some plants ready to move upstairs. At the floor drain, she found a pool of water. She knew there were periodic backups, but it had only been eight months since she and her neighbors last called a plumber to clear the pipes. She had been going through some challenges lately, including financial struggles, a major change in her job situation, and other house repairs that needed attention.

"Oh Lord, really!" she exclaimed. "I don't need another problem. I'm going to break."

But the Lord cut her off: "Your father just called. He's sending you a check. I've got this covered. You don't need to complain."

Immediately, her attitude changed. "That's right. Thank you, Lord," she breathed.

The backup was on Sunday. The check arrived Monday, but at 4:30 p.m. instead of the usual noontime. Despite the late hour, when she called the plumber, he said he'd be there in thirty minutes. The plumber cleared the drain, and after paying him $79, she had $121 left over.

These two people moved from grumbling and complaining to shining like stars. Likewise, Christians with pure, Spirit-filled hearts should find it natural to rejoice and shine. What a message it sends to everyone around us when we do!

47

Food You Do Not Know

"My food," said Jesus, "is to do the will of him who sent me
and to finish his work."
John 4:34

On November 20, 1955, at nine o'clock in the evening, Jesus Christ walked into my heart. I was so thrilled to have him as a guest that I invited him to visit every area of my heart, his newfound home.

We sat at the table together in the dining room—the room of the appetites and desires. The Lord Jesus did not touch the food placed before him, which still had the flavor of the world in it.

When I asked him why he did not touch his food, he turned, and looking me straight in the eye, he said, "I have food to eat that you know nothing about. . . . My food . . . is to do the will of him who sent me" (vv. 32, 34).

Right there at the table of my heart, he gave me a taste of what it means to do God's will. Since then, I have found everything else dissatisfying.[20]

48

Love to the Limit

---

20. Previously published in *Come Ye Apart* January–February–March 1964 (Kansas City, MO: Nazarene Publishing House), 35. Used by permission. (This publication became *Reflecting God*.)

I pray that you, being rooted and established in love, may have power, together with all the Lord's holy people, to grasp how wide and long and high and deep is the love of Christ, and to know this love that surpasses knowledge—that you may be filled to the measure of all the fullness of God.
Ephesians 3:17–19

How much love can you hold? A lot, apparently. Paul prays the following for the Ephesians and for us:

- To be rooted and established in love
- To grasp the full extent of the love of Christ
- To know this love that surpasses knowledge

When you realize the extent of Christ's love—a love so deep that he went to the cross to die for our sins—you might doubt that you could ever love like that. Yet Paul surrounds us with assurances that God has the power to bring us to that kind of love.

He says that God has "glorious riches" from which he can draw to strengthen us with power by his Spirit in our inner being (Ephesians 3:16). He prays that Christ may settle down and be at home in our hearts (v. 17). It's our privilege to be "filled with all the fulness of God" (v. 19, KJV). And if you still think this is too big an order, Paul concludes by telling us that God can do "more than all we ask or imagine" (v. 20).

It helps if we can see a present-day human being living with that kind of love. I'm blessed because I have seen them. At a conference in Manila, Philippines, I met such a person—Carl, a missionary to Smoky Mountain. The city of Manila was so overwhelmed with the volume of garbage they produced that they began dumping it in the Pasig River. Soon, the site was a mountain of garbage, so city officials set it on fire to diminish its size. Garbage doesn't burn well, but it generates a lot of smoke—thus, the spot became known as Smoky Mountain.

Twenty thousand people in desperate poverty flocked to the mountain to find a place to live. They built shacks out of cardboard, plywood, or discarded tin. Their floors were dirt, and they had to walk a quarter-mile to get water from one community spigot.

Carl was enthusiastic about what the Lord was doing at his ministry assignment. He told us he had ten men who had become disciples of Christ. They had been changed: they had victory over tobacco, alcohol, and gambling; they were treating their wives with love and kindness; Carl was helping them build better homes. He loved these ten disciples.

When we asked Carl what he planned to do next, he was excited. Soon he would have a furlough and return to his native Sweden, where he would get to see his family.

And then what? With great enthusiasm, he said, "Oh, I can't wait to get back to Smoky Mountain!" That day, in a real live human being, I saw a love like Christ's—love to the limit.

To Be Presented Holy

Now he has reconciled you by Christ's physical body
through death to present you holy in his sight,
without blemish and free from accusation.
Colossians 1:22

If I were going to be presented to God, I'd want my Sunday best on. Yet somehow, I don't think that's what he's going to look at. I've been living in the kingdom for years now and have seen many blemishes. I have my own memorized.

There's a path of forgiveness at our house, a well-worn one. Sometimes I'd rather not use it because it's easier to "do unto others as they do to me." It's not easy to choose love, but it works. It's not easy to respond instead of reacting, but it works. It's not easy to confront a problem that needs resolution when I'd rather not face it, but it works. It's not easy to let a little thing go, but it works.

God must look and not see my blemishes, just as I looked at each of my three newborn babies and said, "They are perfect." Because of God's gift to me, I am reconciled. What was broken is mended. What was separated was brought back together. What never was now is. It works!

Nancy Shaver[21]

---

21. Previously published in *Come Ye Apart* March–April–May 1996 (Kansas City, MO: Nazarene Publishing House), 29. Used by permission. (This publication became *Reflecting God*.)

You Were the Only One

*Let us hold unswervingly to the hope we profess, for he who
promised is faithful. And let us consider how we may spur one another
on toward love and good deeds, not giving up meeting together,
as some are in the habit of doing, but encouraging one another—
and all the more as you see the Day approaching.*
Hebrews 10:23–25

"We really do need each other" was Reuben Welch's famous and oft-quoted phrase. The writer of Hebrews believed that too—and so do we.

The early church frequently met in private homes. The wealthy businesswoman, Lydia, came to faith in Christ under Paul's ministry (Acts 16:14–15). Later, we read, "After Paul and Silas came out of the prison, they went to Lydia's house, where they met with the brothers and sisters and encouraged them" (16:40). A major focus of this house church meeting was this: "they . . . encouraged them."

Eventually, churches came to be more often established in public meeting places—often, in a building set aside as a house of worship. Even in these new settings, a major goal of these church gatherings was still to encourage one another and "spur one another on toward love and good deeds."

One man approached an ordained minister and stated that he did not see the need for an organized church. He went on to explain that he called his wife and children together each Sunday, preached to them, and served them Communion from time to time—and that was sufficient. But since this gathering was only one small family, who held them accountable? To whom did they pay their tithe? No wonder the writer of Hebrews warned that we should not give up meeting together. More than just one family, "we really do need each other."

During the COVID-19 lockdown, many governments promoted social distancing and urged or even required churches to stop having physical gatherings. Many churches conducted worship with a pastor, a few musicians, and an empty sanctuary, using digital technology to communicate to parishioners in their homes. This was a good action under the circumstances, but everywhere Christians were saying, "I can't wait 'til we get back to church together."

A minister was the guest speaker at a church outside of his regular parish. Gary, a pastor on staff at the church, approached the minister and recounted an experience from more than forty years earlier, when Gary and his wife had just begun a church assignment in a new district. At the time, the guest speaker was serving in the same district. Gary recalled, "When we arrived, we didn't know anybody. You were the only one who paid any attention to us. You and your wife took us out to lunch." How shocking. May this never happen again.

So do your part. Get neck-deep in a church that is true to the Bible and honors Jesus Christ. Join those around you in "spurring one another on toward love and good deeds" and "encouraging one another." Later, may people say not, "You were the only one," but rather, "You were one of many people who loved and paid attention to us."

No Other Name

Salvation is found in no one else, for there is no other name under heaven given to mankind by which we must be saved.
Acts 4:12

It would be rare for someone to willingly suffer jail time for a myth or a hunch. Peter and John, imprisoned for preaching Christ, had known Jesus in his life, death, and resurrection—they knew for sure that Jesus was God come in the flesh.

Though the lame man spent every day in a religious place surrounded by religious people who were constantly praying, he had never been healed through them. But in the name of Jesus, he was healed instantly (Acts 3:6–7).

Though the authorities challenged him, Peter was emboldened by the fullness of the Spirit (4:8), and preached that Christ offers not only healing but also salvation. Peter is very specific: "There is no other name under heaven given to mankind by which we must be saved" (4:12).

A Vietnamese pastor spent more than forty weeks of a year in jail. Most Sundays, he preached, then authorities arrived to arrest him and jail him. Upon his release, he was given an official document recording his arrest. The pastor saved these documents because, in Vietnam, a church can only be registered after fifteen years of operation—and his arrest documents prove the fifteen years. All the while, he has been preaching, "Salvation is found in no one else" but Christ.[22]

How Sacred Is Sunday?

You shall have no other gods before me.
Remember the Sabbath day by keeping it holy.
Exodus 20:3, 8

The true, amazing, only God had rescued Israel from Egyptian slavery. They were to be his people alone. In a momentous meeting with Moses on Mount Sinai, God issued the Ten Commandments. Right away, he told the people to have no other gods—only "the LORD your God." He issued further laws to protect his people and help them keep him first in their hearts and lives. One of these laws was to keep the Sabbath holy.

After Jesus was crucified, Mary Magdalene and the other Mary went to his tomb. Matthew 28:1 specifies the time: "After the Sabbath, at dawn on the first day of the week." While they were there, an angel announced, "He is not here; he has risen, just as he said" (v. 6). The resurrection of Jesus Christ became the most important event in Jesus's life and ministry. As the new Christian movement spread, Christians began increasingly to meet on Sunday, the first day of the week. In 1 Corinthians 16:2, Paul urges the Christians, "On the first day of every week, each one of you should lay aside a sum of money in keeping with your income, saving it up, so that when I come no collections will have to be made." In the modern world, probably 95 percent of all Christians consider Sunday, the day Jesus rose from the dead, to be their day of worship.

He was often criticized for the way he treated the Sabbath; certain Pharisees even plotted to kill him because he performed a healing on the Sabbath, which violated the strict laws the Jews had developed to keep the Sabbath holy (Mark 3:2–6). Jesus answered their outrage with a rhetorical question: "Which is lawful on the Sabbath: to do good or to do evil, to save life or to

---

22. Previously published in *Reflecting God* June–July–August 2010 (Kansas City, MO: WordAction Publishing Co.), 23. Used by permission.

kill?" (3:4). During his time on earth, Jesus revealed a new understanding of the Sabbath—he showed us that "to do good" is appropriate activity on the day of worship.

At another time, Jesus further addressed the issue with another question: "If one of you has a child or an ox that falls into a well on the Sabbath day, will you not immediately pull it out?" (Luke 14:5). It is okay to respond to the emergencies of your children or animals on the days of worship.

In my early life, I treated the Lord's Day with carelessness. The slightest inconvenience would keep me from church. But after I came to know Christ personally, I became very sensitive about honoring the Lord's Day. I came to believe it was a day for worship, fellowship, service, and rest.

Once, I was visiting the home of a childhood friend and their family. We went to church. My friend's mom had put a roast in the oven before we left. Upon arriving home, we found that the roast had burned, and the resulting smoke had left an oily residue all over the furniture. At first, I was troubled—was it a worship day or a work day? But I knew I needed to pitch in and help, so we all worked together to clean the furniture. It was a case of "the ox in the well."

To this day, I am conscientious about maintaining Sunday as a day of worship. If company comes to visit, they are warmly welcomed to come to church with us. If they decline, they know that my priority will be to visit the house of the Lord. If I am traveling, I make a travel schedule that preserves Sundays as worship days.

I once heard an old saying: "The Jews kept the Sabbath, and the Sabbath kept them." I believe I can honestly say that in the more than sixty-five years since I first met Christ, "I have kept the Lord's Day, and the Lord's Day has kept me." And that keeping has been rich, joyful, abundant, and overflowing.

Here's a good exercise—finish this sentence by filling in the blank: "Lord, I'm skipping church this morning because meeting with you is not as important as _____."

Will I Be Like You?

*Jesus replied, "Very truly I tell you, no one can see
the kingdom of God unless they are born again."*
John 3:3

But grow in the grace and knowledge of our Lord and Savior Jesus Christ.
2 Peter 3:18

"If I accept Jesus Christ tonight, will I be like you tonight since you have followed Christ for many years?" This was Peggy's sincere and serious question to me. I and two other people from the church sat with Frank and Peggy in their living room. We discussed in detail what it meant to receive Christ and follow him. We explained that when someone truly accepts Christ into their life, the person is so transformed that Jesus called it being "born again."

Now Peggy wanted to know if, one minute after accepting Christ, she would be just like me—someone who had followed Christ for years. The next part of our conversation went something like this:

"Peggy, you've told me about your son, Brent. How old is he?"

"Three."

"How's he doing in algebra?"

Shocked, she replied, "He doesn't do algebra."

"That's right. He's been born. He's truly alive. He talks, he walks, he runs, he plays. He's healthy and fully alive. He's all he's supposed to be for three years old. But he's not yet all he is going to be. Someday he will go to school, learn his numbers, learn to add and subtract, then to multiply and divide. And someday he will learn algebra."

I continued, "When you are born again spiritually, you become truly and fully alive in Christ. You now have a real spiritual life. But you have a whole life of growing ahead of you. God will be patient with you. He will lead you step-by-step, as you can handle it, into a stronger and more mature life. There are some lessons he taught me my first week, some he taught me a year later, and some just last week. It is an exciting way to live, with God himself growing you week by week."

Peggy was satisfied. That night, both Frank and Peggy received Christ into their lives and began a journey with Jesus. And did they ever grow!

No wonder we have both admonitions: "Be born again," and, "Grow in the grace and knowledge of our Lord and Savior Jesus Christ."

Grow

But grow in the grace and knowledge of our Lord and Savior Jesus Christ.
2 Peter 3:18

I'm having surgery tomorrow morning. It's nothing major—just cataract sur-gery. Yet there are so many steps to get there. With twenty-four hours to go, I've had a preliminary medical exam and three rounds of eye drops. I still need to thoroughly wash my face tonight and in the morning; have no food or water after midnight; take only certain, allowed prescriptions upon waking; have someone drive me to and from the surgery center; leave my valuables at home; present my medical history paperwork, driver's license, insurance card, and credit card at the admissions desk; and more.

All these little steps are taken to get to one successful surgery, then a life-time of improved vision. I have taken each step with a positive spirit because I like the final outcome. I believe it is all worth it because I've already had successful surgery on one eye, and life is so much brighter.

Peter has had many things to say in his two letters to early Christians. He speaks about "the sanctifying work of the Spirit" (1 Peter 1:2); "new birth into a living hope" (v. 3); an "inheritance" in heaven (v. 4); "be holy" (v. 16); and "rid yourselves of all malice and all deceit" (2:1). He says, "Like newborn babies, crave pure spiritual milk, so that by it you may grow up in your sal-vation" (2:2).

There are times in spiritual life when you take small baby steps, knowing you will attain great advances and victory in the future. As a young Christian, I read biographies of great mature Christians like Hudson Taylor's *Spiritual Secret* and Rees Howell's *Intercessor*. These men had great answers to prayer and victories. I was drawn to more in my spiritual life because of them, but I knew it would take many years of growth to get there. But I was not dis-couraged that I was not there yet. Even as you read through these devotional pages, you will see great things done by God. Let this inspire you to greater heights, rather than dismay because it's not yet your experience.

In my early Christian life, I might pray ten minutes a day and read one New Testament chapter a day. But I knew there were richer things ahead. At one point, I felt great temptation and tried to pray through it, but could not. Only after running over to my spiritual mentor's college dorm room and pouring my heart out to him did I find the answer.

In the church where I had recently found Christ, I noticed an older Chris-tian living an inconsistent life and complained to my pastor about him. My pastor encouraged me, counseled patience, and cautioned against a judgmen-tal spirit. How much these little steps have shaped my present life.

I share all of this so that you will grow in God's grace. I know you can do it.

A Knock at the Door

Here I am! I stand at the door and knock. If anyone hears my voice and
opens the door, I will come in and eat with that person, and they with me.
Revelation 3:20

A picture can be the means of a person receiving Jesus into their heart and life.

Above is Warner Sallman's famous picture of Christ knocking at a door. Sallman's *Head of Christ, Christ at Heart's Door,* and other paintings have appeared in one billion images of Christ that have circulated around the world.[23]

Christ at Heart's Door is based on the appeal to the church in Laodicea in Revelation 3:20. Though the call is specifically for the lukewarm to open their church and lives afresh to Christ, it also establishes a broader spiritual principle: wherever there is an opened door, there will be an entering Christ. Thus, the passage can be applied to individuals in need of salvation.

Here is a summary of my conversation with Fred and Patty after a previous discussion showed their understanding of the gospel:

---

23. Based on research done by Chaplain Don Weston at Anderson University, Scheierman Gallery, Anderson, Indiana, and Weston's article, "Christ at Heart's Door Painting." Order from TheFoundryPublishing.com or 1-800-877-0700. Use item number AW-250 for package of 100.

Chic Shaver: Fred and Patty, here is a famous picture of Christ knocking at the heart's door. It is based on Revelation 3:20, "Here I am! I stand at the door and knock. If anyone hears my voice and opens the door, I will come in and eat with that person, and they with me." Notice the light over the door's stone archway, and then to the left under the wooden arch? The light then tapers down to Jesus's feet. If you use your imagination, you can see the shape of a heart. Can you see that?

Fred: Yes, we can!

Chic Shaver: Let's think of that as Jesus knocking at your heart's door. Notice the thorns growing around Jesus's feet, as though he has been knocking for a long time. It seems to me that Christ has been knocking at your heart's door for a long time. Do you sense that?

Patty: I think we'd both have to say yes—he has been knocking for a long time.

Chic Shaver: See the little window? It's dark inside because a life is always dark within when Christ is left out. Then, notice Christ only knocks; he doesn't try to push open the door. This is because the door must be opened from the inside.

Fred: I get it.

Chic Shaver: A common way to lock doors in that day was to drop a plank in a metal bracket on each side of the door. To open the door, the one inside would have to push the plank out of the brackets and to one side of the door. The verse before Revelation 3:20, verse 19, ends with the word "repent." If we are going to open our heart's door to Christ, we must tell God we are sorry for our sins and, with God's help, turn from our sins. In the imagery of this picture, if we really want to open the door to Christ, we must push the plank of sin away. Is this making sense to you?

Fred: It sure is.

Patty: Yes, it does.

Chic Shaver: If you open your heart's door to Christ, he promises to come in. But you must understand that when you open that door, you are accepting him as Savior, the forgiver of all your sins, and as Lord, the leader of your life. That means that starting now, you would do what he wants you to do. You let him call the shots. Is this what you are willing to do?

Fred: Yes, it is.

Patty nods yes.

Tomorrow's devotional will tell you what happened next.

The Power of a Picture

Those whom I love I rebuke and discipline. So be earnest and repent.
Here I am! I stand at the door and knock. If anyone hears my voice and
opens the door, I will come in and eat with that person, and they with me.
Revelation 3:19–20

Chic Shaver: It seems to me, Fred and Patty, that Christ is asking you right now if you would like to receive him and his gift of eternal life by opening the door of your heart to Christ. If I could help you do that by praying with you, is that what you would like to do?

Patty: Oh, yes!

Fred: That's what I want to do.

Chic Shaver: Would you like to pray your own prayer, or repeat a prayer after me if you can really mean it?

Fred: You pray, and we'll repeat if after you.

I prayed the following prayer, and they repeated after me.

Chic Shaver: O God, I am sorry for my sins, and with your help, I turn from them. Just now, I open the door of my heart to you, Jesus. I receive you as the one who forgives all my sins and the one to take charge of my life. Just now, I receive you into my heart and life. Amen.

I then asked them to keep their heads bowed while I asked several questions.

Chic Shaver: Fred, did you mean it when you told God you were sorry for your sins and turning from those sins?

Fred: Yes, I did.

Chic Shaver: Did you mean it when you invited Christ to come into your heart and become the leader of your life?

Fred: Yes, I did.

Chic Shaver: Jesus said that if anyone opens the heart's door, he will come in. Do you think he meant that?

Fred: Yes, he did.

Chic Shaver: If you turned from your sins and meant it; if you opened your heart's door and meant it; and if Jesus said that if you opened the door, he would come in; then where is Jesus right now?

Fred: He's in my heart.

At the end of our conversation, Fred got very serious, and I asked Patty similar questions. She told me, "He's in my heart," and began to weep.

We all raised our heads. I shook their hands and said, "Welcome into the kingdom of God!" They were all smiles. Big smiles.

I immediately started a discipleship process with them that included starting them on *Basic Bible Studies for New and Growing Christians*. I took the picture of Jesus and wrote on the back: "Fred Smith opened the door of his heart to Christ on February 13, 2018—Revelation 3:20." I asked Fred to sign the spiritual birth certificate and asked any who came with me to sign it too. I also gave Patty a similar picture and statement.

The picture of Christ knocking at the door is a natural illustration of the gospel message with each element of the painting reminding you what to say next. The power of a picture! A knock at the door! Have you invited Christ into your heart and life? Do you know someone who needs you to explain this picture to them?

May God Bless You

That night the L ORD appeared to him and said, "I am the God of your father Abraham. Do not be afraid, for I am with you; I will bless you and will increase the number of your descendants for the sake of my servant Abraham." Isaac built an altar there and called on the name of the L ORD. There he pitched his tent, and there his servants dug a well.
Genesis 26:24–25

Let's summarize the context of the passage above:
- The Lord had a personal meeting with Isaac.
- The Lord told Isaac not to be afraid. Why? Because the Lord would be with him.
- God promised to *bless* Isaac and give him many descendants.
- Isaac did not take this meeting lightly. He immediately built an altar and worshiped the Lord.
- Isaac's *blessing* included the presence of God; immediate relief of physical suffering (a successful well of water in a desperately dry place); and a chain of descendants resulting in the birth of Jesus Christ.

In the Bible, a blessing is bestowed for good—often a material and a spiritual good.

Matthew 7:11 recounts Jesus's teaching on prayer: "If you, then, though you are evil, know how to give good gifts to your children, how much more will your Father in heaven give good gifts to those who ask him!" Luke 11:13 explains further what Jesus said at that time: "If you then, though you are evil, know how to give good gifts to your children, how much more will your Father in heaven give the Holy Spirit to those who ask him!" Apparently, the Holy Spirit is the best of all the gifts. No wonder we say that anyone who receives the Holy Spirit is truly blessed. When you have the Holy Spirit, you have God himself.

What a blessing it is to receive the Spirit in his sanctifying fullness. As Galatians 5:25 puts it, "Since we live by the Spirit, let us keep in step with the Spirit." This can truly be called "living in the blessing." *May God bless you.*

Self-Discipline

Therefore I do not run like someone running aimlessly;
I do not fight like a boxer beating the air. No, I strike
a blow to my body and make it my slave so that after I have
preached to others, I myself will not be disqualified for the prize.
1 Corinthians 9:26–27

Can you believe that the man who said, "For it is by grace you have been saved, through faith—and this is not from yourselves, it is the gift of God" (Ephesians 2:8), and, "No, in all these things we are more than conquerors through him who loved us" (Romans 8:37), and, "My God will meet all your needs according to the riches of his glory in Christ Jesus" (Philippians 4:19) would put such an emphasis on self-discipline as to say, "I strike a blow to my body and make it my slave"?

I told my young friend who had recently accepted Christ and had a background of serious alcohol abuse, "You cannot afford to even take one drink." Another friend had often felt defeated by her overeating and excess weight, but I saw her finally discipline her eating and bring her weight under control.

I decided to honor God in my thought life by countering the first glimpse of suggestive TV scenes with the two-second rule: within two seconds, I would use the remote to change the channel.

God may have given you a clean heart, but you will have to discipline your feelings about the hurts of life. Dr. Jim Diehl once said that if you don't give your heart to Jesus, the hurt may become bitterness, which may become resentment, which may become hatred. He said, "If you don't self-discipline, you will never stay in victory." Even the apostle Paul self-disciplined so that he would not be "disqualified for the prize."

And what is the end result of the self-discipline? The woman who lost weight told me she felt good about herself, felt victorious, and experienced joy. Imagine how *you* will feel when you see the fruits of self-discipline in your own life. When you draw on the grace of God to discipline yourself, victory happens. You will run the race with purpose and finish well.

Why So Much Killing?

When the Lord your God has delivered them over to you and you have defeated them, then you must destroy them totally. Make no treaty with them, and show them no mercy. Do not intermarry with them. Do not give your daughters to their sons or take their daughters for your sons, for they will turn your children away from following me to serve other gods, and the Lord's anger will burn against you and will quickly destroy you.
Deuteronomy 7:2–4

After the Lord your God has driven them out before you, do not say to yourself, "The Lord has brought me here to take possession of this land because of my righteousness." No, it is on account of the wickedness of these nations that the Lord is going to drive them out before you.
Deuteronomy 9:4

"Why is there so much killing in the Old Testament?" is a question I've been asked many times over the years. I admit that it is troubling. Here are some thoughts on the issue:

1. Israel is to take possession of the nations not because of Israel's righteousness but rather because of those nations' wickedness (Deuteronomy 9:4). They are evil.

2. Israel is to destroy these populations totally. If they don't, and the nations' daughters marry Israel's sons, the daughters' influence will eventually draw Israel into worshiping false gods. God is endeavoring to establish a new land in which he is honored as the only true God (Deuteronomy 7:3–4).

3. The total destruction of the evil nations is a picture of what spiritual life should be—the removal of *all* sin from our hearts and lives, and a total yielding to the one true God. There can be no rivals—our hearts must be 100 percent God's.

After Jesus comes to our world, we see a new emphasis. He fulfills what the Old Testament portrayed, and now we have a New Testament.

1. Jesus teaches, "Love your enemies and pray for those who persecute you" (Matthew 5:44). We are called not to the sword, but to love: "Do not be overcome by evil, but overcome evil with good" (Romans 12:21).

2. We are not to allow any traces of evil in our lives, lest they pull us back into a life of sin: "Let us throw off everything that hinders and the sin that so easily entangles. And let us run with perseverance the race marked out for us" (Hebrews 12:1).

3. God calls Christians to a *full* surrender of our entire lives: "Therefore, I urge you, brothers and sisters, in view of God's mercy, to offer your bodies as a living sacrifice, holy and pleasing to God—this is your true and proper worship" (Romans 12:1). The New Testament even speaks of totally killing all evil in our lives. As Paul puts it, "I have been crucified with Christ and I no longer live, but Christ lives in me" (Galatians 2:20).

This is the sort of killing I would be most concerned with today—the killing of sin. Matthew 5:8 says, "Blessed are the pure in heart, for they will see God." Are you willing to become one of the pure in heart?

God So Loved Us

Dear friends, let us love one another, for love comes from God.
Everyone who loves has been born of God and knows God.
1 John 4:7

Rees Howells's room was in the basement of the mission house. He was the only human occupant there. But Rees said he had visitors during the night—creeping things that thrive in hot climates. One morning, as he prepared to eat his breakfast of oatmeal and cheese, he found that insects had beaten him to it. At first, Rees could not help but have hard feelings against his friend who had given him such a place to live. Then God spoke to Rees, saying that Jesus had loved him when he treated Jesus worse than his friend had treated him.

Out on the hills of that tropical island, Rees prayed. He lost sight of his friend and saw the Savior who loved those who put him to death! By the time God had worked on Rees's inner nature, the Holy Spirit in him gave him perfect love for the one who had wronged him. No imitation forgiveness here—when Rees saw that "God so loved" him, he was able to love the hard-to-love.[24]

If Your Brother or Sister Sins, Go . . .

If your brother or sister sins, go and point out their fault,
just between the two of you. If they listen to you, you have won them over.
But if they will not listen, take one or two others along.
Matthew 18:15–16a

What the passage above describes seems too demanding, too hard, too loaded with danger—many will avoid doing what it says. Yet these facts stand out about the scenario of a brother or sister caught in sin:
- Sin is damning, and this person is valued.
- Christians care for each other.
- The one who sins can be restored.

---

24. Previously published in *Come Ye Apart* January–February–March 1964 (Kansas City, MO: Nazarene Publishing House), 36. Used by permission. (This publication became *Reflecting God*.)

This was such a big issue that Jesus taught that the faithful shepherd would leave the ninety-nine sheep to search for one lost sheep. Then, he concluded, "In the same way your Father in heaven is not willing that any of these little ones should perish" (Matthew 18:14).

I was a young pastor, and Cal was elected Sunday school superintendent in our newly formed church. One night, I received an anonymous phone call. The unidentified caller said, "Do you know that Cal is drunk and is now at another woman's house?"

After the call, I felt I had to go to the house—there, a very drunk Cal met me at the door and cursed me. I had caught him in sin. I returned home and called my district superintendent for advice. He told me, "The people of your new church have known Cal longer than they have known you. They will not believe your word against his. Tell your church board what you have discovered. Take two or three men with you. Get Cal to admit his drinking problem in front of your men. Get his resignation as Sunday school superintendent."

The church board agreed; we selected three men. The board prayed for Cal that night, and the three men said they wanted to pray for Cal in the home. So we went to see him.

When we arrived at the house, Cal, who was now sober, admitted his alcohol problem. I asked for his resignation, and he pleaded, "Let me keep my job, and I'll get victory over my drinking."

I said, "No, you get victory over your drinking, and then at a later date the church will decide if you may serve in this role." He reluctantly agreed. And, oh, you should have heard those board members' compassionate prayers for him.

We elected a new superintendent, and the men of the church surrounded Cal with love, prayer, and accountability. Cal stayed in the church, and his wife continued to serve as a board member and a faithful example to others. Their preteen son was saved for the church and for the kingdom.

It was hard, but we followed biblical principles in confronting a brother who had sinned. And so a lost sheep was brought back into the fold.

I'm Going—He's Coming

But very truly I tell you, it is for your good that I am going away.
Unless I go away, the Advocate will not come to you;
but if I go, I will send him to you.
John 16:7

Thomas Edison was known for owning more than a thousand patents—more than any other person in history. He invented the electric light bulb. But his light bulb has gone away, and now it is for our good that we use LED bulbs and other modern, improved bulbs.

At one point, Henry Ford gave Edison a 1916 Ford Model-T. In the earliest days of the Model-A and the Model-T, you could buy a new Ford for $450. Now the Model-T has gone away and, for our good, far better cars have become available.

Jesus conducted his powerful ministry for three years, but he never went beyond the area we know as Palestine. As he was approaching death on the cross, his disciples were in considerable anguish. He comforted them, saying, "It is for your good that I am going away," because, "if I go, I will send him [the Advocate, the Holy Spirit] to you." The Holy Spirit would be able to exist and work anywhere in the world at the same time.

Jesus said, "When the Advocate comes, whom I will send to you from the Father—the Spirit of truth who goes out from the Father—he will testify about me" (John 15:26). The Spirit's major task is to point to Jesus, to represent Jesus. When you accept Christ as your Savior, it is the Spirit who makes Christ real to you. John 3:8 calls it "born of the Spirit." Romans 8:9 calls the Holy Spirit "the Spirit of Christ."

Consider God's Holy Spirit to be your great privilege. Think of all the blessings he wishes to give you:

- "I will ask the Father, and he will give you another advocate to help you and be with you forever—the Spirit of truth. The world cannot accept him, because it neither sees him nor knows him. But you know him, for he lives with you and will be in you" (John 14:16–17).
- "But the Advocate, the Holy Spirit, whom the Father will send in my name, will teach you all things and will remind you of everything I have said to you" (John 14:26).
- "When he comes, he will prove the world to be in the wrong about sin and righteousness and judgment" (John 16:8).
- "But when he, the Spirit of truth, comes, he will guide you into all the truth . . . he will glorify me" (John 16:13–14).

- "But you will receive power when the Holy Spirit comes on you; and you will be my witnesses in Jerusalem . . . and to the ends of the earth" (Acts 1:8).
- "Then the church . . . was strengthened. Living in the fear of the Lord and encouraged by the Holy Spirit, it increased in numbers" (Acts 9:31).
- "The two of them, sent on their way by the Holy Spirit, went down to Seleucia" (Acts 13:4).
- "Keep watch over yourselves and all the flock of which the Holy Spirit has made you overseers" (Acts 20:28).
- "For those who are led by the Spirit of God are the children of God" (Romans 8:14).
- "In the same way, the Spirit helps us in our weakness. We do not know what we ought to pray for, but the Spirit himself intercedes for us through wordless groans" (Romans 8:26).
- And even more!

Rees Howells, a Welsh layman (1879–1950), founder of the Bible College of Wales, was a man of much prayer. Though he had accepted Christ and been born of the Spirit, he testified about a later, in-depth meeting with the Holy Spirit: "He said to me, 'As the Saviour had a body, so I dwell in the cleansed temple of the believer. I am a Person. I am God, and I am come to ask you to give your body to me that I may work through it. I need a body for my temple (1 Cor. 6:19).' It meant every bit of my fallen nature was to go to the cross, and he would bring in his own life and his own nature."[25]

What do you most need the Holy Spirit to do for you just now? Are you born of the Spirit? Are you filled with the Spirit? What a blessing—the Holy Spirit has come.

Whatever!

So whether you eat or drink or whatever you do,
do it all for the glory of God.
1 Corinthians 10:31

---

25. Norman Grubb, *Rees Howells, Intercessor: The Story of a Life Lived for God* (Philadelphia: Christian Literature Crusade, 1952), 36.

When someone says "whatever," it usually means indifference. But that's not what Paul meant when he said, "Whether you eat or drink or *whatever* you do, do it all for the glory of God." Paul's "whatever" meant total concern that all life be lived for God's glory.

Even though they were permitted to eat market-purchased meat, concerned Christians would refrain from doing so if it would offend another's conscience. We can summarize Paul's message to the church thus:

- Down to the smallest detail, do all to God's glory.
- Seek the good of many.
- The greatest good is that people be saved.
- Follow my example, as I follow Christ's.

After accepting Christ, one man became sensitive. He thanked God for even a drink of water. He could no longer put a cigarette in his mouth and pray, "O God, thank you for this cigarette. Bless it to my body's strength and your service." So he quit.

A woman I know went out of her way to spend time with, care for, entertain, and invite those around her. Now her friend and the friend's husband have accepted Christ and are active in church. Dr. Larry Garmin gave up his homeland to reach Indians in the Peruvian jungle. In both cases, these believers are "seeking . . . the good of many, so that they may be saved." They are doing "whatever" it takes, "for the glory of God."[26]

Expect Victory

I saw the Holy City, the new Jerusalem, coming down out of heaven from God, prepared as a bride beautifully dressed for her husband.
Revelation 21:2

Those who are victorious will inherit all this,
and I will be their God and they will be my children.
Revelation 21:7

---

26. Previously published in *Reflecting God* June–July–August 2010 (Kansas City, MO: WordAction Publishing Co.), 14. Used by permission.

"Do you have the victory?" was the question my loving Pastor Ferrioli asked me every Sunday when I arrived at church. I was a baby Christian, living on a very secular Ivy League campus, surrounded by pressures and temptations. The pastor's question was valid in light of his concern for my ongoing Christian life. The question was also valid for John, the author of Revelation. He saw that one group of people would inherit the Holy City, the new heaven, the new earth (21:1–2), the "victorious."

Earlier, in chapters 2 and 3, John stressed this issue repeatedly in recording Christ's message to the seven churches:

- To Ephesus—Repent at your loss of your first love for Christ; then, you will be victorious (Revelation 2:7).
- To Smyrna—Be faithful to Christ even under persecution and even to the point of death; then, you will be victorious (2:10–11).
- To Pergamum—Repent of having embraced false teaching; then, you will be victorious (2:14–17).
- To Thyatira—Do God's will to the end; then, you will be victorious (2:26).
- To Sardis—Wake up. You are spiritually dead and your deeds are unfinished. Repent; then, you will be victorious (3:1–5).
- To Philadelphia—Hold on to what you have; then, you will be victorious (3:11–12).
- To Laodicea—Repent of your lukewarmness and open your heart, life, and church to Christ afresh; then, you will be victorious (3:15–21).

Earlier, this same John wrote a letter to early Christians. In 1 John 1:7, he said, "But if we walk in the light, as he [Christ] is in the light, we have fellowship with one another, and the blood of Jesus, his Son, purifies us from all sin." This is another way to describe what it means to be victorious. So, what do you say? Do you have the victory?

God Has an Army

The end of all things is near. Therefore be alert and of sober mind so that you may pray. Above all, love each other deeply, because love covers over a multitude of sins. Offer hospitality to one another without grumbling.

Each of you should use whatever gift you have received to serve others,
as faithful stewards of God's grace in its various forms.
1 Peter 4:7–10

In 2020, an order was issued by our city and surrounding counties requiring people to stay at home unless their activities were essential for the health and safety of themselves or others. The order was an attempt to slow the spread of the coronavirus that swept through the world in 2020.

In another day of severe persecution and challenge, Peter wrote to Christians with instructions to pray, love, offer hospitality, or use whatever gift they had to serve others. In their day and in ours, in the most difficult of times, God still has an army: the millions of faithful Christians who use whatever gifts they have to serve others.

In this crisis, numbers of Christians have told me that they are praying that God will use this crisis to draw people to himself; that he will empower scientists to find a cure or a vaccine; that he will give strength to medical workers and others who care for the sick; and that he will do all this for our nation and for the rest of the world.

I felt loved when my pastor phoned me to see how we were getting along during the pandemic. Church services were canceled due to the danger of the virus spreading in crowds. So I decided that for the next thirty days, I would phone at least one person a day from my Sunday school class or my neighborhood and encourage them.

A previous government directive told us that gatherings must be limited to ten people or fewer. My friend Scott said that, since church services were canceled, he was inviting eight people, believers and nonbelievers, to his home to watch our pastor preach remotely. Then all his guests would be invited to Sunday dinner. Talk about hospitality!

My neighbor John phoned me to say I was free to ask him to run any errand for me, even if it was a late-night run to the drugstore. Christians everywhere used whatever gifts they could to serve others during the pandemic.

God has an army, and in a time of crisis, it swings into action. And if the efforts of this army do not seem like enough, remember one other thing: When the hostile king of Aram surrounded the city of Dothan to capture the prophet Elisha, Elisha's servant saw the city surrounded with horses and chariots. In distress, he called out to Elisha, "Oh no, my lord! What shall we do?"

"'Don't be afraid,' [Elisha] answered. 'Those who are with us are more than those who are with them.' And Elisha prayed, 'Open his eyes, LORD, so that he may see.' Then the LORD opened the servant's eyes, and he looked and saw the hills full of horses and chariots of fire all around Elisha" (2 Kings 6:14–17).

Join God's army of servants today. And remember that God has a backup army of his direct miraculous forces: "horses and chariots of fire."

Two Lost Sheep

Suppose one of you has a hundred sheep and loses one of them.
Doesn't he leave the ninety-nine in the open country and go after the lost
sheep until he finds it? I tell you that in the same way there will be
more rejoicing in heaven over one sinner who repents than over
ninety-nine righteous persons who do not need to repent.
Luke 15:4, 7

One of the most troubling things to me is people who accepted Christ in the past but, years later, display little evidence of following the Lord. Paul was concerned enough about this issue to write the following to the Colossians (2:6–7): "So then, just as you have received Christ Jesus as Lord, continue to live your lives in him, rooted and built up in him, strengthened in the faith as you were taught, and overflowing with thankfulness."

Jesus, too, was serious about this issue when he said, "If you do not remain in me, you are like a branch that is thrown away and withers; such branches are picked up, thrown into the fire and burned" (John 15:6).

More than twelve years ago, Alan and Martha became very involved in our church. They gave evidence of being committed to and zealous for Christ. I don't know exactly how it happened, but they drifted off—dropped out. I reached out to them, but received no response. Over those twelve years, I contacted them periodically.

Here are two letters from Alan and Martha about what has happened in the last three years:

> *Pastor Shaver,*
> *Thank you for being a wonderful example of Christ and his love for us.*
> *A few years ago, God began bringing to my mind and heart that it was time to get back to church. I noticed that after we had no jobs to go to Monday–Friday, it was harder to tell which day of the week it was. Each time he*

brought it to mind, I asked if he would make it a solid move for us, as I wanted us both to desire a deeper relationship with Christ.

Each time I sent the church a check, I prayed we would someday be back. It just so happened that after you sent us a card inviting us to come back, you would be teaching the next day. I read the card to Alan, and his response was, "We are going tomorrow."

I am so thankful for your dedication for lost or stray sheep. We had been wandering for a while. We were faithfully reading our Bibles but lacked guidance. Disciple class is the perfect place for us at this time, and we are enjoying all aspects of our church home.

We love you and thank God for you and your drive to draw others into a deeper relationship with our Lord.

God bless you!
Alan & Martha

Chic & Nancy,

Wow! What a wonderful year God has blessed us with. In January 2019, Alan had open-heart surgery; February, back to the cath lab for a stent; July, back to the cath lab for two stents; and the presence of God has been with us the whole time. The fact that he has not had a cigarette since January 23, 2019, is a miracle that only God could accomplish.

We thank you both and the Sunday school class for supporting us through it all with prayers and food and cards. God is so good, and we feel so very blessed.

Love always,
Alan & Martha

Alan and Martha have been found; they have returned; two sheep are back. They have become strong spiritual leaders—and there is rejoicing here and in heaven.

Obedience and Courage

Do not be yoked together with unbelievers. For what do
righteousness and wickedness have in common?
2 Corinthians 6:14

Settle it therefore in your hearts, not to meditate before what ye shall answer: For I will give you a mouth and wisdom, which all your adversaries shall not be able to gainsay nor resist.
Luke 21:14–15, KJV

Yes, the Spirit-filled life will repeatedly call for obedience to God, and that same Spirit will empower you with the courage to obey!

I was increasingly uneasy with a decision I had made in my sophomore year in college. Now, in my junior year, as a young follower of Jesus, that decision kept coming back to trouble me.

I had joined a national Greek-letter fraternity. Now, I was sensing I had to get out! There were three reasons for this:

- This secretive organization had certain controls over me. I sensed I was unequally yoked.
- I was required to pay a regular social tax. The funds were mainly to purchase alcohol. However, I had felt convicted to cease drinking alcohol.
- Many decisions in the fraternity were based on discrimination and prejudice.

When I approached the vice president to let him know I wanted to resign from the fraternity, he told me it was not my choice. I would have to plead my case before the Interfraternity Council.

The date was set. This council was made up of twelve or fourteen members—half fraternity presidents, half faculty who were highly invested fraternity members. I had written the required letter to the council requesting to be released from my fraternity "due to religious conviction." As I was in my room, trying to prepare myself mentally for this council meeting, I was nervous. How would these council members react when I said, "I'm quitting the fraternity because I've become a Christian"? What should I say?

I was reading Scripture when I saw a passage I had never seen before: "Settle it therefore in your hearts, not to meditate before what ye shall answer: For I will give you a mouth and wisdom." I sensed that I should not prepare a speech but instead depend on the Spirit of God to give me the words.

Soon, I was sitting in the waiting room outside the heavy oak doors of the interfraternity council meeting. It was twenty-five minutes past my appointment time, and I had butterflies in my stomach.

Suddenly, the Lord moved into the room. He seemed to have a huge bucket of peace that he poured into my heart. With that, all the butterflies flew away.

Just then, the oak doors opened, and a spokesman said, "Mr. Shaver, we're ready for you." And I was ready for them.

When the council members asked me to explain why I wished to leave the fraternity, I said I had found Christ as my Savior and Lord, and was now sensitive to issues that had not bothered me before. These fraternity-committed men grew angry and raised their voices at me. Finally they announced, "You may leave. We will let you know in a few days if we will allow you to leave your fraternity."

A few days later, I received a letter granting me permission to leave the fraternity.

Later, in my senior year, an outstanding speaker from InterVarsity Christian Fellowship was scheduled to visit our campus. I contacted my old fraternity to ask if they would like this person to speak to them on the meaning of Christianity. They agreed—on the condition that I would come with the speaker and tell my own story of how I found Christ. I did!

Jesus promised that they would "not be able to gainsay nor resist." They could not! He gave me the courage to be obedient!

Gospel Power

For I am not ashamed of the gospel, because it is the power
of God that brings salvation to everyone who believes.
Romans 1:16a

Paul was no spiritual wimp. Note his boldness: he is "obligated" (Romans 1:14), "eager" (v. 15), and "not ashamed" (v. 16). This was because the gospel contained such amazing power.

Roy and Doris Baker became present-day examples of this power. For most of his life, Roy was antagonistic to religion. Yet he was successful by most counts, with a Harvard PhD and position as an accounting professor at the University of Missouri-Kansas City.

Roy and Doris visited a church and began asking questions. When new Christian friends visited them in their home and shared the gospel with them, they were intrigued. One visitor explained the forgiveness described in Isaiah 53:6: "The LORD has laid on him the iniquity of us all."

"Roy, Doris," he said, "what happens to my sins? They're all laid on Christ. I'm forgiven and free."

Roy and Doris fell on their knees, wept, turned from sin, and opened their hearts to Christ. They grew, displayed a righteousness received from God, and became leaders in the church.

When Roy later spoke at a seminary class, a student asked, "Dr. Baker, what was the great truth Dr. Shaver shared that convinced you?"

Roy replied, "Jesus died for me!"

This is the gospel: the "power of God for . . . salvation."[27]

MARCH 10   69

Engaged

When you believed, you were marked in him with a seal, the promised Holy Spirit, who is a deposit guaranteeing our inheritance until the redemption of those who are God's possession—to the praise of his glory.
Ephesians 1:13–14

When couples tell their stories, one of the greatest moments of their courtship is always their engagement. Some engagements happen after a walk through a beautiful park; others take place at the most enchanting site in the city; some even happen on athletic fields before thousands of fans. Rarely is the event forgotten.

In modern Greek, the word for "deposit" is the same word for "engagement ring." When you were sealed by the promised Holy Spirit, he became your deposit of something better to follow. As the engagement ring is the promise of something better to follow (marriage), so the Holy Spirit is the promise of something better to come—the marriage supper of the Lamb in heaven.

This idea of sealing also shows up in 2 Timothy 2:19: "God's solid foundation stands firm, sealed with this inscription: 'The Lord knows those who are his,' and, 'Everyone who confesses the name of the Lord must turn away from wickedness.'" The themes here are ownership and holiness. If you are

---

27. Previously published in *Reflecting God* June–July–August 2010 (Kansas City, MO: WordAction Publishing Co.), 19. Used by permission.

tempted to doubt your relationship with God, remember Acts 15:8–9, which refers to the Spirit's outpouring on Gentiles. This outpouring proved that the Gentiles too were accepted by God: "God, who knows the heart, showed that he accepted them by giving the Holy Spirit to them, just as he did to us. He made no distinction between us and them, for he purified their hearts by faith." Even if you do not understand the full depths of your heart, God does. The result of his action in our hearts is purity, ownership, and holiness. When the Spirit marks you with a seal, he makes you more like Jesus.

A minister once complained to E. Stanley Jones that the mention of the Holy Spirit made cold chills run up and down his spine; he feared that discussing the Spirit would result in rampant emotionalism in the congregation. Jones replied, "My friend, you are patterning the Holy Spirit after certain people who have gone off into extremes. Christ is our pattern. He was more filled with the Holy Spirit than anyone who ever walked the face of the earth. Are you afraid to be like Christ?"[28]

The Holy Spirit is your down payment to heaven. When Dan, a college student I knew, was filled with the sanctifying Spirit, he said, "Oh, if heaven is anything like this!"

It's as if God is saying to you, "Son, daughter, I can't usher you into my presence just yet. I have a task for you to do first: live to the praise of my glory. But I'll do the next best thing. I'll give you my presence in the person of the Holy Spirit, and he will settle down to live inside you—he will be there day or night, in sickness and in health, in joy or in sorrow. I can't bring you up to heaven just yet, but I'll put a little bit of heaven inside you."

Sir, Give Me This Water

The woman said to him, "Sir, give me this water so that I won't
get thirsty and have to keep coming here to draw water."
John 4:15

He paced the room, hands clasped behind his back. He exclaimed to his friend, "Oh, Mr. Judd, God has made me a new man! God has made me a new

---

28. Sermon notes, original source unknown.

man!" Hudson Taylor had long been a Christian and a zealous missionary to China, but recently he had come to a new spiritual experience.

Under the pressure of his work, Taylor received new light from the Lord: "Whoever drinks the water I give them *will never thirst*" (v. 14). To think that "will" means *will*, that "never" means *never*, and that "thirst" means *any unsatisfied need*! From that day forward, there was new power in Taylor's ministry, greater faith in his prayer, and deeper rest in his soul.

No wonder the Samaritan woman pleaded, "Sir, give me this water." We all have thirsts: heart-thirst, soul-thirsts, mind-thirsts. So did she. She was still confusing the physical with the spiritual (v. 15), but she was asking the right person to supply the needs of her life. If you are drinking continually at the source in Jesus, you "will never thirst."[29]

Don't Sin—But What If You Do?

*My dear children, I write this to you so that you will not sin.
But if anybody does sin, we have an advocate with the Father—
Jesus Christ, the Righteous One.
1 John 2:1*

Make the lawn pretty—that was my job. I was ten or twelve years old, and the grass was still green. One day, I raked up rows of leaves for pickup. My dad then set the rows on fire for quick disposal. I was so upset by this act that I yelled at him and kicked him in the shins. I will never forget the look on his face—such disappointment. How could I have done that to a dad who loved me so much?

And then there is our heavenly Father. Imagine how he feels when we rebel against him, sin against him. John writes, "so that you will not sin" (2:1), and hammers this point home: "No one who lives in him keeps on sinning" (3:6). Later, he writes, "The one who does what is sinful is of the devil . . . The reason the Son of God appeared was to destroy the devil's work" (3:8).

---

29. Previously published in *Come Ye Apart* January–February–March 1964 (Kansas City, MO: Nazarene Publishing House), 33. Used by permission. (This publication became *Reflecting God*.)

Jesus healed the invalid at the pool of Bethesda and commanded him, "See, you are well again. Stop sinning or something worse may happen to you" (John 5:14). Apparently, Jesus thought he could stop sinning—otherwise, this man was now under a terrible curse. You and I need not sin.

But if you do—oh, here is great mercy: "But if anybody does sin, we have an advocate with the Father—Jesus Christ" (1 John 2:1). If you should disobey or displease the Lord, stop right there and ask God to forgive you, restore you, and strengthen you to follow him. Christ will intercede for your forgiveness. This is why we have the promise: "If we confess our sins, he is faithful and just and will forgive us our sins" (1:9).

Driving home after a service one day, I said, "My, didn't I give a good altar call."

I heard God say, "My glory I will not share with another."

I confessed my pride, and God forgave me.

If I speak harshly to my wife, I quickly ask both God and Nancy for forgiveness.

The apostle Peter disowned the Lord and sinned. He was forgiven and restored and then became a powerful, holy, major leader of the young church. God still offers this kind of forgiveness—I saw him do it for a person I know who followed Christ, went back into sin for twenty years, then repented, was restored, and is a mighty power for God today.

God Knows My Name

These are the names of the men who are to assist you: from Reuben,
Elizur son of Shedeur; from Simeon, Shelumiel son of Zurishaddai;
from Judah, Nahshon, son of Amminadab.
Numbers 1:5–7

Moses and Aaron were the big human names in God's miraculous feat of delivering Israel from Egypt and starting them on their wilderness journey to the promised land. It was the second month of the second year since the Israelites had been set free from Egyptian slavery (1:1). God speaks to Moses and tells him to count all men twenty years old and over who are able to serve in the army. Since this is a huge task, the Lord names to Moses twelve men who will assist in the task. This group of specific men includes Elizur, Shelumiel, and Nahshon. When they finish the count, there are 603,550 men capable of military service.

This shocked me at first—that out of 603,550 men, God named twelve specific men, and even told Moses their fathers' names. Elizur, Shelumiel, and Nahshon out of 603,550—think of it. These men were not as famous as Moses or Aaron, but God knew their names.

In Luke 10:20, Jesus tells seventy-two of his followers, "Rejoice that your names are written in heaven." The only possible conclusion is that the Lord knows *your* name too.

Whenever people ask my son, Paul, how he can function after five cancer surgeries and the removal of his voice box, he quotes the lyrics of a song that is very meaningful to him: "He knows my name, he knows my name." Sometimes, he quotes the words of another famous song: "His eye is on the sparrow, and I know he watches me."

He knows your name! Yes, yours!

For the Long Run

So then, just as you received Christ Jesus as Lord, continue to live your lives in him, rooted and built up in him, strengthened in the faith as you were taught, and overflowing with thankfulness.
Colossians 2:6–7

But the one who stands firm to the end will be saved.
Matthew 24:13

Tom and Agnes knew they had to do something—the increasing Communist pressures in Guyana's political climate was making life there extremely difficult. Their plan was to take their four children with them to the United States. However, the government put restrictions on their departure—the two older children would not be allowed to leave. Out of all their resources, Tom and Agnes were only allowed to take $400 and one suitcase for each person. They found an apartment in Kansas City, took a bus, and walked the remaining distance uphill to a church.

"Would we be welcome here?" they asked.

"Would you ever!" said the greeter.

Tom and Agnes settled into the life of the church, and the church surrounded them with prayers for their two older children left behind in Guyana. One year later, on July 7, 1978, both children walked into church with the rest of their family—and the church broke into applause!

What was the background of this heroic family? Let me tell you Agnes's story. Her grandmother wanted to raise her as a Hindu. Her father said, "No way!" She began attending a Wesleyan church near her Guyanese home. As a child, she accepted Christ and joined the church. When her father died and her mother went to work, twelve-year-old Agnes assumed major responsibilities and dropped out of school to care for her six younger brothers and sisters.

For the rest of her life, Agnes served Christ. At age eighty-nine, as Agnes approached the end of her life, her son said, "Daddy and Mom were our bridge to Jesus."

Agnes prayed each morning, at each meal, and each night. If anything was bothering you, Agnes urged you to pray. When her adult son suffered an untimely death, Agnes never showed bitterness or blamed God. She attended her granddaughter's college graduation in weakness, in a wheelchair, without complaint.

When her health failed and she moved to a nursing home, Agnes said, "This is where I'm supposed to be." Days before her death, she was repeating, "I love Jesus," and praying fervent, anointed prayers for her pastor and church.

Do you get the picture? She stood firm to the end. That is the Christian life the Bible teaches.

The Church with Enough Love to Keep Them Warm

When he came to Jerusalem, he tried to join the disciples, but they were
all afraid of him, not believing that he really was a disciple. But Barnabas
took him and brought him to the apostles. He told them how Saul on his
journey had seen the Lord and that the Lord had spoken to him, and how
in Damascus he had preached fearlessly in the name of Jesus.
Acts 9:26–27

And to know this love that surpasses knowledge—that you
may be filled to the measure of all the fullness of God.
Ephesians 3:19

We almost lost him. Saul, later called Paul, had just received the Lord, but the Jerusalem church was afraid of him—and for good reason. Until he met Jesus, he had been arresting Christians and approving their deaths. A man with much love and wisdom reached out to Saul and "took him and brought him" to the apostles. Feeling loved and accepted, he stayed in church. This Saul (Paul) eventually became the leader of the Christian movement. Acts 14:21–22 tells, "Then they returned to Lystra, Iconium and Antioch, strengthening the disciples and encouraging them to remain true to the faith." Now Paul was the master of follow-up, nurture, and support.

Early in my ministry, evangelist Modie Schoonover taught me to ask: Does my church have enough love to keep them warm? Just as a newborn baby needs attention, love, special care, and warmth, so does the newborn Christian. I saw this lived out in the case of Dan and Judy.

Dan was raised in a parsonage, but by age twelve, he was smoking; by sixteen, he was bitter and resentful. When he married Judy, he warned her to never become a Christian. While Dan was in the military, his mom got really sick, and he sent Judy to comfort her. To Judy's surprise, she found a loving atmosphere in that parsonage home. She went to church with her in-laws on Sunday and was saved.

Dan was angry at the news. After his discharge, they moved to a Midwestern U.S. city. Soon afterward, Judy got sick and learned she had a tumor. Scared, she called Dan's parents for prayer. In surgery, the doctor examined Judy before he made a cut and exclaimed, "The cancer we came to remove is already gone." When Dan heard the report, he admitted it was an answer to prayer, and he didn't know why he'd been so bitter.

Dan and Judy decided to go to church that Sunday. But the church people were busy enjoying the company of their old Christian friends and barely noticed Dan and Judy. They sat alone. Few people greeted them; no one invited them for Sunday dinner. Dan was amazed at the lack of friendliness. The next week, they tried another church. They went looking for a warm heart and got a cold shoulder.

With the encouragement of friends, they tried a third church that greeted them warmly. By Friday, a lay couple visited their home. When the pastor visited them, Dan bragged about the church's love. That next Sunday they returned, and Dan came to the altar, weeping all the way. When the pastor asked if he'd been forgiven, his reply was, "I only had to ask once."

Later, Dan called his dad and told him, "I met a lifelong friend of yours." "Who was it?"

"The Lord Jesus Christ."

The next Sunday, Dan and Judy were sanctified. The Sunday after that, they joined the church. After that, they brought friends to a Billy Graham crusade. And after that, the church had a revival—they came every service but one.

Soon, a new couple showed up. Immediately, Dan and Judy were at their side, inviting them to their home. They had now become the church with enough love to keep them warm.

The Heart-Changing Spirit

I will give you a new heart and put a new spirit in you;
I will remove from you your heart of stone and give you
a heart of flesh. And I will put my Spirit in you and move you
to follow my decrees and be careful to keep my laws.
Ezekiel 36:26–27

Bill was so low and so weak. Finally, it had to be done—heart surgery. A few days ago, I sat beside him at breakfast and saw his energy, his clear thought and speech, his new joy in living. What a difference a heart surgery made.

The Old Testament prophet Ezekiel said Israel had profaned the holiness of God's great name. Because of their sin, they had been exiled to Babylon. But now God had promised to bring them back to their land (Ezekiel 36:24). They would have to experience a heart change and the indwelling of the Spirit for this to happen. Their willpower would not be enough; God's forgiveness that cancels guilt from past sins was not enough. Deep down, their hearts would be changed. The Spirit would so inhabit them that he would move them to obedience.

George shared his testimony of being ordained to ministry:

I always felt I had more wisdom than anyone else. So, no one could minister to me. It was so deeply ingrained that I was no longer conscious of it.

But you can't love a person like Jesus does when you think you're better than them.

Then, he told of his cleansing: "If God hadn't done that, this church would be ruined. I had to be a servant; I had to stay long enough to see victory. The Lord really owns me."

Searched by the Spirit. Cleansed to serve. A new heart.

As you, reader, are making your spiritual journey, will you open your heart to the Spirit's changes?

The Parts Are Working

Just as a body, though one, has many parts,
but all its many parts form one body, so it is with Christ.
1 Corinthians 12:12

"Come, follow me," Jesus said, "and I will send you out to fish for people."
At once they left their nets and followed him.
Matthew 4:19–20

Bill and Irene knew Laura from a work contact. They must have invited Laura and her husband, Keith, to church eight times before a "church and brunch" invitation worked. Then someone from the church delivered a homemade pastry to Keith and Laura. The children's director took an interest in their son, Andy, and he began attending Sunday school. An adult Sunday school teacher invited Keith and Laura to an adult class and to stay after church for a potluck meal.

New friends from the church visited Keith and Laura by appointment and discussed spiritual issues that got Keith and Laura to begin doing some heavy thinking. They attended a Gospel of John Bible study, where God spoke to Laura as they read about the woman at the well.

On August 28, one of the church pastors, along with Scott and Angie, shared the gospel in Keith and Laura's home, and both accepted Christ. John and Helen led them through eight weeks of *Basic Bible Studies for New and Growing Christians* to establish them. After membership instruction, Keith and Laura joined the church.

Keith took a church-sponsored class on evangelism. He befriended his coworker Marta and her husband, Waynard, shared the gospel with them, and led them to Christ. They eventually joined the church.

Today, Keith and Laura are spiritual leaders at their church because many parts of the body of Christ in that church worked together as one to evangelize, nurture, and disciple.

Perfume Is in the Air

Here a dinner was given in Jesus' honor. Martha served,
while Lazarus was among those reclining at the table with him.
Then Mary took about a pint of pure nard, an expensive perfume;
she poured it on Jesus' feet and wiped his feet with her hair.
And the house was filled with the fragrance of the perfume.
John 12:2–3

I was preaching at a church in Bedford-Stuyvesant in Brooklyn, New York, where most of the parishioners were island people—from Trinidad, Bahamas, Barbados, Jamaica. Nearly all the women wore hats. And did the congregation ever sing!

The pastor was driving four ladies and me back to our respective homes when a lady said, "Oh, Brother Shaver, your preaching is like the label off the perfume bottle." I wasn't quite sure what she meant, but I think it was a compliment.

In today's scripture, John is reporting a dinner scene with Jesus where the fragrance of a pint of perfume filled the air. Jesus was heading to his death on the cross—but in that moment, it was time to enjoy a tremendously uplifting social break.

Think of all the elements. Dinner, prepared by Martha, in honor of Jesus. Lazarus, next to Jesus, now famous since he had recently been raised from the dead. People who had come to see Lazarus (12:9).

In the midst of all this, Mary, in a great expression of love, anointed Jesus's feet with expensive perfume. But even with the honor to Jesus, the rejoicing over Lazarus, a great meal, warm fellowship, and the beautiful fragrance, evil lurked. Judas complained about the waste of costly perfume, but the text shows us his real character when it notes that he was stealing from the treasury (12:6).

There are lessons in all this. With all the demands of everyday living—maybe even the demands of Christian service—we need to take time to rejoice and celebrate. Rejoice, relax, and raise up Jesus! We need to honor Jesus; to gain from fellowship of the meal; to marvel at the evidence of God's grace and miracles, like Lazarus. We need to pour out our love in extravagance. And even though evil lifts its ugly head, we do not let that thwart our praise and joy. Christian friend, be sure to include some events like this.

I just got off the phone with Rev. Jack Hamilton. He has been a little lonesome since the passing of his neighbor and dear brother, Dr. Jim Hamilton, at age ninety-four. Jack was a public school teacher and evangelist who held more than 250 revivals in the states of Missouri and Kansas alone. Jack is ninety-nine now.

On our phone call, we talked about the Lord, the church, the family, old times, and present victories. I learned more about Jack in twenty-five minutes than I ever had known before. We rejoiced; we were encouraged. There was the fragrance of a rare perfume in our talk.

If you think all this relaxing, remembering, and rejoicing is not spiritual enough, I remind you of Revelation 19:7 and 9: "Let us rejoice and be glad and give him glory! For the wedding of the Lamb has come, and his bride has made herself ready. . . . Blessed are those who are invited to the wedding supper of the Lamb!"

MARCH 19   78

Tragedy to Triumph

You intended to harm me, but God intended it for good to accomplish what is now being done, the saving of many lives.
Genesis 50:20

On April 28, 2020, at somewhere between eighty-eight and ninety-one years old, Mincaye died at his home in an Ecuadorian village. He is survived by his wife, thirteen children, and more than fifty grandchildren. This man, born into the violent culture of the Amazon rainforest in eastern Ecuador, was known throughout the world because tens of thousands of people saw him as proof of God's redeeming and transforming power.

Mincaye was one of six warriors who speared missionaries Nate Saint, Jim Elliot, Pete Fleming, Roger Youderian, and Ed McCully to death on a river sandbar in 1956. Nearly all the news media coverage reported the murders as a great tragedy. How could such an event ever result in triumph?

In today's scripture, Joseph, who has become prime minister of Egypt, says to his brothers who sold him into slavery, "You intended to harm me, but God intended it for good." God used Joseph to provide food and property for his brothers and their families during a terrible famine. In other words, God used Joseph to accomplish the saving of many lives. The brothers meant evil, and God brought good out of it.

After the five murders, the wives and family members of the missionaries who were killed went back to the tribe. Eventually, some tribe members came to know Jesus Christ. Mincaye's new life in Christ was depicted in *End of the Spear*, a book that was also adapted into a movie. The movie is now translated into the languages of one-quarter of the world's population.

Mincaye, who could only count up to twenty (using his fingers and toes), shared the gospel throughout the USA and Canada to crowds as large as forty-five thousand. He often said, "We lived angry, hating and killing for no reason, until they brought in God's markings. Now, those of us who walk God's trail live happily and in peace."

Steve Saint, the son of one of the murdered missionaries, has been Mincaye's regular traveling companion. He said, "I have known Mincaye since I was a little boy, when he took me under his wing and had his sons teach me to blowgun hunt. He was one of my dearest friends in the world. Yes, he killed my father, but he loved me and my family."[30]

Yes, "you intended to harm me, but God intended it for good." It has been more than sixty years since the murders, so we remember to give God time to bring about the last part of the sentence: "God intended it for good."

Have you watched and listened long enough to see God's good?

30. Steve Saint, "Remembering Mincaye: Obituary for Mincaye," ITEC, itecusa.org/mincaye/.

Circumstances

I have learned to be content whatever the circumstances.
I know what it is to be in need, and I know what it is to have plenty.
I have learned the secret of being content in any and every situation,
whether well fed or hungry, whether living in plenty or in want.
I can do all this through him who gives me strength.
Philippians 4:11–13

When Ralph left a stable job to answer God's call to pastor, he took a church plant that was meeting in a remodeled two-car garage. His circumstances had changed, but he was content.

Peter went from living his everyday life to extensively caring for his seriously ill wife. His circumstances changed, but he was content.

Rachel went from enjoying a happy marriage to mourning her husband's premature death. Her circumstances changed, but she learned the secret of being content.

Scott went from pastoring a thriving church in a beautiful American city to serving as a missionary to eight nations with Communist and other non-Christian influences. His circumstances changed, but he was content.

The apostle Paul was imprisoned for preaching Jesus, and in the passage above, he writes to the church he had planted in Philippi. Meanwhile, he was chained to guards. He couldn't get away from them—but on the other hand, they couldn't get away from him. So Paul witnessed to them about Christ, and many guards came to know the Savior. Paul couldn't get out to preach, but he had a lot of time to write letters to his churches. Of course, these letters later became key parts of the New Testament.

During Paul's powerful ministry in Lystra, a man lame from birth, who had never walked before, was healed, jumped up, and began to walk (Acts 14:8–10). Paul himself had a physical ailment—"a thorn in my flesh," as he called it (2 Corinthians 12:7). Three times he pleaded for God to take it away. While God did not heal him, he gave Paul these words: "My grace is sufficient for you, for my power is made perfect in weakness" (12:9). By grace, under these circumstances, he was content, even victorious. Even in prison, writing to Philippi, he cited the primary reason for his contentment as, "I can do all this through him who gives me strength" (Philippians 4:13).

Mrs. Dutcher was a godly Baptist woman who was bedridden. Yet she was radiant, joyful, and maintained a ministry of intercession. One day, she asked me to call on a young man for whom she had been praying. Chuck was in jail, but Mrs. Dutcher believed he had accepted Christ. I called on Chuck, we connected, and we began a discipleship Bible study. He grew, lived a godly life in jail, brought others to Christ, and was finally released. At last report, he was heading to Bible school to study for the ministry.

Samuel and Gladys were natives of England and Wales but had spent most of their adult lives as missionaries to South America. During their deputation in America, they lived across the street from us, and we became close with them and their three children. After their retirement, we kept in contact with them.

When I heard that Samuel had passed away, I phoned Gladys. Expressing my sympathy, I asked, "How are you doing under the circumstances?"

With her rich Welsh accent, she exclaimed, "Oh, Brother Shaver, I'm not under the circumstances, I'm on top of the circumstances!"

How is this possible? Through Christ who gives us strength.

If You Believe

If you believe, you will receive whatever you ask for in prayer.
Matthew 21:22

Our daughter, who was raised in church, divorced her husband and entered into an ungodly lifestyle. My wife and I learned how to get stomach ulcers and broken hearts at the same time. For five years we prayed and saw a few spiritual movements but no clear-cut return to Christ and a new life.

"Have faith" or "believe" are the most cited conditions for answered prayer in the New Testament. Is my human exertion of faith or belief all there is? J. G. Morrison used to teach that besides saving faith and sanctifying faith, there is also achieving faith. By this, he meant a faith that God uses to achieve miraculous feats beyond our personal spiritual needs.

There is much teaching in Scripture about waiting on God and spending time before him in prayer. These practices allow God to work in us. Faith is both a gift of God and an ability the believer must exercise. In Matthew

21:22, the phrase "if you believe," emphasizes this need to exercise faith. In 1 Corinthians 12:9, faith is a gift from God by the Spirit.

In a letter to Theophilus Lessey, John Wesley also gives us a key insight: "When we urge any to believe, we mean, *Accept that faith which God is now ready to give.* Indeed, believing is the act of man, but it is the gift of God. For no one ever did believe unless God gave him the power."[31]

One day, after five years of prayer for our daughter, God enabled me to have faith, and I saw a vision of my daughter going to the altar to pray. It was so real that I ran upstairs to tell my wife, "I just saw Rachel getting saved."

That night, I received a phone call from my weeping daughter. "Dad," she said, "I've been listening to your conversion story, and for the last half hour I've been praying and confessing my sins. Christ has come back into my heart, and God has never been so real as he is tonight." She has been different ever since and is a powerful follower of Jesus to this day.

I'll Die before I Disobey

Be faithful, even to the point of death,
and I will give you life as your victor's crown.
Revelation 2:10

It was the hardest day of my Christian life. My dad was angry with me for becoming a fully devoted follower of Jesus Christ. Maybe it was because I hadn't explained my new life well. Maybe it was his ungodly lifestyle. Or maybe it was his disappointment that I might not fulfill *his* dream for my life—that I might be a doctor or lawyer.

Whatever the case, the pressures he put on me were tremendous. He cut me off financially as I was finishing my junior year, knowing there was no way I could raise enough money for my senior year at my expensive Ivy League school. He told one friend he would rather have me be a criminal than be a Christian. He hired a husband-and-wife legal team, both atheists, to put me

---

31. John Wesley, *The Works of John Wesley* (Kansas City, MO: Nazarene Publishing House, nd), XIII, 136.

through a grueling cross-examination and prove it was impossible for a human being to know God.

The two lawyers invited me to their apartment for a steak dinner. They were my dad's friends, so I thought I was invited to a pleasant social evening. They began to question me about my dramatic conversion experience. However, they didn't wait for my answers—rather, they shot off rapid-fire questions with the goal of beating me into submission, or confusion.

Finally, one of them said to me, "You may have had a dramatic experience, but it's all just psychological."

In other words, "It was just your emotional experience—it couldn't be God."

I was only several weeks old in the Lord, and I was shaken. This event happened during a break in my school year. A few days later, back in my college dormitory, I was having a morning devotional time with the Lord. I was still troubled over the lawyers' verbal assault. As I thought about the conversation with the lawyers, I heard a sinister voice repeating, *But it's all just psychological.*

I wondered, *Is this real? Have I made a mistake? Is this just an emotional, psychological experience arising from my own personality? Was this really God? Should I just give this all up?*

Then I heard the whisper of a loving voice: *Chic, you know what happened to you.*

My heart responded, *Yes, Lord, I know that was you.* I looked back down at the page I had been reading in my Bible: "Therefore everyone who hears these words of mine and puts them into practice is like a wise man who built his house on the rock. The rain came down, the streams rose, and the winds blew and beat against that house; yet it did not fall, because it had its foundation on the rock" (Matthew 7:24–25).

My heart rejoiced. *Yes,* I thought, *my life is on the rock! I have come to know Christ! God is real! I will hear your words and put them into practice! I will not turn back!*

That experience with the lawyers and the sinister voice put steel in my soul. What is the worst thing anyone could do to me? Kill me. So I decided, "I'll die before I disobey." I will be part of the Revelation crowd: "Be faithful, even to the point of death, and I will give you life as your victor's crown" (2:10). That determination has never left me.

This Judge Is Just

Against you, you only, have I sinned and done what is evil in your sight;
so you are right in your verdict and justified when you judge.
Psalm 51:4

"You, David, you are the man," said Nathan the prophet. And immediately David began a journey to that inmost place where no one is allowed entrance without permission, except for God. He went behind the wall of protection, behind the mask, behind the judgments, behind the *oughts* and *shoulds* to where he stood stripped naked without the covering of an excuse.

David didn't say, "My father's sins left stains on my life."

He didn't say, "I am the king—I am above keeping God's commandments."

He didn't say, "I was her smitten victim."

He didn't say, "What kind of game can I play so God will believe that this wasn't my fault?"

He didn't say, "What about you, Nathan?"

He simply stood there, naked in his shame, and agreed with God. He asked for mercy, compassion, and forgiveness, knowing the just judge had unfailing love—knowing there was no other way to receive cleansing for his inmost self.

When God came, David held up a sign reading, "I am guilty."

When God left, David held up a sign reading, "I am forgiven."

Down in that inmost place, what does *your* sign say?

Nancy Shaver[32]

Real Christians—Better Workers

---

32. Previously published in *Come Ye Apart* March–April–May 1996 (Kansas City, MO: Nazarene Publishing House), 26. Used by permission. (This publication became *Reflecting God*.)

Slaves, obey your earthly masters in everything; and do it,
not only when their eye is on you and to curry their favor,
but with sincerity of heart and reverence for the Lord. Whatever you do,
work at it with all your heart, as working for the Lord, not for human
masters, since you know that you will receive an inheritance
from the Lord as a reward. It is the Lord Christ you are serving.
Colossians 3:22–24

Slavery was an established institution in the Roman Empire (and a wholly different system from the American chattel slavery system that was abolished in the nineteenth century). In fact, perhaps half of the population of the Roman Empire were slaves. Many slaves were well-educated people who carried great responsibility in the homes of the wealthy, including educating the children. A bit later in this letter, masters are told of their responsibility for right and fair treatment of slaves.

At the time, Christianity was a minority group with little political power. As the church and her influence grew, eventually the church became a major force for ending slavery.

Today, the slave-master relationship may become a model for the worker-boss relationship. In effect, the worker's Christianity will make him or her a better and more efficient worker. Working for the boss is regarded as working for the Lord.

I know a Christian woman who has worked for her company for more than twenty-five years and has twice won the president's award. She prays for and with her boss and coworkers, practices compassion (like a generous check to a coworker battling cancer), and shares her faith effectively.

Recently, her boss said to her, "Your loyalty to the company is unprecedented; it's the same with your loyalty to your coworkers. The sales reps love you."

This worker responded, "It's natural for me because I invest in people."

Recently, as this woman was perusing one of her hundreds of emails, she saw that one of her coworkers was asking for assistance. She said she could have fired off a quick email, and that would have been acceptable. Instead, she phoned her coworker and, for twenty-five minutes, gave her thorough and caring counsel.

"Where did this work ethic come from?" I asked her.

She responded, "I was raised in a Christian home. I saw it in my parents."

I urge you to take your Christian lifestyle into your workplace.

In the context of Paul's letter, slaves were not allowed to own property. But amazingly, God promised these conscientious Christian workers "an inheritance from the Lord as a reward" (3:24). Yes, this is like the president's award, but far greater—it is Jesus's reward.

Perfect?

Be perfect, therefore, as your heavenly Father is perfect.
Matthew 5:48

Every three seconds, our kitchen faucet dripped. It had one of those long handles that could swivel in all directions. Hard to the right was cold water; hard to the left was hot. When you shut the water off, you couldn't pull it straight down—you had to angle it a little to the right. But it always dripped.

When my backhoe operator, master trench digger, and friend Dave told me his good friend Jim was a plumber I could stake my life on, I almost shouted for joy. Dave and Jim came on a Monday, and we gave them every plumbing project in the house. (We'd been saving for a long time.) But the big project was the kitchen faucet.

My wife, Nancy, had purchased a mid-price faucet with all the fittings at the local Lowe's. Dave and Jim worked long and hard, and the new faucet was in. We turned it on—there was a nice flow of water. But when we turned it off, it dripped.

We went back to the store and bought the same style of faucet in a new, sealed box. But when we opened the box, we saw the faucet was damaged, the handle disconnected. We went back to the store for a second time.

The third new faucet took more work, but it was finally installed. We turned it on—the water flowed. We turned it off—and it *did not drip*! I thought, *That's perfect!* It wasn't the most expensive faucet or the fanciest, but it was perfect because it fulfilled the purpose for which it was built.

Does it surprise you that God says to us, "Be perfect, therefore, as your heavenly Father is perfect" (Matthew 5:48)? In verses 43–47, Jesus told us to love others like the Father loves. William Barclay says, "A man is perfect if he realizes the purpose for which he was created and sent into the world."[33]

---

33. William Barclay, *The Gospel of Matthew*, Vol. I (Philadelphia: Westminster Press, 1975), 177.

You may not be the most talented, the most brilliant, or the greatest communicator, but you can fulfill your purpose of love. You can be perfect in showing love to others—that's the purpose for which you and I were created. This sort of love is high-caliber, but by God's grace, we can do it.

By the way, it's been a few days—the faucet still has not leaked or dripped. That's perfect! I'm happy that it's serving its purpose.

It Can Be So Specific

And the LORD told him, "Yes, go after them.
You will surely recover everything that was taken from you!"
1 Samuel 30:8b, NLT

An Alzheimer's diagnosis brings a lot of problems to a family. It has affected our family. We hear a lot of "I can't find my . . ." It strikes fear into your heart when it's your credit card.

One Tuesday, Nancy called me to tell me she was leaving the store and heading home. That Saturday, she told me, "I can't find my cell phone." We tried to retrace her steps. It had been missing since the call from the store, but she had been reluctant to tell me because she didn't want to upset me. By Saturday night, I had thoroughly searched four purses and rummaged through the entire house. The more I searched, the more anxious I felt.

Early Sunday morning, I was reading from 1 Samuel. David's city of Ziklag had been attacked, and raiders had carried off the wives, sons, and daughters of David and his soldiers. David sought God's guidance: "Then David asked the LORD, 'Should I chase after this band of raiders? Will I catch them?' And the LORD told him, 'Yes, go after them. You will surely recover everything that was taken from you!' (1 Samuel 30:8, NLT).

These words, this truth, was so impactful to me. I wrote in my journal, *Lord, I feel a little like David. Nancy has lost her cell phone. Will you guide me? Will you tell me where it is? Will you help me find it?*

A bit later, as I was preparing to get in my car to head to Sunday school and church, I felt compelled to search our other car—the one Nancy had been driving on Tuesday. I searched under the front seats and some storage areas—no phone. What about the back seats? In a niche on the floor, next to the center console, *there was the phone.* I took the phone into the house to show Nancy, and we both said, "Thank the Lord!" What relief.

How amazing that the living God can and will speak to us and guide us. He provides us with a sense of well-being and an assurance that he will be with us—and, at times, his guidance can be so specific to our needs!

Bid Alienation Goodbye!

Consequently, you are no longer foreigners and strangers, but fellow citizens with God's people and also members of his household.
Ephesians 2:19

Bid alienation goodbye!

Does that sound good? It means finally having a place to be included, loved, validated, and cheered on. It means having a safe space in the world—the same world that found it difficult to make space for God.

I have seen many people hesitate to ask about membership in his kingdom, for a number of reasons. Some don't believe they deserve to be in God's kingdom. Some aren't used to being loved. Some are fearful of what God will ask them to do. Some are abusing others and creating victims; some are themselves the victims. Some believe they must be in control at all times; others are out of control. Some deny they need anything—even God's love. Some come with their walls up and their doors locked and barricaded. Some are in pain and believe there is no relief. Some are spiritually dead and don't believe they can really live before they really die. Some are filled with anger and shame. Some are exhausted caretakers of the world.

"Is God going to let them in?" you ask. Yes, if they open their heart's door. You see, I was like several of those mentioned above, and he let *me* in. Farewell, alienation!

Nancy Shaver[34]

---

34. Previously published in *Come Ye Apart* March–April–May 1996 (Kansas City, MO: Nazarene Publishing House), 28. Used by permission. (This publication became *Reflecting God*.)

Heaven

*Then I saw "a new heaven and a new earth," for the first heaven and the
first earth had passed away, and there was no longer any sea. And I heard
a loud voice from the throne saying, "Look! God's dwelling place is now
among the people, and he will dwell with them. They will be his people, and
God himself will be with them and be their God. 'He will wipe every tear
from their eyes. There will be no more death' or mourning or crying or pain,
for the old order of things has passed away."*
Revelation 21:1, 3–4

"Hey, Siri!" I said. "What's tomorrow's weather?"

She replied, "Forty percent chance of thunderstorms, high of eighty-eight
degrees, low of seventy-seven degrees."

Amazing! She can tell you tomorrow's weather.

Hey, Revelation! What is our future eternity?

Amazing! Revelation can tell you about your future in heaven.

When a Christian dies today, their spirit goes immediately to be with the
Lord. Paul testified, "For to me, to live is Christ and to die is gain. . . . I desire
to depart and be with Christ, which is better by far" (Philippians 1:21, 23).
He further wrote, "We are confident, I say, and would prefer to be away from
the body and at home with the Lord. So we make it our goal to please him"
(2 Corinthians 5:8–9).

Beyond that, a day is coming when our physical bodies will be redeemed.
First Thessalonians 4:16–17 tells us, "The Lord himself will come down from
heaven, with a loud command, with the voice of the archangel and with the
trumpet call of God, and the dead in Christ will rise first. After that, we who
are still alive and are left will be caught up together with them in the clouds
to meet the Lord in the air. And so we will be with the Lord forever."

When one person was asked, "Why should God let you into heaven?" the
reply was, "Because I want to see my mother again."

That may be a good desire, but it is not a basis for entry into heaven.
Revelation tells us who enters and who doesn't: "Those who are victorious
will inherit all this, and I will be their God and they will be my children. But
the cowardly, the unbelieving, the vile, the murderers, the sexually immoral,
those who practice magic arts, the idolaters and all liars—they will be consigned to the fiery lake of burning sulfur" (21:7–8).

Or, "Nothing impure will ever enter it, nor will anyone who does what is shameful or deceitful, but only those whose names are written in the Lamb's book of life" (21:27).

Or, "Blessed are those who wash their robes, that they may have the right to the tree of life and may go through the gates into the city. Outside are . . . the sexually immoral, the murderers, the idolaters and everyone who loves and practices falsehood" (22:14–15).

Revelation says that this heavenly city is 1,400 square miles; its walls are 200 feet thick; twelve gates bear the names of the twelve tribes of Israel; its guards are angels; its foundation is made of stones bearing the names of the twelve apostles; its walls are decorated with jewels; its gates are made of pearl; its main street is made of gold; its temple is the Lord God and the Lamb; its lights are the glory of God. It will have no tears, no death, no crying, no pain. It will have the water of life, the tree of life, twelve crops of fruit, healing for the nations, and bright light.

My Aunt Mary's last words before she died were, "Oh, oh, oh, the angels, the angels, they're all around me!" Oh, there is a heaven.

"The Spirit and the bride say, 'Come!' And let the one who hears say, 'Come!' Let the one who is thirsty come; and let the one who wishes take the free gift of the water of life" (Revelation 22:17).

What I Have, I Give

Then Peter said, "Silver or gold I do not have, but what I do have
I give you. In the name of Jesus Christ of Nazareth, walk."
Acts 3:6

Ethiopian missionary Howie Shute reported that among the one thousand people gathered for the Holiness Conference were some skeptical Muslims who doubted the power of Christ. While the pastor was preaching, four Muslim men brought their friend who had been disabled all his life and was well known in the community. They laid him on the altar. During prayer, his dead muscles grew, his legs strengthened, and the man began to run and praise God. Forty Muslims ran to the front and exclaimed, "We need Jesus."*

It still happens. Spiritual power attends fully devoted followers of Christ—power from the Spirit's fullness (Acts 1:8; 2:4). In the context of today's scripture, the man is disabled and has to be carried to a place to beg (3:2)—he is both helpless and hopeless. If only their pockets weren't empty, Peter and John could give the man cash for his needs for the day. But because they are in touch with the power of Christ, they instead give him what he most needs, with long-term results.

As always, this healing, this kind deed, is performed to point to Christ as Savior. Witnesses are amazed (3:10), opportunities for preaching and evangelism open up, and many people accept Christ (4:4). Likewise, in the power of the Spirit, let us give what we have (3:6).

*Reported by Howie Shute, Holiness Summit, Colorado Springs, Colorado, September 7, 2008.[35]

He Went So Low

Christ Jesus: Who, being in very nature God, did not consider equality with God something to be used to his own advantage; rather, he made himself nothing by taking the very nature of a servant, being made in human likeness. And being found in appearance as a man, he humbled himself by becoming obedient to death—even death on a cross!
Philippians 2:5–8

Moscow—I was there for just one week to teach seventeen Russians, eight hours a day, how to better witness for Jesus. I was taken to a small apartment for my lodging. As I unpacked, I noticed a single wastebasket filled with garbage. I didn't know the apartment complex's protocol for disposing of trash, so I asked my host missionary about the basket. Almost lovingly, he got on his hands and knees, removed the contents by hand, and scrubbed the basket.

I could have wept. Here was a lifetime missionary who had left his homeland in the US to give himself to the call of Jesus, to bring Russians to the

35. Previously published in *Reflecting God* June–July–August 2010 (Kansas City, MO: WordAction Publishing Co.), 20. Used by permission.

Savior. Now, in addition, he was on his knees cleaning out my wastebasket to make things more comfortable for my one-week visit.

Consider Jesus Christ, who is truly God but came to earth as a human; who willingly went to the cross to die so that your sins and my sins could be forgiven. To identify with lost humanity even more completely, he hung between two thieves and died just as they were dying. Just imagine! E. Stanley Jones said, "This meant that He went so low that He could get under the lowest sinner and lift him to undreamed heights."[36]

He did this for you and me!

Crucified

I have been crucified with Christ and I no longer live, but Christ lives in me. The life I now live in the body, I live by faith in the Son of God, who loved me and gave himself for me.
Galatians 2:20

Jesus Christ was crucified for our sins. Christians everywhere recognize this central truth. But did you know it is possible for you to be crucified too? Paul actually claimed it: "I have been crucified with Christ."

In the Greek, Paul's word for "I" is "ego." When we describe someone by saying, "He has a big ego," we mean he is self-centered. Likewise, when Paul states, "I have been crucified," and references "the life I now live in the body," Paul means that his self-centeredness has been slain. When you experience this, your self-centeredness is crucified but not your essential selfhood—you will still have a personality. And you will still experience limitations, weaknesses, and temptations. You will "live by faith in the Son of God," making Christ-centered choices. Paul reveals the secret of such power: "Christ lives in me." He doesn't sleep or rest—he lives.

If you let him crucify you, you will hold all things loosely, because it is hard to hold anything with a spike in your hand. Dennis Kinlaw tells of hearing a woman named Mary play the violin in the most exquisite way and to the

---

36. Eli Stanley Jones, *How to Be a Transformed Person* (New York: Abingdon-Cokesbury Press, 1951), 12.

glory of God. Mary explained to him that her relationship with her violin had not always been God-glorifying.

The Lord told her, "Mary, give me your violin."

She responded, "Lord, it's all I've got."

"Give me your violin."

"But Lord, it's my life."

"I know. I want to be your life."

Mary explained to Kinlaw, "That violin possessed me. I didn't possess it. So I gave it to the Lord. For the first time I was free. He gave it back—now I possess it because he possesses me. And I'm free!"

Crucified, yet abundantly alive. The result—the most beautiful music.

The Best Out of the Worst

And Jesse the father of King David. David was the father
of Solomon, whose mother had been Uriah's wife.
Matthew 1:6

Matthew reports the genealogy of Jesus Christ, the Messiah, son of David, son of Abraham. He goes all the way back to Abraham, who obeyed God's call to leave his homeland and establish a new nation. Matthew highlights David, who became Israel's greatest king. This is significant because during his ministry, Jesus is repeatedly called the "Son of David."

But notice what Matthew does: When he reports that David is Solomon's father, he specifies that Solomon's mother had been Uriah's wife. Now this gets very messy—King David had many wives (2 Samuel 5:13), which was considered acceptable in that day.

Then, one day, from the roof of his palace, David sees a beautiful woman bathing and sends a servant to get her. The woman, Bathsheba, comes to the king, and David has sex with her. He sends her back home, and eventually she sends word she is pregnant with his child.

After learning this, David calls Bathsheba's husband, Uriah, back from battle, and arranges for him to return home in hopes he will sleep with his wife. But Uriah refuses to go home and instead, in solidarity with his troops, elects to sleep on a mat with the king's servants. David sends Uriah back into battle and tells his commander, Joab, to put him on the front lines. Soon, Uriah is killed. David then marries Bathsheba, and eventually, she bears David's child. Thus, David both commits adultery and arranges Uriah's death.

So, as Matthew reports Jesus Christ's genealogy, he truthfully lists the flawed King David in the line of relatives, and he further identifies Bathsheba as Solomon's mother. One reason I believe Scripture is true and reliable is because it does not cover up the unpleasant, sinful realities. Here is the best coming out of the worst: The Savior of the world descended from a line that included such egregious sin. This tells me that God can take the worst out of your life or mine and make something good come from it.

God does not treat David's sin lightly—God's prophet Nathan confronts David to reveal his sin and rebuke him (2 Samuel 12:7). During this encounter, David immediately confesses, "I have sinned against the LORD" (12:13). Nathan responds with God's forgiveness, but tells David that his unborn son will die. David's full prayer of repentance is recorded in Psalm 51: "Hide your face from my sins and blot out all my iniquity. Create in me a pure heart, O God, and renew a steadfast spirit within me" (vv. 9–10).

After this, David follows God faithfully. By the time we get to the New Testament, Peter preaches about David and recalls God's assessment of him: "I have found David son of Jesse, a man after my own heart; he will do everything I want him to do" (Acts 13:22). David becomes the greatest king in Israel's history, and eventually, he is the channel for the Savior of the world.

The best out of the worst!

He Bore Our Sins

"He himself bore our sins" in his body on the cross, so that we might
die to sins and live for righteousness; "by his wounds you have been
healed." For "you were like sheep going astray," but now you
have returned to the Shepherd and Overseer of your souls.
1 Peter 2:24–25

It felt like a joke—I worked all summer and saved most of my wages. In the fall, I returned to my Ivy League college for another year and plunked down all I had saved for tuition, fees, room, and meals. Still, it was a small drop in a big bucket. What about the rest of my huge balance?

Wait a minute—I remembered that I carried in my pocket a big check from my dad. You see, he had worked hard and saved a lot. Now, because his great love for me, he bore my college cost himself so I could be completely financially free.

A lot of blood was shed for the sins of humanity. If you read the Old Testament, you will see that thousands upon thousands of bulls, rams, and lambs were sacrificed to atone for the sins of people. Still, all this blood did not solve the problem of sin. The only way to solve it was for God to show up.

This is why God sent his divine Son. Christ said, "'I have come to do your will.' . . . And by that will, we have been made holy through the sacrifice of the body of Jesus Christ once for all" (Hebrews 10:9–10). One sacrifice, once for all, not repeated. My sins, completely atoned for. All my sins forgiven in a moment. My privilege—die to sin. My destiny—live for righteousness! Because he bore our sins!

Brought Near by the Blood

But now in Christ Jesus you who once were far away
have been brought near by the blood of Christ.
Ephesians 2:13

When Jesus knocked on my door, he found it tightly locked. Even though I wanted him to come in, I didn't know how to give him entrance. I slipped him a message under the door with a list of all my wonderful qualities—all the reasons why I would be an asset to the kingdom and not a liability.

There was no answer. So then, I sent a list of my liabilities—why I wasn't worthy of God's love, why I didn't deserve to be a member of the kingdom. Sad to say, this list was longer than the first. Again, no answer.

So I called out and asked someone who was already a member to show me the way. This person told me of a cross upon which Jesus hung at great personal cost and gave his greatest gift—his life's blood—so that I could be included in his family.

Precious was the moment when I asked through the door, "For me too?"

"Yes, for you too."

I swung the door wide open, the bells rang, the band played, and Love walked in.

Do you need to ask someone to show you the way? Is there someone asking *you* to show them the way?

Nancy Shaver[37]

APRIL 4   94

So Great

And who through the Spirit of holiness was appointed the
Son of God in power by his resurrection from the dead:
Jesus Christ our Lord.
Romans 1:4

Have you ever thought about things that are just so great? I've thought of a few:

- Making the Rocky Mountain drive from Red Lodge, Montana, into Yellowstone National Park
- Witnessing the hourly eruptions of Old Faithful
- Seeing a male bison orchestrating a road crossing for a dozen females and their young
- Hearing Christians pray in other languages
- Seeing my mom get saved
- Recognizing God's grace in my marriage

We serve so great a Savior—Romans 1 gives us a picture of him. Let's break it down by phrase:

- "The gospel he promised beforehand through his prophets in the Holy Scriptures" (Romans 1:2)—Hundreds of years before Christ came, the prophets told us about him.
- "His earthly life . . . a descendant of David" (1:3)—Christ was truly human and, as promised, descended from Israel's greatest king.

---

37. Previously published in *Come Ye Apart* March–April–May 1996 (Kansas City, MO: Nazarene Publishing House), 27. Used by permission. (This publication became *Reflecting God*.)

- "Through the Spirit of holiness was appointed the Son of God in power" (1:4)—The Spirit—who is truly holy and the creator of holiness in others—works in power. Christ is truly God.
- "By his resurrection from the dead" (1:4)—The resurrection, established as a great historical fact by more than five hundred witnesses, was the conquest of humanity's greatest enemy, death.
- "Jesus Christ our Lord" (1:4)—Our hearts reach out to worship him.
- "Through him" (1:5)—So much comes to us through him, only through him—he gives us what no one else can.
- "We received grace" (1:5)—We can think of this in terms of an acronym, in which G.R.A.C.E. stands for "God's Riches at Christ's Expense." God does for us what we don't deserve—and his gift is receivable.
- "Apostleship to call all the Gentiles" (1:5)—We are Christ's representatives, tasked with calling others to come to him.
- "To the obedience that comes from faith" (1:5)—It is possible to be obedient to God, and we can do it by the power of faith—not any other way.

This is the one you know and serve—the *so great* Jesus Christ, who is with you right now.

Through Death to Risen

He has risen from the dead and is going ahead of you into Galilee. There you will see him.
Matthew 28:7

More than sixty times I've heard joyous Christians sing, "Up from the grave he arose, with a mighty triumph o'er his foes,"[38] or songs like it on Easter Sunday. This event was so monumental that Romans 1:4 describes Jesus as the one "who through the Spirit of holiness was appointed the Son of God in power by his resurrection from the dead."

---

38. Robert Lowry, "Christ Arose" (1874), *Sing to the Lord Hymnal* (Kansas City, MO: Lillenas Publishing Co., 1993), #258.

Your death, my death, can be a fearful thing. As a matter of fact, Paul says, "The last enemy to be destroyed is death" (1 Corinthians 15:26). However, there is also a last answer: "But thanks be to God! He gives us the victory through our Lord Jesus Christ" (v. 57).

I've asked God to bring glory to himself through all aspects of my Christian life—even in my death. To be honest, I have had a sense of concern about dying. I've passed through many challenges in my more than sixty-five years of Christian life: financial challenges prayed through, sicknesses overcome, victory despite awful opposition, release for those in drug addiction, love and patience in the face of Alzheimer's, and more. Each of these past victories gives me a sure pattern when I face them again.

Yet, dying—I've never passed through that experience before. But I am reminded of this Savior who became fully human—"because he himself suffered when he was tempted, he is able to help those who are being tempted" (Hebrews 2:18). After all, the Lord "knows how we are formed, he remembers that we are dust" (Psalm 103:14). As Frances Ridley Havergal puts it, "He is remembering all the time," and, "We have not passed this way before, but the Lord Jesus has."[39]

Even though I've never been through anything that can truly prepare me for my death, my Lord Jesus has personally been through death—and he arose. Since I am in a living connection with him, he will walk me through my death: "We have not passed this way before, but the Lord Jesus has." Will you receive that assurance too?

If You Suffer

Those who sow trouble reap it.
Job 4:8

Joni was a vibrant, active teenager. She had been a Christian for two years. Many things were going well in her life, but she was troubled by some of her

---

39. Quoted in Mrs. Charles E. Cowman, *Streams in the Desert: 366 Daily Devotional Readings* (Grand Rapids: Zondervan, 1996), 112.

old attitudes cropping up—anger, jealousy, resentment, possessiveness—so she asked God to change her.

On July 30, 1967, Joni dove into a shallow lake, broke her neck, and was paralyzed from the neck down. She began to experience bitterness, anger with God, and unanswered prayers. Slowly she realized that, although God had not caused her accident, he was using it to bring her to a greater reliance on him. She said God used the tragedy "to turn a headstrong, stubborn, rebellious kid into a young woman who would reflect something of patience, something of endurance, something of long-suffering."[40] Eventually, Joni Eareckson Tada became an artist who painted by holding the brush in her teeth; an author; an advocate for the disabled; and a powerful speaker for God.

But wait a minute! Doesn't Joni's suffering prove that there was unconfessed sin in her life? That was the argument that Job's "comforter," Eliphaz, made when he said, "Those who sow trouble reap it." Because all Job's flocks had been taken away in one day through death or capture; because all of his children had died in one day in a house collapse; because Job was afflicted with painful sores from his head to his feet—there must be some secret sin behind it all.

It's true that Galatians 6:7 says, "A man reaps what he sows." But that verse is true when we include eternity, not just this life. I conclude that yes, all who sin will suffer—but not all who are suffering have sinned. Jesus clarified this issue in John 9:2–3 when his disciples, referring to a blind man, asked, "Rabbi, who sinned, this man or his parents, that he was born blind?"

Jesus answered, "Neither this man nor his parents sinned . . . but this happened so that the work of God might be displayed in his life."

Here are some reasons why people suffer:

- *Your sin results in your suffering.* A friend of mine was approached by a stranger who sucker-punched him and knocked him out. The man who threw the punch is now *suffering* in jail.
- *Your sin results in others' suffering.* As a teen, my wife suffered from anxiety and feelings of rejection because her dad abandoned the family for alcohol and another woman.
- *Your sin brings suffering to a nation or organization.* Over the years, we've seen many examples of this in the headlines, where the actions of a sin-

---

40. Quoted in Rick Williamson, "Adult Leader," Mike Wonch, editor, June–July–August 2014, Vol. 37, No. 4 (Kansas City, MO: WordAction Publishing Co.), 74–75.

gle person—whether politician or church leader—can cause suffering for an enormous group of people.

- *Adam and Eve sinned, and our whole world has been suffering ever since.* God said to Adam, "Cursed is the ground because of you" (Genesis 3:17). We also see this pain reflected in Romans 8:18–23, especially verse 22: "The whole creation has been groaning as in the pains of childbirth right up to the present time." True, a day is coming when it "will be liberated from its bondage to decay" (8:21), but for now, we still suffer from tornadoes, tsunamis, fires, flood, hurricanes, and more.

Dr. Orval Nease, a church leader, was in great anguish over problems that seemed insurmountable. He read Romans 8:28 in his King James Bible: "And we know that all things work together for good to them that love God." His suffering was so deep that the words didn't seem true. He picked up his Greek New Testament and read the verse in its original language. It read, "And we know that in all things God works for the good of those who love him." In that moment, the lights went on for Dr. Nease. He realized it was not that "all things work," but rather, "in all things *God works*." God can take what even the devil sends and, given time, work it into a pattern for good for those who love him—for Joni; for Dr. Nease; for you; and for me.

Humbly March Right Up!

*In him and through faith in him we may approach God
with freedom and confidence.*
Ephesians 3:12

When I am with my heavenly Father in that safe place we call home, I can talk to him about anything. I can boldly approach because:

He invites me to.

He has an open-door policy.

He's never said, "Don't come."

He was there the last time.

He's never too busy to listen.

He has my "to-do" list.

He takes my burdens (if I leave them).

He binds up my wounds.

He teaches me about life.

I don't need a passport.

I don't have to "pass go."

I don't have to measure up.

I don't have to get past a secretary.

I don't have to be important, and my topic of conversation doesn't have to be important.

I don't *need* a topic of conversation—I can sit with God and just *be*.

I can boldly go there because I know he loves me, and perfect love casts out fear. So what can man do to me when I have God?

Nancy Shaver[41]

Courage Is . . .

My soul is overwhelmed with sorrow to the point of death.
Stay here and keep watch with me.
Matthew 26:38b

My Father, if it is possible, may this cup be taken from me.
Yet not as I will, but as you will.
Matthew 26:39b

Look, the hour has come, and the Son of Man is delivered into the
hands of sinners. Rise! Let us go! Here comes my betrayer.
Matthew 26:45b–46

Jesus Christ speaks all the words above as he prays in Gethsemane, knowing he will soon go to the cross for our sins.

Here, we gain insight into Jesus's humanity: he feels deep sorrow. He prefers an easier, less painful way to do God's will. He is probably afraid. Yet he chooses to do God's will despite the humility and pain: "Let us go!"

---

41. Previously published in *Come Ye Apart* March–April–May 1996 (Kansas City, MO: Nazarene Publishing House), 31. Used by permission. (This publication became *Reflecting God*.)

This glimpse into Jesus's experience proves that you may be very close to God and still not receive what you ask for. It teaches the necessity of prayer when times are hard. Jesus prays the same prayer three times until he settles on a final plea: "May your will be done" (26:42).

Early in my Christian life, I thought that any truly Spirit-filled Christian would be free from feelings of fear. But now I have a new definition of courage. New Testament courage is not the absence of fear—it is doing what God wants you to do even though you're afraid.

Jesus felt sorrow, and probably fear, yet he chose God's will. Likewise, the Spirit-filled apostle Paul said, "I came to you in weakness with great fear and trembling" (1 Corinthians 2:3), but in the very next verse, proclaims that his message came to the Corinthians "with a demonstration of the Spirit's power." Despite his fear, Paul did God's will.

As a young Christian, despite my fears, I had to go back to my former boss and apologize for my gossip about him. Despite my fears, I had to face the Interfraternity Council to explain why I wanted to leave my fraternity. To this day, I have to repeatedly resist my fears whenever I witness for Jesus Christ.

Thankfully, there is help for those of us who are fearful. Even in Jesus's agonizing time in Gethsemane, Luke 22:43 tucks in this little sentence: "An angel from heaven appeared to him and strengthened him." Paul reports, "Therefore, my dear friends, as you have always obeyed . . . continue to work out your salvation with fear and trembling, for it is God who works in you to will and to act in order to fulfill his good purpose" (Philippians 2:12–13).

So be courageous in spite of your fears. Do what God wants you to do.

Jesus Is Alive!

Jesus said, "Do not hold on to me, for I have not yet ascended to the Father. Go instead to my brothers and tell them, 'I am ascending to my Father and your Father, to my God and your God.'" Mary Magdalene went to the disciples with the news: "I have seen the Lord!"
John 20:17–18

What's real? What's true? Our world so completely depends on the scientific method that we may believe that only quantifiable things are true. In math, from simple addition problems to complex calculus formulas, we depend on very specific outcomes. Yet science and math do not answer the whole of life. Do you believe there is such a thing as justice? Do you believe that love is real? Then please show me a yard of justice or a pound of love. You can't—because these truths are neither scientifically nor mathematically quantifiable. In court cases, we accept evidence. Personal testimony is highly important. Verdicts are reached when the evidence provides proof beyond a reasonable doubt.

Christianity makes an amazing claim about its leader, Jesus Christ, "who through the Spirit of holiness was appointed the Son of God in power by his resurrection from the dead" (Romans 1:4). The four Gospels are careful reports of Jesus Christ's life and ministry. The Gospels of Matthew and John were written by two of the twelve apostles who were carefully chosen by Jesus and had intense contact with him for three years. Mark became a follower of Christ and traveled with Paul and Barnabas doing powerful missionary work; Luke was a careful historian who interviewed eyewitnesses and wrote an orderly history of Christ (Luke 1:1–4). Later books of the New Testament were written by major Christian leaders who were in living relationship with Christ and faithfully proclaimed his message.

Christ repeatedly told his followers he would be killed and rise from the dead. See Luke 18:31–33: "Jesus took the Twelve aside and told them, 'We are going up to Jerusalem, and everything that is written by the prophets about the Son of Man will be fulfilled. He will be delivered over to the Gentiles. They will mock him, insult him and spit on him; they will flog him and kill him. On the third day he will rise again.'" Jesus also promised to send the Holy Spirit back to the disciples after his death, resurrection, and ascension to testify about Jesus, to make him real to people (John 15:26–27).

On the cross, Jesus said, "It is finished," and gave up his spirit (19:30). Shortly after this, when soldiers came to check on Christ, they "found that he was already dead" (19:33).

The Gospel writers are transparent; they do not hide the doubt that Jesus's followers experienced. Despite all his teachings, when Mary Magdalene discovered that Jesus's tomb was empty, she did not assume he was resurrected. Rather, she ran to Peter and said, "They have taken the Lord out of the tomb, and we don't know where they have put him!" (20:2). But finally, Mary saw him.

Thomas, one of the Twelve, refused to believe that Jesus was alive when the other disciples told him, "We have seen the Lord!" (20:25). It was only when Jesus appeared among his disciples in a locked room, only when he offered Thomas the chance to touch the wounds in his hands and side, that Thomas believed (20:26–28).

By the time these divine meetings were over, all twelve of the disciples (plus Mary Magdalene and several other women) had seen the Lord. After Jesus ascended back to his Father, the Father and Son poured the Holy Spirit out upon the 120 praying disciples (Acts 2:33). A great spiritual surge flowed through the people as Jesus' followers told his story. Later, when the devout Stephen was being stoned, he looked up to heaven and saw Jesus "standing at the right hand of God" (7:56).

Saul was heading to Damascus to persecute Christians when suddenly, a light from heaven flashed around him. He fell to the ground, then heard, "I am Jesus, whom you are persecuting" (9:5). Saul became the apostle Paul, the powerful leader of a worldwide Christian movement. Later, Paul reported that the resurrected Christ had "appeared to more than five hundred of the brothers and sisters at the same time, most of whom are still living." (1 Corinthians 15:6).

What can we say? Only this: Jesus is alive!

Two men were walking to Emmaus, a village about seven miles from Jerusalem, soon after Jesus's resurrection. Jesus joined the two men, and they got into an extended conversation, but did not recognize him. Only later, as they were all sharing a meal, did the men realize this was the living Jesus. They went back to Jerusalem and reported to the Eleven, "It is true! The Lord has risen and has appeared to Simon" (Luke 24:34).

In light of the fact that Jesus is alive, how many people today need to be alert as they walk through their daily lives—to watch for him who goes before us in every step? It would be wise to pray, "Reveal yourself to me, Lord Jesus."

Destined for the Throne

To the one who is victorious, I will give the right to sit with me on my
throne, just as I was victorious and sat down with my Father on his throne.
Revelation 3:21

What is the greatest goal and purpose of your life? What is God's greatest role and purpose for your life? By the full measure of God's redemptive action, he is preparing people to sit with Christ on his throne. Do you get it? God's plan is for you to sit on Christ's throne.

Sin is the major block to this plan. So God works through Christ's life, death, resurrection, and intercession, and the ministry of the Holy Spirit to forgive and cleanse us of our sin and selfishness—all so we will be able to sit with Christ. Embrace the fact that God is doing everything possible to shape and refine you for your destiny.

Hear the Word of the Lord on this truth:

Romans 8:29: "For those God foreknew he also predestined to be conformed to the image of his Son, that he might be the firstborn among many brothers and sisters."

Hebrews 2:10–11: "In bringing many sons and daughters to glory, it was fitting that God, for whom and through whom everything exists, should make the pioneer of their salvation perfect through what he suffered. Both the one who makes people holy and those who are made holy are of the same family. So Jesus is not ashamed to call them brothers and sisters."

Hebrews 11:16—"Instead, they were longing for a better country—a heavenly one. Therefore God is not ashamed to be called their God, for he has prepared a city for them."

Hebrews 13:12–13: "And so Jesus also suffered outside the city gate to make the people holy through his own blood. Let us, then, go to him outside the camp, bearing the disgrace he bore."

Hebrews 12:10–11: "They [our fathers] disciplined us for a little while as they thought best; but God disciplines us for our good, in order that we may share in his holiness. No discipline seems pleasant at the time, but painful. Later on, however, it produces a harvest of righteousness and peace for those who have been trained by it."

Think of it—you and I are destined for the throne! Our sensitivity to the sanctifying Spirit of God will prepare us.

Power to Forgive

This proposal pleased the whole group. They chose Stephen,
a man full of faith and of the Holy Spirit.
Acts 6:5a

While they were stoning him, Stephen prayed, "Lord Jesus,
receive my spirit." Then he fell on his knees and cried out, "Lord, do not
hold this sin against them." When he had said this, he fell asleep.
Acts 7:59–60

It's amazing that people who are so mistreated have the power to forgive those who abuse them. Stephen did! Jesus did! Dying on the cross, Jesus prayed for his executioners and the jeering crowd, "Father, forgive them, for they do not know what they are doing" (Luke 23:34).

We see this also in the story of Jacob DeShazer, who was imprisoned and tortured by the Japanese for years during World War II, then forgave his guards. In prison he received Christ, was sanctified and filled with the Spirit, and felt called to preach. After the war, he returned to Japan as a missionary to preach forgiveness and Christ's love.

And this power of forgiveness is still at work today. Kathy Cagg, a sanctified, Spirit-filled woman, gave and received that forgiveness. Here is her story:

In April of 2007, my brother Dave did a mass shooting at the Ward Parkway Shopping Center in Kansas City, Missouri. Four people lost their lives including my brother, who had to be stopped by the police.

For months after, I wasn't able to feel any sadness about Dave's death. I could only feel sadness for his victims and their families. Running through my mind was, *How dare he bring so much pain into the lives of so many people!* It took God's intervention to help me process my complicated emotions. I did a press conference in front of my church the day after the shooting. My pastor prayed, and then I made some statements intending to offer my condolences and apology for my brother's act of violence. The mother of one of my brother's victims was watching, and seeing me make those statements somehow started some healing in her.

Several months later, she got in touch with my pastor and requested a personal meeting with me. We met in the pastor's office, hugged, cried, talked, and continued our commitment to our mutual healing by going to the site of the shooting together. In an ocean of cars in the mall parking lot, the space was empty where Carolee's precious daughter, Leslie, took her last breath. We stood in the middle of that space holding each other and crying. During our conversations, she told me that she forgave my brother, knowing it's what Jesus requires of us. Up until then, I hadn't even allowed myself to see the level of rage I was carrying toward my brother.

Immediately I knew I had the task of forgiving Dave ahead of me. That night, at home in bed, I asked God to help me forgive, and he did. For four months prior to the mass shooting, I had been sleeping with my head at the foot of the bed, concerned that Dave would try to shoot me through my bedroom window. I reasoned, *Better my feet than my head.* After the shooting, I had not been able to switch my sleeping position. After forgiving Dave, I was able to, and that night I got the best sleep ever—the peaceful rest of an obedient child!

After recognizing my anger and choosing forgiveness, I still had the grief to process. It took time, and in the end, it brought me to the place of God placing a ministry call on my life to lead grief recovery at my church. It is a precious honor and blessing to walk with people through their journey from grief to joy. Forgiveness is almost always a component of their healing. Forgiveness is a choice we have the power to make when we make our relationship with Jesus bigger than the pain.

Carolee forgave Dave. Kathy forgave him too. Even more amazingly, Carolee, whose daughter was murdered, and Kathy, the sister of the murderer, became good friends. Carolee decided to join Kathy's Sunday school class. You would see them sitting together Sunday after Sunday with the glow of God on their faces. They had discovered the power of forgiveness.

Resurrection Power

*I pray that the eyes of your heart may be enlightened in order
that you may know the hope to which he has called you, the riches
of his glorious inheritance in his holy people, and his incomparably
great power for us who believe. That power is the same as the mighty
strength he exerted when he raised Christ from the dead and
seated him at his right hand in the heavenly realms.*
Ephesians 1:18–20

John was raised in a coal miner's family. On the nights he stayed late at school for football practice, he often came home to find that all the supper had been eaten by the rest of his family.

He became a top athlete. He was high scorer in basketball for the final tournament of the year. He joined the track team and won three victories in the district championship: the 220, the 440, and as anchor on the relay team. At Colorado State he was elected to the All-Conference scholastic football team. He's now in the Pennsylvania Football Hall of Fame, Eastern Conference. And for thirty-three years, he worked as a high school teacher, football coach, and wrestling coach.

Nancy and I stayed in John and Gloria's beautiful log cabin during revival services at their local church. Now eighty-four years old, John told me that, up until ninth grade, he had only been to church once. After that, he became a bit more involved. One of the first things he said to me was, "Help me with religion."

On April 2, the local pastor and I shared the good news of Jesus Christ with John. Early in our discussion, John said, "I don't think I can go to the Lord because I have unfinished business."

That morning, John prayed and received Jesus Christ into his heart and life. Over the next few hours, he said the following:

- "I feel different now."
- "I can put most of my problems in the Lord's hands."
- "Because of what the Lord has done for me."
- "I felt something came into my body—just going to church wasn't enough."
- "I feel different—I guess I found him—he found me."
- "You helped me so much."

That night, he gave a testimony at the revival service: "I used to be five foot eleven inches, but I've shrunk to five foot eight inches. Now I feel five foot eleven inches again—I felt I was off the floor."

Two days later, while planning an out-of-town trip, John went to his friend to recruit his help in dog-sitting. He said, "Ray, I've got something great to tell you. I'm a born-again Christian."

How could such a change occur? After eighty-four years, John had been transformed from being dead in sin to living in Jesus Christ. It's all because of the great power available to those of us who believe—that same power that raised Christ from the dead. Resurrection power is available to John, to you, to me!

Packing Up for Home

I have fought the good fight, I have finished the race, I have kept the faith.
Now there is in store for me the crown of righteousness, which the Lord,
the righteous Judge, will award to me on that day—and not only to me,
but also to all who have longed for his appearing.
2 Timothy 4:7–8

We're packing our stuff—all the stuff we thought we needed to spend time with twenty family members in our beloved Treasure Island, Florida. Early tomorrow morning, we will start our journey home. As great as our two weeks here have been, I can honestly say it will be so good to get back home.

As the apostle Paul packed up for his departure to his heavenly home, his testimony was strong. He did not say, "*If* I fought the good fight," or, "*Maybe* I finished the race," or, "I *tried* to keep the faith." Rather, he declared that he *had* fought the good fight, finished the race, kept the faith.

As Paul prepared for his journey, he didn't pack any physical stuff. Instead, he packed the record of what God had done in his life. He had already laid out the issue to the Philippians when he wrote, "For to me, to live is Christ and to die is gain . . . I desire to depart and be with Christ" (1:21, 23).

There will be neither time nor storage for physical stuff when we get to heaven. At Christ's future coming, the dead in Christ, then the living, will rise to be with the Lord forever (1 Thessalonians 4:16–17). Followers of the Lord today who die before Christ's return will enter his presence, just as Paul testifies.

No, we won't take stuff—there is a much more important goal we should have in mind before going home to heaven. First John 3:2–3 tells us plainly, "But we know that when Christ appears, we shall be like him, for we shall see him as he is. All who have this hope in him purify themselves, just as he is pure." So don't pack stuff for your heavenly home—just be sure you have a pure heart.

When a Saint Goes Home

Those who are victorious will inherit all this,
and I will be their God and they will be my children.
Revelation 21:7

Dr. Robert Coleman, a gracious man of God, a Christian leader, and the author of *The Master Plan of Evangelism*, wrote a letter to friends in 2017. Here are portions of that letter:

My dear wife, Marietta, died early in the morning on January 3.

When given the terminal cancer diagnosis just four months earlier, Marietta calmly looked at the doctor and said, "Then I am going home to heaven."

In this waiting period while she still had a measure of comfort, we read again her favorite book, *The Pilgrim's Progress*, an allegory of a Christian's pilgrimage to heaven. As [the] Pilgrim traveled, he was repeatedly asked where he came from and where he was going. He always replied he left the City of Destruction and was on his way to the Celestial City.

She began her journey as a young girl when she fell in love with Jesus. Her quiet, deep Christian faith flowed through her life like an artesian spring of refreshing water.

Our home became a gateway to heaven. Hospitality was her passion, and she made our house a veritable inn with students, missionaries, friends often sitting at our table. For sixty-five years, Marietta and I ministered together.

During the last months of her illness, I canceled all meetings to be with her. She died at home in my arms. Now that she is gone, it's time for me to get back to working, preaching, and discipling. Oh, how I will miss Marietta beside me! Sometimes I can almost feel her gentle touch on my hand. Thankfully, my daughter, Angie, and her husband live ten minutes away. Wherever I am, there is a faraway look in my eye, for I am on my way to the Celestial City where there's going to be a wonderful reunion around the throne of God.

Thank you for your prayers and remembrances of love.

Robert Coleman

You and I can be part of that reunion too.

Trash It? Never!

So do not throw away your confidence; it will be richly rewarded.
Hebrews 10:35

I could just hear one of Wormwood's cohorts saying, "She's down. I don't think she's going to get up. The dart I threw pierced her heart clear through, and she's finished with God."

As I lay there in my pain, bewilderment, and disappointment, God came along and picked me up. I laid my head on his chest, and he just held me.

"Lord, I thought all my pain was in the past."

"Pain," he said, "is part of life, but so is joy. I don't force my love on anyone. Everyone is free to choose. It took you awhile to choose me."

"Yes, Lord, and you are my special treasure. I have a relationship with you that no one else can destroy. Wormwood's cohort got a surprise today, Lord. He came back to find me, and he found your footprints. Doesn't he know that you take care of your own, whether down here, or up there? I'm feeling better. I think I can walk now. I think I'm ready to bind up someone else's wounds, help someone celebrate because they have discovered your love, tell that person a story, or . . ."

Once upon a time, God looked down—and sent his Son.

Nancy Shaver[42]

The Payoff for Suffering

---

42. Previously published in *Come Ye Apart* March–April–May 1996 (Kansas City, MO: Nazarene Publishing House), 32. Used by permission. (This publication became *Reflecting God*.)

We also glory in our sufferings, because we know that suffering produces perseverance; perseverance, character; and character, hope. And hope does not put us to shame, because God's love has been poured into our hearts through the Holy Spirit, who has been given to us.
Romans 5:3–5

Even the most casual football fans became highly excited by this game—two teams, Houston playing Kansas City—were on their way to be the potential finalists for the 2020 Super Bowl championship. At the end of the first quarter, Houston led 24–0.

The young Kansas City quarterback, Patrick Mahomes, moved among his players on the sidelines. With a wisdom beyond his years, he did not berate them, yell at them, or lose his temper. Instead, he encouraged them, supported them, and projected hope—all while staying calm. He challenged the team and the crowd with the words, "We're going to fight until the end," and, "Let's go do something special." Mahomes was the picture of perseverance and composure.

Then, from their misplays and a 24-point deficit, Kansas City came alive, scored four touchdowns in under sixteen minutes, and won the game 51–31.

The characteristics on display during that playoff game are trumpeted in the Word of God. Suffering, when used and managed by God's help, produces perseverance, which produces character, which produces hope. And this hope will not put us to shame or disappoint us, because it anticipates a far better reward than an incredible football victory. It is about God's love poured (not dripped) in our hearts (where we need it most) through the Holy Spirit (God's personal presence) given to us.

Yes, there is a payoff to suffering when we cooperate with God's help and develop awesome character. And then, there is another and bigger payoff—the hope of the glory of God, in which we'll someday live in his eternal presence in heaven.

A Real Live Letter

You show that you are a letter from Christ, the result of our ministry,
written not with ink but with the Spirit of the living God,
not on tablets of stone but on tablets of human hearts.
2 Corinthians 3:3

Letters—we get stacks and stacks of them. What kind of letters do you like to receive? Perhaps the kind that say:

"We're having a great event—come over and help us celebrate."

"Thanks, you did a great job! We couldn't have done it without you."

"I'm sorry. Forgive me. "

"Your behavior is grieving me, but I still love you."

"Eventually you will find something good in this storm."

"Just had to let you know: I met your Jesus and I'm a kingdom member now too."

"It's okay—we all make mistakes. What did you learn from this one?"

"Nothing is impossible. God is unstoppable. Trust him."

"I know I can count on you; I know because you stand upon the Rock."

"Have I told you lately that I love you more than you'll ever know?"

If so, pick up God's letter. Your name is on its pages.

"Wear your whole armor today." (See Ephesians 6:13.)

"Thou wilt keep him in perfect peace, whose mind is stayed on thee" (Isaiah 26:3, KJV).

By the way, did you know that you are a letter too? God's love, when engraved upon our hearts, is there for all the world to read.

Nancy Shaver[43]

With Regard to the Smoke, Put Out the Fire

43. Previously published in *Come Ye Apart* March–April–May 1996 (Kansas City, MO: Nazarene Publishing House), 30. Used by permission. (This publication became *Reflecting God*.)

You were taught, with regard to your former way of life, to put off
your old self, which is being corrupted by its deceitful desires;
to be made new in the attitude of your minds; and to put on the new self,
created to be like God in true righteousness and holiness.
Ephesians 4:22–24

The college chaplain was angry with me. Students who attended the voluntary chapel services were often asked to speak, and he asked me, a brand-new Christian. I preached on the verse, "For the kingdom of God is not a matter of eating and drinking, but of righteousness, peace and joy in the Holy Spirit" (Romans 14:17). I was joyous in expressing my new, changed life in Christ.

The chaplain spoke to me after the service: "If you think you're better now than you were then, you're worse now than you were then." Wow! Apparently, he embraced the teaching that even a Christian can only be sinful. What happened to God enabling us "to serve him without fear in holiness and righteousness before him all our days" (Luke 1:74–75)? Yet beyond our outward sins, there is a deeper issue.

E. Stanley Jones testifies that he experienced a life-changing conversion. He writes that in Christ, "life has a new center around which to revolve. But all the life forces and affections are not gathered up around Christ. There are some who do not bend the knee and accept this new allegiance." There are urges that are "used to having their way—they have had their way for a long time."[44]

Paul wrote to the Ephesians, "With regard to your former way of life, to put off your old self." God challenges us to go to the deepest chasms of our hearts for a full cleansing. The New Living Translation puts verse 22 this way: "Throw off your old sinful nature and your former way of life." Behind your deeds there is a disposition; behind actions, an attitude; behind movements, a motive; behind sins, self-centeredness. To combat this, we must take strong action—"put off"—and positive action—"put on the new self, created to be like God in true righteousness and holiness."

When it comes to smoke, put out the fire. When it comes to your former way of life, put off your old self.

Sometime after he accepted Christ as his Savior, Rees Howells, the Welsh layman who founded the Bible College of Wales, had an in-depth meeting with the Holy Spirit. Of that experience, he said, "It meant every bit of my

---

44. E. Stanley Jones, *Abundant Living* (New York: Abingdon, 1942), 150.

fallen nature was to go to the cross, and he would bring in his own life and his own nature."[45]

Add Your Testimony

If I testify about myself, my testimony is not true. There is another who testifies in my favor, and I know that his testimony about me is true.
John 5:31–32

"Gentlemen, the Gospels were written by men who *thought* Jesus was the Messiah. We must regard it as so much *propaganda*." This was my college Bible professor's opening statement.

His words sent a chill through my recently converted soul. What a negative testimony! Far truer and more moving were the words I heard a few weeks earlier from the man who led me to Christ: "Chic, I'm different than I used to be because I found the Lord."

To testify is to tell another what Jesus has done for you—to testify is to affirm all that Jesus really is.

In dealing with the hostile people of his day, Jesus said that if he only testified to who he really was, that would not be good enough—he would not be accepted. Jesus then began to list the other people and facts who testified to his true identity. Would it be possible to sway his antagonists?

He first mentioned John the Baptist, who was well-regarded as a prophet in that day: "You have sent to John and he has testified to the truth. Not that I accept human testimony; but I mention it that you may be saved" (John 5:33–34).

Second, he cited the works, signs, and miracles he performed as valid evidence: "For the works that the Father has given me to finish—the very works that I am doing—testify that the Father has sent me" (5:36).

Third, the Father himself testified to Christ's message: "And the Father who sent me has himself testified concerning me" (5:37).

---

45. Norman Grubb, *Rees Howells, Intercessor: The Story of a Life Lived for God* (Philadelphia: Christian Literature Crusade, 1952), 36.

Finally, there is the scriptural evidence: "These are the very Scriptures that testify about me" (5:39).

Jesus presented four strong, respected testimonies as though he were in a court of law. And how did his audience respond to this evidence? Jesus said of them, "I have come in my Father's name, and you do not accept me" (5:43). How sad!

Then, another witness emerged: the man who had been healed spoke up to Jesus' opponents. John 5:15 reports, "The man went away and told the Jewish leaders that it was Jesus who had made him well."

How beautiful it is to listen to people like Jolene. On a September 30, she accepted Christ and said, "It was incredible. I was instantly different."

Recounting the moment in which God brought down his last wall of resistance, Mike said, "I felt I just had to get away from people that night; and all alone at 11:00 p.m., I cried out and asked Christ into my heart." Later, he said, "God has helped me incredibly."

Shahrzad was depressed on April 14 because of income taxes. But when some Christian friends told her that Christ was knocking at the door of her heart, she prayed and opened the door. She began to rejoice and said, "Oh, oh, oh, I have such peace! I have such peace!"

She ran across the room and hugged her husband, exclaiming, "Albert, what do we do next?"[46] Let's answer for her—go tell someone!

Would you like to join the testifiers?

Standing on the Promises

But if we walk in the light, as he is in the light, we have fellowship with one another, and the blood of Jesus, his Son, purifies us from all sin.
1 John 1:7

As an outstanding singer and an accomplished pianist, Frances Ridley Havergal could have had a glittering career in front of cheering crowds. However,

---

46. Portions of this report are from *Holiness Today*, October 2000 (Kansas City, MO: Nazarene Publishing House), 3–4. Used by permission.

she was convinced that her gifts were on loan from the Lord. Thus, with the goal of winning souls, she only sang sacred music.

Born in 1836, Frances began writing at age seven. She studied in England and Germany and became proficient in biblical Greek and Hebrew. In 1874, she went into a home where the ten people residing there either didn't know the Lord or were not joyful Christians. By the time she left the home, all ten were joyful Christians. Afterward, she was so filled with joy that she couldn't sleep. That night, she wrote "Ever, Only, All for Thee," which became part of a hymn.

Many Christians who seek a deeper spiritual life experience dramatic sanctification. Frances's search was less dramatic. Frances knew and loved the Lord yet longed for a deeper relationship with him. Gradually, she approached what she called a "second experience."

Recalling December 2, 1873, Frances wrote:

> I first saw it in a flash of electric light . . . There must be full surrender before there can be full blessedness . . . I was shown 'the blood of Jesus Christ his Son cleanseth from all sin' . . . He who had thus cleansed me had power to keep me clean . . . That one word 'cleanseth' . . . I had never seen the force of the tense before, a continual present, always a present tense, not a present which the next moment becomes a past. It goes on cleansing . . . Not a coming to the fountain only, but a remaining in the fountain, so that it may and does go on cleansing.

She joyously concluded, "I see it all and I have the blessing."[47]

Out of her spiritual overflow, she wrote hundreds of hymns, and her joyous words can still be found in hymnals today.

You may be struggling; you may be asking the Lord to sanctify you. You can stand on the promise that he will do it—he will cleanse you, purify you, sanctify you. Reach out to him as you stand on his promises.

Every Thought Captive to Christ

---

47. J. Sidlow Baxter, *His Deeper Work in Us* (Grand Rapids: Zondervan, 1967), 70.

*We demolish arguments and every pretension that sets itself up
against the knowledge of God, and we take captive
every thought to make it obedient to Christ.*
2 Corinthians 10:5

It is with some apprehension that I include Ed's personal testimony here. Even though his story is raw and painful, it illustrates God's powerful deliverance and the need for continual self-discipline.

I was first carried into the church at ten days old. Thereafter, throughout my childhood, my parents took me to church every time the doors were open. I was raised in Sunday schools and educated in Christian colleges; I even went to seminary for eighteen months. I had given my life to God in 1966, at the age of fourteen—but prior to that, I laid the foundation for a sexual addiction.

By the end of my teenage years, I had created a secret life. By the middle of my first marriage, my mind was so perverted that I believed my sinful choices were justified. My out-of-control sexual behavior cost me two marriages and one career. I have hurt many people.

By the summer of 1992, I was so suicidal that, within the same week, my pastor asked for my shotgun, and my therapist offered to put me in a psychiatric hospital. But God had other plans!

In May 1993, I attended a twelve-step retreat and admitted I was a sex addict. God then led me through several healing experiences in the form of church-related conferences and retreats. But because I thought I could control them, my out-of-control sexual behaviors continued to escalate.

In June 2000, I attended my first recovery support group for sexual addiction. By this time, I knew I was powerless over my sexual thoughts, and my life was nearly destroyed. My concept of God was one of judgment and condemnation—how could a God like that forgive me for the things I had done? But my recovery brothers accepted and loved me. I decided that if they could accept me, maybe God could too.

Through my recovery group and the biblical preaching at my church, I learned that the God of Scripture is a God of love, grace, redemption, and acceptance. I came to realize that he was the God of second, fifth, tenth, and twentieth chances. But my compulsive thinking still drove my sexual behavior.

In 2001, on the Sunday night before Palm Sunday, my pastor led the church in a Communion service. As the elements were passed, I visualized Christ on the cross, and he said to me, "Give me your guilt and shame."

After thirty-five years as a sex addict, I had plenty of guilt and shame. I struggled with the decision, but Christ kept speaking to me. He couldn't take it—I had to lay it on him.

The very moment I laid my guilt and shame on him, the power of addiction left. The chains of sin were broken—I was free!

But was I really free? Scripture says that Satan prowls like a lion seeking someone to devour. He is still seeking to devour me. I still have the thoughts and mental images—I burned them into my mind over many years. Every day, Satan tries to use them against me.

But Scripture tells me that the only way I can overcome Satan is by the blood of the Lamb and the word of my testimony. Christ has already shed his blood, and the word of my testimony is found in 2 Corinthians 10:4–5 (NASB95): "For the weapons of [my] warfare are not of the flesh, but divinely powerful for the destruction of fortresses. [I am] destroying speculations and every lofty thing raised up against the knowledge of God, and [I am] taking every thought captive to the obedience of Christ."

The Love Channel

This is how God showed his love among us: He sent his one and only Son into the world that we might live through him.
1 John 4:9

God's love has been poured into our hearts through the Holy Spirit, who has been given to us.
Romans 5:5

Dear friends, since God so loved us, we also ought to love one another.
1 John 4:11

Bill's mom died at age forty-four, when Bill was fifteen. The next year, his dad died. Bill's older sister took Bill and his two siblings into her home, and at seventeen, Bill went to Kansas City to find work. He got a job at a lumber company and went to accounting school at night.

Dick befriended Bill and urged his company to hire Bill. Afterward, Dick began taking Bill to gatherings for Christian business professionals. On a retreat, after hearing the testimonies of his colleagues, Bill went to his room and prayed, "Forgive my sins. I want to be part of your family. Guide my life."

Back at work, Bill told Dick, who had missed the retreat due to illness, about his prayer. With further guidance, Bill realized he had been born again.

Bill started at the company where Dick got him a job in 1966, became a partner in 1976, and became sole owner in 1986. Afterward, for three years in a row, the *Kansas City Business Journal* featured Bill's company as one of the top ten fastest-growing Kansas City businesses. Bill later married a godly woman named Gwen. In 1990, after years of spiritual growth, Bill experienced God's sanctifying grace.

Bill has a blessed connection with his Savior that is defined by love:

- Christ's love for him (1 John 4:9)
- Christ's love in him (Romans 5:5)
- Christ's love through him (1 John 4:11)

Bill invests in people, mentors them spiritually, and maintains lifelong friendships. More than forty years ago, he and Jim became friends. Whenever Jim got a two–month break from Merchant Marine duty, he stayed at Bill's. To this day, they share prayer requests, and Bill periodically visits Jim and his wife in New Jersey, where Jim works at a Christian school.

Dave and Bill became friends when Dave attended seminary. They made calls together to visitors to their local church. Dave helped build Bill's house; Bill visited Dave at his pastorate in Maine; and Bill attended Dave's marriage to Maybeth in Washington. To this day, when Dave is back from missionary assignments in Georgia (the European country) or Poland, he stays at Bill's.

Bill became friends with Michael, a seminary student, when they made calls to church visitors together. Michael is now a chaplain, and Bill has visited him, his wife, and their five children at military assignments in Savannah, Georgia, and Monterrey, California. Bill and Michael support each other in prayer.

Bill is an amazing, consistent channel of Christ's love for scores of people. You can be a channel of Christ's love too.

Filled for Courage

When they saw the courage of Peter and John and realized that
they were unschooled, ordinary men, they were astonished and
they took note that these men had been with Jesus.
Acts 4:13

After they prayed, the place where they were meeting was shaken. And
they were all filled with the Holy Spirit and spoke the word of God boldly.
Acts 4:31

Have you ever been thrown into an uncomfortable situation in which you knew everyone around you was unsympathetic to your faith? Have you ever been threatened because of your beliefs?

If you have been in either of these situations, you know what Peter, John, and other early disciples went through for following Jesus. Peter and John met the lame beggar at the temple, and in the name of Jesus Christ, he was healed. When he immediately began walking, leaping, and praising God, the man attracted considerable attention in the temple courts (Acts 3:1–10). Peter used the event to preach about Jesus. The priest, captain of the temple guard, and Sadducees were greatly disturbed at this, and they seized and jailed Peter and John.

The next day, the authorities asked Peter to explain himself. Peter proclaimed a searching message. How? "Filled with the Spirit," Peter was so empowered that his hearers marveled at his courage. Eventually, Peter and John were further threatened and released. They went back to their fellow disciples and reported these events. The larger group went to prayer, and "they were all filled with the Holy Spirit and spoke the word of God boldly."

Whether a Christian is living in a Spirit-filled state or experiencing a fresh outpouring and filling of the Spirit, the result is courage. Sometimes the Spirit's filling is for cleansing (Acts 15:8–9), but here, it is for courage.

Early in my Christian life, I encountered the issue of courage. I was beginning my senior year at my Ivy League College. Just before returning to campus, I had experienced the sanctifying, empowering filling of the Holy Spirit. Every senior was required to attend the "Great Issues" course, in which major figures came and spoke out of their expertise on major topics in business, government, international relations, finance, and religion.

The administration had chosen a Unitarian minister to represent Protestantism. Drawing heavily on psychology, he promoted the idea that humanity is basically good. The next day, students came back to the class to ask the speaker questions.

Back in my room, God began to prod me: "You can't let his message stand without challenge." I knew that the next day, I had to ask the speaker a question in front of all the seniors.

The next day, I posed the following question to the presenter: "How can you say humanity is basically good when the Bible says, 'All have sinned'; and when Freud says, 'Man has a hollow heart filled with filth'; and when, in my own experience, I was sinful and self-centered until I took Christ into my heart and life?"

People in the crowd groaned unsympathetically. The speaker again tried to answer out of psychology.

I admit that in the moment that I stood up to ask that question, I was afraid. But I was willing to do what God had asked me to do. Courage by the power of the Spirit—it is possible today.

Yes, Flee from Sexual Immorality

Or do you not know that wrongdoers will not inherit the kingdom of God? Do not be deceived: Neither the sexually immoral nor idolaters nor adulterers nor men who have sex with men nor thieves nor the greedy nor drunkards nor slanderers nor swindlers will not inherit the kingdom of God. And that is what some of you were. But you were washed, you were sanctified, you were justified in the name of the Lord Jesus Christ and by the Spirit of our God.
1 Corinthians 6:9–11

Though Steve and Jackie had only been to the church a few times, they came to the Sunday morning revival service. After the Monday night service, Steve walked over to talk to me. He said something like, "I was impressed by the story you told in the Sunday morning service. I think I've led a good life—never used tobacco, alcohol, or drugs, but, boy, do I swear. A lot. But when I swore on my construction job today, I felt so guilty. Look at my hands, just shaking." I offered to pray with Steve, but he didn't respond to that. He simply said he would be back for more services.

Steve and Jackie came back on Tuesday. Of all things, I preached that night on "People, Sex, and God," based on 1 Corinthians 6. In that sermon, I defined immorality as a man living in a sexual relationship with a woman to whom he was not married—which was this couple's exact situation.

On Wednesday night, they were back again. During the altar call, Steve and Jackie joined hands and came forward. When I knelt down beside Steve, he had been praying fervently. He exclaimed to me, "My sins, my sins, they've been all forgiven. They're gone."

I asked Steve where Christ was, and he boldly replied, "He's in my heart."

Filled with Joy, Steve and Jackie had begun to walk away from the altar when, after a few steps, Steve turned around and came back to me. He asked, "And those other sins—are they all forgiven too?"

I knew what he was talking about—the topic of my sermon from the night before. I said, "Yes, they are all forgiven too."

"We've been living together," Steve said. "We're not married—we're both divorced. We plan to get married, though. We already have the rings."

In response, I urged Steve to talk to his pastor and marry Jackie as soon as possible.

Note what the apostle Paul said to the Corinthians: After his list of sinful behaviors, he wrote, "That is what some of you were. But you were washed, you were sanctified, you were justified in the name of the Lord Jesus Christ and by the Spirit of our God" (v. 11). For all of us who have engaged in sexual sins in the past, we can be forgiven; we can be changed; we can be clean; we can be new. God's Spirit can make it happen. He did for the Corinthians; he can do it for you and me.

In front of me, I have a photograph of Steve and Jackie walking out of the church after their wedding ceremony. Three weeks after their prayer at the altar, they held their wedding right after worship on Sunday morning. And what a smile on Jackie's face!

Since their wedding, Steve has been baptized, and both have joined the church and completed *Basic Bible Studies for New and Growing Christians*. Now Steve is learning to play bass guitar so he can contribute to the worship team.

So yes, we say, "flee from sexual immorality" (v. 18). If you think this is too difficult for you to do, remember your body is the temple of the Holy Spirit (v. 19), and that Spirit gives you great power.

Grace Shows!

*When he arrived and saw what the grace of God had done, he was glad
and encouraged them all to remain true to the Lord with all their hearts.*
Acts 11:23

Grace shows on the outside when God has done a work on the inside. Sometimes one can see that hearts are held down, held back, hurting, harried, hiding, hanging on with little hope, or living in harm's way. Others harbor resentment and are haughty, high-minded, and too proud to believe they need God. Are they unworthy of asking? Are they too good to ask? Many are the walls that keep us separated from God's love.

When Jesus comes, he washes away the dirt and grime of life and raises us up to respectability. His love gives us new life and allows us to live knowing he gives strength for another day. He matters and he makes you matter. He wipes our tears and takes away our fears, and then he laughs as our hearts are filled with him.

Nancy Shaver[48]

She Was a Giver

I was in prison and you came to visit me.
Matthew 25:36

Suzie was either very frank or very close to her pastor. One day, in the middle of a conversation, she said to him, "Do you know you're going bald?" Don't worry, he took it in good humor—he's the one who told the story.

More of Suzie's story emerged as we talked with her family about her memorial service. She had passed away suddenly at age seventy-two.

---

48. Previously published in *Come Ye Apart* July–August–September 1964 (Kansas City, MO: Nazarene Publishing House), 90. Used by permission. (This publication became *Reflecting God.*)

When Suzie was about twelve, she went forward to the altar to pray, and that day, she accepted Christ. Years later, after getting married and having three children, she was mainly a stay-at-home mom. At a prayer meeting, Suzie heard God speak to her: "I have many things in store for you." Those who knew her say she was sanctified in a prayer meeting—maybe this same one.

Suzie eventually became Kansas secretary for Prison Fellowship ministries and an ordained minister. She founded In His Service Ministries and ran a network that helped prison inmates and their families find jobs, housing, and counseling.

On at least three occasions, Suzie and her friend Chaplain Vickie invited me to preach in prisons in Lansing, Kansas. I was amazed at how well they knew the prisoners personally. These prisoners' openness and reverence led them to cooperate with the women.

Suzie's concern was that inmates would come to know Christ personally as their Savior and Lord. And for those who had become Christians, she prayed that they would experience God's sanctification. Suzie and Vickie also made sure that new believers joined a Bible study so that they might continue to grow and mature in their faith.

Suzie's family relationships were incredibly loving. Her husband, Harry, said, "She was the best thing that ever happened to me. She was always doing something for others."

Her son Stephen said, "We talked by phone every day for eighteen years. My mom was my best friend."

Her son Paul spoke of his mom's joy when he took a mission trip to Argentina.

In 2007, Suzie developed a serious liver disease. Even though she was hospitalized at least once a month, she never slowed down or had a pity party. Instead, she made time for those around her and listened to them. She had so much joy to give.

Her son Stephen said, "I wouldn't change a single moment growing up."

Her son Paul said, "When she passed, I had peace; there is no question where she is."

Why go into so much detail about a single individual? Because it's important to see how much God can do through one life. Fifteen years after she heard the Lord say, "I have many things in store for you," Suzie's prison ministry had bloomed into full flower. What a giver! What do you think God will do through your life?

Twenty Good Years

So then, just as you received Christ Jesus as Lord, continue to live
your lives in him, rooted and built up in him, strengthened in the faith
as you were taught, and overflowing with thankfulness.
Colossians 2:6–7

Though he was raised in church, as a teenager, John was a rebel. He started drugs at age twelve and alcohol at fifteen. He established a twenty-year record of smoking pot. At eighteen, he married his fifteen-year-old girlfriend. He made attempts at being a husband, but he enjoyed hunting, fishing, and late-night partying too much.

One day at work, John saw a truck driver fail his drug test and lose his job. John had given him the drugs! That woke him up—John realized the same could happen to him. So John climbed into his truck and prayed. That day, he was saved.

That week, his wife's church was having revival. There, John went to the altar for reaffirmation, and then again for sanctification. He testified that his sanctification took away the desires for his former vices.

During the revival, the Lord challenged him to give his last $50 as an offering. John hesitated—that was his gas money, and he needed it. But the Lord told him, "I'll take care of you." So John did as God asked. The next day, he received an unexpected utility reimbursement of $120.

John immediately saw changes in his life: He was freed from drugs. He had already quit tobacco. He began spending more time with his family, including his two children. He began attending church regularly, reading his Bible, and praying. His wife said, "He was a different person right away."

These days, John and his wife still participate in all the church's revival services. He now says, "It's been twenty good years." John has been following Christ and is in it for the long run.[49]

---

49. Adapted from *The Good News: The Chic Shaver Center for Evangelism Newsletter* (June 2014).

Why Doesn't God Remedy Every Wrong?

The LORD God took the man and put him in the Garden of Eden to work it and take care of it. And the LORD God commanded the man, "You are free to eat from any tree in the garden; but you must not eat from the tree of the knowledge of good and evil, for when you eat from it you will certainly die."
Genesis 2:15–17

Bill and Donna were one of the sweetest, most loving, most godly couples you could imagine. Bill was a pastor and eventually a denominational leader who produced adult Sunday school literature that blessed hundreds of thousands of people.

A few years ago, on their way to Sunday school, as Bill and Donna were just one block away from the church, their car was hit by an alcohol-impaired driver. Both Bill and Donna died as a result of the accident.

How unfair—how wrong. Couldn't God have stopped the accident?

Back in the beginning, when God created humans, he said, "You are free to eat from any tree in the garden; but you must not eat from the tree of the knowledge of good and evil."

When it came to his highest creation—humans—God chose to limit his own power by giving us free will ("You are *free* to eat from any tree in the garden"). He gave humanity the privilege of choice. But of course, our choices have consequences ("But you must not eat from the tree of the knowledge of good and evil, for when you eat from it you will certainly die"). Thus, our world is a product of God's love and humanity's choices.

God's plan for the world provided a wide range of good, healthy choices—more than enough to satisfy anyone ("eat from *any* tree"). Only one option was prohibited.

Peter Marshall, chaplain to the United States Senate, dealt with these issues in his sermon during World War II. Here is a portion of that sermon:

> There is no use trying to evade the issue. There are times when God does not intervene—the fact that He does nothing is one of the most baffling mysteries in the Christian life. It was H. G. Wells who voiced the dilemma that many troubled hearts have faced in wartime: "Either God has the power to stop all this carnage and killing and he doesn't care, or else he does care, and he doesn't have the power to stop it." But that is

not the answer. . . . As long as there is sin in the world. As long as there is greed, selfishness, hate in the hearts of men, there will be war. . . .

It is only because God is God that he is reckless enough to allow human beings such free will as has led the world into this present catastrophe. God could have prevented the war! Do you doubt for a moment that God has not the power? But suppose he had used it? Men would then have lost their free agency. . . . They would no longer be souls endowed with the ability to choose. . . . They would then become puppets, robots, machines, toy soldiers instead. No, God is playing a much bigger game. He is still awaiting an awakened sense of the responsibility of brotherhood in the hearts of men and women everywhere. He will not do for us the things that we can do for ourselves.[50]

Despite the mess we have made of our world, God will have another word. He endeavors to teach us to plan for two worlds—this and the next. Where there has been unfairness on earth due to humanity's disobedience in the first garden, he will make possible a second garden for those who will possess it. The second garden is a place where wrong will be made right. Revelation 22:1–5 describes it:

Then the angel showed me the river of the water of life, as clear as crystal, flowing from the throne of God and of the Lamb down the middle of the great street of the city. On each side of the river stood the tree of life, bearing twelve crops of fruit, yielding its fruit every month. And the leaves of the tree are for the healing of the nations. No longer will there be any curse. The throne of God and of the Lamb will be in the city, and his servants will serve him. They will see his face, and his name will be on their foreheads. There will be no more night. They will not need the light of a lamp or the light of the sun, for the Lord God will give them light. And they will reign for ever and ever.

This is the city, the garden, where Bill and Donna will live.

Many people have used their God-given free will to accomplish incredible things. Think of the following heroes:

- Martin Luther King, Jr., who called for racial reconciliation
- Charles Colson, a prison inmate who found Christ and became the world's leading force in prison reform
- William and Catherine Booth, who established The Salvation Army to uplift the poor and save their souls

---

50. Catherine Marshall, *Beyond Our Selves* (New York: McGraw Hill Book Company, 1961), 26–27.

- John Wesley, whose influence in the British Isles, America, and beyond prompted millions to turn to Christ

These are people who used their free will in concert with God's ideal will—by their cooperation with the Spirit, suffering was healed. Likewise, you and I have the opportunity to decide how to use our free will—choose well.

Love Fulfills the Law

Love does no harm to a neighbor. Therefore love is the fulfillment of the law.
Romans 13:10

My lawyer friend Albert estimates that America's statute books contain fifty million laws intended to make people good. But the Christian has only one law: "You shall love."

When a law expert asked Jesus, "Which is the greatest commandment in the Law?" Jesus replied, "'Love the Lord your God with all your heart and with all your soul and with all your mind.' This is the first and greatest commandment. And the second is like it: 'Love your neighbor as yourself.' All the Law and the Prophets hang on these two commandments" (Matthew 22:36–40).

In God's book, this love is not a sloppy love. Prior to stating that "love is the fulfillment of the law" (Romans 13:10), Paul quotes from the Ten Commandments (v. 9). If you love your neighbor, you will not commit adultery with his wife. If you love your neighbor, you will not murder him, steal from him, or covet his property. If you have true love, you will naturally fulfill all the Ten Commandments.

Paul admits to the Galatian Christians that a battle may still be raging in their hearts: "For the flesh desires what is contrary to the Spirit, and the Spirit what is contrary to the flesh. They are in conflict with each other, so that you are not to do whatever you want" (Galatians 5:17).

Paul then gives a series of statements to further spell out the law and love issue. In Galatians 5:14, he writes, "For the entire law is fulfilled in keeping this one command: 'Love your neighbor as yourself.'"

But if the flesh or sinful nature wars against the Holy Spirit and leads to unloving attitudes, what can we do? Paul gives the following answers:

- Galatians 5:24—"Those who belong to Christ Jesus have crucified the flesh with its passions and desires."
- Galatians 5:16—"So I say, walk by the Spirit, and you will not gratify the desires of the flesh."
- Galatians 5:22–23—"But the fruit of the Spirit is love . . . Against such things there is no law."

Jesus had strong words for the critical Jewish leaders who considered themselves law experts: "But I know you. I know that you do not have the love of God in your hearts" (John 5:42). This was a valid charge against leaders who exhibited so much hypocrisy. Yet many conscientious Christians who accept the command to love others also struggle with internal spiritual warfare as they continue in un-Christlike attitudes and dispositions. They try to be more loving, but they cannot produce sufficient love on their own strength.

Be alert to the previously quoted Galatian passages. Sense Paul's repeated references to an outside power; a divine source; the work of the Holy Spirit. Elsewhere, in Romans 5:5, Paul gives us the most complete answer to this predicament: "And hope does not put us to shame, because God's love has been poured out into our hearts through the Holy Spirit, who has been given to us." When you can't muster up enough love, God's Holy Spirit will pour it into your heart.

The testimony of Dr. Daniel Steele, a professor at the University of Boston, illustrates this point. He came to know Christ as his Savior when he was eighteen, but he had struggles in his Christian life. He sensed that he was "free from the guilt and dominion of sin, but not from strong inward tendencies thereto, which seemed to be a part of my nature." For a year, he struggled with these tendencies, and eventually, he began seeking God more earnestly. "Then," he said, "the Spirit uncovered to my gaze the evil still lurking in my nature."

One November night, he was earnestly seeking the Lord when, as he reports, "Suddenly I became conscious of a mysterious power exerting itself on my sensibilities . . . as if an electric current were passing through my body with painless shocks, melting my whole being into a fiery stream of love." He said this was best described as "the love of God shed abroad in the heart by the Holy Spirit."

He became more certain of God's love for him than of the existence of the earth beneath his feet. He realized that this was "the elimination of the sin-principle by the cleansing power of the Paraclete." He had experienced "that perfect love which casts out all fear." Dr. Steele went on to live in a new level of victory and became a great spiritual leader and author.[51]

As Dr. Steele's story demonstrates, "Love fulfills the law." The Holy Spirit's filling and presence and power will make it happen in your life too!

What about the Hypocrites?

When Simon saw that the Spirit was given at the laying on of the apostles' hands, he offered them money and said, "Give me also this ability so that everyone on whom I lay my hands may receive the Holy Spirit."
Acts 8:18–19

The Spirit told Philip, "Go to that chariot and stay near it."
Acts 8:29

Have you ever heard someone say, "What about the hypocrites in church?" The question usually precedes an excuse for why the person doesn't attend church. I like to ask these people about their jobs: "Do you have any coworkers who talk big about how hard they work, but you see them standing around the water cooler shooting the breeze, playing video games at their desk, and loafing a good part of the time? They're really hypocrites, aren't they? Does the fact that you have hypocrites in your workplace keep you from going to work?" Usually, they get the point.

In Acts 8:14–40, we have the story of two men, Simon and Philip. Both are interested in the Holy Spirit, but there are differences between them:

- Simon wanted to use the Holy Spirit; Philip wanted the Holy Spirit to use him.
- Simon wanted to pay for the Holy Spirit; Philip surrendered to the Holy Spirit.
- Peter rebukes Simon and tells him he is not right with God; he is captive to sin and must repent. Conversely, God honors Philip and uses him to lead the Ethiopian secretary of the treasury to Christ.

---

51. Quotations from Daniel Steele are taken from J. Sidlow Baxter, *His Deeper Work in Us* (Grand Rapids: Zondervan Publishing House, 1967), 71–73.

Note that both men's stories are in the Bible. The Bible is frank, and by telling Simon's story, acknowledges that there are hypocrites in the church. The same Bible also tells Philip's story to illustrate that there are genuine Christians in the church. So, what should our stance be?

We have a defining guideline: "By their fruit you will recognize them" (Matthew 7:16). We must exercise discernment and learn to tell the difference between the hypocritical and the genuine. Then, we must decide to not let the hypocrite stand in our way and instead follow the model of the genuine Christian. I know thousands of such Christians, and I want to be like them.

The Talk That Comes out of Your Mouth

*Do not let any unwholesome talk come out of your mouths, but only
what is helpful for building others up according to their needs, that it may
benefit those who listen. And do not grieve the Holy Spirit of God, with
whom you were sealed for the day of redemption. Get rid of all bitterness,
rage and anger, brawling and slander, along with every form of
malice. Be kind and compassionate to one another, forgiving each other,
just as in Christ God forgave you.*
Ephesians 4:29–32

In effort to give me some "wisdom," a layperson once advised me, "You'll never make it in this denomination because you don't have any relatives in the church." Maybe he had been hurt; maybe he was cynical; but he told me in no uncertain terms that if you wanted to move up the church ladder, you had to have family members in positions of power.

His words definitely didn't build me up, but they didn't break me down either—I was not concerned about climbing a ladder. I was happy pastoring the little church I was serving. Another time, this same man had more words for me: "When are you going to get a promotion?"

I knew our church was in a humble setting—we met in a remodeled horse shed. But new people were finding Jesus; some were being sanctified; our church was growing; and we were on the way to a beautiful, newly built sanctuary and educational unit. I responded, "I'm in the center of the will of God. I can't go any higher than that."

To live by the exhortations of Ephesians 4:29–32, we may ask the following questions about our words:

1. Is it true?
2. Is it necessary?
3. Is it wise to share this?
4. Will it build up the hearer?
5. Will it help or hurt someone else?

Our words to others can grieve the Holy Spirit. Jessie Penn Lewis once said that "grieve" is a love word. When you love the precious Holy Spirit, you will not want to grieve him. It is even possible to grieve him out of your life. Please note the verses both before and after verse 30 describe ways to grieve the Spirit.

I am shocked when I realize how long someone's words remain in my heart or mind. The words, "You'll never make it in the church," are more than sixty years old. The words, "I pray for you and Nancy every day," go back more than forty years. I'm impressed how a single sentence can carry so much weight.

There sits in front of me a note from someone who thanked me for my words:

Dear Chic,

For about the last twenty-five years, your words at seminary that day gave me hope that I had done the right thing. No one else gave me any support—it was God who sent you to speak to me, I believe. I have always been so *grateful*!

My words blessed her twenty-five years ago, and her note blesses me today. Make another person happy with your words. Make the Holy Spirit happy with the talk that comes out of your mouth.

How Are You What You Are?

By the grace of God I am what I am, and his grace to me was not
without effect. No, I worked harder than all of them—yet not I,
but the grace of God that was with me.
1 Corinthians 15:10

If grace could be bottled and sold, many people would sell all and buy it—but since it's free, they can't believe it has any value. Many of us could say, "There but for the grace of God go I," meaning that if I had never heard or responded to grace, I would still be lost and serving my old master.

Jim Elliot said, "He is no fool who gives what he cannot keep to gain what he cannot lose." Likewise, the apostle Paul never stopped giving away the love that God put inside him. He didn't let his past offenses and failures keep him from serving in the present moment. He did not let the present obstacle, resistance, or suffering keep him from his goal. He gave his all every day, trusting that if there were to be a tomorrow, God would be enough.

Is God enough for us? Yes, because there's never not enough of his grace. He's available twenty-four hours a day. As believers, we owe all we are to his wonderful grace.

Nancy Shaver[52]

MAY 3   123

From "What Can I Get?" to "What Can I Give?"

Peter answered him, "We have left everything to follow you!
What then will there be for us?"
Matthew 19:27

Peter was not the only Christ follower who wondered, *What can I get?* James and John's mother said, "Grant that one of these two sons of mine may sit at your right and the other at your left in your kingdom" (Matthew 20:21). Mark reports that when Jesus asked his disciples what they were arguing about, "they kept quiet because on the way they had argued about who was the greatest" (Mark 9:34). Yet something must have changed in the deepest level of their hearts, because in describing these same disciples a few months later, Acts says, "No one claimed that any of their possessions was their own, but they shared everything they had" (4:32).

I saw the same pattern in Frank and Peggy's lives. As a young couple, they accepted Christ. Our local church surrounded them with love and care

---

52. Previously published in *Come Ye Apart* July–August–September 1964 (Kansas City, MO: Nazarene Publishing House), 93. Used by permission. (This publication became *Reflecting God*.)

as they grew spiritually. Eventually, after Frank finished his watch-making training, they moved back to their native Omaha, Nebraska, for Frank to begin work as a watch repairman. After spending several weeks looking for a church in Omaha, they sent word back to us: "We cannot find a church here in Omaha as loving as yours."

They went across the state line into Iowa. They couldn't find a church as loving there either. I became concerned for them. I urged the people of our church to pray for them and phone them.

Finally, Frank and Peggy said, "We've decided to stop looking for a church as loving as your church. Instead, we're going to find a church that needs love and give them love like yours gave us." They did—and they became great spiritual leaders in that church.

All of us—Peter, James, John, Frank, Peggy, you, and I—will make spiritual breakthroughs when we move from "What can I get?" to "What can I give?"

Can a Teenager Be Sanctified?

Don't let anyone look down on you because you are young,
but set an example for the believers in speech,
in conduct, in love, in faith and in purity.
1 Timothy 4:12

He has saved us and called us to a holy life—not because of anything
we have done but because of his own purpose and grace.
This grace was given us in Christ Jesus before the beginning of time.
2 Timothy 1:9

One year, I was tasked with preaching and teaching responsibilities at the 137th annual camp meeting of the Iowa Holiness Association. My daily challenge was to teach sanctification, holiness, and the Spirit-filled life in a way everyone could understand.

One night, a teenager named David testified, "On Tuesday, I went down to the altar—surrendered, asked God for cleansing and the Holy Spirit. I have experienced the Spirit over the last several days, and I thank God for his power of sanctification."

I met a sixteen-year-old named Donna at the beginning of camp. She was the only person in her family who attended church, and at first she seemed shy, hesitant, uncertain. At the end of camp, she made this report: *A couple of weeks before Iowa Holiness Association, I was praying to God that there would be a great spiritual victory and that God would transform and change my life. Then I saw that Reverend Chic Shaver would be preaching the message over sanctification, and God pointed out to me that that was for me. Monday, I gave my heart and life completely to the Lord, and the Holy Spirit just flooded my soul throughout the entire week. I was so filled that I am a new human being. I have died out to the old Donna and am new in the Lord and his Holy Spirit. Then, later on during this week, I was praying to God that he would make known to me his will for my life, and on Wednesday, God told me he wants me to be a missionary. I am still praying for what department God is calling me to. God's Holy Spirit has just been with me throughout the entire week. Praise his holy name.*

Oh yes, a teenager can be sanctified![53]

A Single Issue, Part 1

Do you not know that your bodies are temples of the Holy Spirit,
who is in you, whom you have received from God? You are not your own;
you were bought at a price. Therefore honor God with your bodies.
1 Corinthians 6:19–20

Sometimes overcoming a single struggle propels you to greater courage and victory in broader areas of your Christian life. To face, fight, and flatten that obstacle empowers you to overcome even greater challenges.

Once we see others gaining victory, we believe the same can happen to us. As Joshua faced the Jordan River, the mighty city of Jericho, and two million Israelites behind him who looked to him for leadership, God encouraged him by reminding him of his work in another life, "As I was with Moses, so I will be with you; I will never leave you nor forsake you" (Joshua 1:5).

I'm going to pick a single issue—addiction to tobacco. I'll even be more specific and pick smoking. This may or may not be your struggle, but bear

---

53. *The Good News: The Chic Shaver Center for Evangelism Newsletter* (September 2015).

with me. Hear and see how others found victory on that one point and flourished in so many other areas.

When Jerrold Atchison was a young man, he decided to change masters. He had been mastered by liquor and tobacco; he now chose Jesus Christ as his master. After his decision for Christ, he readily quit drinking, but smoking seemed to have the stronger pull. One day, the urge for tobacco seemed unusually strong, and he feared he would give in and smoke. Just then, the phone rang, and a new Christian friend expressed his confidence in him. Jerrold realized he couldn't fail when God had so loved him and his friends believed in him. He turned in his Bible to Jude 1:24 (KJV) and read, "Now unto him that is able to keep you from falling, and to present you faultless before the presence of his glory with exceeding joy." He trusted, God kept him, and he never returned to his habit.[54]

Walter Jackson was a real tobacco addict—he smoked about three packs a day. Then, he accepted Christ as his Savior and Lord and found he had one on whom he could fully depend. He quit smoking immediately, but his wife said that, for two weeks, he was pretty edgy. After two weeks, the cravings let up—Walt had won a victory. He admitted there were still times when he compulsively reached into his shirt pocket for a cigarette. But that reach always reminded him of the change in his heart, for in that same pocket over his heart, he now carried a small copy of the New Testament—about the size of a pack of cigarettes but a lot more powerful. "Why take a cigarette when I could inhale the knowledge of the Lord?" Walt exclaimed.[55]

Walter understood that place in his New Testament where Paul wrote, "No, I strike a blow to my body and make it my slave so that after I have preached to others, I myself will not be disqualified for the prize" (1 Corinthians 9:27).

A Single Issue, Part 2

❖

---

54. Charles "Chic" Shaver, *You Can Quit Smoking* (Kansas City, MO: Beacon Hill Press of Kansas City, 1975), 18–19.
55. Shaver, *You Can Quit Smoking*, 20–21.

Do you not know that your bodies are temples of the Holy Spirit,
who is in you, whom you have received from God? You are not your own;
you were bought at a price. Therefore honor God with your bodies.
1 Corinthians 6:19–20

For police officer Vincent Hutchens, it was a bit of every kind of miracle. For twenty-two years, he smoked two to three packs a day. But after twenty years of watching his wife live a consistent Christian life, Vincent finally quit rebelling and accepted Jesus Christ. God was now real to him, and things that had once seemed crucial lost their importance. For Vincent, cigarettes were in this category.

He quit, but it wasn't easy. He was so addicted that, as his miraculously strengthened will told him to stand firm, he endured what he described as withdrawal symptoms. Yet God did not allow the temptation to exceed what Vincent could bear. In fact, God provided a small physical miracle to help him: In the past, Vincent's sleep was often broken by frequent awakenings. Now he spent his nights in deep, uninterrupted sleep. He gratefully accepted this gift from God's hand. It gave him the physical strength he needed and made it possible for him to maintain victory.[56]

Vincent lived out Paul's promise to the Corinthians: "No temptation has overtaken you except what is common to mankind. And God is faithful; he will not let you be tempted beyond what you can bear. But when you are tempted, he will also provide a way out so that you can endure it" (1 Corinthians 10:13).

When Robert Ferguson found Christ, he felt convicted about his stealing—he had worked at a book bindery for years, and he had stolen a book every week. He knew he had to face his boss, confess his crimes, and pay for the books. Of course, Robert was scared. But he did it.

The boss was amazed at his honesty and treated him graciously. Robert left the boss's office encouraged. He thought, *If God can give me courage to do that, he can give me another kind of courage.* With that, he took a pack of cigarettes out of his pocket, drop-kicked them across the room, and never smoked again.

Robert experienced the truth of 1 John 4:4: "You, dear children, are from God and have overcome them, because the one who is in you is greater than the one who is in the world." And soon afterward, Robert learned another truth: "You have been faithful with a few things; I will put you in charge of

---

56. Charles "Chic" Shaver, *You Can Quit Smoking* (Kansas City, MO: Beacon Hill Press of Kansas City, 1975), 25-26.

many things" (Matthew 25:23). Robert was called to ministry and became a great force for God.

It might just be "a single issue"—but remember that your body is a temple of the Holy Spirit. Treat it well!

Where They Heal Broken Hearts

I will sprinkle clean water on you, and you will be clean; I will cleanse you from all your impurities and from all your idols. I will give you a new heart and put a new spirit in you; I will remove from you your heart of stone and give you a heart of flesh. And I will put my Spirit in you and move you to follow my decrees and be careful to keep my laws.
Ezekiel 36:25–27

"Is this the place where they heal broken hearts?" a Korean girl asked at a mission station.[57] So many hearts need healing—forgiveness, hope, encouragement, strength, love, acceptance.

My own mother needed healing for a broken heart. My dad's abuse and alcoholism had beaten her down for years. She largely abandoned her rich Methodist background of revivals, altar calls, and camp meetings as she tried to walk on the edge of the world's pressures and demands. In the process, she committed some serious sins. She lived feeling guilty—because she was. She needed help. She often visited her Christian neighbor, whom she regarded as her best friend, and they talked by the hour. She even visited church a few times with the same neighbor. One Sunday, she mustered enough boldness to raise her hand to request prayer.

The summer after my conversion to Christ, my mother began to attend church. One night, during a youth revival service, she found she could no longer handle the brokenness. She rushed to the altar, poured out her sins, and received the living, loving, healing Jesus into her heart and life. As we left the church, she confided in me that she had been considering suicide. Only then did I realize how broken her heart had been.

---

57. E. Stanley Jones, *Abundant Living* (New York: Abingdon, 1942), 94.

Jesus immediately began repairing her heart. She knew that *all* her sins were forgiven—what a relief! She immediately had joy, peace, and the presence of God.

She began reorganizing her whole life. She threw her cigarettes into the toilet and became tobacco-free. She quit alcohol. She got into the Word of God. She began praying for other family members to find the Lord. She went deeper in her Christian life and found that God could fill her with his Spirit and sanctify her deepest dispositions. She witnessed to many family members and won her sister to Christ.

God gave her heart strength, and she witnessed to my dad with love and wisdom. When he tried to persuade her to compromise her faith on certain issues, she replied, "Remember, you used to tell me I didn't have a mind of my own. Well, now I do!" Ultimately, he couldn't take her combination of love and strength—finally, he accepted the Lord.

My mother never turned back to her old ways—she was on fire for Jesus the rest of her life. She became a leader in her church, a witness to others, and an influence in her apartment complex. At age ninety-two, she prayed, "When I get old, don't let me get crabby." That prayer was answered. At age 103, she went peacefully to be with Jesus. She had found the place—the person Jesus, who heals broken hearts.

The Family

*Husbands, love your wives, just as Christ loved the church
and gave himself up for her to make her holy, cleansing her
by the washing with water through the word.*
Ephesians 5:25–26

*However, each one of you also must love his wife as he loves himself,
and the wife must respect her husband.*
Ephesians 5:33

Children, obey your parents in the Lord, for this is right.
Ephesians 6:1

*Fathers, do not exasperate your children; instead,
bring them up in the training and instruction of the Lord.*
Ephesians 6:4

"The most important area of life you prepare your children for is marriage and family, and their best preparation is to live with a dad who loves their mom," says Crawford Loritts.[58] I would add, "and live with a mom who loves their dad."

According to Ephesians 5:25, Christ is the model for a husband's love. His is a sacrificial, self-giving, purifying love. This love will not drag down, demean, deceive, or weaken moral fiber. As Christ gave himself to make the church holy, so should the husband encourage his wife's holiness. The idea is to keep loving.

Nancy and I hit a challenging spot in the thirty-third year of our marriage. We talked together and came up with the following vision statement for our thirty-fourth year:

Because we matter, we share our days with each other. Having fun together is a high priority. We enjoy romantic sex. We regularly talk and listen to each other, express our love in word and action, and express our deep thoughts and feelings. We gain closure on some issues by agreeing that it's okay to disagree. We support each other in career and personal endeavors. We are sensitive to each other's changing needs. We take time to keep God in his rightful place in our lives, and we still give each other our rightful places.

Now, after more than sixty years, our marriage is rich and alive.

Today, we recognize that many homes do not have both a husband and wife present. In a sense, all marriages are temporary—either a partner dies or, sadly, a couple divorces. Thus, it is crucial to build a marriage on the foundation of Christ. If your partner is gone, you still have your foundation. If the marriage itself is your foundation, it will depart when your partner does.

Children learn to be obedient to their parents. This improves their initiative to obey God when opportunity arises. Fathers, discipline your children, but don't break their spirits. Give more "You can do it," and "I'm proud of you." For every no, give a yes. May Jesus, Mom, and Dad be their biggest cheerleaders.

As a teen, our son, Paul, lived on the edge. We loved him and prayed for him. How joyous I was the night at a camp meeting when he rushed to the altar, prayed, jumped to his feet, and said, "Dad, God saved me"—and then, with a hug, "Dad, I love you."

58. Crawford W. Loritts, Jr., "Ten Ways to Be a Better Father" (Garland, TX: American Tract Society, 1993), https://jhfamilysolutions.com/10-ways-to-be-a-better-father/.

Kangaroo Hold

Just as you received Christ Jesus as Lord, continue to live your lives in him.
Colossians 2:6

Taste and see that the Lord is good;
blessed is the one who takes refuge in him.
Psalm 34:8

The beloved Dr. Ralph Earle used to teach that there are three ways people understand the Christian life: the cat hold, monkey hold, or kangaroo hold.

The cat-hold theory of Christianity is based on the behavior of a mother cat. If she thinks her kitten is in danger, she simply picks him up by the scruff of the neck and moves him. The kitten goes completely limp—he does nothing to remove himself from danger. Some understand Christianity like this—God picks us up and carries us. We have nothing to do with it, no responsibility, and are maybe even carried against our will—it's all God.

The monkey-hold theory is based on the way a baby monkey is transported. When a mother monkey is ready to travel, the baby is fully responsible for climbing on her back and holding on for dear life. Some Christians consider faith to be all our responsibility to hold onto God—it's all our effort.

Finally, the kangaroo-hold theory is based on the fact that a mother kangaroo has a pouch that offers safety, protection, and nurture to her offspring. Even after the baby kangaroo has matured enough to navigate on his own, he has the responsibility and opportunity to return to his mother's pouch when he's in danger. It is the joey's decision and action, plus the mother's full protection and support—the joey jumps into the pouch in faith. This is the best analogy for Christianity: God is our source of support and protection, but at the same time, we must choose to get (and stay) in the pouch.

Of course, Scripture offers a wide variety of illustrations for the Christian life. Whether they appear in epistles or in the parables of Jesus, these illustrations differ depending on the need of the audience. Sometimes they emphasize God's grace; sometimes they highlight human will, responsibility, and obedience. But in light of Scripture's overall message, surely the kangaroo hold best captures this dynamic.

After teaching that his sheep are those who listen to his voice and follow him, Jesus promises that his flock will have have eternal life. He promises his hearers that "no one can snatch them out of my Father's hand" (John 10:29). However, the individual Christian could choose to leave the Father's hand.

Stay in the Father's hand! "Live your lives in him," and "take refuge in him." The kangaroo hold!

An Ingredient Is Missing

When Samuel reached him, Saul said, "The LORD bless you! I have carried out the LORD's instructions." But Samuel said, "What then is this bleating of sheep in my ears? What is this lowing of cattle that I hear?"
1 Samuel 15:13–14

It was her first attempt at oatmeal-chocolate-chip cookies. She pulled out a detailed recipe and began pouring ingredients into a mixing bowl. Uh-oh— she didn't have baking soda. She sent a family member to the grocery store to buy some. Finally, she mixed the ingredients, preheated the oven, and spaced out the balls of dough on two sheets. When she checked on the cookies in the oven, something looked suspicious. Finally, she pulled them from the oven and sampled them—something tasted strange.

What was wrong? She double-checked the recipe. Then she saw it—she'd forgotten to add three-quarters of a cup of white sugar. Only one ingredient was missing—still, the strange-tasting cookies went into the trash. Only one ingredient!

When it comes to knowing, loving, and serving the almighty God, we have to make a clear decision: if the Lord is the Lord, will we take his recipe, his guidance, his direction to heart, and follow him 100 percent?

By divine leadership, Saul was chosen as the first king of Israel. Handsome, striking, capable, skilled, leadership evident, he had everything going for him.

The Lord's command came to him through the prophet Samuel: "Now go, attack the Amalekites and totally destroy all that belongs to them. Do not spare them" (1 Samuel 15:3). Saul and his army are greatly successful. But Saul spares King Agag and the best of the sheep and cattle. Saul claims he has obeyed. Samuel asks how come he hears bleating sheep. It's as if Saul set his supposed wisdom above the Lord's clear command. Samuel challenges him,

"He sent you on a mission, saying, 'Go and completely destroy those wicked people, the Amalekites.' . . . Why did you not obey the LORD?" (15:18–19). Saul claims he kept the animals to sacrifice to the Lord. Samuel responds, "To obey is better than sacrifice" (15:22). And, "The LORD has rejected you as king over Israel!" (15:26).

Only one ingredient was missing—full obedience.

Oh, God, help us to trust you, the Lord, as the Lord and give you full obedience.

Six Teen Boys on the Front Row

*Remember your Creator in the days of your youth, before the
days of trouble come and the years approach when you will say,
"I find no pleasure in them."*
Ecclesiastes 12:1

What was behind that unusual sight on the closing night of revival at the church in Bowling Green, Missouri? I'd say it was Nick Stumbaugh, one of the teens. The previous summer, at the district's camp meeting, Nick had a deeper experience with God. When he returned home, his pastor sensed that something special had happened to Nick. When his pastor led him through *Basic Bible Studies for the Spirit-filled and Sanctified Life*, Nick realized God had sanctified him and filled him with the Spirit.

Nick was a football player, a basketball player, and popular at school. As he began speaking to his friends at school about the gospel, his mom said, "He's been on a mission."

His pastor said, "Nick's on fire."

After that revival service, as others knelt at the altars, the six teen boys stood around it and talked. As I was packing up to leave, one of them approached me.

Very politely, Nathan Kneib said, "I don't mean to interrupt you, Dr. Shaver. I just wanted you to know I've accepted Christ tonight." I rejoiced and urged him to start studying the Bible.

On April 12, I talked to the pastor of that church again. He reported that exceptional things had been happening since the revival. He had met with five teens individually and reviewed the plan of salvation with them to solidify their commitments. Two weeks later, six revival respondents were baptized. The teens' parents were beginning to attend church. Nick had been leading the teens' Wednesday night worship service with dedication and enthusiasm. The board had called a youth pastor.

Praise God for Nick, the six teen boys on the front row, and others like them.[59]

Would you like to be part of a picture like this?

Lay Testimony, Dennis Kinlaw, and Paul

It is God's will that you should be sanctified.
1 Thessalonians 4:3

After the service, the room erupted with testimonies.

Vickie said, "I was not raised in a Holiness denomination. I've been taking notes all night and cleaning house." Later, she declared, "This is sanctification. I've been sanctified! I've been sanctified!"

Melissa testified, "I've been a Christian for ten years, but tonight, he got into my hall closet. I gave him all the junk, and I'm sanctified."

On this subject, scholar Dennis Kinlaw wrote: "We certainly cannot cleanse our own hearts, for the very will that would choose to be clean is itself unclean. . . . Sanctification is as much the result of faith as justification is because it is something only God can do. . . . This is what Paul was telling the Thessalonians when he prayed for their sanctification. He knew they could never sanctify themselves."[60]

Paul prayed, "May God himself, the God of peace, sanctify you through and through. May your whole spirit, soul and body be kept blameless at the coming of our Lord Jesus Christ. The one who calls you is faithful, and he will do it" (1 Thessalonians 5:23–24).[61]

---

59. *The Good News: The Chic Shaver Center for Evangelism Newsletter* (June 2010).

60. Dennis Kinlaw, *This Day with the Master* (Grand Rapids: Zondervan, 2002).

61. This devotional was previously published in *The Good News: The Chic Shaver Center for Evangelism Newsletter* (September 2013).

What to Do When God Asks You . . .

Then God said, "Take your son, your only son, whom you love—
Isaac—and go to the region of Moriah. Sacrifice him there as
a burnt offering on a mountain I will show you."
Genesis 22:2

When they reached the place God had told him about, Abraham
built an altar there and arranged the wood on it. He bound his son Isaac
and laid him on the altar, on top of the wood.
Genesis 22:9

Six-foot-seven-inch Steve played pro basketball in France. He was raised in a non-Christian home, but when Steve went to a Christian college, he saw a display of Christ in sports. In a church service, he was a blur down the aisle as he rushed to the altar to give his heart to Christ. He went on to become the head basketball coach at a Christian college. There, he led students to Christ, held discipleship classes, and led prayer meetings. Steve said this life was more fun than the one he'd had before. Evidently, he had placed his whole life on the altar.

Abraham developed a close relationship with God, and he obeyed God's command to move to a new land (Genesis 12:1–3). Though Abraham was an old man, God promised him a son (15:1–6). Moreover, in his covenant with Abraham, God promised that through this son, Abraham would be the father of nations (17:1–27).

Years later, God tested Abraham by asking him to sacrifice his son—the very same son God had promised to him. When God asks you for your best, you can only obey if you are sure that God is faithful, loves you, cares for you, and has a purpose for you. Abraham believed all of this. But just as he was about to sacrifice his son, God provided a ram for the offering instead. God said, "Now I know that you fear God, because you have not withheld from me your son, your only son" (22:12).

Just as God promised, many nations have come through Abraham's son, Isaac. Jesus Christ, the world's Savior, also came through Isaac. The heavenly Father allowed his only Son, Jesus Christ, to die in order to save you and all who receive him.

God will ask you to put everything on the altar. Then, when you do, watch how he provides.

After being raised in a Christian home, Jim built his business from the ground up to become a millionaire. He paid his tithes, but he had no joy. He was empty. However, he saw commitment and love in his pastor. Jim realized he'd been harboring wrong attitudes and wasting his life.

One night, as Jim sat in his Mercedes, God challenged him by asking, "Jim, do you really love me?"

"Of course."

"Would you love me if I took it all away? If I took your abilities away?"

"God, I'm willing. Show me anything that would block you from working through me."

By bedtime, Jim had compiled a list of things that were hindering God's ability to work through him, and he began to work through them. Finally, everything was on the altar. Jim's family began responding to the changes he was making. God began opening doors for him to speak to thousands of people every year, and his local church grew from 250 to 2,000. As Jim recalls all the ways God has worked in and through him, he says, "I never dreamed it could be so fulfilling."

My Cat Lucky

As the Father has loved me, so have I loved you. Now remain in my love.
If you keep my commands, you will remain in my love, just as I
have kept my Father's commands and remain in his love.
John 15:9–10

Lucky is the most loving, sweet-hearted cat, but he can be rebellious and disobedient sometimes. I met Lucky after my neighbor moved and chose not to take Lucky with her. She simply kicked Lucky out of her house. He kept showing up at my open window, crying to come in. Anytime I was outside, he showed up and seemed to be begging for a home and security. I decided to adopt Lucky and make him part of my family. He's been with me for about fifteen years now.

A few weeks ago, Lucky was acting up and being disobedient all day. Worn out from dealing with the stresses and pressures of daily life, I found myself making this speech to him: "Lucky, I saved your life! You had nothing—no home, no food, no security, no protection. I provide *everything* for you. I work hard to make money so you have a home and food. I give you my time, energy, and love. I've given you everything. Can't you at least do what I want you to do? Can't you at least obey me?"

Then, silence—as God's Spirit fell on me and showed me a direct parallel in my own life. God said, *Don't you think I feel the same way about you?*

It's so true. God saved me, and he gives me provision and everything I need. He's always been trustworthy. He comforts me, protects me, and meets all my needs. He even gave his life for me.

Why don't I obey him 100 percent of the time? Why don't I always immediately obey, and know he is looking out for me, and fully trust him?

Miriam Burch

They Found Their Freedom—and Lost Their Lives

Whoever follows me will never walk in darkness,
but will have the light of life.
John 8:12

Angelfish, Siamese fighting fish, kissing gouramis, and so many more lived in my aquarium when I was in seventh grade. I treated my fish well—they could have lights on or off, temperature controlled between seventy and seventy-eight degrees, and aeration to provide their oxygen. Mystery snails cleaned the aquarium glass, and Amazon River catfish vacuumed the sandy floor. I fed them dry food, but also I raised mosquito larvae and white worms for my fish to eat—the steak and prime rib of the fish world. I'm sure the fish were happy.

Usually, one fish emerged as the boss or bully of the aquarium, usually claiming a favorite spot and driving other fish away. One night, just before my bedtime, I observed the boss acting uneasy, but I couldn't tell why.

During the night, the boss called a meeting of all the fish in the tank. I'm not sure how fish talk, but I imagine he said something like this: *You all know we've been treated real well by Shaver. We have light, warmth, oxygen, regular maid service, and the best food. You know I've been happy, married the fish of my dreams, had children and now grandchildren. But there's one thing I don't like about Shaver—he keeps us enclosed in these glass walls. I'm tired of it, and I'm making a break for it. Who wants to join me?*

When I came downstairs for breakfast the next morning, I found the boss and three other fish lying on the living room floor, very dry and very dead. By jumping out of the tank, they had found their freedom—but lost their lives.

I was sad. The glass walls of the aquarium were never meant to be a barrier to the fishes' happiness. They were simply the boundaries that kept the fish in the only atmosphere where they could survive and thrive—the warm waters of the tank. I had provided it all with the utmost care for them.

I've noticed that some people treat God's commands as harsh barriers to their happiness. The truth is that God, in his infinite love and wisdom, is trying to keep us in the atmosphere where we can survive and thrive. Outside of his will, there are deadly dangers to our physical and spiritual lives.

God's boundaries as revealed through Moses were the Ten Commandments (Exodus 20:1–17). Moses told the Israelites, "Walk in obedience to all that the LORD your God has commanded you, so that you may live and prosper and prolong your days in the land that you will possess" (Deuteronomy 5:33).

Through Paul, God instructed us, "[Grace] teaches us to say 'No' to ungodliness and worldly passions, and to live self-controlled, upright and godly lives in this present age" (Titus 2:12).

Jesus said, "Whoever follows me [the barrier] will never walk in darkness, but will have the light of life [the blessing]" (John 8:12).

False freedom and death lie outside God's commands. Inside his commands, we find the light of life.

When Jesus Prays for You

Simon, Simon, Satan has asked to sift all of you as wheat. But I have prayed for you, Simon, that your faith may not fail. And when you have turned back, strengthen your brothers. Luke 22:31–32

"I pray for you and Nancy every day," a friend told me. He then indicated he had been doing so for years. How that warmed my heart.

Jesus said Simon Peter's name three times in announcing that he prayed for him. How touching, how powerful, that even as he faced the cross with the weight of the entire world on his shoulders, Jesus prayed for one specific person. He prayed with the knowledge that Peter would soon betray him. Jesus was also aware of Satan's evil influence among all the disciples. Jesus prayed with confidence that Peter would return to the faith, and that the end result of this story would be better because Peter would strengthen his Christian brothers. His experience of falling away and returning to the faith would give him a wisdom and strategy for dealing with the other members of the Twelve. More than that, it would prepare him to deal with thousands of future Christian converts as he became one of the major leaders of the new church. No wonder Peter later wrote, "Be alert and of sober mind. Your enemy the devil prowls around like a roaring lion looking for someone to devour. Resist him, standing firm in the faith, because you know that the family of believers throughout the world is undergoing the same kind of sufferings" (1 Peter 5:8–9).

When Jesus prayed his high-priestly prayer before going to the cross, he included you. He first spoke for his immediate disciples: "My prayer is not that you take them out of the world but that you protect them from the evil one. They are not of the world, even as I am not of it. Sanctify them by the truth; your word is truth. As you sent me into the world, I have sent them into the world" (John 17:15–18). But then, Jesus prayed for you when he said, "My prayer is not for them alone. I pray also for those who will believe in me through their message, that all of them may be one, Father, just as you are in me and I am in you" (vv. 20–21).

Jesus promised that he would send the Holy Spirit back to his followers, and the Holy Spirit would represent him. In Romans 8:26 we read, "In the same way, the Spirit helps us in our weakness. We do not know what we ought to pray for, but the Spirit himself intercedes for us through wordless groans." The Spirit, Jesus' representative, helps us pray despite our limits.

Now Jesus has ascended to his Father and ours. What is Jesus doing today? Hebrews 8:1 reports, "We do have such a high priest, who sat down at the right hand of the throne of the Majesty in heaven." And his specific activity? Hebrews 7:25 tells us, "Therefore he is able to save completely those who come to God through him, because he always lives to intercede for them."

Do you get it? Jesus prays for you.

Repentant and Refreshed

Repent, then, and turn to God, so that your sins may be wiped out,
that times of refreshing may come from the Lord.
Acts 3:19

I once participated in a five-day seminar attended by about sixty people. After sitting down and talking with many of the participants, I wondered, *Why are they so bitter against religion and the church?* As I listened to more and more of their stories, I finally learned the answer. These individuals had been raised in churches that preached, "You have sinned, and God will judge you." That was it—there was no promise of forgiveness. No wonder they were so bitter.

Peter's message was different: "Repent, then, and turn to God, so that your sins may be wiped out, that times of refreshing may come from the Lord" (Acts 3:19). In this statement, he promises that our sins will be wiped away, that the Lord will refresh us, and that our repentance will pave the way for Christ's second coming (3:20–21).

When our son, Paul, had a melanoma on his shoulder, the surgeon cut deep and removed a hunk of his flesh. Was I angry at the doctor? Did I demand, "What right did you have to invade my son's body?" Of course not—I was thrilled that the surgeon removed all the cancer through this radical surgery. As a result, my son lived.

No wonder Romans 2:4 says, "God's kindness is intended to lead you to repentance." By repentance, God removes the cancer of sin so you may be blessed and refreshed.[62]

Power Where It Counts the Most

---

62. Previously published in *Reflecting God* June–July–August 2010 (Kansas City, MO: WordAction Publishing Co.), 22. Used by permission.

*I pray that out of his glorious riches he may strengthen you
with power through his Spirit in your inner being.*
Ephesians 3:16

The Ephesians were good Christians. Yet Paul prays a powerful prayer for a power-filled reality through the work of the powerful Holy Spirit. The Spirit will work in their and your "inner being." One person described it as "power where it counts the most by the one who means the most."

Every true Christian has the Holy Spirit (Romans 8:9) and has been born of the Spirit. Yet there are deeper dimensions to the work the Spirit wants to do in the Christian's heart. The Spirit strengthens you inwardly, and can even bring you to a point where you are "filled with all the fullness of God" (Ephesians 3:19, NRSV).

Grant attempted to save himself with his intellect and good works, but there were massive doses of sin mixed into his efforts. Finally, a day came when he turned from works and sin and was saved by grace at the altar. Incredible changes occurred in his life—yet there was a nagging insecurity about his faith. He had the assurance of salvation but a lack of confidence. He was afraid of failure. In a camp meeting service, he heard the preacher quote Philippians 1:6: "I am confident of this very thing, that he who began a good work in you will perfect it until the day of Christ Jesus" (NASB95). The Spirit moved on Grant's heart. He went forward to pray and, that night, accepted the promise of the gift of the Holy Spirit and was sanctified.

I have watched his life for twenty-five years since. He has consistently lived in the power of the Spirit with quiet but real confidence and strength. He has made a powerful impact on others—he has power where it counts the most.

A Chunk of Life

*This is how we know what love is: Jesus Christ laid down his life for us.
And we ought to lay down our lives for our brothers and sisters.
If anyone has material possessions and sees a brother or sister in need
but has no pity on them, how can the love of God be in that person?*
1 John 3:16–17

In some countries, death is the price some people pay for following Jesus. I have personally known some who paid the price of imprisonment. In my country, following Jesus may result in verbal or legal persecution—but probably not death.

After reminding us of Christ's great love in laying down his life for us, John says we ought to be willing to lay down our lives for others. John then emphasizes the importance of taking part of our material possessions and giving to a brother or sister in greater need. In doing so, John makes it clear that even when we're not called to lay down our physical life for the gospel, we will be called to lay down a "chunk of our lives."

I've done this multiple times. Both in my pastoral duties and as a Christian living my everyday life, I have been called to lay down a chunk of my life.

A vivid example comes out of one of my pastoral experiences. An older couple named Roy and Nora were faithful participants in our local church. They had no children but had had a powerful spiritual impact on their niece who had come to Christ. One Christmastime, Nora was hospitalized, and her leg was amputated due to a chronic illness.

On Christmas morning, we were getting ready to unwrap gifts with our three children, all of whom were under the age of six. Then the phone rang— Roy had just had a severe heart attack and was in the same hospital as Nora.

What should I do? Should I lay down Christmas morning with my children to be with Roy and Nora? They had no children to support them. I asked Nancy, my wife, to explain to the children that we would open gifts a little later in the day. I had to be with Roy and Nora.

Upon laying down a chunk of my family time, I had a sweet, God-touched time with Roy and Nora. Both survived and soon were active in church again. Nancy, the kids, and I had a fun time opening gifts later in the day. To this day, our three adult children talk about seeing sacrifice bring blessing to others.

Think about it—you may not be called to lay down your whole physical life at once, but what chunks of life will Jesus call you to lay down for him and others?

The Holy Spirit Visited Us

In the last days, God says, I will pour out my Spirit on all people.
Acts 2:17

For the seventy-fifth anniversary of Nazarene Theological Seminary in Kansas City, alumni were asked to tell stories about the school. As I reflected on my three years as a student and thirty years as professor of evangelism, one event stood out above all others.

It happened in February 1970—I was only a few weeks into my first year of teaching there. We had gathered for chapel service, and Rev. Paul Cunningham was the chapel speaker. He had just returned from speaking in a week of special services. In those services, two students from Asbury College in Wilmore, Kentucky, had shared their testimonies. This led to a powerful movement of the Holy Spirit among the one thousand students at Asbury, including a chapel service that lasted 185 hours without a break.

As Rev. Cunningham reported on the movement of the Spirit, the Holy Spirit settled on the seminary chapel crowd. Suddenly, a student left his seat and rushed down the aisle on the crowd's left with his face buried in his hands, weeping. Unable to see where he was going, he bumped into the piano, spun off it, and fell weeping at an altar of prayer. Within two minutes, nearly twenty other students had come to the altar, many weeping. Rev. Cunningham looked at the president as if to say, *What do we do now?* He was in the middle of his message. They decided to sing a song of invitation, and Rev. Cunningham urged others to come forward. About twenty more approached. There was no room at the altar, so these students simply knelt between the filled altar and the first row of seats.

As a faculty member, it would have been normal for me to go forward and help the students pray. But that day, I had such a sacred sense, such an awareness of the Holy Spirit's presence, that I dared not leave my seat, lest I interfere with the Spirit's work. Not a single faculty member moved.

The student who had first come forward finished praying, went to the microphone, and asked permission to speak. He testified that he had made his way through college selling Bibles, but he'd kept the last set of payments he had collected—he had never sent them in to the company. He assured the crowd that his dishonesty was forgiven and that he would send in the funds within hours.

By the time he'd finished, other students were lining up to speak. A student admitted he had lied about completing a reading report he had never done, and he asked the professor's forgiveness. Another student spoke of hard feelings against a professor. Another student confessed he had a broken relationship with another student, and asked forgiveness. Before he could step away from the microphone, the offended student was on the platform, and the two embraced. There was praise and singing and rejoicing. Though the bell sounded for the end of chapel, the service continued for two hours.

After that service, the whole semester was different. Chapels were well attended and praise-filled. Classes sometimes became so absorbed in prayer that they never got to the lesson. Other classes were filled with singing. Students acted with love and integrity.

That service still stands in my mind as the greatest worship I've ever been part of. I learned more about the Holy Spirit in two hours than I had in many hours of study. The atmosphere of love and understanding throughout the rest of the semester was so uplifting. The Holy Spirit had visited us.

God Will Know

For we must all appear before the judgment seat of Christ,
so that each of us may receive what is due us for the things done
while in the body, whether good or bad.
2 Corinthians 5:10

And I saw the dead, great and small, standing before the throne,
and books were opened. Another book was opened, which is the book of life.
The dead were judged according to what they had done as recorded
in the books. Anyone whose name was not found written in the
book of life was thrown into the lake of fire.
Revelation 20:12, 15

I lost my wife's birth certificate. Because she needed it to obtain other legal documents, it was important to replace it. I phoned the office of vital statistics, made my request, and gave my wife's birth information—but that was not enough. The polite and helpful clerk I spoke with wanted to be sure that my wife's need and my representation of her were legitimate.

The clerk began to ask me a strange set of questions. She read me five street addresses and asked me if I'd ever lived at any of them. They were all unknown to me, so I said no.

Then she listed five cities in Texas and asked if I'd ever lived in one of them. When she said Houston, I replied, "Yes, I did a four-month assignment there." She was pleased and completed the steps to send us the new birth certificate.

After this conversation, I began thinking about the Texas question. It dawned on me that this government agency knew my life so well, had records so complete, that they even knew that, in the course of my eighty-five years of life, I'd spent four months in Houston.

It dawned on me that if the office of vital statistics knew that much about me, it would be no problem for the almighty God to know all the details of my entire life. So please be ready, my friend, for what will happen at the end of your life. Scripture tells us, "The dead were judged according to what they had done as recorded in the books" (Revelation 20:12), and, "We must all appear before the judgment seat of Christ, so that each of us may receive what is due us for the things done while in the body, whether good or bad" (2 Corinthians 5:10).

What Kind of Law Is This?

Because through Christ Jesus the law of the Spirit who gives
life has set you free from the law of sin and death.
Romans 8:2

Your city council is meeting. One council member, upset about careless driving, argues that the fine for running a stop sign should be raised from $150 to $300. The council votes seven to six that, at midnight on Thursday, the stop sign law will change, and the fine will be raised to $300.

Another council member is concerned about a different law that has been troubling him and persuades his colleagues to repeal it altogether. Thus, the council votes thirteen to zero that, next Thursday, your city will suspend the law of gravity.

Of course, it wouldn't matter two cents if they suspended the law of gravity. While the law of stop signs is a human-decided law intended to encourage safe driving, the law of gravity is not decided by people. It is simply a description of a force at work in our world.

So we should not be disturbed that at the end of Romans 7 and the beginning of Romans 8, the apostle Paul uses the word "law" six different ways: "God's law" (7:22); "another law at work in me" (7:23); "law of my mind" (7:23); "law of sin" (7:23); "law of the Spirit who gives life" (8:2); and, "law of sin and death" (8:2). God's law is outlined in the Ten Commandments; the other laws refer to forces at work in the human personality.

The law of sin and death is a force, a controlling power, a law of operation in the human personality. It is called the law of sin and death because that is always what sin produces—death. As Romans 6:23 attests, "The wages of sin is death." As the law of gravity causes people to fall, so the law of sin and death causes people to sin.

The law of the life-giving Spirit is a force at work, a controlling power, a law of operation at work in other personalities. As Romans 8:2 says, the law of the Spirit of life will set you free from the law of sin and death. Some translations say "set *me* free," which would make this Paul's personal testimony—either way, we are set free.

Ezekiel 36:27 describes this law of the Spirit: "And I will put my Spirit in you and move you to follow my decrees and be careful to keep my laws." Paul also outlines the effect of this law in Philippians 2:13: "For it is God who works in you to will and to act in order to fulfill his good purpose."

The Greek term for "set free" is a strong word. In Romans 6:18 and 6:22, it appears in the phrase "set free from sin." In Romans 8:2, its verb form indicates something that is done in a moment in time. The New Living Translation of Romans 8:2 is, "Because you belong to him, the power of the life-giving Spirit has freed you from the power of sin that leads to death."

Most people don't like to be told what to do. However, imagine that I preached in your church on Sunday morning starting at 11:00 a.m. and ending 3:00 p.m., then gave you the following command: "Go to lunch now." You would be thrilled to do as I said—the law of hunger written all over your stomach would rise up to embrace the command.

I've met some Christians who finally obey God begrudgingly, haltingly, with heels dug in, because a selfish internal force resists the Lord. These people might say with disgust, "Okay, God, I'll do it."

No! That is not God's way. His Holy Spirit will so work within you that you can say with the psalmist, "I desire to do your will, my God; your law is within my heart" (40:8). You will joyfully and happily obey because something has happened inside you: "The power of the life-giving Spirit has freed you from the power of sin that leads to death."

How Free Can You Be?

*Through Christ Jesus the law of the Spirit who gives life
has set you free from the law of sin and death.*
Romans 8:2

As my mother got older, I made a point to visit her more often. She lived in Sanford, Florida, and I lived in Leawood, Kansas. One January, after experiencing twenty-six-below-zero temperatures in the Kansas City area, I figured it was time for a visit. I had booked three weeks of revival services in differing locations and only had one free week.

I wondered, *Would it be worthwhile to go from Kansas to Florida and back—2,600 miles—within one week?* If I walked, I couldn't make it. If I jogged, I couldn't make it. If I did an adult version of the kids' game "giant steps," I couldn't make it. You see, ever since I was born, I've been bound by a law I've never been able to break—the law of gravity. All the downward pull of that law would mean the longest, fastest steps I'd take would always be so severely limited as to not cover the 2,600 miles in a week. I figured it was no use even to try to go to Florida to see my mom.

About that time, one of my friends got my attention: "Haven't you heard of that higher law—the law of aerodynamics? We have jet planes now." He continued, "If you will commit yourself in total trust to this new law, you will be set free from the old law." I decided to try it.

Soon, I was on a powerful jet racing down the runway. Suddenly, the downward pull of gravity lost its power and the law of aerodynamics set me free. In fifteen minutes, I was at 32,000 feet, and in three hours, I had a soft landing in Orlando. Yes, the law of aerodynamics set me free from the law of gravity!

The apostle Paul wants you and me to know a similar "setting free" power.
- "The law of sin and death"—a spiritual force at work in hearts
- "The law of the Spirit who gives life"—a spiritual force at work in human hearts
- "Set free"—a strong term, similar to Romans 6:18 ("set free from sin").
- "Set free"—something that happens in a moment, not little by little

If I was excited to finally experience that "the law of aerodynamics" set me free from "the law of gravity," how much more exciting that September

2 night when, after a year of my new Christian life and a struggle with a downward pull of remaining self-centeredness in attitude and disposition, the law of the sanctifying Spirit of God set my heart free from the law of sin and death.

Only If You're Walking

. . . in order that the righteous requirements of the law might be fully met in us, who do not live according to the flesh but according to the Spirit.
Romans 8:4

. . . that the righteous requirement of the law might be fulfilled in us who do not walk according to the flesh but according to the Spirit.
Romans 8:4, NKJV

There is only one group of people who completely fulfills the righteous requirements of the law. (Note that Romans 8:4 does not say "partially"—it says "fully.") That group is those who "live" or "walk" according to the Spirit. Once the Spirit has set you free from "the law of sin and death," you will need to walk step by step in the Spirit thereafter. Or, as Galatians 5:25 puts it, you will need to "keep in step with the Spirit." How many who were once filled with the Spirit have failed to walk in the Spirit?

Let's go back to the jet plane illustration from yesterday. Imagine that after the law of aerodynamics sets me free from the law of gravity, I have been flying for two hours at 32,000 feet. While flying over the state of Georgia, I begin to feel dissatisfied on several points:

- Twelve people have not approached me to tell me how wonderful I am.
- The plane interior needs a makeover.
- The meals on planes have declined in quality (if you can call peanuts a meal).
- The pilot probably feels superior to me because he's flown millions of miles, and I've never flown an inch. I think he's got a smart-aleck attitude.

I don't have to take this—I'm pretty smart. I've never flown a jet, but I'm sure I could if I had to. Just then, I notice the emergency exit next to my seat.

I disengage the red handle, pull the cube to one side, and jump out of the plane announcing, "I'm going to fly to Orlando on my own!"

Of course, I crash to my death. Why? For one simple reason: as soon as I remove myself from the law of aerodynamics, the law of gravity is the only power left to control my life.

And so it is with the spiritual realm. It's the same as if I had been active in God's work, but became dissatisfied with the church for the following reasons:

- Twelve people failed to approach me on Sunday morning to tell me how wonderful I am.
- The church installed green carpet when I knew bubblegum pink would be best.
- The food at the potlucks is not what it used to be.
- The leader of the church is so sure that he's right. He's always pushing some agenda or another. (You'll need to decide if that leader is the Lord or the pastor.)

What is happening here? It's simple: As soon as we remove ourselves from "the law of the Spirit of life," the law of sin and death is the only power left to control our lives.

Do you see it? "The righteous requirements of the law" can only be "*fully met in us*" if we are walking in the Spirit.

Sweet Fragrance

For we are to God the pleasing aroma of Christ among those who are being saved and those who are perishing.
2 Corinthians 2:15

Fourteen pots of chili at our annual cook-off spread a mouth-watering aroma throughout the church building. On the other hand, there was the odor of the broken eggs that had been left on the kitchen counter for two days—it was awful.

In each case, the odor produced was based on what was happening on a deeper level. For those of us who, by God's grace, are triumphantly following Christ, "through us spreads the fragrance of the knowledge of him everywhere" (2 Corinthians 2:14, ESV). When we yield everything to Christ and his mission on a deep heart level, the fragrance is perceptible to both God and people. The scent that people around us perceive depends on their own heart commitment (2:16).

It has now been eleven days since Evan and Jody accepted Christ. Evan reports that he has a new sense of peace, and Jody says she feels calm. Jody expressed her amazement at this, saying, "For years, I'd been deceived into thinking that you couldn't share your faith—that it was a private matter. But I've been telling people at work all week what the Lord has done for us, and nobody's gotten mad."

There is a sweet fragrance in Evan and Jody's lives, just as there was in those who shared Christ with them. What kind of fragrance are you leaving?[63]

Faithful with a Few Things, Part 1

*Well done, good and faithful servant! You have been faithful
with a few things; I will put you in charge of many things.
Come and share your master's happiness!*
Matthew 25:21

Faithfulness is a big deal with God. This point is reiterated elsewhere in Scripture:
- Matthew 24:46–47—"It will be good for that servant whose master finds him doing so when he returns. Truly I tell you, he will put him in charge of all his possessions."
- Luke 16:10—"Whoever can be trusted with very little can also be trusted with much."
- Luke 19:17—"Because you have been trustworthy in a very small matter, take charge of ten cities."

In all of these cases, present faithfulness results in greater fruitfulness.

Paul was called to ministry, but he had been struggling in seminary. Finally he yielded himself entirely to God, and God sanctified him through and

---

63. Previously published in *Reflecting God* June–July–August 2010 (Kansas City, MO: WordAction Publishing Co.), 15. Used by permission.

through. At graduation, several churches called him to pastor. In the end, he bypassed calls from larger churches because he felt led to pastor a church of forty-six members.

The church had some wonderful people in it—but it would grow a little, then decline a little. Paul threw himself wholeheartedly into his assignment and began praying, studying, preaching, and calling. One day he pleaded in prayer, "Oh, God, bless this church."

The Lord answered him: *If you really want me to bless this church, you can start by raising at least a thousand dollars for missions.*

This was several years ago, and the church had never raised a thousand dollars for missions. Paul responded, "But Lord, if we have to raise a thousand dollars for missions, I'll have to give a hundred dollars." He was scared—he didn't have a hundred dollars.

No, the Lord said, *I'm going to ask you to give two hundred dollars.*

Paul was troubled. He didn't have two hundred dollars either. But then he thought, if he wanted to buy a car and didn't have the money, he would get a loan. If he wanted to honor King Jesus, why not get a loan for missions? He went to his bank, and his interview was set with the bank president. The president questioned him, "Why would a preacher want to borrow two hundred dollars?"

How do you explain to a bank president whose interest is local business investment that you will give it to your church and that they will use it for missionary work in Mozambique, Papua New Guinea, and Peru? Paul simply told him of hospitals, schools, churches, and lives changed by God in more than 160 nations. The banker granted him the loan and said, "I believe in a program like that. Here's my check to go in the offering."

Paul took his checks, challenged the church, and they raised more than a thousand dollars. God was looking on, and he saw a church and a pastor who were faithful in a little thing. Now he could trust them with a greater thing.

Faithful with a Few Things, Part 2

Well done, good and faithful servant! You have been faithful
with a few things; I will put you in charge of many things.
Come and share your master's happiness!
Matthew 25:21

After the missions offering, Paul's church began to grow—attendance rose into the seventies, eighties, nineties, then up to one hundred twenty. They ran out of space, so Paul gathered the church leaders together and asked, "Should we cut back on our efforts, or should we seek larger facilities?" The leaders wanted to grow.

Paul's denomination was known for planting Christian liberal arts colleges in key locations across the country, and they were planning to build a new one in a central part of the United States—the area where Paul's church was located. Paul met with his bank's president, and together, they decided to ask local business leaders to donate land for the new college. Soon, the local leaders were prepared to donate a tract of land—eighty acres located just off the interstate, worth millions of dollars—as a gift to the denomination if they would build their new college on it.

Denominational leaders were contacted, arrangements were made, buildings were constructed, and provision was made for Paul's church to have a portion of the land. The church used the space to construct a larger building. The new college grew, Paul's church grew, and soon they needed an even bigger building. The bank president gave a gift of $100,000 for it.

As the college grew, the town grew, and more and more people were attracted to the church. After twenty-nine years of Paul's leadership, membership had grown, and the church had become one of the largest in the denomination.

At the denomination's 1993 General Assembly, Paul, who had only pastored one church in his life, was elected general superintendent—the most significant worldwide leadership position in the denomination. He exercised powerful leadership in that position for sixteen years. God had found a man who was faithful with a few things, so God entrusted him with many things. Paul was a man God could trust.

That man was Paul Cunningham; the college is MidAmerica Nazarene University; the church was College Church of the Nazarene in Olathe, Kansas.

How far can God trust you?

What the Spirit Will Do through You

But Stephen, full of the Holy Spirit, looked up to heaven and saw the glory
of God, and Jesus standing at the right hand of God. While they were
stoning him, Stephen prayed, "Lord Jesus, receive my spirit." Then he fell on
his knees and cried out, "Lord, do not hold this sin against them." When he
had said this, he fell asleep. And Saul approved of their killing him.
Acts 7:55, 59–60, 8:1a

On September 11, 2001, four commercial airliners were hijacked by terrorists in a planned attack against the United States. Two planes struck the World Trade Center in New York City, and more than two thousand people were killed. Another plane struck the Pentagon in Washington, DC.

At 9:28 a.m., a fourth plane, Flight 93, was hijacked by terrorists who intended to crash it into the nation's capitol. At 9:57, passenger Todd Beamer yelled, "Let's roll!" and led a charge to regain control of the plane from the terrorists. At 10:03, the flight crashed in Shanksville, Pennsylvania, at 563 miles per hour. All on board were killed. They were only eighteen minutes of flying time from Washington, DC—the capitol and its people were spared.

What is it that makes some people so powerful and able to do great things, even heroic things? We now know the following details about Todd Beamer: He was raised in a godly Christian home. He graduated from Wheaton College, a Christian school. He married Lisa, a godly woman. Shortly before the crash, he had been studying *A Life of Integrity* with his men's discipleship group. He phoned Lisa Jefferson, an air-phone operator in Chicago, and they recited the Lord's Prayer together. In the midst of the hijacking, he prayed, "Jesus, help me." Shortly after that prayer was when he said, "Let's roll," and led the attack on the cockpit. Behind Todd Beamer's heroism, we discover a relationship with Jesus Christ.

Though not all feats are so heroic, Scripture shows us many examples of people accomplishing good works by the Holy Spirit's help and power:

- We see it in Peter (Acts 4:8–12). Filled with the Spirit, he courageously confronted persecuting authorities and proclaimed salvation through Christ alone.
- We see it in Stephen (Acts 7:55–60). Filled with the Spirit, he saw Jesus in heaven and prayed for the forgiveness of those who were stoning him.

- We see it in a group of Christians (Acts 4:31–35). Filled with the Spirit, they shared their possessions until there were no needy persons among them.
- We see it in Barnabas (Acts 11:24). Filled with the Spirit, he encouraged a great number of people who were brought to the Lord.
- We see it in Paul (Acts 13:9–12). Filled with the Spirit, he looked straight at the evil Elymas and rebuked him.
- We see it in Philip (Acts 6:1–5; 8:26–30). Filled with the Spirit, he led the secretary of the treasury for the queen of Ethiopia to Christ.
- We see it in Saul, who saw the Spirit-filled Stephen being stoned to death and was so impacted that he accepted Christ and became Paul.

The list could be so much longer. The Holy Spirit empowers people to do great, good, and gracious things.

This is true today with Jenee. Her parents abandoned her when she was two months old. She started using drugs at age eleven. As a juvenile, she was arrested more than twenty-four times. Jenee was arrested by the FBI and facing a life sentence when, on March 6, 2005, she met Jesus through a life-long Christian. Christ delivered her from a nineteen-year drug addiction and transformed her by God's grace. Five months after her conversion, as Jenee was studying *Basic Bible Studies for the Spirit-filled and Sanctified Life* and do-ing her last thirty days in a detox program, she accepted the gift of the Holy Spirit's fullness and experienced entire sanctification.

Today, Jenee is an ordained minister and serves as a pastor on staff at a Kansas City church. At the time of this writing, she has just finished lead-ing twelve young people through the sanctification study that so impacted her. She won the Evangelism Award at the seminary she attends. Jenee's life and ministry are powered by the Holy Spirit. What will the Holy Spirit do through you?

The Best Gift

If you then, though you are evil, know how to give good gifts
to your children, how much more will your Father in heaven
give the Holy Spirit to those who ask him!
Luke 11:13

How much more will your Father in heaven give good gifts
to those who ask him!
Matthew 7:11

What's the best gift another person has ever given you? God will give you more than that kind of gift—he will give you the Holy Spirit. Our parallel passage in Matthew tells us that God gives "good gifts." Thus, we may assume that the Holy Spirit is the best of all good gifts. By this Holy Spirit, you may be born of the Spirit, filled with the Spirit, and led by the Spirit.

Perhaps the most dramatic answer to prayer I've ever experienced happened when I was pastoring my first church. Our church was growing, and I'd invested a lot in Bev and Floyd. Floyd had been saved, joined the church, and elected to the board.

After being fully involved in the church for over a year, Floyd asked to meet me one Sunday afternoon. To my total shock, he said, "Bev and I are quitting the church."

"Why?" I responded. "Are you mad at me about something?"

Floyd said, "Yes, but I'm not telling you about what."

I said, "If you won't even tell me what it is, it's difficult to address it. All I can say is I'll pray about it."

"You can pray all you want. We're leaving." With that, Floyd handed me his treasurer's records from one of our auxiliary organizations.

I was depressed as I walked back to the parsonage and told my wife. We had recently been invited to pastor a larger church—double the size, double the parsonage, double the salary. I'd turned it down, believing God's will was for us to continue in our present assignment. But after my conversation with Floyd, I said to Nancy, "If that's how the people feel about us here, then maybe it's time for us to move."

Nancy replied, "I wouldn't let the devil trick you into thinking that's how everyone feels. This is how two people feel."

I realized she was right. I went to my prayer room and closed the door.

"Lord," I prayed, "I'm ready to leave this church in disgrace if it will advance your kingdom—or I will stay and fight. Tell me what to do."

In that moment, the image of a bulldog drifted across my mind's eye. I knew the bulldog's reputation: they hold on no matter what.

"All right, Lord, I'll stay," I said. "But what about Floyd?"

The Lord told me, *I'll talk to Floyd.*

"Good!" I shouted.

Then God gave me an additional instruction: *Don't tell anyone about this for seven days.*

Sure enough, on the seventh day, Floyd came to me. "Have you told anybody I've quit the church?" he asked.

I told him that I hadn't.

Floyd said, "If you haven't told anyone, Bev and I have decided to stay. I'll take my treasurer records back."

I stayed at that church three more years. By the last year, the church was at its highest attendance, highest membership, and highest financial giving. Floyd got into the church neck-deep and became a major force in our building program. The next year, we had a beautiful new sanctuary and educational unit.

I'm glad I stayed and waited seven days. I'm grateful God spoke to Floyd. And how many more prayers I've seen God answer since I've been filled with the Spirit.

The Holy Spirit Wasn't Finished

To know the love of Christ that surpasses knowledge,
so that you may be filled with all the fullness of God.
Now to him who by the power at work within us is able to
accomplish abundantly far more than all we can ask or imagine.
Ephesians 3:19–20, NRSV

I learned a lot from seeing the Spirit's leadership over Floyd and Bev. When you are depressed, it's easy to generalize. When they told me they were leaving the church, I thought, *If that's how the people feel about us*—when, in reality, that was only how Floyd and Bev felt. I learned that you should never make a major decision when you are tired, nervous, sick, or depressed. (Though, as someone once joked, "That's all the time.")

Part of my prayer had been, "What about Floyd?" About the time we finished building the new church building, Floyd came to me and said, "Pastor, I've been offered a good job back in Michigan. I feel I need to take it. We've got three children now. I'm not well educated, and my jobs here are low-pay. We need to move."

"Floyd, I hate to see you go—you're like a son to me. But I understand."

Before Floyd and Bev left, they took us to the finest restaurant we'd eaten at since moving to Kansas City. Back at the parsonage, Floyd shifted on his feet nervously. After a few moments, he finally said to me, "Pastor Shaver, you're the greatest man I know." It wasn't true, but in light of how he had once felt about me, I'm glad he thought it was.

The family moved to Michigan, and Floyd started his new job. Within a few days, he had to withdraw. The job was above him. He lamented to Bev— what should they do next? He felt that his skills were limited.

Floyd went to the bank and got a job mopping the floors after hours. Then he got the contract for supplying the chemically treated track rugs at the bank's doorways. He had to take the rugs to the Laundromat since they were too heavy for Bev's washing machine. While he was there, he noticed the condition of the Laundromat and got the contract for mopping *their* floors and supplying their track rugs. Next, he got the hardware store and the grocery store.

Meanwhile, the family got involved in their local church, which was twice as big as mine. Floyd was elected to the church board and to lead a key committee.

When I phoned to see how they were doing, Bev said Floyd was giving heavily to the church. I asked Floyd how his janitorial business was going.

"Oh," he said, "I sold it. Now I own the shopping mall in this city. In the mall, I operate the clothing store. I have another clothing store in the city north of here."

A while back, I met up with Bev and Floyd at a Michigan camp meeting. They were both rejoicing and on fire for Jesus.

In my initial prayer, I had asked God, "What about Floyd?" In response, the Lord was "able to accomplish abundantly far more than all we can ask or imagine." The Holy Spirit wasn't finished with Floyd yet. He's not finished with you either!

You Need the Power of the Spirit

I am going to send you what my Father has promised;
but stay in the city until you have been clothed with power from on high.
Luke 24:49

Two ladies sat on the front pew of D. L. Moody's church. At the close of the service, they said to him, "We've been praying for you."

"Why don't you pray for the people?" Moody asked.

The women replied, "Because you need the power of the Spirit." They came to talk to Moody and prayed that he might be filled with the Holy Spirit.[64]

Jesus had a similar concern for his disciples. He had already taught them about the coming of the promised Holy Spirit (John 14–16). Their faithfulness in following Jesus had been erratic. At times they were all in; other times, they argued over who was greatest, sought high honors, or deserted Christ when the pressure was on. In Luke 24, Jesus was resurrected and giving the disciples some final instructions. He knew it was best for them to go to a specific place and wait before the Lord—they would need Christ's power for the monumental task of being his witnesses. They obeyed and were filled with the power of the Spirit (Acts 1:8 and 2:1–4).

Around age eighteen, Dwight Moody was led to Christ by his Sunday school teacher, Mr. Kimball, in the back of the shoe store where Moody worked. After that, his whole life changed. He said, "Before my conversion, I worked toward the cross, but since then I have worked from the cross; then I worked to be saved, now I work because I am saved."[65]

Moody moved to Chicago and started a Sunday school that grew to 1,500. Eventually, he began preaching.

He went to England to study methods of Christian workers in that country. He began hungering for a deeper Christian experience when he heard Henry Varley say, "The world has yet to see what God will do with and for and through and in and by the man who is fully consecrated to him."[66]

Moody went to New York City to collect funds for rebuilding Chicago after its great fire. But his heart was not in the task. He later reported, "I was crying all the time that God would fill me with His Spirit. Well, one day, in the city of New York . . . I can only say that God revealed himself to me, and I had such an experience of His love that I had to ask him to stay His hand.

---

64. James Gilchrist Lawson, *Deeper Experience of Famous Christians* (Anderson, IN: Warner Press, 1911), 347.

65. Lawson, *Deeper Experience of Famous Christians*, 342.

66. Lawson, *Deeper Experience of Famous Christians*, 345–46.

I went to preaching again. The sermons were not different . . . yet hundreds were converted."[67]

Moody traveled back and forth between the British Isles and the USA. As many as forty thousand heard him preach in Glasgow. His last crusade was in Kansas City; there, he was seized with heart trouble and went home to die. In 1899, some of his last words were, "This is my triumph. This is my coronation day. I have been looking forward to it for years."[68]

The Holy Spirit's power is available for Jesus's disciples; for Dwight Moody; for you and me.

Make Yourself at Home

. . . so that Christ may dwell in your hearts through faith.
Ephesians 3:17a

Here is a phrase that troubled me from Paul's great prayer for the Ephesians, 3:14–21. The Ephesian church was not a problem church; these people were good and true Christians. Paul prayed for them to be strengthened by the Spirit (3:16) and that they would be established in love (3:17). That is understandable, but to pray "that Christ may dwell in your hearts" for people who've already accepted Christ is not understandable.

The answer lies in understanding the richness of the word "dwell." Bible scholar Willard Taylor says: "The word for 'dwell' in the Greek is derived from a word meaning 'to settle down,' 'to take up permanent residence.' Christ comes therefore not as a guest, precariously detained, but as a Master resident in his proper home."[69]

We use an expression in my country: "Make yourself at home." It gives guests permission to make themselves as relaxed and comfortable as if they were in their own homes.

As an evangelist, I've traveled a lot; I've packed many suitcases and stayed in many laypeople's homes. I am grateful for the hundreds of people who have

---

67. Lawson, *Deeper Experience of Famous Christians*, 348.

68. Lawson, *Deeper Experience of Famous Christians*, 351.

69. Willard Taylor, *Beacon Bible Expositions Vol. 8, Galatians and Ephesians* (Kansas City, MO: Beacon Hill Press of Kansas City, 1981), 165.

opened their homes to me with unselfish love. Frequently, upon arriving, I am shown to a guest bedroom and told, "Dr. Shaver, please make yourself at home." I begin unpacking and take a suit and two sport coats to hang in the closet, only to find the closet jam-packed with the clothes the family will use in the next change of seasons. I lay my suit and sport coats on the bed until I figure out a solution. I unpack my shirts, carefully folded to be nearly wrinkle-free. I take four shirts to a chest of drawers and find each of the four drawers jam-packed. What do I do? When the revival meeting is over and I return to my own home, a full closet or a full drawer is no problem. As the owner of the house, I have full liberty to remove clothes from the closet or drawer to make room. In this place, I truly make myself at home.

So Paul is praying that the Ephesians who have received Christ into their hearts will go deeper—that they will allow him to settle in and be completely at home in their hearts through faith. Someone once said that in the lives of many Christians, "Christ is resident, but he is not yet president." To put it another way—is Christ a guest, or is he the owner of the house?

Thus, Christians are to enter a deeper dimension of Christian life in which they are empowered by the Spirit (3:16) and filled with the fullness of God (3:19)—they are to give Christ total ownership of their heart and life. Can you honestly say to Jesus, "Make yourself at home in my heart"?

Surrendering the Hall Closet

So that Christ may dwell in your hearts through faith.
Ephesians 3:17a

One of the godliest professors I've sat under is Robert Boyd Munger. He is famous for many reasons, but he is best known for his vivid description of Christian life in his booklet *My Heart—Christ's Home.*

In *My Heart—Christ's Home,* a man invites Christ into his heart, then takes Christ on a tour of the rooms of his heart. The library represents the thought life; the dining room, appetites and desires; the living room, devotional life; the workshop, talents and abilities; the rec room, social life. The man surrenders each area of his life to Christ. Finally, there is the hall closet, kept under lock and key, which contains dead and rotting things. Finally, the man surrenders even that to Christ for cleansing and possession. Then, he signs the whole property over to Christ as the full owner, not just a guest. It conveys a powerful message.

One day after class, Dr. Munger invited me to lunch. During the meal, Dr. Munger lovingly questioned me: "How do you say sanctification is a crisis moment when other evangelicals know it is a process?"

"Dr. Munger," I answered, "do you remember when the man allows Christ to take over the hall closet of his heart?"

"Yes," he said.

I continued, "Does that happen in a moment, or is that a process?"

"Oh," he said emphatically, "that happens in a moment!"

"Dr. Munger, that's what we are talking about—it happens in a moment. Not only that, I have preached your story across the country and have seen hundreds of people come forward in a moment, kneel, pray, and surrender their hall closet to Christ."

Immediately, tears burst from Dr. Munger's eyes—so forcibly I thought they would hit me. In that moment, we both knew that when we talked it through in love, we both believed the same thing—surrender and cleansing happens in a moment, with a process before and after.

After lunch, I went back and read the hall closet story again. "[Christ] walked over to the door, opened it, entered it, took out the putrefying stuff that was rotting there, and threw it all away. Then he cleansed the closet, painted it, and fixed it up all in a moment's time."[70]

Is it time for you to surrender the hall closet of your heart to Christ for his cleansing and full possession? It could happen right now—it depends on your choice.

More than All We Ask or Imagine

Now to him who is able to do immeasurably more than all we ask or imagine, according to his power that is at work within us . . .
Ephesians 3:20

---

70. Robert Boyd Munger, *My Heart—Christ's Home* (Downers Grove, IL: InterVarsity Press, 1986), 25–26.

Once, the pastor of a local church gave me a list of laypeople, each of whom was outstanding in a certain area. Every line started with "not everybody."

Not everybody can bake coffee cake like Kathy.

Not everybody can fix things like Ed.

Not everybody can organize dinners like Stacy and Shirley.

Not everybody can sing and play like our praise team.

Not everybody can fish like Ken.

Not everybody can teach kids like Susan.

Not everybody can greet people like Kevin.

Not everybody can visit people like John and Lester.

But on the day of Pentecost, Scripture says of 120 followers of Jesus, "All of them were filled with the Holy Spirit" (Acts 2:4). Not everybody can . . . but they were *all* filled with the Holy Spirit.

Do you realize that everyone who has come to Christ and been born of the Spirit may go deeper and be filled with the Spirit? Earlier, in our Ephesians 3:14–21 prayer, verse 19 is translated, "that you may be filled with all the fullness of God" (NRSV).

Once, after I urged Christians to press on and "be filled with the Spirit," a somewhat angry young man challenged me. He shouted, "What do you mean, 'be filled with the Spirit'? Do you think the Holy Spirit is divided? Do you get half the Holy Spirit when you're converted and all the Holy Spirit when you're sanctified?"

"No," I responded, "I don't think the Holy Spirit is divided. From the moment of your conversion, the Spirit wants to possess all of you. But as long as there is a part of your heart held back from his full control, you cannot be filled. The problem is not the Spirit's problem—it's your problem."

Think of all Paul has prayed for the Ephesian Christians and for you:

- That he *may strengthen you* with power through his Spirit in your inner being (3:16)
- That *Christ may settle down* and be at home in *your* hearts through faith (3:17)
- That *you may grasp how* wide and long and high and deep is the love of Christ (3:18)
- That you *may be filled* with all the fullness of God (3:19, NRSV)

All these verbs indicate what God will do in a moment.

Your reaction may be something like, "That's too much—I could never get to that place in my spiritual life." However, the Word tells us, "Now to him who is able to do immeasurably more than all we ask or imagine, according to his power that is at work within us" (3:20). He can do it—even more than you ask or imagine. When will you trust him?

I Will Guide You

I will instruct thee and teach thee in the way which thou shalt go:
I will guide thee with mine eye.
Psalm 32:8, KJV

With some measure of fear, I sat in the dean's office to discuss my new teaching assignment. President William Greathouse had phoned me some months earlier and invited me to come to the seminary to teach evangelism. I had been happy in my work as a full-time evangelist, preaching in a different church each week. Yet, when the phone call came, I sensed immediately that this was God's will for me.

Now I faced the reality with Dean Mendell Taylor. I said, "I've never planned to teach. I've never taken a single class in education—yet I think this is what God wants me to do."

The dean thrust a box with Scripture verses in it toward me. "Take one," he said. Understand, I had two semester-long classes assigned to me and not a single lecture ready. I pulled out one verse at random. It said, "I will instruct thee and teach thee in the way which thou shalt go: I will guide thee with mine eye."

And did God ever guide me. Late at night at my desk, and with obvious divine leadership, I developed my lectures. And did the students ever respond! Thirty grace-filled, joyous years of teaching followed.

What happened in the dean's office that day revealed a basic privilege of the Spirit-filled life—to be led by the Spirit of God. As Romans 8:14 says, "For those who are led by the Spirit of God are the children of God."

In guiding Philip to the Ethiopian, "The Spirit told Philip, 'Go to that chariot and stay near it'" (Acts 8:29). Philip had already been described in Acts 6:3: "Brothers and sisters, choose seven men from among you who are known to be full of the Spirit and wisdom."

Are you Spirit-filled? Are you Spirit-led? Do you know what it means when God says, "I will guide you"?

Advocate

And I will ask the Father, and he will give you another advocate
to help you and be with you forever—the Spirit of truth.
John 14:16–17

Twenty family members were gathering for the annual reunion on Treasure Island, Florida. Some were driving, and some were flying. Chad's family—two adults and four children—arrived by plane. My son phoned me and asked if I would lend Chad our car so they could shop for groceries. My son, who had a closer relationship to me than Chad did, was pleading on behalf of Chad and his family—he was advocating for them.

Jesus would soon leave his disciples, so he asked his Father to give them the Holy Spirit, whom he described to the disciples as "another advocate to help you." As Jesus had pled with the Father on the disciples' behalf, the Holy Spirit would take Jesus's place and help them just as Jesus had.

The Holy Spirit could not be accepted by the world (people living without God), but only by those who followed Christ. As a matter of fact, this Spirit would live in them.

Furthermore, Jesus said, "The Advocate, the Holy Spirit, whom the Father will send in my name, will teach you all things and will remind you of everything I have said to you" (John 14:26). Later, he gave more detail: "When the Advocate comes, whom I will send to you from the Father—the Spirit of truth who goes out from the Father—he will testify about me" (15:26).

The word "advocate" is used again in 1 John 2:1: "My dear children, I write this to you so that you will not sin. But if anybody does sin, we have an advocate with the Father—Jesus Christ, the Righteous One." Now Christ is our Advocate. Christians should expect to live in victory over sin—but if sin does occur, we can take the matter immediately to Christ, who will plead for us before the Father. We can be assured that "if we confess our sins, he is faithful and just and will forgive us our sins and purify us from all unrighteousness" (1 John 1:9).

Imagine—the Holy Spirit is your Advocate. Jesus Christ is your Advocate.

You Can Know

I write these things to you who believe in the name of the Son of God
so that you may know that you have eternal life.
1 John 5:13

Larry, my college roommate, had been searching. Though he was raised in church, had strong values, and cared about spiritual matters, he wasn't *sure* he was a Christian. After attending a college Bible study group, he noted that many people in the group had assurance of their salvation.

Planning to be a research scientist, Larry approached his relationship with God rationally. In his study room in the library, he turned out the light so no one else would see, and knelt. He read promises like, "Him that cometh to me I will in no wise cast out" (John 6:37, KJV), and "Here I am! I stand at the door and knock. If anyone hears my voice and opens the door, I will come in and eat with that person, and they with me" (Revelation 3:20).

Larry prayed, "If you really are who you claim to be in the Gospels, I give you permission to come into my life to reveal yourself to me. And I'm not setting any time limits."

Six months later, Larry said, "I had all the evidence I needed. Prayer was becoming a living conversation with God, and the Bible became an exciting, life-transforming book, as if God were speaking to me personally. My whole attitude and character were being transformed." With the Word of God, a changed life, and evidences of Christ at work in his life, Larry came to *know* that he was a real Christian. Today, he is a minister of the gospel and a man of remarkable spiritual power.

God wants you to know that you are a Christian. It is a dominant theme in 1 John, as in 5:13: "I write these things to you who believe in the name of the Son of God so that you may *know* that you have eternal life."

You can *know* you are a Christian by:

- The witness of the Word: "If we confess our sins, he is faithful and just and will forgive us our sins and purify us from all unrighteousness" (1 John 1:9). Note that God is faithful to forgive and purify.
- The witness of the will: "If we walk in the light, as he is in the light, we have fellowship with one another, and the blood of Jesus, his Son, purifies us from all sin" (1 John 1:7). When my personal commitment

of my willpower can say, "I am walking in all the known light God has given me," I may be confident that I am a Christian.

- The witness of the walk—"By their fruit you will recognize them" (Matthew 7:20). Your life will show it.
- The witness of the Spirit—"The Spirit himself testifies with our spirit that we are God's children" (Romans 8:16). The Spirit gives inner assurance, peace, and an awareness of God so that you *know* you are God's child.

Fourteen weeks ago as of this writing, Rob accepted Jesus Christ. A few days ago, I asked Rob how he knew for sure that he was a Christian. The words flowed out of him:

> I gave my heart to Christ. I knew it in my heart. I have peace and confidence. I am walking and talking with Jesus. My walk is different. I have never doubted since February 19.

The wonderful, amazing truth is that you can know that you are a Christian, that you are saved, and that you are right with God. It is best when all four witnesses join together in a life. It delights God for you to have this assurance.[71]

Assurance for Sanctification Too

The one who calls you is faithful, and he will do it.
1 Thessalonians 5:24

In the last one hundred years, one of the greatest powers in the Methodist Church was E. Stanley Jones. For a year after his conversion to Christ, he lived in great joy. Then, he found that ugly tempers, moodiness, and deep conflicts began to rise from the basement of his soul. He sought God for a deeper relationship.

The Lord asked him, "Will you give me your all?"

Jones answered, "Yes, Lord, of course I will. I will give you my all—all I know and all I don't know."

---

71. Previously published in *Standard*, June 5, 2016 (Kansas City, MO: WordAction Publishing). Used by permission.

The Lord replied, "Then take my all—take the Holy Spirit."

Jones saw this as "my all for his all." He eagerly replied, "I will take the Holy Spirit." He arose from prayer with no evidence of this promise except the word of God. Doubts began to close in, but he pushed them back with prayer.

As he walked around the room, God's Spirit witnessed to his heart. Later, he testified, "Suddenly I was filled—filled with the Holy Spirit. Wave after wave seemed to be going through me as a cleansing fire . . . I knew this was no passing emotion; the Holy Spirit had come to abide with me forever."[72]

John Wesley said, "None, therefore, ought to believe the work is done till there is added the testimony of the Spirit witnessing his entire sanctification as clearly as his justification."[73] When Peter was establishing the fact that God also accepted Gentiles who feared him, Peter built on what the Spirit had done for the earlier followers of Jesus: "God, who knows the heart, showed that he accepted them by giving the Holy Spirit to them, just as he did to us. He made no distinction between us and them, for he purified their hearts by faith" (Acts 15:8–9). Later, John proclaimed, "This is how we know that we live in him and he in us: He has given us of his Spirit" (1 John 4:13).

Gary was the manager of the local grocery store. He had known Christ for a year, and his pastor rejoiced over his Christian growth. During the church's spiritual renewal services, he heard a sermon on entire sanctification from 1 Thessalonians 5:23–24. Afterward, he came forward to pray.

"What do you want God to do for you?" the preacher asked.

"I want him to sanctify me," Gary replied.

They read 1 Thessalonians 5:23–24: "May God himself, the God of peace, sanctify you through and through . . . The one who calls you is faithful, and he will do it." The preacher urged Gary to yield his whole forgiven life back to God and ask God to cleanse him from any remaining self-centeredness. He told him to reach out in faith and believe that God would do it. Gary asked what faith meant.

The preacher asked, "Gary, why did you come down here to pray?"

"God called me," Gary answered.

"Why did God call you?"

"To sanctify me."

"Well, the Bible says the one who called you is faithful, and he will do it. When do you think he will do it?"

---

72. E. Stanley Jones, *A Song of Ascents* (Nashville: Abingdon Press, 1968), 52–53.

73. As quoted in H. Orton Wiley, *Christian Theology II* (Kansas City, MO: Beacon Hill Press, 1953), 514.

"Right now!" Gary exclaimed.

After thirty seconds of more prayer, Gary was beaming. "Oh," he said, "I *know* it. This is terrific."

Like E. Stanley Jones, John Wesley, and Gary, you can *know* that God sanctifies you; you can *know* that the Spirit fills you now. Fill me now![74]

God Sent This Moses

This is the same Moses they had rejected with the words, "Who made you ruler and judge?" He was sent to be their ruler and deliverer by God himself, through the angel who appeared to him in the bush.
Acts 7:35

Ironic, isn't it, how people refuse God's chosen representatives? The Israelites refused Moses; many of the prophets found that no one listened to them; the people also rejected Stephen, even as he reminded them that Jesus, whom they had crucified, was sent from God.

John Wesley knew what it was to be refused a hearing. Once it was a stoning; another time, his enemies attempted to beat him with a club. Often, he received a note from the minister or lay leaders of a church reading, "Sir, you are to preach no more at this place." Yet those who did hear him were saved. And now, history tells us that the revival that followed Wesley's preaching saved England from terrible revolution.

Even in the face of violent opposition, a person who is truly sent from God finds a way to get the message across. Moses led his people out of captivity; Stephen made his last words an astounding witness; Wesley preached despite the hostility against him.

Don't be guilty of ignoring God's message by ignoring those he sends to speak from the pulpit.[75]

---

74. Previously published in *Standard*, June 5, 2016 (Kansas City, MO: WordAction Publishing). Used by permission.

75. Previously published in *Come Ye Apart* July–August–September 1964 (Kansas City, MO: Nazarene Publishing House), 18. Used by permission. (This publication became *Reflecting God*.)

Why the Lord Delays

❖

The Lord is not slow in keeping his promise,
as some understand slowness. Instead he is patient with you,
not wanting anyone to perish, but everyone to come to repentance.
2 Peter 3:9

You ought to live holy and godly lives as you look forward
to the day of God and speed its coming.
2 Peter 3:11b–12a

There are at least two reasons why the Lord has delayed his second coming:

1. To allow time for more people to repent, including those to whom you will witness.
2. To give us the opportunity "to live holy and godly lives."

I am so glad Jesus delayed his coming a little longer.

I suppose he could have come in 1954—but I'm so glad he waited because I received him as my Savior in 1955, as a twenty-year-old college student.

I'm glad he waited because, the next year, at age forty-two, my mother accepted Christ.

I'm glad he waited because, four years later, my dad accepted Christ at age fifty-nine.

I'm glad he waited because my grandfather received Christ at age eighty-eight.

I'm glad he waited because my grandmother accepted Christ at age ninety-two.

I'm glad he waited because my son accepted Christ at age seventeen.

I'm glad he waited because my daughter came back to the Lord at age twenty-seven.

I'm glad he waited because my next daughter returned to the Lord at age thirty.

No wonder Peter said, "Our Lord's patience means salvation" (2 Peter 3:15). It's sure true for my family.

But there is the second element: "You ought to live holy and godly lives as you look forward to the day of God." Peter established this issue early on when he wrote, "Be holy, because I am holy" (1 Peter 1:16). But how could my heart be made holy—so prone to cover-up, so unaware of deep, lurking selfishness? Once again, Peter speaks: "God, *who knows the heart*, showed that he accepted them by giving the Holy Spirit to them, just as he did to us. He did not discriminate between us and them, for he *purified their hearts by faith*" (Acts 15:8–9).

The Spirit went down deep in my heart, and he purified it by faith. Now, daily, I "make every effort to be found spotless, blameless and at peace with him" (2 Peter 3:14) and to grow in grace (3:18). Thank you, Lord, for waiting.

By All Means . . . Save Some

If my people, who are called by my name, will humble themselves and pray and seek my face and turn from their wicked ways, then I will hear from heaven, and I will forgive their sin and will heal their land.
2 Chronicles 7:14

In 1949, in a community called Barvas located in the Hebrides islands off the coast of Scotland, six Presbyterian laymen and their pastor met. They prayed for a spiritual awakening of the nearby towns, where young people rarely darkened the door of a church. Their promise was 2 Chronicles 7:14.

For months, on three nights of the week for six hours per night, those men sought God with no apparent results. Finally, one night, one man in the group reminded them that only men with clean hands and pure hearts would receive blessings from the Lord (Psalm 24). They fell on their knees again and confessed their own need—and then, God and revival came.

Two weeks later, on the first night of their revival services, there seemed to be no results—but the Christians held on in faith. The next night's service was interrupted by a policeman. He asked the evangelist to come to the police station to minister to a weeping crowd there. That night, nearly six hundred people sought God around that police station—people whose spirits had been convicted on their way to the services. For five weeks, an awakening swept over that parish with four services a night. Then it spread to other towns.

Fourteen young men who had been drinking at the tavern were converted. In one village, nearly every young person between twelve and twenty years old had surrendered to Christ within forty-eight hours.

By 1952, the results of revival could be seen in family worship in nearly every home. Of the hundreds who turned to Christ in the first wave of the Spirit, only four ceased attending prayer meetings. More than eighty hymns were composed by the converts. In one place, the awakening caused an increase in attendance from 27 on Sunday morning to 875 at a prayer meeting. All of this because some believe: "If my people . . ."[76]

Waiting

God has said, "Never will I leave you; never will I forsake you."
Hebrews 13:5

Surely I am with you always, to the very end of the age.
Matthew 28:20

I waited patiently for the LORD; he turned to me and heard my cry.
Psalm 40:1

The surgeon was running late. The patient was prepped but was still third in line for surgery. All he could do was wait.

His daughter texted him sweet and comforting words: "So sorry for the delay. Jesus is waiting with you."

Repeatedly, Jesus told his disciples that he would be with them, often through the presence of the Holy Spirit. In light of his upcoming crucifixion, he assured them that he would be with them in all their circumstances. He was waiting to go with me today to an important, prayed-over lunch engagement with a key person.

We too are told to wait—we are to wait patiently for the Lord. When we wait before the Lord, it gives him the opportunity to search the deepest parts of our hearts. And while we're waiting, we can hear his voice. E. Stanley Jones urged Christians to be sure they maintained a "listening post" with the Lord.

Waiting before the Lord is especially important to the Christian seeking the sanctifying fullness of the Spirit. Many people report an extended time

---

76. Previously published in *Herald of Holiness* (Kansas City, MO: Nazarene Publishing House, September 30, 1970), 20. Used by permission. (This publication became *Holiness Today*.)

of seeking the Lord about this before they receive God's answer. Likewise, Jesus said to the disciples of his day, "Do not leave Jerusalem, but wait for the gift my Father promised, which you have heard me speak about. For John baptized with water, but in a few days you will be baptized with the Holy Spirit" (Acts 1:4–5).

Jesus is waiting with you; God is waiting for you. You are waiting on the Lord.

Whispering Distance

But when he, the Spirit of truth, comes, he will guide you into all truth.
He will not speak on his own; he will speak only what he hears,
and he will tell you what is yet to come.
John 16:13

After the earthquake came a fire, but the LORD *was not in the fire.*
And after the fire came a gentle whisper. When Elijah heard it, he pulled
his cloak over his face and went out and stood at the mouth of the cave.
Then a voice said to him, "What are you doing here, Elijah?"
1 Kings 19:12–13

In our senior years, my wife and sweetheart, Nancy, has had to face the challenge of memory impairment. We are trying to work together to effectively manage everyday living.

We decided it was best for both of us to order MedicAlert bracelets, which list a twenty-four-hour phone number to call if anyone should discover us in distress. After several website visits and ten weeks of discussing our plans, the day arrived when I would call in the order. But first I had to fill out an extensive questionnaire and make a phone call to the California office. I felt stress over this phone call, but increasingly, I have been learning to pray about everything—even everyday affairs. So I prayed that the Lord would give me the right counselor on the phone. In a positive, compassionate, one-hour conversation, a wonderful counselor got the information she needed from me and answered my questions. In less than a week, we had our engraved bracelets.

Every spring, Nancy decorates our lawn and garden with live flowers that she buys and plants. After thoroughly doing so this spring, she felt a compulsion to buy more flowers whenever she saw a sale. After several days of such purchases, she arrived home to show me one more flower. I felt tempted to explain about too many flowers, extra work, and the flower budget. Instead I paused and asked God to show me what to say. Then I heard a whisper: "Rejoice with her over her flower. Tell her how pretty it is. Don't worry about one more flower. It's made her happy. And besides, it didn't cost that much."

So we rejoiced together. You see, I read the following in Samuel Logan Brengle's devotional book, *Take Time to Be Holy*: "Now if you want to keep the blessing [entire sanctification], you must constantly lift your heart to God for light, not only in the crises of life, but in all its details. By practice, you can get into such a habit of this that it will become as natural for you as breathing. . . . Keep within whispering distance of God always."[77]

That's what I want to do: "Keep within whispering distance of God always."

Be Filled—Keep Filled

Do not get drunk on wine, which leads to debauchery.
Instead, be filled with the Spirit.
Ephesians 5:18

Afterglow: The Excitement of Being Filled with the Spirit is the title of an outstanding book by Sherwood Wirt, the former editor of *Decision* magazine for the Billy Graham organization. It is the story of his own experience of being filled with the Spirit, and of others with whom he has fellowshipped or to whom he ministered.

Paul's exhortation to the Ephesians in 5:18, "Be filled with the Spirit," is in the present tense. The idea is to *stay* filled with the Spirit. Of course, you can't stay filled unless there is a moment you are first filled. But once you

77. Samuel Logan Brengle, *Take Time to Be Holy*, ed. Bob Hostetler (Carol Stream, IL: Tyndale Momentum, 2013), 200.

have been first filled, it is very important that you stay filled. Sherwood Wirt is definite about the time he was filled:

As I read Scripture, at my conversion all the resources of God's power had been made available to me by his Spirit. I just wasn't drawing on them!

And do I know when I was *filled* with the Holy Spirit? I certainly do. It took place when I asked the Lord to take me out of the way, to nail me to the cross, and to fill me with his love.

"I have been crucified with Christ, and it is no longer I who live, but Christ who lives in me" (Galatians 2:20).[78]

Sherwood Wirt realized the truth of Acts 1:8: "But you will receive power when the Holy Spirit comes on you; and you will be my witnesses." Wirt also testified: "A young man who came to an afterglow asked God to make him a better witness for Christ to strangers. The next day he stopped for breakfast at a restaurant. The man sitting beside him at the counter said to him, 'You look as if you were out having a big time last night.' It was an open door, and he walked through it."[79]

Wirt was impacted by the power of love imparted by the Spirit: "No one has ever seen God; but if we love one another, God lives in us and his love is made complete in us. This is how we know that we live in him and he in us: He has given us of his Spirit" (1 John 4:12–13). Wirt says, "If that is true, then the Holy Spirit is love. The power of the Spirit is the power of love. The breath of the Spirit is the breath of love. The flame of the Spirit is the flame of love. The unction of the Spirit is the unction of love. The baptism of the Spirit is the baptism of love. The filling of the Spirit is the filling of love."[80]

This love is also the major factor in pastoral leadership. Again, Wirt writes, "When a minister loves his congregation, really loves the people, and communicates that love so that they get the message, he can just about write his own ticket. I mean, the effective potential of that church has no limits."[81]

Staying filled with the Spirit is so important. Wirt tells the following anecdote about a pastor:

A pastor friend of mine who had been revived was asked by a member of his church, "Reverend, why do you insist on talking all the time about being filled with the Spirit?"

78. Sherwood Wirt, *Afterglow: The Excitement of Being Filled with the Holy Spirit* (Grand Rapids: Zondervan, 1976), 39.
79. Wirt, *Afterglow*, 65.
80. Wirt, *Afterglow*, 93.
81. Wirt, *Afterglow*, 95.

My friend looked solemn. "Because," he said, "I leak."[82]

Romans 5:5 says, "God's love has been poured out into our hearts through the Holy Spirit, who has been given to us." This scripture also made a tremendous impact on Wirt. He explained it this way:

I began thinking about that expression *poured out*. It seemed to me that my life could be described as a glass. (In the old days it would probably have been called a "vessel.") I saw that God has a golden pitcher, and he proposes to fill that glass with living water. He wants to fill it and keep on filling it until it overflows. He wants it to splash into other glasses around, and that's witnessing . . .

When the water is spilling over the brim, talking about Jesus becomes easy. The Lord prepares everything; he sets up the appointments, arranges the interviews, draws the interest, brings off the result.

The problem was, God couldn't fill my glass. There was no problem at the Source; the artesian wells of Infinity are inexhaustible. The problem was with me. There was already water in my glass, and it was polluted. Sediment lay on the bottom. It had to be tipped upside down and emptied.

Jesus said in John 7:38, 39 that living water would flow from those who believed in him. He was speaking about the Holy Spirit.

But God will not mix pure water with impure. He will not pour from his golden pitcher until our glass has been drained. He will not send his love into a heart that is already in love with itself, or his power into a life operating under human power.

Now I saw more clearly what Paul meant by saying, "I am crucified with Christ."[83]

What a life of love and overflow awaits you when you are filled with the Spirit—when you keep filled with the Spirit.

The People Believed

---

82. Wirt, *Afterglow*, 71.
83. Wirt, *Afterglow*, 114–115.

*And they believed. And when they heard that the LORD was concerned
about them and had seen their misery, they bowed down and worshiped.
Exodus 4:31*

He was just a young preacher, and his preaching co-laborer was only a bit older. Frankly, they were scared. It was only a weekend revival too—not much
time! But they did notice people were talking about the revival. And the
prayer power was so evident. The teenagers had been praying and fasting!

On Saturday they both preached, and victory came. On Sunday morning, the young preacher spoke. When he came to the point of inviting people
to the altar, he thought, *I don't even know how to give an altar call.* But with
trembling, he made the invitation.

Before the first five notes of the final hymn, the first seeker came—a
big fellow who hit the altar so hard that it splintered. Then they came from
everywhere—on every verse of the hymn—even as the song was sung for
the third time. All the altars were filled, and behind them, the front seats
were filled too. That morning, six divorces were stopped by grace—the couples loved God and each other. Many were saved and had every sin forgiv-
en—"And they believed."

Moses and Aaron were a much earlier preaching team. They weren't
young, but they were scared. But wait a minute! The God who called them
prepared the people and the way. They believed—and there was a break-
through![84]

From Bombs to Love

*And hope does not put us to shame, because God's love has been poured
out into our hearts through the Holy Spirit, who has been given to us.
Romans 5:5*

On December 7, 1941—"a day that shall live in infamy," as President Roo-
sevelt famously called it—Commander Mitsuo Fuchida led 360 Japanese

---

84. Previously published in *Come Ye Apart* July–August–September 1964 (Kansas City,
MO: Nazarene Publishing House), 17. Used by permission. (This publication became *Reflecting God.*)

planes in the bombing of U.S. ships at Pearl Harbor. On April 18, 1942, the Doolittle Raiders took off from the *USS Hornet* to bomb Japan. Staff Sergeant Jacob DeShazer dropped his bombs and, after thirteen hours in the air, parachuted over Japanese-held China. He was captured and tortured in prison for forty months.

Though he had been raised in a Christian home, DeShazer was careless, indifferent, skeptical, and weak in both self-control and willpower. At some point, one of the guards slipped a Bible into his hands. For three weeks he devoured it, then had to pass it on to another prisoner. The knowledge of Christ's sacrificial death for his sins impacted him. On June 8, 1944, he prayed to God: "You know I do repent of my sins. Even though I am far from home and though I am in prison, I must have forgiveness."[85]

There came into his soul a divine joy—an inner witness that God, for Christ's sake, had forgiven him. DeShazer said, "What a great joy to know that I was saved."[86] No longer did hunger, starvation, or a freezing cold cell hold horrors for him. Now, as a Christian, DeShazer knew he had to love others—even his enemies. He knew God expected obedience.

One day, one of the guards rushed him into his cell and slammed the door on his bare foot. The guard then kicked DeShazer's foot with his hobnailed boots. Afterward, he felt resentment and hatred for the guard.

DeShazer knew he had to go to a deeper level in his Christian life—so he determined to befriend the guard. He sensed that his nature had been changed. He realized that, as a Christian, he could lead a victorious life.

Later, as illness wracked his body in prison, DeShazer neared death. As he prayed, he heard a voice say, "The Holy Spirit has set you free from sin."[87]

He began experiencing an unusual communion with God. The days passed, and he was led to pray for peace. The voice then spoke to him again: "You are called to go and teach the Japanese people."[88] Of this encounter, DeShazer later said, "I know I was baptized with the Holy Spirit and that a great flood of love came into my heart."[89]

On December 28, 1948, DeShazer, his wife, Florence, and their children began their missionary service in Japan. In early 1950, DeShazer felt led to do a forty-day fast for a spiritual awakening in the country.

---

85. C. Hoyt Watson, *DeShazer: The Doolittle Raider Who Turned Missionary* (Winona Lake, IN: Light and Life Press, 1950), 95.

86. Watson, *DeShazer*, 96.

87. Watson, *DeShazer*, 118.

88. Watson, *DeShazer*, 123.

89. Watson, *DeShazer*, 142.

One of the first fruits of the fast came on April 14, 1950, when Commander Mitsuo Fuchida was converted to Christ. The next month, Fuchida and DeShazer were together, giving their testimonies in the largest auditorium in Osaka. Five hundred people came forward to seek Christ. Imagine—the bomber of Pearl Harbor and the bomber of Japan, both forgiven, made new in Christ, and preaching forgiveness and love.

Could you have done it? Only the power and purity of the Holy Spirit's fullness can make it happen.

Courageous Singles

But while Joseph was there in the prison, the LORD was with him; he showed him kindness and granted him favor in the eyes of the prison warden.
Genesis 39:20–21

He could have been bitter. Twice he was grievously mistreated: first, his brothers sold him into slavery; then Potiphar's wife falsely accused him. This single man was now in prison. But *the Lord was with him*. By following the Lord, he became prime minister of Egypt and led a food program that saved the country and his own relatives from famine.

Let's give a salute to courageous singles. Lisa had gone through a messy divorce; her husband had left her with the children and one chair. That Sunday, she visited a Nazarene church, and by the end of the week, the church delivered furniture to her. Lisa said, "It was even color-coordinated. God has been so kind. I could feel his arms around me. Would I have ordered it? No, but God is using it." Instead of getting bitter, Lisa decided to get better as she faced the rest of her life.

After Kelli's marriage broke up, she and her son Brian started going to church. The youth pastor took a special interest in Brian. Kelli said, "We had no family, but now I've found a family."

Corrie ten Boom, the Dutch watchmaker, was taken to a Nazi concentration camp because her family had been hiding and protecting Jews during the war. After both her father and sister died in the camp, Corrie came out of the camp with so much of God's grace that she was able to forgive her captors. She wrote a powerful book titled *The Hiding Place*, and by age eighty, she had worked and spoken in sixty-one countries of the world. In her singleness, she was able to do what she probably couldn't have if she'd had a husband and children.

God uses some single people in special ways. At age forty-three, chaplain Oswald Chambers died from appendicitis. His now-single wife gathered her written notes of his sermons and published them as *My Utmost for His Highest* in 1927. The book is still in print as the most popular daily devotional book in the world.

Christian history is not clear on whether the apostle Paul ever married. Considerable evidence suggests that he never did. And of course, he became the major force in spreading the message of Jesus in his day.

Courageous singles, we salute you.

JUNE 17   168

Understanding Evangelism

We are therefore Christ's ambassadors, as though God
were making his appeal through us. We implore you
on Christ's behalf: Be reconciled to God.
2 Corinthians 5:20

I'm helped by the four "Ps" of marriage:

Presence—Living a life of kindness, compassion, and good deeds; paying attention to her, and developing a relationship with her.

Proclamation—"I love you."

Persuasion—"Will you marry me?"

Preservation—Nurturing and growing the marriage relationship throughout a lifetime.

Likewise, these four "Ps" are a part of wholesome and holistic evangelism:

Presence—Living a life of kindness, compassion, and good deeds; paying attention to and developing a relationship with the unsaved person.

Proclamation—"God loves you"; sharing the facts of the gospel both in preaching and personal witness.

Persuasion—"Will you receive Jesus Christ as your Lord and Savior?"

Preservation—Nurturing, growing, and developing the Christian into maturity and service.

Almost no American I've met has gotten married without a persuasion question: "Will you marry me?" Living a life of love and proclaiming that love without asking a decision question will not result in marriage. And a missional or discipleship strategy without an intentional question—"Would you like to receive Christ as Savior and Lord?"—will short-circuit our Christian mission.

Wholesome biblical evangelism will include all four "Ps." Paul pleaded for a ministry of reconciliation in 2 Corinthians 5:11–21. Within his appeal he said, "Since, then, we know what it is to fear the Lord, we try to *persuade* others" (v. 11). He also said, "Christ's love *compels* us" (v. 14), and "We *implore* you on Christ's behalf: Be reconciled to God" (v. 20).

So I urge you, my Christian brothers and sisters, include the "persuasion"—include all four "Ps"![90]

In the Fishbowl—"Let Them Look"

However, I consider my life worth nothing to me; my only aim is to finish the race and complete the task the Lord Jesus has given me—the task of testifying to the good news of God's grace.
Acts 20:24

She runs the 400-meter race, does the long jump, and lettered in track and field. But beyond that, she is determined to finish the race on which Christ has set her.

Kelly is seventeen, a high school senior, and is mainly homeschooled, with several classes at the public high school. Both her parents are ministers and have pastored lovingly and influentially in rural Pennsylvania for fourteen years. Kelly is the youngest of their eight children, all of whom are college graduates, college students or, in Kelly's case, will start college next year. She will impress you as smiling, happy, shining, peaceful, and filled with quiet strength.

Kelly gets up at 2:15 a.m. four days a week, spends devotional time with Christ, and gets to work by 3:00 a.m. With one helper, she milks 130 cows. She's off by 7:00 a.m. Why does she do such demanding work? She says, "I

---

90. Previously published in *The Good News: The Chic Shaver Center for Evangelism Newsletter* (March 2012).

like to be helpful, do a job no one else wants to do, and work with animals. And the money helps."

Kelly found Christ as Savior as a four-year-old in Vacation Bible School. Over the years, her relationship with Christ has developed increased trust. She loves the fact that she can approach God anytime, and God never lets her down. She finds value in realizing that God doesn't always answer prayers like she asks—because it keeps her coming back to God.

"People know I'm a Christian and act differently around me," she said. She recently witnessed at work, and when her coworker responded that there wasn't time to go to church, Kelly replied, "If you trust the Lord with your time, he will bless you."

Her mission trip to Peru at age seventeen was a highlight of her young life. She spoke to a congregation about resisting fear, telling the story of how, although her trip cost $1,550, she never held a fundraiser—people just came up to her and handed her money.

She won a first-place award in the Festival of Life event with her first painting. She loves Bible quizzing, and her favorite memorized verse is Acts 20:24.

She doesn't see the need to date in high school. She says she will date when she is more mature; it may even be that the first one she dates will be the one she marries. To Kelly, seeing seventh graders holding hands in school seems out of place.

One of her future dreams is to work in the national parks. The idea of doing Christian ministry in the parks appeals to her.

The verses her parents chose for Kelly at her infant dedication were 1 Thessalonians 4:11–12: "Make it your ambition to lead a quiet life: You should mind your own business and work with your hands, just as we told you, so that your daily life may win the respect of outsiders and so that you will not be dependent on anybody." You're living it, Kelly!

Recently, during a Monday night revival service at her local church, Kelly went forward to pray and seek God at a deeper level. She had just heard a dramatization of Robert Boyd Munger's *My Heart—Christ's Home*. Kelly testified: "I gave everything over to the Lord last night. I asked him to clean up all the rooms of my heart. I gave him everything, and I felt good. I felt a sense of peace knowing I was sanctified. Now, for future spiritual stability and growth, I will ask, *What rooms do the Lord and I specifically work on today?*"

All of Kelly's previous spiritual radiance and influence will be greatly amplified by her full surrender and God's full cleansing.

When someone remarked that being in the pastor's family is like living in a fishbowl, Kelly's brother said, "Let them look!"

Kelly added, "It doesn't bother me to be in the fishbowl."

Your Heavenly Father

*If you, then, though you are evil, know how to give good gifts
to your children, how much more will your Father in heaven
give good gifts to those who ask him!*
Matthew 7:11

Our world has a heavenly Father who loves you and wants the best for you. He longs to be close to you and give you good gifts.

Join in Linda's story: Between the ages of fourteen and sixteen, she had only attended church two or three times, through the influence of an aunt and uncle. Her mother left when she was five. Her daddy tried to raise her with the help of her aged grandmother.

One night, while she was helping her grandmother in the kitchen, Linda heard a thud. She stepped into the living room to see her dad pitched forward onto the floor, newspaper crumpled under him—dead of a heart attack at age forty-two.

That night, she called the pastor of the church and asked, "Would you do my daddy's funeral?"

Later, she wrote, "I felt I never could go on living because Daddy was all I really had."

At the funeral, the pastor quoted Psalm 23:4 (KJV): "Yea, though I walk through the valley of the shadow of death, I will fear no evil: for thou art with me." He explained these words could only be true if we will let the Lord be our shepherd.

Linda picked up that truth. She and her aunts, uncles, grandparents, and cousins came to the following Sunday night service. By the end, Linda and six of her relatives had come to the altar to seek the Lord. Thoroughly disgusted with the meaninglessness life, Linda said, "For the first time Christ actually seemed *real* to me."

A few weeks later, when the pastor spoke to her about the deeper life of sanctification, Linda told him that she had just received that experience. Soon, Linda and two of her cousins joined the church by profession of faith.

When Linda's grandmother moved out of town, Linda went to live with one of her aunts. She had to maintain the old Ford she'd inherited from her dad and pay living expenses out of the $96.80 a month she received as a minor under her dad's social security. When it came time for college plans, Linda and her friend Lois (whom Linda had led to Christ) got short-term jobs to earn money for a student motorcade to a Christian college in Bethany, Oklahoma. Soon, Linda was a student there.

Linda could not keep quiet about what Jesus had done for her. She brought more new people to her church than anyone else. During a five-day youth revival, she brought eleven different teens—all new to the church—and four of them sought God in the services.

Linda met Paul in college; they fell in love and were married. Paul was from a musical family, and soon Linda was singing in a gospel quartet that toured the American southeast. They eventually settled in Florida and became active in their local church, where Paul led music and Linda taught children and teens from broken homes.

As Linda looks back on her life, she proclaims, "I lost my earthly father, but I found my heavenly Father!" That Father loves you and would like for you, too, to truly find him.

The Source of Achievement

He was a good man, full of the Holy Spirit and faith,
and a great number of people were brought to the Lord.
Acts 11:24

Thomas Edison owned more than a thousand patents—probably more than any other person in history—but is best known for inventing the light bulb. When you visit his home and museum in Fort Myers, Florida, you cannot help but wonder—what was the inner motivation, the internal force, the personal drive, that made him such a great inventor?

We might ask similar questions about the inner motivation and spiritual lives of Bible heroes. When we see great result, great fruit, great quality, and great achievement, we ask—what is behind it?

Look at Barnabas, who became the main source for getting the newly converted Saul (later Paul) to be accepted by the church (Acts 9:26–28; 11:25–27). Barnabas was known as the "son of encouragement" (4:36) and repeatedly encouraged others. He is one of the Bible's best examples of "follow-up" on new Christians. He was a generous giver and truly "good." Acts 11:24 reveals the source of this kind of life: "He was a good man, full of the Holy Spirit and faith."

Consider Philip. He was a layman and a great personal evangelist. He led the Ethiopian secretary of the treasury to Christ, and that man took Christianity back to Ethiopia. He was part of the first local church board with a compassionate ministry devoted to feeding widows. In Acts 6, we learn about his internal source of strength: "Choose seven men from among you who are known to be full of the Spirit and wisdom . . . They chose Stephen, a man full of faith and of the Holy Spirit; also Philip" (vv. 3, 5).

This verse also calls Stephen to our attention. He was the early church's first recorded martyr for the cause of Christ. As he was being stoned to death for preaching Jesus, he prayed, "Lord, do not hold this sin against them" (7:60), forgiving his killers just as Christ had. Scripture tells us what captured his attention before he was attacked by the angry mob: "But Stephen, full of the Holy Spirit, looked up to heaven and saw the glory of God, and Jesus standing at the right hand of God" (7:55).

Then there is the apostle Paul, the miraculously converted Saul of the Damascus road. He did more to expand the church than any other person in history. What was his source? We see it as he faces the evil Elymas: "Then Saul, who was also called Paul, filled with the Holy Spirit, looked straight at Elymas and said, 'You are a child of the devil and an enemy of everything that is right! You are full of all kinds of deceit and trickery. Will you never stop perverting the right ways of the Lord? Now the hand of the Lord is against you. You are going to be blind for a time, not even able to see the light of the sun'" (13:9–11).

In more recent history, you have one of the most powerful leaders in the Methodist Church, E. Stanley Jones. He left behind many achievements, including his books, which include *How to Be a Transformed Person*; *Christian Maturity*; *Way to Power and Poise*; *Victorious Living*; *Victory Through Surrender*; *Abundant Living*; *Unshakable Kingdom*; *Song of Ascents*; and *The Divine Yes*. A year after his conversion to Christ, Jones testified, "Suddenly I was filled—filled with the Holy Spirit. Wave after wave of the Spirit seemed to be going through me as a cleansing fire."[91]

All these heroes of the faith drew their strength, perseverance, and hope from the Spirit of God.

Intentional Parenting

These commandments that I give you today are to be on your hearts.
Impress them on your children. Talk about them when you sit at home and
when you walk along the road, when you lie down and when you get up.
Deuteronomy 6:6–7

Hear an impassioned plea from a denominational leader to parents for the sake of their children. Whatever your religious background, hear his heart.

"Hear, O Israel: The LORD our God, the LORD is one. Love the LORD your God with all your heart and with all your soul and with all your strength" (Deuteronomy 6:4–5). Jesus, of course, quoted the *Shema* when asked, "What is the greatest commandment?" Adding the command to "love your neighbor as yourself" (Leviticus 19:18), Jesus revealed that all of the other commandments flow from these two commands!

These two commands continue to hold the most vital place in the hearts of holiness people today. As Nazarenes, we hold firmly to the belief in the work of entire sanctification. It remains our point of theological distinctiveness in a sea of Protestant churches, and was part of the reason for the birth of the Church of the Nazarene in 1908. *The Manual of the Church of the Nazarene* states, "We believe that entire sanctification is that act of God, subsequent to regeneration, by which believers are made free from original sin, or depravity, and brought into a state of entire devotement to God, and the holy obedience of love made perfect" (Article of Faith X). Loving God and loving others are the greatest expressions of the life of an entirely sanctified believer.

In my twenty-six years of pastoring, however, I must admit that I have not seen this same passion and intentionality in Nazarene parents when it

---

91. E. Stanley Jones, *A Song of Ascents* (Nashville: Abingdon Press, 1968), 53.

comes to helping their children experience God's gift of entire sanctification. While we believe in this second work of grace, sadly, we don't seem committed to helping our children experience the joy of walking in such a wonderful relationship of full surrender to God. I don't hear parents pleading with God for their children to be entirely sanctified. I rarely hear testimonies of children who have entered this wonderful relationship of abundant life in Christ. Think about this for a moment: Do we want our children to know the forgiveness of sins but never experience the "holy obedience of love made perfect"?

We have devised a new global framework for discipleship. This framework will serve to guide our discipleship efforts with intentionality. Our new framework defines Nazarene discipleship as A Journey of Grace. We recognize that discipleship is a journey that lasts for a lifetime. Along that journey, we encounter the grace of God and are called to respond to his grace. The journey of grace includes God's prevenient grace, saving grace, and sanctifying grace. Through prevenient grace, God goes before us to make a way and draw us into relationship. Through saving grace, Jesus rescues us from sin and leads us into the truth that sets us free. Through sanctifying grace, the Spirit empowers us to live a life fully consecrated to God. As Nazarenes participate in the mission of God in this world, we commit to joining others along the journey from grace to grace through grace.

My wife, Jenni, and I want to declare our desire for both of our daughters, Bekah and Sarah, to experience not only the grace of salvation in Christ but also the Holy Spirit's work of entire sanctification by grace through faith. We pray that our girls "may be filled to the measure of all the fullness of God" (Ephesians 3:19). We earnestly pray, "night and day . . . that we may . . . supply what is lacking in [their] faith" (1 Thessalonians 3:10). We pray that "the God of peace, [will] sanctify [our daughters] through and through. May [their] whole spirit, soul and body be kept blameless at the coming of our Lord Jesus Christ" (1 Thessalonians 5:23). We commit to impressing this on our children and calling other parents to do the same. We will not rely on the children's ministry of the local church to lead them into this relationship with God, but will be thankful for the support we receive from our church community. We receive this responsibility personally as parents, and we commit to discipling our children through the entire journey of grace! Will you join with us in making this commitment to intentional parenting?[92]

Scott Rainey

The Greatest Lessons in Fifty Years of Marriage

For this reason a man will leave his father and mother and
be united to his wife, and the two will become one flesh.
Ephesians 5:31

At Sunday school, Nancy and I taught "The Ten Greatest Lessons We Have Learned in Fifty Years of Marriage." Here are the lessons, in very brief form (the first four are from Nancy, and the rest are from me):

1. Keep the passion alive throughout your marriage.
2. A sense of security is needed for healthy marriage, and we provide that for each other—but find an even higher security in leaning on the Lord.
3. Create the intimacy that allows you to get really close to one another, at heart level.
4. Commitment—to each other, 'til death do us part—is the wisest and healthiest path. But most of all, commitment to the Lord is the greatest secret to deep love in marriage.
5. Marriage is part of a bigger plan—God's. Your foundation is Jesus Christ, not your marriage.
6. Don't take her for granted. Every day, say thank you; compliment her; say I love you; and give seven hugs a day.
7. Amid the temptations of a pornographic world, the Lord told me, "You don't have the right to look at any other body [in picture, or in person] but Nancy's."
8. When the hardest times have come, like our daughter's divorce, Nancy and I experienced broken hearts and stomach ulcers at the same time. We also learned, "At the end of broken dreams, he's the open

---

92. Adapted from *The Good News: The Chic Shaver Center for Evangelism Newsletter* (March 2020).

door." After God healed our hearts, we found that in the process, he also stretched our hearts. Today, we are able to hold more love and more of God than we ever could have otherwise.

9. Maintain a note-writing ministry to each other—in a suitcase, on the kitchen table, in a card.
10. When you have a hard time understanding your spouse, let this question guide your interaction: "How would Jesus Christ treat him/her?"
11. Bonus: We continually play a game in which I try to be nicer to her than she is to me. She tries to be nicer to me than I am to her. (Nancy says I'm winning.)

There it is—eleven lessons in fifty years. What an adventure with such an awesome woman. Thank you to all of you who have supported us on this journey, and thank you to Jesus Christ who has blessed us so much that it has worked![93]

Fruit That Will Last, Part 1

You did not choose me, but I chose you and appointed you
so that you might go and bear fruit—fruit that will last—and so that
whatever you ask in my name the Father will give you.
John 15:16

It must have been about 1989 when First Church embarked on the Neighbor-to-Neighbor project. Its goal was to introduce ourselves and invite nearby neighbors to church through a packet left at each door. Nancy and her daughter, Jennifer, responded. Now the same Jennifer and her husband, Jonathan, teach a class at church. How did this happen over a span of thirty-plus years? Here is the story in their own words:

Jennifer

My story begins when I was roughly the same age as our fifth and sixth graders. My parents decided to move to a new home in Kansas City during

---

93. Previously published in *The Good News: The Chic Shaver Center for Evangelism Newsletter* (September 2009).

my fifth-grade year, and it just so happened that our new home was built a few streets northeast of a church called First Church. At that time, the church did not look like it does now; it didn't have a steeple or a sanctuary, and my mom even told me that, for a while, she thought it may have been an electric company. Up to this point in my life, I had only been in church a handful of times.

Then, one day, my mom and I returned home to find a simple packet on our doorstep. When we opened it, we discovered that it was from First Church as part of a community outreach program. I remember it being enough to spark the idea in my mom that it wouldn't hurt to give First Church a try.

Since Dad worked on Sundays, it was just my mom and me who began attending. I remember from that first Sunday feeling so welcomed and such a warmth that made us feel right at home. The pastor during those first months of our attendance was Keith Wright, and I remember eagerly listening to his sermons on Sundays and soaking up his messages, thinking that church was not boring at all! After a few weeks, I began attending Sunday school. I remember going to the children's department and immediately recognizing a girl from my fifth-grade class at school. One of my first Sunday school teachers was Beulah Postlewait, who has also taught my son, Jackson, and is currently teaching my daughter, Hadley, in the four-year-olds' class. During that first year at First Church, my mind was becoming open to the plans God had for me.

During this time, my mom was approached by a pastor who was interested in coming to our home and learning more about us. I remember him showing us a card of Jesus standing at a door and knocking. He explained that the door represented the doorway to our hearts and that Jesus wanted to be invited in. I felt excited to do so, and my mom and I both prayed with Pastor Shaver for the Lord to come in. It has been such a journey since then!

I have no doubt in my mind that God was leading and guiding us to him all along through our initial move, the packet found on our doorstep, and through the many wonderful people of First Church.[94]

---

94. Previously published in *The Good News: The Chic Shaver Center for Evangelism News-letter* (March 2017).

Fruit That Will Last, Part 2

*You did not choose me, but I chose you and appointed you so
that you might go and bear fruit—fruit that will last—and so that
whatever you ask in my name the Father will give you.*
John 15:16

Jonathan

*My story of accepting Jesus Christ into my heart happened when I was
twenty-one years old—a little later in life than my wife's story.*

*I was raised Catholic. My family regularly attended church for a while,
but for whatever reason, that sort of faded away sometime in my later ele-
mentary school years.*

*It wasn't until I met Jennifer that I started going to church again. I began
accompanying her off and on throughout our dating years. At that time, I
wouldn't say I was a religious person, but I was open to attending with her.
The services we were attending at First Church were often impactful and
meaningful to me, and my faith was growing, but I still hadn't fully committed myself to the Lord.*

*After I proposed to Jennifer in the summer of 2000, we knew we wanted
to be married at First Church. We chose Pastor Shaver to officiate our wedding and met with him several times to discuss our spiritual lives going into
our marriage and the details of our ceremony. Being that I had not yet fully
accepted Christ at that time, Pastor encouraged us to do a Bible study with
another couple, Fabian and Kandy Pearson, at their home. Fabian had a
career in the financial industry similar to mine, and he was taking courses
through seminary to become a pastor, so Pastor thought we would be a good
match. Through the course of our meetings over several months, I came to
understand what it meant to be a Christian and to have Jesus as the center of
my life. During one of those meetings, sitting at the Pearsons' kitchen table, I
felt the call to pray and accept Jesus into my life and heart. In that moment, I
felt an inner contentment and a warmth I had not felt before. I am so thankful
for the path on which God put me and look forward to whatever my future
holds, good and bad, because I know I can rely on him to guide me.*

Just think—an unchurched fifth grader who came to Christ is now teaching fifth graders about Jesus more than thirty years later. What a payoff for
a church involved in outreach and witness. Or as Jesus put it, "You did not

choose me, but I chose you and appointed you so that you might go and bear fruit—fruit that will last."[95]

Tempted—But No Sin

For we do not have a high priest who is unable to empathize with our weaknesses, but we have one who has been tempted in every way, just as we are—yet he did not sin.
Hebrews 4:15

Our dear friends were moving into their newly purchased condo. During the thirty minutes they left to return a borrowed truck, their condo caught fire, and several units were destroyed. On the advice of the homeowner's association, they then hired a contractor. After clearing out the damage and barely starting the rebuilding, the contractor disappeared with their repair funds. Lawsuits ensued, and I asked my lawyer friend to help them. When he found out the state district attorney was involved, my lawyer friend said to stick with him—he had more clout than any other attorney they could hire.

Jesus Christ is our high priest before God, and he has more clout than anyone else to present our case. Lest you think that he is so high and holy that he cannot understand you, please know that in his humanity, Jesus was tempted in every way you are tempted. Not once did he cave in; he never sinned. There is a difference between temptation and sin: Everyone, including Jesus, is tempted, but he did not sin, and you need not sin.

Some temptations come from without and are very blatant, as when Satan tempted Jesus in the wilderness (Luke 4). Sometimes Satan is brazen and attacks like a roaring lion (1 Peter 5:8). Other times, he is subtle and deceptive, disguising himself as an angel of light (2 Corinthians 11:14).

But temptations can also come from within. God has created us with certain drives and desires as part of healthy, robust humanity. These drives are healthy and good if disciplined and guided.

---

95. Previously published in *The Good News: The Chic Shaver Center for Evangelism Newsletter* (March 2017).

There is the social drive—a healthy desire for people to like you. But if that drive is allowed to get out of control, you may disobey God in order to get people to like you.

There is the sexual drive, which is part of God's plan for the propagation of the human race, and is meant to be an experience of love between a married man and woman. But if that drive is undisciplined, and you consider it only a matter of your own pleasure, it becomes sin.

There is the security drive, which protects your life. This drive causes you to jump out of the way of a speeding car. But it can also become perverted and make you into a grasping, possessive, selfish person. In this case, again, a good drive has become sin.

Be smart. Be alert. Your internal drives are good—don't let them become twisted. While Jesus is our high priest on high, the present Holy Spirit "helps us in our weaknesses" (Romans 8:26).

Paul used strong words in 1 Corinthians 9:27 when he wrote, "I strike a blow to my body and make it my slave so that after I have preached to others, I myself will not be disqualified for the prize." Tempted, yes, even from within—but with godly discipline, you need not sin.

Out of the Blue

There he met a Jew named Aquila, a native of Pontus, who had recently come from Italy with his wife Priscilla, because Claudius had ordered all Jews to leave Rome. Paul went to see them, and because he was a tentmaker as they were, he stayed and worked with them.
Acts 18:2–3

"Out of the blue" is an expression we use to describe a totally unexpected event or occurrence. God is doing his work in the world, and although we try to understand God's will and follow it, he will sometimes surprise us.

You might describe Paul's meeting with Aquila and Priscilla as "out of the blue." Paul met the couple in Corinth because Emperor Claudius had ordered all Jews to leave Rome—God will use political and social events, even evil ones, to advance his kingdom. The first connection of these three people was in their secular work as tentmakers.

Paul left his synagogue preaching in Corinth due to opposition from the Jews. Then, out of the blue, Crispus, ruler of the synagogue, accepted the Lord, along with his whole family (Acts 18:7–8). Soon afterward, "the Lord spoke to Paul"—again, seemingly out of the blue—telling him not to be afraid because he had "many people in this city" (vv. 9–10).

His new tentmaker friends, Priscilla and Aquila, now worked with Paul in his ministry and accompanied him on his trip to Ephesus. In the end, he left them there to minister (vv. 18–19). Priscilla and Aquila discipled the powerful orator Apollos, who eventually went to Achaia to proclaim Jesus as Messiah (vv. 26–28). Such developments might have seemed out of the blue, but God made them happen!

Likewise, your actions for God can produce out-of-the-blue results. Nancy and I visited a local church to sing, teach, and preach. While we were there, we met members of the pastoral staff. At one point, one of the pastors, Gary, approached us and reminded us of our first encounter. He said something like this: "When we arrived to pastor a little church, hardly anybody said anything to us. You were the only people who welcomed us. You and Mrs. Shaver took us out to lunch."

I had not remembered this connection—Gary was speaking of a meeting that had happened about fifty-five years earlier. I was amazed and humbled to learn that our simple kindness had made such an impact. This report came to us completely out of the blue.

Get ready for your out-of-the-blue experience from the Lord; get ready to become such an influence for God that reports like this will come back to you out of the blue.

Grace—Gracious

*For if the many died by the trespass of the one man, how much more
did God's grace and the gift that came by the grace of the one man,
Jesus Christ, overflow to many!*
Romans 5:15

A ten-second tornado tore through Pierce City, Missouri, at 6:45 p.m. on May 4, 2003. One person died. Additionally, the city hall, forty-two of the town's forty-five businesses, and eighty-one homes were demolished.

The owner of the town's supermarket was hospitalized in Springfield during the tornado. He and his wife had owned the store sixteen years. When he returned to the spot where his store once stood, it was being scooped up and tossed in a Dumpster.

Finally, once the town had settled a bit, the grocery store owner approached the Baptist church and asked if he could buy their property. The church had previously made plans to build a new sanctuary outside of town. After the church board met, they refused to sell to the grocer—instead, they simply gave him the property. After all, the town needed a grocery store.

The town pharmacist also needed a new property, so he approached the grocery store owner about buying *his* old property. The grocer wouldn't sell it; he simply gave it.

City Hall had to be rebuilt, so the mayor approached the pharmacist about selling *his* old property. The pharmacist said the city could have it for free.

How amazing that in a place of devastation, gracious deeds proliferated. None of it was forced.

When we see God's grace portrayed in the Bible, it is clear that it tends to make its recipients gracious in turn. The grace of God and grace of Jesus Christ is overflowing to many today. Are you caught in that flow?[96]

The Place Is Holy Ground

Then he said, "I am the God of your father, the God of Abraham,
the God of Isaac and the God of Jacob." At this, Moses hid his face,
because he was afraid to look at God.
Exodus 3:6

---

96. Drawn heavily from a report in Marilyn Meberg, *Assurance for a Lifetime* (Nashville: W Publishing Group, 2004), 55–57.

He hungered to know God better. At times, something unholy still raged within him. Alone at home, he sat praying.

Then, God came to him as fire—as "condensed light." His soul was transformed, lifted to new spiritual heights, and his needs were supplied.

He began to preach the holiness of God and people's need for holiness as never before. The churches he pastored thereafter grew with amazing vitality—more than once, his churches would double in membership in a year. Dr. Phineas F. Bresee thus became God's man to deliver a people for God. Before long, holy fire burned across the American continent in a new group called the Church of the Nazarene.

The man who received the Ten Commandments from God's hand first learned that God is holy. In order to answer the cry of a people in bondage (Exodus 2:24), the Lord spoke to Moses from fire on ground made holy by his presence (Exodus 3:5) Oh, that today more would take off their shoes after having heard the voice and felt the fire! Then they could lead the people.[97]

How to Know the Will of God

Therefore, I urge you, brothers and sisters, in view of God's mercy, to offer your bodies as a living sacrifice, holy and pleasing to God—this is your true and proper worship. Do not conform to the pattern of this world, but be transformed by the renewing of your mind. Then you will be able to test and approve what God's will is—his good, pleasing and perfect will.
Romans 12:1–2

Cheri wept as she said, "I'm afraid God won't let me have him." The teenage girl was in the midst of a conflict: God's will versus Cheri's will.

The first step to finding God's will is to make sure you have offered yourself to him as a living sacrifice. Once you are in that surrendered state, there are five practical ways to discern God's will:

1. **The Bible**. The Word of God provides certain overarching principles, such as Romans 12:1–2. The Bible doesn't tell you whether you're sup-

---

97. Previously published in *Come Ye Apart* July–August–September 1964 (Kansas City, MO: Nazarene Publishing House), 14. Used by permission. (This publication became *Reflecting God*.)

posed to be a doctor or a truck driver—however, it makes it clear that the choices you make must stem from a life fully surrendered to God.

2. **The Leadership of the Spirit in Prayer.** Here is where the Spirit may give you more specific guidance: which job, which person, which choice. What does the voice of the Spirit sound like? According to A. J. Russell, "The divine voice is not always expressed in audible words. It is made known as a heart-consciousness."[98]

3. **Open and Closed Doors.** These should support the Spirit's leadership. If you feel led to be an engineer but have failed all your math and science courses, that sounds like a closed door.

4. **Advice of Mature Christian Friends.** When I was invited to teach at seminary, I asked five of my trusted Christian friends for their opinion. Four said I should accept the position. (Of course, I also consulted the Scriptures and prayed about the decision.)

5. **Sanctified Reason.** You should use your logic and understanding to grasp the facts of the situation. This is the practice of "sanctified" reason—that is, reason that keeps the major place for God. Just now, one of my loved ones is trying to decide whether he should refinance his home mortgage. In the process, he is using his sanctified reason to make a list of all the financial options.

In reviewing these resources, I'm reminded of a friend who has had a series of monumental decisions before him. In the process, he has used all five guidelines to discern God's will. As a result, he is able to test and approve of God's will—his good, pleasing, and perfect will. And it is very good.

"Perfect"—Are You Kidding?

It is by God's will that we have been sanctified through the offering of the body of Jesus Christ once for all.
Hebrews 10:10, NRSV

For by a single offering he has perfected for all time those who are sanctified.
Hebrews 10:14, NRSV

---

98. A. J. Russell, *God Calling* (New York: Arthur James Ltd., 1953).

It is possible to create confusion around perfectly good words, phrases, or ideas. It's like the Seattle fifth grader who took a science test on the human body. Instead of identifying the cranium, thorax, and abdominal cavity, he wrote "branium," "borax," and "abominable cavity."

The word "perfect" has had a troubled history. My teen son's constant excuse for wrongdoing was, "Nobody's perfect, Dad."

Hebrews portrays the superiority of Christ's sacrifice to the old sacrificial system—"once for all" versus "again and again." The Old Testament priest remains *standing* day after day; Christ died once for all and is now *seated* at the right hand of God (Hebrews 10:11–13).

It appears the first item of God's will is that we should be sanctified (v. 10)—but we cannot do this for ourselves. It is only through the body of Christ. His perfect offering has brought perfection to those who are sanctified. In verses 16–17, God deals with sin two ways: in verse 17, he remembers sins no more (that is, he forgives sin); in verse 16, he puts his law in our hearts. In the process, he cleanses and imprints our hearts with Christlikeness. Now God has gone beyond outward behavior to transform our inward selves.

In the New Testament, the word "perfect" means complete; brought to a desired level; fulfilling the purpose for which something was intended or designed. It brings us to a complete love, in which we love God with all our heart, mind, and soul. First John 4:17 18 describes this kind of love when it says, "Love has been perfected among us in this: that we may have boldness on the day of judgment, because as he is, so are we in this world. There is no fear in love, but perfect love casts out fear" (NRSV).

This perfection is limited. It is not perfect strength, perfect knowledge, perfect wisdom, perfect communication, perfect judgment—but perfect love. The words "once for all" and "for all time" in today's scriptures emphasize the superiority of Christ's sacrifice.

Imagine that after studying long and hard, a little boy earns 100% on his spelling exam. He brings his test home and shows his dad that his teacher has written "A perfect paper" across the top. Dad looks at it for a moment, then says, "But Son, don't you think you could improve your penmanship?" Of course, that would be missing the point entirely—the son was perfect in the area in which he was tested.

No wonder Romans 13:10 says, "Love is the fulfilling of the law" (NRSV) and Romans 5:5 says, "God's love has been poured out into our hearts through the Holy Spirit, who has been given to us." God has created us to love him and others—now the purpose for which we were made is being fulfilled by the work of the Holy Spirit.

We're not kidding! As Hebrews 10:14 testifies, God has "perfected for all time those who are sanctified" (NRSV).

The Lord, the Heart Mover

In the first year of Cyrus king of Persia, in order to fulfill the word of the LORD spoken by Jeremiah, the LORD moved the heart of Cyrus king of Persia to make a proclamation throughout his realm and also to put it in writing: "This is what Cyrus king of Persia says: 'The LORD, the God of heaven, has given me all the kingdoms of the earth and he has appointed me to build a temple for him at Jerusalem in Judah.'"
Ezra 1:1–2

When President Harry Truman recognized Israel as a nation in 1948, Jews from around the world streamed back to their reestablished nation. Could this have been a case of the Lord moving the president's heart?

Our passage tells us that the Lord moved the heart of Cyrus, a heathen king. The Babylonian conquest of Judah in 586 BCE had led to the deportation of many Jews to Babylon. Judah fell due to its sin; then Cyrus, king of Persia, defeated Babylonia. But in 538 BCE, Cyrus issued a decree permitting the people of Israel to return to their homeland and rebuild the temple. Forty-two thousand returned.

The prophets had predicted that God would bring his people back to their homeland. Jeremiah 32:37 says, "I will bring them back to this place and let them live in safety." Likewise, Isaiah 45:13, "I will raise up Cyrus in my righteousness . . . he will rebuild my city and set my exiles free." Yes, God is the heart mover, the heart stirrer even of great people—even of people who do not yet serve him.

I know a woman whose present employer's business has been sold—now there is a new, bigger showroom, an expansion plan, and a new owner. Soon, the employee will meet with the new owner to discuss her responsibilities, hours, and salary. Her friends are praying that the Lord will move the heart of the new owner to appropriate and considerate treatment of said employee.

One Friday morning, I was with a dozen men at a men's prayer breakfast. At the time, I was serving as professor of evangelism at Nazarene Theological

Seminary. The man sitting next to me, the vice president of a prestigious financial institution in town, leaned over to me and whispered, "I'm on the board of a charitable trust, and we like to give money to Christian causes, especially evangelism. Make an appeal to us for evangelism scholarships." He then made an appointment for me to meet the president of the trust. In the end, between half a million and a million dollars of scholarship money went to scores of students who today are winning many people to Jesus Christ. I was caught off guard in the moment, but God moved the heart of the man next to me at breakfast.

Whom do you need to pray for—that God will move their heart?

When a Christian Disappoints You

To the church of God in Corinth, to those sanctified in Christ Jesus and called to be his holy people, together with all those everywhere who call on the name of our Lord Jesus Christ—their Lord and ours.
1 Corinthians 1:2

Therefore, since we are surrounded by such a great cloud of witnesses, let us throw off everything that hinders and the sin that so easily entangles. And let us run with perseverance the race marked out for us, fixing our eyes on Jesus, the pioneer and perfecter of faith. For the joy set before him he endured the cross, scorning its shame, and sat down at the right hand of the throne of God.
Hebrews 12:1–2

In writing to the Corinthian church, Paul called them "sanctified." "Sanctified" has two basic meanings: to be set aside for sacred service; and to be cleansed or made pure. Yet things were not quite right with the Corinthians—a few verses later, Paul, disappointed with them, appeals "that there be no divisions among you" (1 Corinthians 1:10). We might call their experience "initial sanctification"—that level of separation and cleansing that comes when a person is converted and accepts Christ.

But the Corinthians needed to go deeper and deal with the self-centeredness that remained within them. When Paul dealt with the deeper sanctification of the Thessalonians, he prayed, "May . . . the God of peace sanctify you through and through" (1 Thessalonians 5:23). This is called "entire sanctification." Today, when preachers call people to be sanctified, they usually mean "entire sanctification." That's clearly what the Corinthians needed, and what many Christians need today.

One of the most troubling things a Christian can go through is when a fellow Christian disappoints you by careless lifestyle choices or by turning away from the Lord. This happened to me: A man I regarded as a most godly person, a dear friend, and a person I looked to for leadership, turned away from the Lord. I was distressed, but I knew that Jesus Christ was so real to me that I *would not turn* from the Lord. I fixed my eyes on Jesus and kept running the race.

Over the years, I kept in contact with this friend—he told me I was one of the few who did so. Years later, he came back to the Lord and lived a life of great spiritual power and influence.

If someone has disappointed you, keep your eyes on Jesus—he will never let you down. And instead of giving all your attention to the one who has fallen, why not look at those who are standing true? After all, we are surrounded by a great cloud of witnesses.

The Lord Was with Him

But the LORD was with Joseph in the prison and showed him his faithful love. And the LORD made Joseph a favorite with the prison warden.
Genesis 39:21, NLT

At an early-morning men's prayer meeting, Kim reported that his colon cancer had moved to his lungs and liver. He was considering participating in an experimental drug trial next. But he also reported, "This is the best I've felt in three years. I thank God for everything. Life is good."

My son, Paul, after five major cancer surgeries from ages thirty-three to fifty-five, said in a raspy voice over the phone, "The blessing of God was on me before my cancer. The blessing of God was upon me after they removed my voice box. The blessing of God is upon me today."

When my wife, Nancy, and I entered the saddest period of our lives after our daughter's divorce and ungodly lifestyle, God repeatedly spoke to us through the words of a song by Steve Green called "People Need the Lord": "At the end of broken dreams, he's the open door."

My friend Tim reported from his prison cell that a Christian friend "visited me the very day I watched my mom's funeral video, which was emotional for me. Again, this Christian brother, through God's love and timing, was there to help comfort me. Some people would call that coincidence. I call it no accident. God's love and timing are perfect. Prison can be a lonely place, but with God's love I have been growing as a Christian. Though my freedom is bound by a razor-wire fence, I have never felt more like a free man, and that is because I have been filled with God's love in my heart."

In the very hard places in life, the Lord will be with you. Going through the hard places does not mean that God is gone from your life—he can be present and real in those difficult places.

It's worth noting that in Genesis 39:3, "Potiphar . . . realized that the Lord was with Joseph, giving him success in everything he did" (NLT). Potiphar noticed this when Joseph was a slave, which was certainly an unfair and difficult time in Joseph's life. Later, Genesis 39:21 affirms this: "The Lord was with Joseph in the prison and showed him his faithful love" (NLT).

Likewise, the Lord may be *with you* in every situation. The living presence of the Lord is the most important factor in all of life.

The Two-Second Rule

Finally, brothers and sisters, whatever is true, whatever is noble, whatever is right, whatever is pure, whatever is lovely, whatever is admirable— if anything is excellent or praiseworthy—think about such things.
Philippians 4:8

In nearly nine hundred revivals and thousands of miles traveled, I've had the privilege of staying in many homes and motels. If lodging in a motel, my goal in getting back to my room after an evening of preaching, praying with people seeking God, and counseling others was to relax and unwind.

Over the sixty-five years I have been doing this, our world has seen many changes and advances in technology. At one point in our home life, we had a simple TV that received six or eight channels via antenna. But as I stayed in certain motels, for the first time, I was exposed to cable channels. With the power of the handheld remote, I could visit many channels in a short time. My favorite programs for relaxation were sports and animal shows. At some point, unplanned, I came across cable channels that were sexually suggestive. I am sorry to say that I lingered over some of these programs.

A cloud began to descend over my relationship with the Lord. At one point, I felt like the Lord said to me, *If you keep this up, you are going to lose your soul.*

I immediately asked for forgiveness and cleansing. I knew my lingering was not acceptable and that I must take decisive action. I then established (and still maintain) the Two-Second Rule: if I come across anything sexually suggestive on TV, I must change the channel within two seconds. What a blessed use of the remote now.

The apostle Paul could not have known there would be cable TV, the internet, Facebook, smartphones, or other modern devices that are now capable of video transmission. But he understood that whatever caught your sight or your mind would eventually *capture* your mind, your will, your actions. So, he made a list of qualities—true, noble, right, pure, lovely, admirable—and said, "think about such things." Whatever gets your mind gets you—so for the sake of your soul, choose the pure, the noble, the true. In previous verses (4:6–7), Paul provided the solution to anxiety. It stands to reason that there must be a connection between verse 8 (thought life) and verses 6 and 7 (anxiety-free living).

One of the best choices I ever made was to adopt the Two-Second Rule. Today, I am living and rejoicing in the sweetest, most intimate, uplifting relationship with God I've ever known. Thank you, Lord! Do you need to adopt the Two-Second Rule or a similar strategy?

We Can't Help It!

As for us, we cannot help speaking about what we have seen and heard.
Acts 4:20

Why don't Christians witness more? In the more than 250 Witnessing without Fear seminars I've taught, the two most popular answers are the following:

- People might reject me.
- I don't know what to say.

Both are, in part, fear issues. Yet Peter and John are known for their courage (Acts 4:13).

Still, there is another big reason Christians don't witness: They are not excited enough about what Jesus has done for them personally.

Hobby had been part of a church for years and lived, by most standards, a good and decent life. Yet, at age sixty, he invited Christ into his heart in a personal way. For the first time, God was real to him.

When we went shopping together for light fixtures for the church, he took the salesman aside before I had finished my purchase. Later, when I asked him why, Hobby said, "Oh, I got a chance to tell him what God had done for our family." Hobby simply overflowed. Or, as Peter said, "We cannot help speaking about what we have seen and heard" (4:20).[99]

Scammed!

[The devil] was a murderer from the beginning, not holding to the truth,
for there is no truth in him. When he lies, he speaks his native language,
for he is a liar and the father of lies.
John 8:44b

In a single day, I've received five phone calls:
- "Hello, Grandpa . . . I've been in an accident and I'm at the medical center . . ."
- "A $999 order for an Apple phone has been charged to your account, unless you cancel . . ."
- "I'm calling on behalf of AT&T. Would you like a discount?"
- "A $599 order for an Apple phone has been charged to your account . . ."
- "Would you like your credit card rate reduced?"

If I had responded to any one of these calls, I guarantee they would have tried to take my information or get me to make a commitment of some kind,

---

99. Previously published in *Reflecting God* June–July–August 2010 (Kansas City, MO: WordAction Publishing Co.), 24. Used by permission.

with the end result of stealing my money. Every appeal sounds beneficial to me, but it's all deception—the end result is always to get something beneficial for them, no matter how much it hurts me.

This reminds me of how Satan operates. He makes an appeal, either calling for your sympathy or promising you a benefit. He has no problem with lying to you. In the end, his goal is to steal, kill and destroy (John 10:10). You will be hurt in the end, maybe even left with your bank account drained or your credit card maxed out.

Satan can be vicious—1 Peter 5:8 says, "Your enemy the devil prowls around like a roaring lion looking for someone to devour." Satan can appear good, even godly. But 2 Corinthians 11:14 warns us, "Satan himself masquerades as an angel of light."

So, "be alert and of sober mind" (1 Peter 4:7). Don't let the devil scam you.

Narrowing the Power Gap, Part 1

Very truly I tell you, whoever believes in me will do the works
I have been doing, and they will do even greater things than these,
because I am going to the Father.
John 14:12

If you have followed American politics and cultural life over the last sixty years, you've probably heard about the missile gap, the credibility gap, and the generation gap. I'd like to suggest another term—the values gap. But perhaps the most important gap is the power gap in the church. It is the gap between what Jesus promised and the power displayed in Christian lives.

Jesus promised that those who believed in him would do even greater works than he had done. While there are several ways to interpret his promise, we do know that whereas Jesus' converts were numbered by the scores, Peter saw thousands converted under his preaching, and Paul had thousands come to Christ through the churches he planted.

Jesus gives three keys to unlock this spiritual power:

1. The key of prayer: "I will do whatever you ask in my name" (John 14:13).

2. The key of loving obedience: "If you love me, keep my commands" (14:15).
3. The key of the Holy Spirit's ministry: "I will ask the Father, and he will give you another advocate to help you and be with you forever—the Spirit of truth" (14:16–17).

I wanted to narrow the power gap in my life. Here's one lesson God taught me in the process: When I made a pastoral call in an unchurched home, I met Clark. He was so mature, so big, so muscular that I thought he was the father in the family. He turned out to be the son, and he played on the high school football team. He began coming to church. Soon enough, he found the Lord, was baptized, and joined the church. He lived a glowing life and even began bringing his cousins to church. After school, he joined the military and was stationed in Europe. For six years, I didn't see him—I only made contact through correspondence. When he came home, he brought a German girl named Rhonda with him. She was a translator, fluent in four languages. They wanted to be married.

I asked Clark where he was spiritually. He answered, "I'm doing all right. I'm not doing anything wrong. I'm doing everything I'm supposed to." His words were flat; the glow was gone. Rhonda assured me she was okay because she was a member of the German State Church.

After their marriage, Clark and Rhonda attended Sunday mornings but did nothing else. I called on them, prayed, and preached but got no response. About that time, an evangelist shared with me, "If you really want to reach people, you must surround them with love and prayer." That was the intense channel I needed for the Lord to do a greater work.

One day, I received a phone call about Rhonda being hospitalized. They were expecting a child, but she wasn't in labor—she was having abdominal surgery.

I visited Rhonda in the hospital. She was distraught. The baby was due shortly, but she wouldn't be able to stand labor after the surgery. It looked like she would have an unplanned C-section. I explained that the Lord understood her condition, and suggested we pray.

If the Lord ever visited a hospital room, he visited Rhonda's room that day. She looked up from the prayer and said, "God has come, God has come" in her German accent. As I left the room, she called out, "Thank you, thank you, Pastor Shaver."

Narrowing the Power Gap, Part 2

*Whoever believes in me will do the works I have been doing, and they will
do even greater things than these, because I am going to the Father.*
John 14:12

I continued surrounding Clark and Rhonda with love and prayer. Later, when
I returned to the hospital, I found Rhonda sitting up with a fried chicken
dinner in front of her. She'd had her baby normally and was entirely free of
pain from both her operation and the delivery. We agreed it was a miracle.

The next day, while I was studying in the church office, I heard a noise.
Out in the church lobby, Clark was proudly bragging about his baby daughter.
We rejoiced together. Prayerfully, I threw another lasso of love around him
and asked, "Clark, how are you doing spiritually?"

He answered, "God's not real like he used to be."

In that moment, the Holy Spirit gave me the gift of discernment. I knew
which sin had broken Clark's relationship with God. I said, "Clark, I know
what your sin is, but if I ever tell you, you'll be mad at me."

He said, "No, I won't, Pastor Shaver. You're my friend, so you can tell
me." So I named his sin.

Suddenly, the powerful football player burst into tears. He said, "I've
been so bad, I've been afraid to pray."

We both headed to the altar in the sanctuary. There, Clark poured out
his heart and got back to God. Then he jumped to his feet, emphatically
pumped his fist in the air, and said, "Now I believe I'm a real Christian!"

Then a look of surprise came over his face. He said, "But I've got to tithe
. . . but I can't afford to tithe . . . but I've got to tithe." Back and forth he
argued with himself. In the end, despite the house payments, car payments,
and new baby, Clark joyfully resolved to start tithing. When I asked if he was
going to tell his wife what had happened to him, he went beyond that and
said, "I've got to tell Mom and Dad." His parents also attended the church.

With that, he rushed out of the church, got into his little black sports car,
and sped off on his mission.

Soon I got another phone call. One of the ladies at church had talked to
Rhonda, who had asked, "What has happened to my husband? He came to
see me last night, but my room was crowded with people, and we didn't get a
good chance to talk. But he acts different, he talks different."

When I heard this, I returned to Rhonda's room and told her, "Clark has found the Lord."

Rhonda began to cry, pulled the sheet over her face, and said, "Oh, I've held back."

The next Sunday, Clark, Rhonda, and the baby were all in church. That morning, Rhonda knelt at the altar for the first time and accepted Jesus Christ.

A few weeks later, Rhonda joined the church by profession of faith, and Clark reaffirmed his broken membership vows. They went on to live lives of spiritual service and power.

Rhonda found Christ; Clark got the glow back; and I learned that, by surrounding others with love and prayer, I could narrow the power gap.

JULY 9   190

Where Does My Help Come From?

I lift up my eyes to the mountains—where does my help come from?
My help comes from the LORD, the Maker of heaven and earth.
Psalm 121:1–2

Truly my soul finds rest in God; my salvation comes from him. Truly he is
my rock and my salvation; he is my fortress, I will never be shaken.
Psalm 62:1–2

When Saul was on a rampage, intent on murdering David—

When Israel was fleeing Egypt, came to the Red Sea, and realized that Pharaoh's army was pursuing them—

When Joshua was trying to lead Israel into the promised land and faced the walled and fortified city of Jericho—

When Paul was imprisoned for preaching Jesus—

—they all found their help in the Lord.

When Israel rejected Joshua and Caleb's report on the promised land, God's judgment fell on the ten other spies who had discouraged Israel from entering the land. After the judgment, Israel decided to reenter the promised land and possess it, but Moses warned, "Do not go up, because the LORD is not with you. You will be defeated" (Numbers 14:42). Sure enough, in their presumption, the Israelites were defeated (vv. 44–45).

Because of choices made by others, I am a citizen of the United States, which has a reputation for being the most advanced nation in the history of the world. We have huge technical skills, an outstanding medical system, tremendous financial strength, great educational opportunities, and opportunities for scientific advancement. Yet, at the time I wrote this, a deadly coronavirus that started in December 2019 spread across the world. Schools closed, businesses shut down, people lost jobs, the stock market plummeted, and most of the world's population experienced lockdowns and quarantines.

I have an Apple iPhone. By simply addressing the phone with the words, "Hey, Siri," I can get answers to all kinds of questions. So far, she has told me today's temperature; tomorrow's weather; when the Major League Baseball season starts; the best route from Naples, Florida, back to Kansas City; and even how to spell "coronavirus." She is so smart that I decided to ask her, "Hey, Siri, what is the cure for the coronavirus?"

She answered that, at present, "there is no cure for the coronavirus."

God, in his mercy, granted some excellent scientists the skill to develop a vaccine that began to be distributed in early 2021, and maybe a more definitive cure or treatment is on the horizon. But above all else, we must remember that, however smart or capable we think we are, there are problems we can't control or solve—we must not presume we can do it on our own.

Then "where does my help come from? My help comes from the Lord." Indeed, as the psalmist writes, "Truly he is my rock and my salvation; he is my fortress, I will never be shaken."

Moses Fled to Midian

Looking this way and that and seeing no one,
he killed the Egyptian and hid him in the sand.
Exodus 2:12

With his spear, he had committed twelve murders. But now Gikita, a member of the Huaorani tribe of Ecuador, was not happy with his past. He had not done well. Now that he knew God, there were tears in his eyes.

In the past, his wrath had caused him to lead an attack on five missionaries on Palm Beach. Nate Saint had been killed in the attack. But now, Nate's

sister, Rachel, heard the powerful testimony—Gikita was leading other Huaorani people to Christ.

This was not the first time God caused "human wrath . . . to praise" him
(Psalm 76:10, NRSV). Moses, who had killed an Egyptian, met God in Mid-
ian. In Egypt, he had tried to correct injustice by taking the law into his own
hands. But after his encounter with the holy God, Moses matured for forty
years in a strange land. By the time God was finished with him, Moses would
do far more than deliver one Hebrew from one Egyptian by the force of his
own hand—now, he would deliver a whole nation from bondage by the force
of God's hand working through him.

Don't you see? God wants to take your past defeats, sins—yes, even your
wrath—and produce a new creation who will bring praise to him.[100]

It Fits

All the curtains were the same size—twenty-eight cubits long and
four cubits wide. They joined five of the curtains together and did the same
with the other five. Then they made loops of blue material along the edge
of the end curtain in one set, and the same was done with the end curtain
in the other set. They also made fifty loops on one curtain and fifty loops
on the end curtain of the other set, with the loops opposite each other.
Then they made fifty gold clasps and used them to fasten the two
sets of curtains together so that the tabernacle was a unit.
Exodus 36:9–13

What are the chances you could make curtains forty-two feet long and six
feet wide, put fifty loops on each, attach loop to loop with fifty gold clasps,
and have it *all fit*? It's as amazing as God calling twelve men by name out of an
adult male population of over six hundred thousand to help with the census
count (see Numbers 1:5–7).

Why specify such intricate construction details? A holy God who had
given ten holy commandments now gives instructions for a holy tabernacle

---

100. Previously published in *Come Ye Apart* July–August–September 1964 (Kansas
City, MO: Nazarene Publishing House), 13. Used by permission. (This publication became
Reflecting God.)

built by holy workers. Yes, God even handpicked the workers: "The Lord has chosen Bezalel . . . and he has filled him with the Spirit of God, with wisdom, with understanding, with knowledge and with all kinds of skills" (Exodus 35:30–31).

As Moses sets up the tabernacle, the text reports, "Moses did everything just as the Lord commanded him" (40:16). Step by step, obedience is emphasized, and the phrase "as the Lord commanded him" appears in Exodus 40:19, 21, 23, and 25.

We see Moses and the workers' implicit obedience to the explicit instructions of God, in which even the construction details are important. Even the fifty loops and the fifty clasps—it all fits.

Our pastor once gave the following illustration: "Have you ever tried to button up a sweater or shirt after you got the first button in the wrong buttonhole? By the time you get to the last button, you realize there's no place for the last button—it doesn't fit." He emphasized that our right relationship with Jesus Christ is the foundation for all elements of life to fit in their right place. As the pastor was still speaking, a young woman who was new to our church leaned over to me and said, "I think I've got a button that doesn't fit." The young woman and her husband later sought Christ.

Imagine—if God could lead workers to construct curtains so that fifty loops of "curtain one" met perfectly with fifty loops of "curtain two," and they were perfectly held together with fifty gold clasps—what could he do with your life yielded to him? Only he can make it fit.

Miracles in the Middle of Evil

Ahab son of Omri did more evil in the eyes of the LORD than any of those before him.
1 Kings 16:30

Then the word of the LORD came to Elijah: "Leave here, turn eastward and hide in the Kerith Ravine, east of the Jordan. You will drink from the brook, and I have directed the ravens to supply you with food there."
1 Kings 17:2–4

Evil Nazi forces burst into the Dutch home and arrested the entire family. Their crime? They had been hiding Jews in the secret panels of their house to save them from persecution.

In the concentration camp, Corrie ten Boom soon learned her father had died in his cell. She later saw her sister Betsie die. Corrie alone survived. Could there be any miracle in the middle of such evil?

Such evil had happened before—Ahab holds the record as Israel's most evil king. In response to the evil, God sent his representative Elijah to pronounce a judgment of an extended drought. In the middle of the evil, the drought, and the suffering, God performed a miracle: He preserved his prophet and sent him to the Kerith Ravine, where he could drink from the brook. God directed ravens to feed Elijah morning and evening.

Months passed, and there was no rain. The brook dried up, and God acted again for Elijah by sending him to a widow in Zarephath. When Elijah asked the widow for a little water and bread, she explained that she had only enough flour and oil to make a final meal for herself and her son—after that, they would starve to death. Elijah assured her the flour would not be used up and the oil would not run dry until rain returned. Sure enough, there was food every day for Elijah and the widow's family—another miracle.

When the widow's son later sickened and died, Elijah prayed over the boy, and God brought him back to life. A miracle! The key in Elijah's life was, "So he did what the LORD had told him" (17:5). Yes, even in the midst of evil and judgment, God can make special interventions for those who belong to him.

The treatment of Corrie and her sister Betsie in the Nazi prison camp would make you weep. And yet, even there, they saw miracles. Betsie was ill, and Corrie gave her doses from a small bottle of liquid vitamins every day. But others in the camp were ill too. Soon, a dozen women a day were taking it; soon, twenty-five. And yet, every time Corrie tilted the bottle, another drop came out. She said it was like the widow of Zarephath.[101]

Even in the midst of their imprisonment, Corrie and Betsie thanked the Lord for all things. At one point, they couldn't understand why the guards had stopped coming into their room—they soon learned it was because their bunk and the room were infested with fleas. And so, they thanked God even for the fleas.

---

101. Corrie ten Boom, Elizabeth Sherrill, and John L. Sherrill, *The Hiding Place* (Washington, CT: Chosen Books, 1971), 184.

The ten Boom sisters learned there was no pit so deep but that God was there. Before she died in prison, Betsie had a vision of a beautiful home where they would minister to suffering people after the war. She told Corrie, "We must tell them [people] what we learned."[102]

Miraculously, Corrie was later released from the concentration camp due to a clerical error. Back in Holland, the wealthy Mrs. de Haan offered her home to Corrie as a refuge for camp survivors.

Upon hearing the offer, Corrie immediately began to describe the home's features. "You've been here then!"[103] Mrs. de Haan said with surprise.

Corrie had not been there—but she knew from Betsie's vision what it looked like. The fifty-four-room home was soon serving others.

Later, at a church service in Munich, Corrie met one of her former prison guards. Knowing that she could not do so in her own power, she asked Jesus to help her forgive him. Corrie later testified that it was as if a current passed through her hand to him, and love sprang into her heart for the man who had formerly persecuted her and her family.[104]

Corrie began to tell people all that God had done. By age eighty, she had worked and taught in sixty-one countries.[105] Her 1971 book *The Hiding Place* and its subsequent film adaptation have spread the power of forgiveness to millions more.

In Corrie ten Boom's story, in Elijah's story, in the story of God—we see miracles in the middle of evil.

Positives from Alzheimer's

Consider it pure joy, my brothers and sisters, whenever you face trials of many kinds, because you know that the testing of your faith produces perseverance. Let perseverance finish its work so that you may be mature and complete, not lacking anything.
James 1:2–4

---

102. Ten Boom, Sherrill, and Sherrill, *The Hiding Place*, 211.
103. Ten Boom, Sherrill, and Sherrill, *The Hiding Place*, 213.
104. Ten Boom, Sherrill, and Sherrill, *The Hiding Place*, 215.
105. Ten Boom, Sherrill, and Sherrill, *The Hiding Place*, 219.

One day, my wife, Nancy, and I had lunch together. Then, about an hour later, she asked me, "Do you want me to fix your lunch?" Sadly, she couldn't remember we'd already eaten.

More challenges began to arise. She came home and told me, "Honey, I left my groceries in the shopping cart at the store without paying for them. I couldn't find my credit card." Five days later, we found the credit card in our home.

My wife has been suffering from Alzheimer's for almost a decade now. Despite difficulties we've experienced, we've also found some positive experiences in managing this disease.

James speaks of trials. Some of our trials may be persecution because of our faith; others may simply be challenges that come with our minds or bodies wearing out. Either way, the result can be trials that test our faith, which produces perseverance, which produces maturity. But it's not automatic—we decide. James says, "Let perseverance finish its work."

I've considered my tendency to impatience to be one of the greatest weaknesses of my Christian life. Guess what? Many Alzheimer's-produced events in our family are teaching me a patience I never knew before. I believe I'm mellowing.

Here are some thoughts that have helped me:

1. Her words or actions are coming from a damaged mind.
2. She does not intend to be hurtful.
3. We talk freely about her condition and are able to laugh at some things together.
4. I'm having the privilege of living out my marriage vow "in sickness and in health, for better or for worse."

When Nancy first became ill with Alzheimer's, she was depressed, agitated, anxious, and angry (which was totally unlike her usual demeanor). As I tried to guide her, she curtly said, "You're trying to micromanage me."

I said, "Yes, I am, because you're facing challenges that need special help."

We began to work together to handle her disease. Through wonderful doctors, Alzheimer's Association sharing groups, medicine, people's prayers, and God's grace, things have changed for the better. The disease hasn't improved—it's still progressing—but our response to it has.

About a year and a half ago, Nancy and I were lying in bed, holding hands and just talking. Nancy said, "I think I'm the happiest I've ever been. And I love you more than ever!"

Wow! I'm taking that to the bank. We are having some of the sweetest days of our marriage. I believe the trials are making me a better Christian.

What trials are you facing?

Two Men and the One Holy Spirit

❖

When Simon saw that the Spirit was given at the laying on of the apostles'
hands, he offered them money and said, "Give me also this ability so that
everyone on whom I lay my hands may receive the Holy Spirit."
Acts 8:18–19

The Spirit told Philip, "Go to that chariot and stay near it."
Acts 8:29

"I don't go to church because there are too many hypocrites there" is a common excuse in today's society. Guess what? It's true—there are hypocrites in
the church. The Bible acknowledges this; in fact, the Bible is so open about
this that it even describes some of the hypocrites, like Simon. However,
it's important to remember that our responsibility toward hypocrites is not
avoidance of the church, but *discernment* about those in the church.

In Acts 8:9–40 (which I suggest you read), two men are featured. Both
are interested in the Holy Spirit. When you read the Acts account, you can
tell who is genuine and who is phony. Cast your lot with the genuine.

This passage is filled with important lessons:

- "Simon himself believed and was baptized" (8:13). He may have believed certain facts about Jesus, but he did not truly commit to him.
  Baptism cannot save you.
- When Simon saw the apostles giving the Spirit to new believers, he offered money to buy that power. Peter rebuked Simon and told him his
  heart was not right with God. He told Simon to repent of wickedness,
  for he was "full of bitterness and captive to sin" (8:21–23).
- Simon then asked for prayer to protect him from judgment (8:24). Motive is important to God, and it is clear that Simon wanted the Spirit
  for his personal glory; he wanted to use the Spirit.
- Philip is a godly lay leader, and one of those elected to the first local
  church board. The apostles had said to choose only those who were
  "known to be full of the Spirit and wisdom" (Acts 6:3, 5). This passage
  makes a distinction between believers who are filled with the Spirit, and believers who aren't—only "Spirit-filled" Christians could be
  elected to this position.

- Philip was full of the Spirit and led by the Spirit (8:29). The Spirit used him.
- Philip led the Ethiopian to a saving faith in Christ (8:38). His personal witness was Spirit-led.
- Philip relied on the power of the Spirit in his life to help others and to glorify God.

Both Simon and Philip were interested in the Holy Spirit. One was right; one was wrong. Both left a legacy.

In Simon's story, we see the sin of simony—paying money to receive appointment to a powerful religious position.

Philip led the Ethiopian to Christ. This man was secretary of the treasury to the queen of Ethiopia (8:27), and he took Christianity back to Ethiopia. Nineteen hundred years later, at the 1966 World Congress of Evangelism in Berlin, Germany, Emperor Haile Selassie of Ethiopia gave the opening address and acknowledged Jesus Christ as his Savior.

What is your interest in the Holy Spirit? What legacy will you leave?

The Ethiopian

He met an Ethiopian eunuch, an important official in charge of
all the treasury of the Kandake (which means "queen of the Ethiopians").
This man had gone to Jerusalem to worship.
Acts 8:27

Does this mean what I think it means?

Yes, "eunuch" means a physically castrated man.

These men often served as keepers of harems, and often rose to high state positions. Because this Ethiopian was a eunuch, he would never know the joys of marriage; would never have children or grandchildren. He may have been a slave. His physical condition was imposed upon him; it was not his choice. Though he had gone to the Jewish temple, he could never be a full-fledged member of Judaism. What a chance to be bitter.

It was the same with Lisa—she had gone through a very messy divorce in which her husband left her with one chair and two children. She visited church on Sunday, and within a week, the church had delivered furniture—

she said it was even color-coordinated. Lisa said, "God has been so kind. I can feel his arms around me. Would I have ordered it? No—but God is using it."

Both Lisa and the Ethiopian made a choice: instead of getting bitter, they would get better.

The Ethiopian had another challenge. He was secretary of the treasury to the queen of Ethiopia, meaning he handled more money than anyone else in the nation. He could have thought, "I have arrived," and become proud. He could have identified with a local businessman who was the president of his own company and said, "I was so busy making a living, I didn't have time to have a life." Both the businessman and the Ethiopian decided pride and position were not enough; they would seek God.

The Ethiopian had been searching—he had traveled from Ethiopia, to Jerusalem, to the Jewish temple to worship. On his way home, he parked his chariot in the Gaza Strip and was reading his Old Testament. Still, his heart was not satisfied.

But God was interested in the Ethiopian. God sent his angel to the Spirit-filled layman, Philip, to go down the desert road from Jerusalem to Gaza. Then the Spirit of God told Philip, "Go to that chariot and stay near it" (Acts 8:29).

The Ethiopian and Philip got into a conversation. When Philip asked the Ethiopian if he understood the passage he was reading, he answered, "How can I . . . unless someone explains it to me?" (8:31) His answer clearly highlights the need for a witness.

Philip led the Ethiopian to Christ and baptized him. The newly converted man rejoiced as he journeyed back to Ethiopia, where he would spread the Christian message.

Neither bitterness nor pride could stop the Ethiopian—nor should it stop you.

Never Doubt in the Dark What God Has Told You in the Light

And surely I am with you always, to the very end of the age.
Matthew 28:20

Marsha had had a big argument with her fiancé. She was crying as she drove through town to get away from it all. Then she remembered a verse that had stood out to her in her Sunday school class: "Do not grieve, for the joy of the LORD is your strength" (Nehemiah 8:10). Marsha composed herself and drove home.

We will all face dark places in life. As you seek to face such challenges with wisdom, remember what God has told you, shown you, led you to, in your brightest moments with him. The greatest enduring truth to sustain us is the resurrected Jesus Christ's promise to his disciples: "I am with you always." This is more than a statement of fact—he promises his personal presence to all who follow him.

However dark the hour, all your past victories with and by the Lord can be your stepping stones to new victories. Other believers' victories can also encourage you. As Joshua faced one of the greatest challenges of his life—leading two million Israelites across the Jordan River into the promised land—the Lord made him a promise: "As I was with Moses, so I will be with you; I will never leave you nor forsake you" (Joshua 1:5).

What are the moments in which God showed you the light? Perhaps they include some of the following:

- When God saved you and gave you a new life (2 Corinthians 5:17)
- When God sanctified you through and through and gave you a pure heart (1 Thessalonians 5:23)
- When God delivered you from deep financial need (Philippians 4:19)
- When God guided you as you made a big decision (Psalm 32:8)
- When God worked out a troubling relationship (Philippians 4:2)

Some of my darkest times have been when my dad cut me off financially because I'd become a Christian; when a car T-boned us as we drove through an intersection with a green light; when our daughter left her husband and the Lord; when I received negative votes on a recall as the pastor of a church; when my wife developed Alzheimer's; and when my son reported a fifth cancer surgery, this time to remove his voice box. Yet, in every case, we drew on the resources God had given us when he spoke to us in the light. As a result, we came through with his new victory.

When our son said that his voice box would be removed, we went to Philippians 4:6–7. Right away, the peace of God descended on me in Mississippi; on my wife, Nancy, in Leawood, Kansas; and on our son in Muncie, Indiana. And it never left—we are all living in the blessing today.

Remember what God has told you in the light!

To Those Who Obey Him

❖

We are witnesses of these things, and so is the Holy Spirit,
whom God has given to those who obey him.
Acts 5:32

Believers may experience as much depth in the Christian life as they desire. Some may live at a level of five minutes of prayer daily: "Oh God, bless my children and make this a pleasant day."

There are others who go to deep levels with God. The mother of Madame Chiang Kai-shek consistently spent so much time with the Lord that if you asked for her advice, she would say, "You must wait until tomorrow so that I can ask my Master all about it and get his guidance."[106]

The 120 followers of Jesus joined in constant prayer for forty days, and on the day of Pentecost, they were all filled with the Holy Spirit (Acts 1:3, 15; 2:4). As a result, a powerful spiritual movement surged through Jerusalem. Many more believed in the Lord, and many were healed. The Jewish authorities, filled with jealousy, arrested and jailed the disciples.

The next day, the disciples were called before the Sanhedrin, and the high priest commanded them to stop teaching about Jesus. Peter responded, "We must obey God rather than human beings!" (Acts 5:29). Once again, he spoke Jesus to the authorities.

Peter then added, "We are witnesses of these things, and so is the Holy Spirit, whom God has given to those who obey him" (5:32).

The disciples were eyewitnesses to the resurrected Jesus and numerous other evidences. Beyond that, God the Father was witnessing to these truths by the activity of the Holy Spirit—healings, miracles, conversions. It was as Peter had previously preached: "I will pour out my Spirit in those days . . . I will show wonders in the heavens above and signs on the earth below" (Acts 2:18–19).

Please note in 5:32 that this Holy Spirit is only given to those who obey him. Someone who has received Christ, been born of the Spirit, and is cur-

---

106. Mrs. Charles E. Cowman, *Streams in the Desert: 366 Daily Devotional Readings* (Grand Rapids: Zondervan, 1996), 169.

rently following Jesus Christ and obeying him is the one who may receive the Holy Spirit in fullness.

My friend Chad had accepted Christ but was living a surface-level, sloppy Christian life. When he finally awakened to his condition, he renewed his relationship with Christ and began walking in obedience. Then he understood his need for the Spirit's deeper work—cleansing his inner motives, sanctifying his heart, and filling him with the Spirit. On a specific day, he was clearly filled with the Holy Spirit.

Have you received Christ? Are you living in a pattern of obedience? Then grasp your privilege to become a Spirit-filled Christian (5:32)!

An Enlarged Heart

And I pray that you, being rooted and established in love,
may have power, together with all the Lord's holy people, to grasp
how wide and long and high and deep is the love of Christ.
Ephesians 3:17–18

If a Christian has been filled with the Spirit, and that spiritual work has produced sanctification—or as Peter puts it, "the sanctifying work of the Spirit" (1 Peter 1:2)—what next? We understand that the Spirit's work is sometimes described as purification. Note Acts 15:8–9: "God, who knows the heart, showed that he accepted them by giving the Holy Spirit to them, just as he did to us. He did not discriminate between us and them, for he purified their hearts by faith." If I'm filled with the Spirit, and I have been sanctified, and my heart has been purified, where is the room for spiritual growth?

Go back to the Ephesians passage for the answer—see that the grasping of the extensive love of Christ is "together with all the Lord's holy people." In my connection with more and more of the Lord's holy people, my heart is enlarged, and my love capacity is expanded.

I particularly think of certain holy people—like Peter, who spent hours telling me how I could know Christ. Like Ralph and Bernice, who showed up at my college dorm with a picnic lunch and strong encouragement to keep following Jesus. Like Clyde, who drove me twenty-six miles home after church when I was a student and didn't have a car. Like Ralph and Mabel, who invited me to dinner when I was the new kid on the block. Like Bengt, who urged his Baptist church to send me funds to help put me through seminary. Like Bill, who prays for my wife and me every day. Like Juanita, who keeps in touch with the Lord so completely and lets me in on her secrets. Like Phil and Joy, who orchestrated the details of my retirement from teaching the same Sunday school class for forty-five years, so that I felt loved. Like Alan and Martha, who keep thanking me for pointing them to Jesus as they face their own physical challenges and surgeries. Like my wife, Nancy, who says, "I love you more than ever." And so many more.

All these holy people keep rubbing off on me—through them, I know the love of Christ deeper than ever. So, I am growing. Think about some of God's holy people you know; name them; and let it grow you.

Once you have been filled with the Spirit of God, sanctified, and purified, that is not the end—rather, it's the beginning of tremendous growth in grace. You will discover God polishing your character and personality.

On that September 2, when God's Spirit filled and sanctified my twenty-one-year-old heart, my whole heart was made 100% pure and filled with God. However, it was a small heart. Now, by rubbing shoulders with many saints and going through heartbreak, pain, and sorrow, something amazing is happening. As God piles more love on me through his saints and heals my sorrow, I notice that he keeps stretching my heart. So today, I have an enlarged heart.

The Spirit's fullness and purity of heart does not cease growth in grace; it increases it. So join me in the enlarged-heart club.

Victory by the Spirit

The sting of death is sin, and the power of sin is the law. But thanks be to God! He gives us the victory through our Lord Jesus Christ.
1 Corinthians 15:56–57

How excited do you get when your favorite team gains the victory? When I think of breathtaking sports victories, I remember how excited Americans were when the USA beat Russia in hockey at the 1980 Winter Olympics in Lake Placid, New York.

Would you get that excited about experiencing victory over sin? God wants you to have full victory, and the Holy Spirit is his special agent who brings you that victory.

Consider these promises:

- "... Our great God and Savior, Jesus Christ, who gave himself for us to redeem us from all wickedness and to purify for himself a people that are his very own, eager to do what is good" (Titus 2:13–14).
- "It is God's will that you should be sanctified ... For God did not call us to be impure, but to live a holy life. Therefore, anyone who rejects this instruction does not reject a human being but God, the very God who gives you his Holy Spirit" (1 Thessalonians 4:3, 7–8).
- "I have been crucified with Christ and I no longer live, but Christ lives in me. The life I now live in the body, I live by faith in the Son of God, who loved me and gave himself for me" (Galatians 2:20).
- "He [Christ] gave me the priestly duty of proclaiming the gospel of God, so that the Gentiles might become an offering acceptable to God, sanctified by the Holy Spirit" (Romans 15:16).
- "I am sending you to them [Gentiles] to open their eyes and turn them from darkness to light, and from the power of Satan to God, so that they may receive forgiveness of sins and a place among those who are sanctified by faith in me" (Acts 26:17–18).

Here is a present-day testimony from Maridel:

My mother died of pancreatic cancer in 2003. She asked me to promise her I would meet her in heaven. I did, and I meant it. I was agnostic, but I began to search. I went to Christian bookstores and bought and read Lee Strobel's books. I asked people if they knew anyone who had a gone-to-heaven experience and returned. As heaven became more real to me, I believed there had to be a God to run it. I asked God to allow me to feel his presence. I found myself in a church in Phoenix. Communion was being served, and I felt I was not worthy to take it. The presence of God came over me, and I wept profusely as I accepted the Lord. I knew I must go deeper. I sought entire sanctification. On a November day in 2003, I died to myself, and God filled me with his Spirit. I can honestly say I have never had a lack of joy or peace since. And not one moment of doubt. What a move from agnosticism to positive, sanctifying faith![107]

May the Holy Spirit produce God's victory in you.

---

107. Previously published in *The Good News: The Chic Shaver Center for Evangelism Newsletter* (March 2016).

Walking after the Spirit, Part 1

*. . . because through Christ Jesus the law of the Spirit who
gives life has set you free from the law of sin and death.*
Romans 8:2

*. . . that the righteousness of the law might be fulfilled in us,
who walk not after the flesh, but after the Spirit.*
Romans 8:4, KJV

In evident frustration someone said to me, "Well, you can't be a walking saint, can you?"

As I thought about it, I concluded, "Yes, you can. As a matter of fact, that's the only kind of saint you can be—a walking saint—for Romans 8:4 says that the righteousness of the law is fulfilled in us who walk not after the flesh but after the Spirit."

A walk is movement one step at a time. Some are confused when they think of the Christian life as a walk—they cannot see the place for a second crisis of grace. However, two crisis experiences are assumed and implied in Romans 8. In verse 1, Paul speaks of freedom from the condemnation that comes with wrongdoing—that is, the peace that comes with justification (5:1).

But Paul also speaks of a second crisis: "For the law of the Spirit of life in Christ Jesus hath made me free from the law of sin and death" (8:2, KJV). Here Paul describes a deliverance from the *being* of sin. How was he delivered? The answer is all at once, by a crisis of grace, as the Greek tense here implies. Paul uses the same word for "make free" here as he does in 6:18 and 22 (KJV): "Being then made free from sin, ye became the servants of righteousness"; and, "But now being made free from sin, and become servants to God, ye have your fruit unto holiness, and the end everlasting life."

Our walk with God is like many of our human relationships. Take the marriage relationship. There is the time of engagement when one person proposes—that is quite a crisis—and the other says, "I will." Then, at the altar of marriage, in complete consecration to each other, the two pronounce, "I do."

One day, after my wife and I had been married for about five years, she said to me, "Honey, do you love me?"

Rather surprised that she should ask, I answered, "Of course. I told you I loved you when we got married. Do I need to tell you again?"

Didn't she ask a ridiculous question? You're thinking *I'm* the ridiculous one—and, of course, you're right. We all realize that in a meaningful and successful marriage, we must day by day and moment by moment abide in each other's love. Mere absence of wrongdoing is not enough—unless I actively indicate my continued love and trust every day, the relationship is hurt. Far too many Christians make the mistake of thinking that once they have received the crisis experience of entire sanctification, they have arrived spiritually. But entire sanctification is just the beginning of a continuing, day-by-day relationship with God. Holiness is not the end but the beginning of what God wants us to be.[108]

Walking after the Spirit, Part 2

That the righteousness of the law might be fulfilled in us,
who walk not after the flesh, but after the Spirit.
Romans 8:4, KJV

And do not grieve the Holy Spirit of God,
with whom you were sealed for the day of redemption.
Ephesians 4:30

Sanctification is not only, or even primarily, an experience to be obtained but a relationship to be continued. It is dangerous to talk about "keeping" or "holding onto" your experience. There's a sense in which these terms are permissible—yet they're not fully accurate. We *keep* an *experience*, but we *walk* with a *person*—with God. Paul wants us not only to know a precise time when we were made "free from the law of sin and death" (Romans 8:2) but also to presently and habitually walk after the Spirit, as the present tense of the verb suggests (8:4).

Our relationship with God must be vital day by day. We must so completely rest in him that we will be kept sweet in every trying situation. Being

---

108. Previously published in Charles "Chic" Shaver, *Keeping Spiritual Victory* (Kansas City, MO: Beacon Hill Press of Kansas City, 1972), 5, 8–10.

sanctified is not something mechanical that is switched on—it means entering into a dynamic relationship with God that must be continual. Keeping our relationship with God as a moment-by-moment affair is pictured in Jesus's parable of the vine and branches in John 15:1–8 (KJV): "Abide in me, and I in you. As the branch cannot bear fruit of itself, except it abide in the vine; no more can ye, except ye abide in me" (v. 4).

Relationships are sensitive; they can be easily damaged. Mere neglect is sufficient to ruin a beautiful friendship. But lack of trust can ruin our relationship with God, for this reflects on both his willingness and his ability to help us. "And grieve not the holy Spirit of God, whereby ye are sealed unto the day of redemption" (Ephesians 4:30, KJV); and "do not quench the Spirit" (1 Thessalonians 5:19), "that the righteousness of the law might be fulfilled in us, who walk not after the flesh, but after the Spirit" (Romans 8:4, KJV).

Keep in Step

Those who belong to Christ Jesus have crucified the flesh with its passions and desires. Since we live by the Spirit, let us keep in step with the Spirit.
Galatians 5:24–25

A self-propelled, walk-behind mower is the means of my neatly cut lawn. The procedure is simple: fill the tank with gas, turn on the ignition, adjust the lever that regulates gas supply and motor speed, adjust the walking speed, compress the activation control—and you're mowing. The gas supplies the power, and I do the walking.

When I mow along the edging in front of our evergreen shrubs, protruding branches sometimes catch the gas control lever and exert enough pressure to turn the gas supply off. Then the motor turns off, and the mower stops. When this happens, I have to stop walking.

In the realm of the Spirit-filled life, there must be a *continual* leaning on, depending on, and listening to the Holy Spirit. He is the source of spiritual power, and his supply is constant as long as we keep in step with him. Get out of step, break your connection, and difficulty arises. There is a moment in time when you are filled with the Spirit, but a continuous dependence on and rest in the Spirit is required for continuous victory.

The Scripture emphasizes this truth many ways. Colossians 1:22–23 says, "But now he has reconciled you by Christ's physical body through death to present you holy in his sight, without blemish and free from accusation—if you continue in your faith." Note the key word: "continue."

Consider the analogy of the vine and branches in John 15:5–6: "I am the vine; you are the branches. If you remain in me and I in you, you will bear much fruit; apart from me you can do nothing. If you do not remain in me, you are like a branch that is thrown away and withers: such branches are picked up, thrown into the fire and burned."

In Acts 2:4, the disciples were filled with the Spirit at a moment in time. When these same disciples were under pressure and threatened, they prayed and experienced a fresh infilling of the Spirit to give them boldness (Acts 4:31). Later, in Paul's admonition to Christians in Ephesians 5:18—"Be filled with the Spirit"—he uses the present tense, meaning "*Keep* filled with the Spirit."

Some may wonder if you have been sanctified, your heart has been made pure, and you are filled with the Spirit, is there any room for growth? Oh yes, even more! Please notice these two glasses, and assume they are both filled with water.

Both glasses are all the way full—yet the larger glass holds more water. Does it make sense to say that a younger Christian can be full of the Spirit of God? Yes—but then imagine that through trials, challenges, and difficulties, their heart is stretched. Their heart is still all the way full, but their capacity is so much bigger—they have grown.

Hudson Taylor, the great British missionary who founded the China Inland Mission in 1865, discovered and experienced the habit of continuous dependence on God. He saw this principle illustrated in John 6:35, which he paraphrased this way: "He who is habitually coming to me shall by no means hunger, and he who is believing on me shall by no means thirst."[109] Or, put another way—keep in step with the Spirit.

She Was Only Twelve

But in a great house there are not only vessels of gold and silver, but also of wood and clay, some for honor and some for dishonor. Therefore if anyone cleanses himself from the latter, he will be a vessel for honor, sanctified and useful for the Master, prepared for every good work.
2 Timothy 2:20–21, NKJV

A missionary called to report on new ministries that had been founded in five new cities in five different countries—all of which had been part of the former Soviet Union. And then he told me about his daughter Bekah.

Bekah has always been spiritually sensitive. When she was three, as the family watched a showing of the *Jesus Film* in Houston, she saw the scenes of Jesus's baptism. When she heard the Father speak over Jesus, "This is my beloved Son," she asked, "Jesus is God, right? How come God spoke?" She was already trying to understand the Trinity.

At age four, Bekah and her mom began discussing sin. Upon Bekah's request, her mom pulled their truck over, they prayed together, and Bekah accepted Jesus. Her parents noticed immediate changes in her demeanor—notably, her former habit of negative stubbornness changed to a determination to follow Jesus.

A while back, in her daily devotions, Bekah read about the rich man who asked Jesus what he must do to inherit eternal life. She understood Jesus's response to be, "You must give me everything." She thought she heard a whisper: *You need to give me all.*

Shortly afterward, Bekah expressed her need to be sanctified. She, her mom, and her dad all got on their knees and prayed, and God sanctified Bekah. Later, her dad asked, "What made you sense this need?"

---

109. Dr. and Mrs. Howard Taylor, *Hudson Taylor's Spiritual Secret* (Chicago: Moody Press, n.d.), 182.

Bekah answered, "I want my heart to be ready for whatever God calls me to."

Yes, "a vessel for honor, sanctified and useful for the Master, prepared for every good work"—and she was only twelve.

Preach by the Spirit, Listen by the Spirit

*All of them were filled with the Holy Spirit and began to
speak in other tongues as the Spirit enabled them.*
Acts 2:4

*Then Peter stood up with the Eleven, raised his voice
and addressed the crowd.*
Acts 2:14a

*When the people heard this, they were cut to the heart and said
to Peter and the other apostles, "Brothers, what shall we do?"*
Acts 2:37

It was a monumental day—the Spirit of God poured out on 120 followers of Jesus. Miraculous events accompanied the Spirit's presence—a sound like violent wind, symbolizing *power*; tongues of fire, symbolizing *purity*; people breaking out into languages, symbolizing *proclamation*. The 120 declared the wonders of God; people of many nations heard these testimonies in their native languages; and, in this Spirit-anointed atmosphere, Peter preached. The crowd listened and, convicted by the same Spirit, asked, "What shall we do?"

And this is still happening today. Here is Nancy's report from when she finally attended church at the invitation of her brother, Craig:

> All during your sermon, I felt like you were talking personally to me—like no one else was there. I remember your message hitting me so hard that I had to keep holding back the tears. Finally, at the end of the service, when you invited people to come up and pray, my heart started pounding . . . I was trembling all over, tears pouring out, and I took a look at my brother. He said, "Do you want me to go with you?"
>
> I really do not even remember walking up to pray, but . . . when I started praying that prayer for salvation, I had a tremendous weight lifted off my shoulders. I cannot honestly explain how I drove that night—I

was so relaxed and at peace with the Lord. I do remember walking in and telling my husband what had happened to me . . . He said, "That's nice. I suppose you're going to be going to that church now."

Six months later, my husband and I were sitting in the last pew of the church, and we were all singing "Amazing Grace" after a very powerful message. And he started crying. He told me he had an enormous burden lifted from him and he felt he had a peace about him . . . On October 4, my husband opened his heart to the Lord.

Their children became involved in the church's Christian school. On January 19, their daughter wrote this note to her parents: "Today was my second day at the Christian school, and it's great. They have really nice kids. Last Sunday, in children's church, I invited Jesus into my heart. I really love you both. Thank you again for putting me in a Christian school."

Preach by the Spirit. Listen by the Spirit.

What Is His Purpose?

And we know that in all things God works for the good of those who love him, who have been called according to his purpose. For those God foreknew he also predestined to be conformed to the image of his Son, that he might be the firstborn among many brothers and sisters.
Romans 8:28–29

What is *your* purpose? At different stages in my life, I've embraced different purposes. In college, my purpose was to learn well in each class and successfully finish school. As I thought about what my work life would be, I had a purpose to find the right job that fit me. An overarching purpose in my life was to do something to help others. Regarding marriage, to meet the right woman and enter into a marriage that would be compatible, fulfilling to both of us, true love—that was the purpose.

Shift your thinking for a moment: What is *God's* purpose? In the Romans passage, we learn that God takes all things that come our way, both good and bad, and works them into a pattern for our good. There is a condition, however: He does this for those who love him, who have been called *according to his purpose.* Those God foreknew (those he knew would respond to his grace), he predestined to be *conformed* to the *image* of *his Son*. In other words, he wants to make you more like Jesus. Even that desire is rooted in the context of bringing more glory to Jesus, so that Christ would not be alone—rather, he would be the firstborn among many people made Christlike by God's grace.

Think of it! God wants to make you and me more like Jesus. Second Peter 1:3–4 emphasizes this: "His divine power has given us everything we need for a godly life through our knowledge of him who called us by his own glory and goodness. Through these he has given us his very great and precious promises, so that through them you may participate in the divine nature, having escaped the corruption in the world caused by evil desires." We may participate in the divine nature to be like Jesus.

Samuel Logan Brengle was an officer in The Salvation Army. More than a million copies of his books have blessed the world. Here is part of his story:

On January 9, 1885, at about nine o'clock in the morning, God sanctified my soul. I was in my own room at the time, but in a few minutes I went out and met a man and told him what God had done for me. The next morning, I met another friend on the street and told him the blessed story. He shouted and praised God and urged me to preach full salvation and confess it everywhere. God used him to encourage and help me. So the following day I preached on the subject as clearly and forcibly as I could, and ended with my testimony.

God blessed the word mightily to others, but I think he blessed it most to myself. That confession put me on record. It cut the bridges down behind me. Three worlds were now looking at me as one who professed that God had given him a clean heart. I could not go back now. I had to go forward. God saw that I meant to be true 'til death. So two mornings after that, just as I got out of bed and was reading some of the words of Jesus, he gave me such a blessing as I never had dreamed a man could have this side of heaven. It was a heaven of love that came into my heart. I walked out over Boston Common before breakfast, weeping for joy and praising God. Oh, how I loved! In that hour I knew Jesus and I loved him 'til it seemed my heart would break with love. I loved the sparrows, I loved the dogs, I loved the horses, I loved the little urchins on the streets, I loved the strangers who hurried past me, I loved the heathen—I loved the whole world.

Do you want to know what holiness is? It is a pure love. Do you want to know what the baptism of the Holy Ghost is? It is not a mere sentiment. It is not a happy sensation that passes away in a night. It is a baptism of love that brings every thought into captivity to the Lord Jesus

(2 Cor. 10:5); that casts out all fear (1 John 4:18); that burns up doubt and unbelief as fire burns tow; that make one "meek and lowly in heart" (Matt. 11:29, KJV); that makes one hate uncleanness, lying and deceit, a flattering tongue and every evil way with a perfect hatred; that makes heaven and hell eternal realities; that makes one patient and gentle with the forward and sinful; that makes one "pure, . . . peaceable, . . . easy to be entreated, full of mercy and good fruits, without partiality, and without hypocrisy" (James 3:17, KJV); that brings one into perfect and unbroken sympathy with the Lord Jesus Christ in his toil and travail to bring a lost and rebel world to God.

God did all that for me, bless His holy name![110]
Conformed to the image of his Son! Make you like Jesus!

Still Trouble

Throw off your old sinful nature and your former way of life,
which is corrupted by lust and deception. Instead, let the Spirit
renew your thoughts and attitudes. Put on your new nature,
created to be like God—truly righteous and holy.
Ephesians 4:22–24, NLT

They wash their dishes by hand because the dishwasher is broken. They sometimes talk of repairing or replacing it but always decide to wait because there's another problem: the drainage system for the house doesn't work very well. Tree roots have grown into the underground pipe that carries wastewater out of the house. Periodically, water that should be going out of the house backs up in the basement. Even if they get a new dishwasher, there is still trouble.

Likewise, in the lives of many Christians, there is deep internal trouble blocking the full blessing of God in their life. One Christian lamented, "There were ugly tempers arising from the basement of my soul." Paul urged the Christians in Ephesus to throw off the old sinful nature as well as the

---

110. S. L. Brengle, *Helps to Holiness* (London: Salvationist Publishing and Supplies, Ltd., 1955), 9–10.

former way of life. They were to put on a new righteous and holy nature, like God.

Paul admonishes the Christians at Corinth: "You are still worldly. For since there is jealousy and quarreling among you, are you not worldly?" (1 Corinthians 3:3). He exclaimed that they were not living by the Spirit (3:1).

Paul warned the Galatian Christians of an internal spiritual battle: "For the flesh desires what is contrary to the Spirit, and the Spirit what is contrary to the flesh. They are in conflict with each other, so that you are not to do whatever you want" (Galatians 5:17). He later seemed to suggest a remedy: "Those who belong to Christ Jesus have crucified the flesh with its passions and desires" (5:24). In 5:16, he wrote, "Walk by the Spirit, and you will not gratify the desires of the flesh."

In Ephesians 2:2–3, Paul spoke of those who used to be dead in sins. He then wrote, "All of us also lived among them at one time, gratifying the cravings of our flesh and following its desires" (2:3). He seems to say that behind the sins are the cravings and desires, and behind them is the "flesh"—or, as some translations say, the "sinful nature."

Often, Christians display positive changes in their behavior yet harbor an attitude or disposition that still needs to change. Maybe that's why James said, "Wash your hands, you sinners, and purify your hearts, you double-minded" (4:8).

Maybe we could understand this issue this way: As a Christian, you might not swear, but you grumble and complain when you don't get your way. As a Christian, perhaps you would not steal, but you're jealous that your friend has something new and you don't. As a Christian, you would not put him down publicly, but it irritates you that your friend got recognition and you did not.

Perhaps a look into the life of John Allan Wood will help us. Though he was clearly converted and preparing for a life of ministry, Wood found his old nature (his self-centeredness) to be his greatest hindrance. He wrote of his struggle:

> During this period I was often convicted of remaining corruption of heart and of my need of purity. I . . . was often conscious of deep-rooted inward evils. . . . They marred my peace. They obscured my spiritual vision. They were the instruments of severe temptation. They interrupted my communion with God. They crippled my efforts to do good. . . . They occupied a place in my heart which I knew should be possessed by the

Holy Spirit. . . . I was often more strongly convicted of my need of inward purity than I ever had been of my need of pardon.[111]

Finally, Wood made a decision. He testified: "Glory be to God! . . . The moment of decision was the moment of triumph. In an instant I felt a giving away in my heart so sensible and powerful that it appeared physical rather than spiritual; a moment after I felt an indescribable sweetness permeating my entire being."[112]

John Allan Wood experienced firsthand the cleansing and filling of the Holy Spirit, as well as the Spirit's sin-defeating power. He could now be included in the apostle Paul's phrase, "So that the Gentiles might become an offering acceptable to God, sanctified by the Holy Spirit" (Romans 15:16)—the answer for any area in which we still have trouble.

The Inner Battle for Your Soul

So I say, walk by the Spirit, and you will not gratify the desires
of the flesh. For the flesh desires what is contrary to the Spirit,
and the Spirit what is contrary to the flesh. They are in conflict
with each other, so that you are not to do whatever you want.
Galatians 5:16–17

He was my best friend and the man who led me to Christ. He was driving his car, and I was riding in the passenger seat, proposing some great idea. However, he didn't seem that impressed. Suddenly, a feeling of resentment rose up within me. When he saw the expression on my face, he asked, "What's the matter?" The fact that he had caught me made me feel even more negative toward him.

Wait a minute—this man was the human instrument for my salvation. Why was I harboring these feelings toward him? Though I'd come to know Christ, there was an inner battle going on inside of me—the flesh (or the sinful nature) versus the Spirit.

---

111. V. Raymond Edman, *They Found the Secret* (Grand Rapids: Zondervan, 1960), 131–132.

112. Edman, *They Found the Secret*, 133.

The Galatian Christians were experiencing this battle, and Paul put it into words. Behind the acts of the flesh (5:19) is the flesh itself—not the meat on human bones, but a selfishness, a sinful force that is sometimes translated as "sinful nature." Paul instructed the Galatians to combat this nature by crucifying the flesh (5:24), living by the Spirit, and keeping in step with the Spirit (5:25).

Someone once said of the Christian life, "Prayer will crowd sin out, or sin will crowd prayer out." The same may be said of the flesh and the Spirit. To live in the Spirit, to live this relationship, you must enter it—you will know the Spirit in his fullness when he fully guides you. As this battle rages within you, you will make a clear decision about where your allegiance lies.

Bud was an active young man with real potential, and as a big-chested power lineman, he made an impressive appearance. However, he had a history of ups and downs. He had once held a local minister's license, but it was not renewed by his church. Along the way, he had been a Navy Seabee, had rehabbed houses, and had dug fence posts. He was in every revival service, but for all his physical strength, he was spiritually defeated—he was losing the battle to the flesh.

He said he was waiting for God to sanctify him. Then someone told him, "Bud, he's ready. He's waiting for you to be ready."

That night, Bud came to the altar. Amid tears, he took his "flesh" to the cross, and the Spirit moved. Afterward, he blurted out to his wife, "I'm free, I'm free."

Then he repeated it to me: "Chic, I'm free, I'm free." Finally, the Spirit had won.

An Act of God

He gave me the priestly duty of proclaiming the gospel of God,
so that the Gentiles might become an offering acceptable to God,
sanctified by the Holy Spirit.
Romans 15:16

There are some things you can do—you can pray, surrender your life, ask for inward cleansing, and reach out to God in faith. But when it comes to being sanctified, it is God who does it—it is a miraculous *act of God*.

The Scriptures tell us this. For instance, in his high-priestly prayer on behalf of his followers, Jesus prayed, "Sanctify them by the truth; your word is truth" (John 17:17). Notice that he asked *God* to accomplish this feat. In the original text, we also see that the word "sanctify" is a verb indicating instantaneous action.

Jesus then prays, "For them I sanctify myself, that they too may be truly sanctified" (17:19). We know Jesus could not become more holy than he already was—when he spoke of sanctifying himself, he meant he was setting himself apart for the sacrificial death on the cross. And when he said his disciples would be "truly sanctified," he meant both "set apart" and "made pure." For us today, the word "sanctified" also refers to a continuing state or relationship.

Hebrews 13:12 (NRSV) speaks of Jesus's great sacrifice: "Therefore Jesus also suffered outside the city gate in order to sanctify the people by his own blood." Here, once again, "sanctify" is an instantaneous action that Jesus performs.

In 1 Thessalonians 5:23–24, Paul prayed, "May God himself, the God of peace, sanctify you through and through. May your whole spirit, soul and body be kept blameless at the coming of our Lord Jesus Christ. The one who calls you is faithful, and he will do it." Note that it is clearly God himself who will sanctify you entirely. Paul then prays for God's preserving power to maintain the believers once they are sanctified. Finally, he stresses that God will accomplish the sanctification he has called them to. Paul is clear: *he will do it*. And now, the sanctified can enjoy great growth in grace.

In Acts 26:17–18, Paul explains the divine commission under which he lives: "I am sending you to them to open their eyes and turn them from darkness to light, and from the power of Satan to God, so that they may receive forgiveness of sins and a place among those who are sanctified by faith in me." The human part of receiving this grace is our exercise of faith in Jesus, but God still does the sanctifying.

Since sanctification is a miraculous act of God, it happens in an instant. John Wesley, leader of the great holiness revival that spread across England and much of the world in the 1700s, affirmed this: "After interviewing 652 members of the society who were exceeding clear in their experience, and of whose testimony I could see no reason to doubt . . . all who believe they are sanctified declare with one voice that the change was wrought in a moment.

I cannot but believe that sanctification is commonly, if not always, an instantaneous work."[113]

Here is the testimony of Danielle, a young woman who was new to the church:

> When I was five years old, I gave my heart to Christ. At thirteen, I rededicated my life to Christ. I still felt like something was missing from my life. Sunday, October 13, 2019, I was sanctified. Everything about sanctification intimidated and scared me. After hearing Rev. Shaver preach, I understood what had been missing from my Christian life. That Sunday evening, I finally surrendered all to Christ and everything has been clearer and brighter. My attitude and outlook on things changed for the better. I have felt freer, closer to God, and cleaner than I have ever felt before in my life. I finally feel complete and I have purpose in my life.

Notice her clear statement: "Sunday, October 13, 2019, I was sanctified." What a wonderful act of God. *He will do it!*

Don't Just Stand There—Walk!

But if we walk in the light, as he is in the light, we have fellowship with one another, and the blood of Jesus, his Son, purifies us from all sin.
1 John 1:7

Would you consider buying a fancy new car, bringing it home, parking in your garage, then just letting it sit there? Would you brag to your friends, "I've got a beautiful new car!" but never pull it out of the garage? Of course not—you'd drive it! That's what a car is for.

Still, some people treat Christianity that way: they accept Christ in a moment, and even tell others about it. But then the relationship stalls out because they do nothing. John says, "Don't just stand there—walk. Walk in the light." Light is any truth God shows you—anything that reveals him, exposes sin, or produces warmth, growth, purity, righteousness, holiness. You are meant to live in a dynamic relationship with a living Lord.

---

113. John Wesley, "On Patience," *Great Holiness Classics, Vol. 2: The Wesley Century*, T. Crichton Mitchell, ed. (Kansas City, MO: Beacon Hill Press of Kansas City, 1984), 147.

I once knew a Christian college student who had lost the glow in his experience with God. But one day, God's Spirit shined light into his mind and reminded him that when he had sold Bibles to pay his way through school, he had never sent the last payment in to the company. He immediately confessed his sin to God, sent the payment in, and began walking in peace, joy, and victory.

This walking calls for heart honesty. If we falsely claim to be without sin, we deceive ourselves. I've heard it before: "I'm a Christian kid—I do a little goofing off, a little booze, a little drugs, a little sex—but that's not the real me. I'm really good at heart." Such deceit!

The result of this walking is absolute: it "purifies from all sin." Don't dilute it—this purification requires constant, joyous walking in the light. He makes us pure, keeps us pure, keeps purifying us, cleanses us whenever we need it—again, if we walk in the light.

So what should you do if you fall into sin?

A little boy once asked on old man, "Will falling in the water drown you?"

"No," the old man said, "it's staying there."

In other words, if you sin, take it immediately to God in prayer and confession.

Charles had been raised in a Christian home, but as an adult, he got careless. He felt he had to take his boat out to his cottage on the weekends, and he kept his daughters out of church long enough that they adopted his lifestyle. He admitted that he didn't really believe in answers to prayer. In his thinking, he said, you go to the altar once, and from then on, just try to live a good life. But last week, Charles received confirmation of his kidney disease and upcoming surgery.

After receiving his diagnosis, Charles told me, "I've been doing a lot of praying. I gave God my boat, my cottage, my weekend, me. Finally, he saved me, and God is real. I've experienced temporary healing, I've been able to attend the week of revival, my friend Eugene was saved on Wednesday, Fred was reclaimed on Sunday, and I'm ready to go to the hospital. I've seen more answers to prayer this week than all my past life."

Yes, Charles, Christianity is a life, not just a moment. So, get the word out: "Don't just stand there—walk!"

The Right Path

He guides me along the right paths for his name's sake.
Psalm 23:3

In seventh grade, I auditioned for the class play. After I'd tried a few times, the drama coach took me aside and said, "You're a monotone. There's no hope for you."

I'm amazed that I wasn't devastated by that. I was a pretty sensitive kid, but somehow, her words didn't bother me.

In eighth grade, I tried out for another play. Amazingly, I got the lead part. The same drama coach said, "What's happened to you?" She was astonished by my improvement, but I couldn't give a reason for it. My confidence soared.

In high school, I had a major part in another play. That play won top ratings in the regional drama festival, then in the state festival, then in the New England drama festival.

Eventually, that play took us into the region of Dartmouth College. A graduate of our Connecticut high school who was now a Dartmouth student showed us around the campus. I had been thinking of applying to Yale, but after seeing the Dartmouth campus, I knew that was where I wanted to go.

When I became a student at Dartmouth, I was awed by the achievements of that same Connecticut high school graduate, Peter. As president of his fraternity, varsity soccer team player, member of the Green Key society, and a straight-A student (when he tried), he was making his mark on the school. Then the news came: Peter's alcohol consumption had ruined him. He flunked out of school and left in disgrace.

In my junior year at Dartmouth, as I was increasingly searching for my life's purpose, I wondered if I could find a personal relationship with God. In the middle of my search, Peter showed back up at a college chapel service. He shook my hand and said, "Chic, I'm different than I used to be because I found the Lord!" Soon afterward, Peter shared his dramatic testimony with me and invited me to his church, where I met and received the living Jesus.

As a pre-law major, I thought I would go to law school and become an attorney. But as I came to the end of college, God called me to the ministry. I then attended seminary in Kansas City. Within a short time, I was receiving invitations to preach. Though many of my seminary buddies were fearful of public speaking, I wasn't, thanks to my training and experience in drama.

Now I look back with joy on a lifetime in ministry as a pastor, seminary professor, evangelist, and author.

Even before I knew him personally, God was guiding me. This is what we call "prevenient grace"—grace before conversion. And since I've come to know him, God continues to guide me.

This can be true for you too. God is longing to guide you "along the right paths for his name's sake." How about it?

I Believe in Jesus Christ

For my Father's will is that everyone who looks to the Son and believes in him shall have eternal life, and I will raise them up at the last day.
John 6:40

I believe in Dr. Carter. She is my eye doctor, and this week, she did cataract surgery on my right eye. For years, Dr. Carter has helped our family with eye exams, glasses, and treatments for eye disease. Because I believe in her, I agreed to her advice to undergo this surgery—I entrusted her to use delicate instruments to remove a cataract from my eye and install a new lens.

Dr. Carter gave me many instructions to prepare for this surgery. They included:

- Before surgery, use a steroid-antibiotic drop in the eye three times a day, continuing in tapered intervals for four weeks after surgery
- Thoroughly wash the face the night before surgery and the morning of surgery
- No food or water after 11:59 p.m. the night before surgery (except for key medications)
- Check back in with the doctor the day after surgery, then one week after surgery, to ensure progress in the healing process

Because I believe in Dr. Carter, I gladly obeyed these instructions.

There was considerable prep time at the surgery center—blood pressure check, heart and lung exam, sedation, oxygen, drops for dilation, injection of numbing solution around the eye. The actual surgery took thirty minutes.

There was a time in history when there was no known correction for cataracts. Now, it's hard to believe that an incision can be made in the eye, a device inserted to break down the cataract, the cataract vacuumed out of the eye, and a new lens inserted that locks in place in thirty minutes! Unbelievable!

At the next-day checkup, I was giving Dr. Carter lots of thanks and praise. I was beginning to see what I had not seen in years. I believe in Dr. Carter.

I believe in Jesus Christ. Many people take the admonition to believe in Christ to simply mean, "I believe he exists." But "believe," as used by Christ, means much more than that:

- James 2:19—"You believe that there is one God. Good! Even the demons believe that—and shudder."
- John 6:36—"You have seen me and still you do not believe."
- John 8:31—"If you hold to my teaching, you are really my disciples."
- John 14:23—"Anyone who loves me will obey my teaching."

So, to "believe" in Jesus Christ means you respect him, trust yourself to him, love him, obey him, and follow his instructions. You even have regular check-ins (called devotions) after you first accept him. And if it is amazing that Dr. Carter could remove my cataract and install a lens in thirty minutes, it is far more astounding to realize that Jesus can perform miracles. And when you really come to *believe* in Jesus, it's natural that you would thank him, praise him, and joyfully spend eternity with him.

Ordinary

*Now Simon's mother-in-law was suffering from a high fever,
and they asked Jesus to help her. So he bent over her and rebuked the fever,
and it left her. She got up at once and began to wait on them.*
Luke 4:38–39

*[Jesus] said to Simon, "Put out into deep water, and let down the nets for a
catch." Simon answered, "Master, we've worked hard all night and haven't
caught anything. But because you say so, I will let down the nets." When
they had done so, they caught such a large number of fish
that their nets began to break.*
Luke 5:4–6

In the big picture, our concern was very small. Yet it seemed big to us.

We have three TVs in our home. None of the TVs had worked for more than three weeks. We pushed all the right (and some of the wrong) buttons on our remotes. We did everything we knew. Finally, we called the Geek Squad to send someone to fix them. I pleaded with the phone representative to send someone who would be understanding toward older people.

After I prayed for the right repairman, the right solution for each TV, and the best answer for the least expense and time, Dominic phoned to say he would be our repairman.

Just before Dominic arrived, we discovered that the cable box of the first TV had been unplugged. Within sixty seconds, it was working again.

The very understanding Dominic made one adjustment to the cable box of the second TV, and in five minutes, it was working too.

The third TV had lines running across the screen and was emitting a strange, chemical-burning smell. Dominic said this old TV would be too expensive to repair—it would be better to replace it. We explained that, because of the government's warnings about shopping in crowds during the coronavirus pandemic, we did not want to go out in public.

"Dominic," I asked, "if we tell you what we want, could you buy it and install it for us?" Dominic said yes.

Once we selected the $149.99 on-sale special, Dominic returned to the store, picked up the TV and the necessary tools, and had it installed within two hours. He even removed our old TV for free. What a relief for us—and what a specific answer to prayer. Thank you, Lord! It is not hard to follow and serve a God who cares even for the ordinary affairs of our lives.

If you think I am too presumptuous, please remember our Scripture passages: Jesus healed Simon's mother-in-law of a high fever. He also led Simon and his fellow fishermen to the best fishing spot after they had caught nothing all night. With Jesus's guidance, they caught so many fish that they filled two boats. In these encounters, Jesus addressed the family, health, and work concerns of one man, Simon. It was personal stuff in the big picture—but it was stuff that mattered to this man's heart and life.

Soon after the fishermen's success, "Jesus said to Simon, 'Don't be afraid; from now on you will fish for people.' So they pulled their boats up on shore, left everything and followed him" (Luke 5:10–11). Simon, later called Peter, became one of the greatest leaders of the early church.

Do you understand how much Jesus cares about the ordinary events in your life? Then why not follow him? Or, put another way, if you're looking for food or drink or clothes, "seek first his kingdom and his righteousness, and all these things will be given to you as well" (Matthew 6:33).

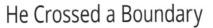

He Crossed a Boundary

The voice spoke to him a second time,
"Do not call anything impure that God has made clean."
Acts 10:15

Years ago, we were having race riots in our city, and I was distressed.

Peter had been a conscientious Jew, but he had come to know, love, and follow Jesus Christ. His Jewish background had taught him to keep separate from Gentiles. Now, in a vision, God was leading him to cross a boundary—to reach out to Gentiles, as well as Jews, with the gospel. While Peter was still processing what he had seen, three men knocked on his door to invite him to the home of the Gentile Roman centurion Cornelius. The Spirit told Peter, "I have sent them" (Acts 10:20). So, Peter went, and in doing so, he and the gospel crossed a boundary (10:23–48).

During the race riots in my city, I wondered what I could do. I didn't think a counter-protest was a healing answer. So I had an idea: what if I did one simple thing? My barber was African-American, and my only contact with him was for haircuts. What if Nancy and I invited Arby (my barber) and his wife, Joyce, over for dinner? We did, and we enjoyed an evening filled with good food, warm fellowship, and mutual understanding and respect. It was a small gesture—but what would happen if ten thousand citizens of my city did the same thing over a two-week period?

My life has been enriched by crossing cultural boundaries. It has been a blessing to interact with ministerial students and foster lifelong friendships with people of many backgrounds. Crossing boundaries is a blessing.

Others

Love the Lord your God with all your heart and
with all your soul and with all your strength and with all your mind;
and, love your neighbor as yourself.
Luke 10:27

If you do what today's scripture instructs, you will inherit eternal life (Luke 10:25–27). The "love God" and "love your neighbor" are both important. Let's think about the "Love your neighbor" part.

When Tim came to our church and our Sunday school class, he had already been arrested for his crimes and was awaiting sentencing. He was hesitant and cautious at first, but the love of people, the witness of many, and powerful preaching won the day. Tim had repented of his sins and received forgiveness a few days earlier in the county jail. At First Church, he gave his life fully to God and grew spiritually. Eventually, he was sentenced to prison and has been incarcerated for six years.

Every Christmas, our Sunday school class sends financial gifts to thirty or so people. Tim received a hundred dollars in his commissary account. With so few of the comforts of life, I assumed he would spend it on himself. But then I received the following letter from him:

I am a blessed individual! Isn't that a wonderful phrase from an inmate in a corrections facility? There are times when doubt creeps into my mind. Then I receive a letter, a Bible study, a visit, or even money, and the doubt is washed away.

I want to thank the Sunday school class for remembering me at Christmas. The class gave, so I was able to give. There were a few of us who donated toward a Christmas treat for all fifty guys in our wing. There were some guys who didn't want it, but most were grateful. I have included a letter of one gentleman's response. Please make sure the class knows I am thankful and greatly appreciate the gift.

The person who runs the chapel service I go to often says, "We weren't arrested; we were rescued." All Christians could say God rescued them, and God is ready to rescue every sinner who asks.

Below is part of the letter Tim received from another inmate:

I would like to personally thank you guys for all the hard work you've done to give everyone such a nice treat. I remember last year you did the same thing. You guys have truly lived up to what I believe the Bible says is a true Christian. . . . You guys have proven to be the shining light I believe the Bible talks about. I appreciate you and pray for your well-being.

Earl from our Sunday school class models what it means to love your neighbor. About every six weeks, Earl drives to the other side of the state, stays overnight in a motel, goes to see Tim and, as allowed by the prison, brings Tim homemade food.

So, whether it's the class sending gifts to those in need, or the imprisoned Tim showing care to the fifty other men in his wing, or Earl making his weekend trips to see Tim, there are Christians out there who are loving others. Who needs your love today?

What If God Asks Me . . .

What must I do to inherit eternal life?
Luke 10:25

He was about to board Malaysian Flight 17 from Amsterdam to Southeast Asia when suddenly, a Dutch young man felt troubled and ran back to his mother. He blurted out, "I'm afraid the plane will crash. What if I die?" His mother assured him that he'd flown before and that his brother would be with him.

He persisted with more questions:

1. What if I die?
2. What if God asks me a question?
3. What should I say to him?

This story came from a television interview with the young man's mother after the Malaysian flight was shot down over Ukraine—the plane was caught in the crossfire between Russian separatists and the Ukrainian military in 2014. Everyone on board—nearly three hundred people—died.

What a sad story! And what a significant question from the young man: "What if God asks me a question?"

What if God asked *you* a question? Dr. James Kennedy wrote, "Suppose you were to die tonight and stand before God and he were to say to you, 'Why should I let you into my heaven?' What would you say?"[114]

---

114. D. James Kennedy, *Evangelism Explosion* (Wheaton, IL: Tyndale House, 1996), 33.

The question is deeper than you might think. In Luke 10, an expert in religious law actually asked Jesus, "What must I do to inherit eternal life?" Jesus told him the answer: You love God with your whole being and love your neighbor as yourself.

Eternal life is more than heaven, but because it is "eternal," it includes heaven. Jesus said, "Now this is eternal life: that they may know you, the only true God, and Jesus Christ, whom you have sent" (John 17:3). Eternal life is *knowing* God the Father and *knowing* Jesus Christ—a relationship.

Loving God and loving your neighbor is the condition Jesus specifies for inheriting eternal life. But who can do that by human effort alone? That kind of love is only possible with divine aid. So Paul tells us in Romans 5:5, "God's love has been poured out into our hearts through the Holy Spirit, who has been given to us."

The question about entrance into heaven is answered by the famous John 3:16: "For God so loved the world that he gave his one and only Son, that whoever believes in him shall not perish but have eternal life." We must understand that the word "believe" here means more than intellectual acceptance; it means a commitment to Jesus. This leads us into an ongoing relationship with Christ.

Thankfully, you can have *assurance* and *know* that you are right with God. Romans 8:16 promises, "The Spirit himself testifies with our spirit that we are God's children."

Tom Phillips, former president of the Raytheon Corporation, knew this for certain. He shared his story with Charles Colson, assistant to former president Richard Nixon, after Colson was sentenced to prison for Watergate-related crimes. Colson later became a Christ follower and a champion of prison reform. Here's what Phillips said:

> I didn't seem to have anything that mattered. It was all on the surface. All the material things in life are meaningless if a man hasn't discovered what's underneath them.
>
> . . . One night I was in New York on business and noticed that Billy Graham was having a crusade in Madison Square Garden . . . I went—curious, I guess—hoping maybe I'd find some answers. What Graham said that night put it all into place for me. I saw what was missing—the personal relationship with Jesus Christ, the fact that I hadn't ever asked him into my life, hadn't turned my life over to him. So I did it—that very night at the crusade.
>
> . . . I asked Christ to come into my life, and I could feel his presence with me. His peace within me. I could sense his Spirit there with me.

Then I went out for a walk alone on the streets of New York. I never liked New York before, but this night was beautiful. I walked for blocks and blocks. Everything seemed different to me. It was raining softly, and the city lights created a golden glow. Something had happened to me, and I knew it.[115]

Let Us Hold Fast

Let us hold unswervingly to the hope we profess,
for he who promised is faithful.
Hebrews 10:23

Raised under camp-meeting preaching in the Methodist church, she knew the importance of a personal relationship with Christ. Yet, for years, she left him out of her life. Then, when she was close to fifty years old, she received the Savior.

Everything around her pressured her to turn her back on Jesus Christ. She considered her situation. Having been given boldness to enter the Most Holy Place (Hebrews 10:19) and a high priest (10:21), she knew there was *provision* sufficient for her victory. So she drew near to God (10:22), held fast to her faith (10:23), and even stirred up others to love and good works in their mutual fellowship (10:24–25). In other words, she put God's grace into *practice*.

The issue came to a head, however, when others began to pressure her to return to a lifestyle of continuous disobedience (10:26). As these people urged her to turn away from Christ, she became rather dogmatic and revealed her determination by blurting out, "I'm not going to disobey and go to hell!" She lived in spiritual victory.[116]

---

115. Charles W. Colson, *Born Again* (Old Tappan, NJ: Fleming H. Revell, 1977), 110.

116. Previously published in *Come Ye Apart* March–April–May 1971 (Kansas City, MO: WordAction Publishing Co.), 87. Used by permission. (This publication became *Reflecting God.*)

When God Shows Up

Jacob also went on his way, and the angels of God met him.
Genesis 32:1

His father-in-law was mad at him, his brother was mad at him, and Jacob was stuck in the middle, trying to protect his flocks, his children, his wives, and himself. Caught between the angry Laban and the angry Esau, Jacob became more open to God, more sensitive than ever before. At that critical moment, the angels of God met him.

By the time of the Acts of the Apostles, the early church expected God to show up—to intervene, to speak up regularly. In the book of Acts, there are twenty-nine instances where we see the Spirit's divine leadership. Acts 13:2 is an example of this: "The Holy Spirit said, 'Set apart for me Barnabas and Saul for the work to which I have called them.'"

So often I pray and pray and receive no answer. Sometimes I wish God would show up and speak to me as I pray. Rees Howells used to say, "The meaning of prayer is answer." However, Howells also said, "Effectual praying must be guided praying."[117] J. G. Morrison wrote of an "achieving faith" and compared it to a cable "that connects the soul with God, over which he operates to deliver His power upon the believer, for the very thing for which his faith stands."[118]

When we were in our first pastorate, a church plant, our income was very meager. I prayed, "Lord, I need a new car. I'm too poor to buy another one and too dumb to fix the one I have." After that prayer, the Spirit of God gave me faith, and I was assured a car was on the way. Within minutes the phone rang, and my mother told me that a friend had decided to give me his new car.

Sometimes the Spirit places a burden or a dream on your heart that will not go away. I had seen Shahrzad, a Muslim woman, accept Christ as Savior and Lord before my eyes. She and her husband, Albert, became my dear friends. At their twentieth wedding anniversary (a renewal of their vows now that they were Christians), I met their Muslim friends. For months afterward,

---

117. Norman Grubb, *Rees Howells, Intercessor: The Story of a Life Lived for God* (Philadelphia: Christian Literature Crusade, 1952), 43.
118. J. G. Morrison, *Achieving Faith* (Titusville, PA: The Allegheny Wesleyan Methodist Connection, n.d.), 34–35.

a burden rested on my heart: "Lead a Bible study for these Muslim friends." After nearly three years, on a Tuesday night, thirteen of us met for Bible study. Except for my wife and myself, everyone came from a Muslim background or was married to someone from a Muslim background.

Oh, may I expect God to show up—and may the Spirit lead me to have faith in God's answers.

Fruit Production

Every good tree bears good fruit, but a bad tree bears bad fruit.
Thus, by their fruit you will recognize them.
Matthew 7:17, 20

Yes, he said it! Jesus said the actions we see in people's lives reveal the true condition of their hearts. Godly words will not count when matched by ungodly actions.

Joe and Carol had been attending our Sunday school class. One day, I went to visit them at their home, and while I was there, we got into a discussion about their spiritual lives. In an appropriate way, I asked Joe if he was sure he would go to heaven.

He answered something like this, "Oh yes, I know I will go to heaven. About twenty-seven years ago, I accepted Christ as my Savior. Of course, I admit I've been immoral with other women, I have a dirty mouth, I take God's name in vain, I—" He paused. "You don't believe me, do you?"

I was startled. I hadn't said a word. I guess the look on my face expressed disbelief. Finally, I said, "Joe, it's not whether I believe you. You claim you're going to heaven, and then you give me a list of the fruit of your life. Jesus said, 'By their fruit you will recognize them.' What else can I assume?"

Contrast that with this event. A Protestant chaplain who was new to us was working with a Catholic community hospice and stopped at our church office to report that Jack Wilson was in hospice care. Jack had told the chaplain that our church was his church. The chaplain thought we'd like to contact Jack.

The office staff was perplexed. The name didn't ring a bell with them. They began a search. A retired minister remembered the name. The last time

Jack attended had been more than fifteen years earlier. Before the day was over, a minister from our church was at Jack's bedside with Scripture, prayer, and comfort.

The chaplain later related her experience. She said, "There were three women in the office. They did a beautiful job. Wonderful! One came out from behind the counter and prayed with me. This is real Christianity! I go to some churches and ask them to check on a person. They say, 'He's not on our giving record.' They seem to have no other awareness of the person. I'm so impressed with your church."

"Beautiful job"—"wonderful"—"real Christianity"—"so impressed." That's good fruit. That's godly fruit. That's proof the Christianity is genuine.

What kind of fruit are you producing?

From Criminal to Christ

I am not ashamed of the gospel, because it is the power of God that brings salvation to everyone who believes: first to the Jew, then to the Gentile.
Romans 1:16

The power of God for salvation—how great is that? Great enough to change Joe!

Joe was raised Catholic. At times, God tried to speak to him. Once, God showed him a vision of Joe behind the pulpit. Joe responded by running away from God. From ages nine to forty-five, he used drugs, sold drugs, and stole. "All my life, I was an out-and-out criminal," he admitted.

He lost his house because of his lifestyle. He lost his marriage. After a time of being drug-free, he was back to prostitutes and selling drugs because he needed the money.

In 2009, Joe was arrested for embezzlement. When the police kicked in his door, they found an abundance of heroin in his home, and they took him to jail. One night, he was suddenly awakened from sleep in his cell. He heard God ask him, *"Have you had enough? Are you ready to follow me?"* In that moment, he committed to follow Christ, and in the years since, his life has changed.

Joe completed his probation in August 2017. He has been ordained by his church and became a biblical counselor at a powerful city rescue mission. Now Joe points hundreds of desperate people to great power: "The power of God that brings salvation." Is that power enough to deliver you from the challenge you face today?

Oh, That My People Would Listen!

I am the LORD your God, who brought you up out of Egypt.
Open wide your mouth and I will fill it. But my people would
not listen to me. Israel would not submit to me.
Psalm 81:10–11

He accepted Jesus, and God delivered him from so much:
- The burden of guilt
- The chaos of undisciplined credit buying
- The harsh-tempered shouting of an arguing spirit
- A hundred cans of beer per week
- The agony of nerves on edge

Imagine my surprise when he began to slip away from the God who'd done so much for him. "Tell me if you ever see me backsliding," he'd told me. But when I took him at his word and did so, he wouldn't accept it.

Finally, he took his life completely into his own hands. He walked in his own counsel. Finally, since he insisted on it, God gave him up to his own heart's lust (Psalm 81:12).

Then, one night, the phone rang, and he asked me to come over right away—he was under arrest.

If only he had listened![119]

---

119. Previously published in *Come Ye Apart* March–April–May 1971 (Kansas City, MO: WordAction Publishing Co.), 84. Used by permission. (This publication became *Reflecting God*.)

Does Your Face Ever Shine?

*When Moses came down from Mount Sinai with the two tablets
of the covenant law in his hands, he was not aware that his face
was radiant because he had spoken with the* Lord.
Exodus 34:29

Finally, after standing up to Pharaoh through the ten plagues of judgment against Egypt, Moses received permission to leave Egypt. He led more than 1.5 million of his people through the opened waters of the Red Sea, and the Egyptian army that tried to cross after them was drowned. For forty years, he guided Israel through the wilderness with God's miraculous provisions of manna, quail, and water from the rock. At last, Moses brought them to the Jordan and passed leadership to Joshua to lead them into the promised land.

All of Moses's powerful leadership was because of his *close relationship with God*. On Mount Sinai, Moses met with God for the second giving of the Ten Commandments. Here is the description of their encounter:

Then the Lord came down in the cloud and stood there with him and proclaimed his name, the Lord. And he passed in front of Moses, proclaiming, "The Lord, the Lord, the compassionate and gracious God, slow to anger, abounding in love and faithfulness, maintaining love to thousands, and forgiving wickedness, rebellion and sin. Yet he does not leave the guilty unpunished; he punishes the children and their children for the sin of the parents to the third and fourth generation." (Exodus 34:5–7)

The Lord then promised Moses, "I will do wonders never before done in any nation in all the world" (34:10).

Thus, we can understand why Moses's face shone when came down from Mount Sinai: "his face was radiant because he had spoken with the Lord."

Does anyone have a shining face after the Christ's coming? Can some, though maybe not as great as Moses, still shine?

Stephen was one of the seven laymen chosen to distribute food to the widows in the early church. He stood so courageously for Jesus that those who opposed Christianity stoned him to death. What was his secret? Regarding his election to the Seven, the record states, "They chose Stephen, a man full of faith and of the Holy Spirit" (Acts 6:5).

Just before his death, as the people argued about Stephen and called false witnesses against him, the record reports, "All who were sitting in the Sanhedrin looked intently at Stephen, and they saw that his face was like the face of an angel" (Acts 6:15). He was shining.

Finally, as he was about to be stoned, we read, "But Stephen, full of the Holy Spirit, looked up to heaven and saw the glory of God, and Jesus standing at the right hand of God" (7:55).

I once walked into a godly home and found that it was shining. I have known Peter, Juanita, Kelli, and others whose godly faces shone. Do you speak with the Lord, and are you filled with the Holy Spirit? Does your face ever shine?

Rivers of Living Water

Whoever believes in me, as Scripture has said, rivers of living water will flow from within them. By this he meant the Spirit, whom those who believed in him were later to receive. Up to that time the Spirit had not been given, since Jesus had not yet been glorified.
John 7:38–39

"Is it true? Does it really say a river of living water will flow?" she asked the minister. He answered her that it was not just a river, but *rivers*. In John 4:14, Jesus had promised "a spring of water welling up to eternal life." Now he raises the quantity to "rivers."

As Roger knelt at a Filipino altar and prayed for God to sanctify him entirely and fill him with the Holy Spirit, God answered. With a beaming face, Roger then testified, "My heart is purified. I am so happy. I could sing, I could shout. I want to be with my Christian brothers and sisters."

The next week, the Spirit flowing through him went beyond his Christian friends. For ten years, Roger's brother had been his enemy because of a disagreement over a business deal. Since being filled with the Spirit, Roger had been praying for his brother. One day, upon arriving home, he found his brother waiting for him. His brother apologized, and they were reconciled. Then Roger witnessed to him, and his brother accepted Christ. The next week, Roger was at dinner at his brother's house.

Roger reported other changes in his interactions with others: "Before, I was afraid to talk to people about Christ. Now I have courage. I'm amazed— I've talked to three people about the Lord, and they've all been converted. I feel like I'm a winner with my Lord."

Rivers of living water are flowing. Be sure you get in on the flow!

Which Pair of Hands?

David inquired of the LORD, "Shall I pursue this raiding party? Will I overtake them?" "Pursue them," he answered. "You will certainly overtake them and succeed in the rescue."
1 Samuel 30:8

Before Jim Elliot became a bold missionary to the Huaorani tribe or stained the Curaray River with his martyr's blood, he was a college student. During that time, he once gave a talk to incoming freshmen that he described as "what I, as a junior, wish someone had told me when I was a freshman." In that speech, Jim shared what he had learned: that beyond believing and behaving, there is being, and you can only *be* when you have learned to put all of your life in God's hands. This truth needs to be held against one of the most common reasons for failure: "I took it into my own hands."

Saul considered David a threat. Though David had soothed Saul's soul with his music and killed giants for Israel's victory, Saul repeatedly lied to David and tried to kill him.

The Philistine king had dismissed David from his military position and sent him away. After three days (fifty miles) of travel, David had his men returned to Ziklag. There, they found that the Amalekites had burned the city and taken all their wives and children captive. David's men were bitter against David, but David did not go that route; he found it better to find strength in the Lord (1 Samuel 30:6). He went to the Lord in prayer and put the problem in God's hands. When he heard from God, David followed his directions. Consequently, David and his army recovered all their family members and plunder (vv. 18–20). By chapter 31, Saul, who had repeatedly taken issues into his own hands, killed himself.

Rhonda had wept her way back to God, yet she was nervous about other people's reactions at her work, where she had been known as a woman of the world. How would she deal with her reputation for drinking and risqué behavior? Should she take the situation into her own hands and compromise? Ultimately, she chose to put it in God's hands, looking to the promise of Philippians 4:6–7: "Do not be anxious . . . present your requests to God. And the peace of God . . . will guard your hearts and your minds in Christ Jesus." She did, and God did.

Ann noticed the nurses like Ruth and Cathy at the hospital where she worked. Their quality of life was a source of strength. Then she noticed Dr. John Cashman, who was intelligent, humble, and godly. He was the only doctor for whom the nurses signed retirement cards—they called him a living saint. Ann joined their church because she met people in her workplace who put their work in God's hands.

Which pair of hands have you put yourself in? Mother Teresa once said, "Pray for me that I not loosen my grip on the hands of Jesus, even under the guise of helping the poor."

All Alone—Oh No!

When my father and my mother forsake me,
then the LORD will take me up.
Psalm 27:10, KJV

Hagar was the second wife, and she was pregnant. Sarai, the first wife, had been barren up to this point. When Hagar began to rub it in, Sarai wouldn't stand for it—after all, Hagar was Sarai's slave. Sarai abused Hagar, and Hagar fled.

Whatever Hagar had done wrong, she was now in a desperate place. On the road to Shur, running from Canaan to Egypt, she stopped at a spring in the desert. It was rare for a woman to travel alone; she was pregnant; she was a slave from Egypt. Whatever family she had in her connection to Abram and Sarai was shattered. Would anyone there help her? She was alone—all alone.

Right there, in that place, that problem, that despair, he showed up: "The angel of the LORD found Hagar" (Genesis 16:7). The angel told her to go back to Sarai, but also promised her a son—Ishmael—and descendants "too numerous to count" (16:10). Where before she had felt alone, she now exclaimed, "You are the God who sees me," and, "I have now seen the One who sees me" (16:13).

As a college junior, I met Jesus Christ; thrilled, I began to follow him. Fewer than three months into my relationship with the Lord, I made a visit to my girlfriend. After all, the questions of the girl I planned to marry had spurred my search for Christ. When I told her how my life had changed, she said, "Some changes I like—some changes I don't." When I went home to tell my mom and dad, my mother was disturbed; my dad was angry. Please understand that the three most important people in my life at the time were my mom, my dad, and my girlfriend.

One day, when I was back at college, two letters arrived. The one from my girlfriend said, "I think you're demented. I don't want to see you again."

In shock, I opened the letter from my mom and dad. My dad's words were, "Because of the stand you have taken, I'm cutting you off from further financial aid."

I wept. I was alone—all alone.

Still new in my faith, I didn't know my Bible well, yet I knew I had to go to the Word. Not knowing that such a line was in the Bible, I read Psalm 27:10: "When my father and my mother forsake me, then the LORD will take me up" (KJV). A few hours later, I was in the daily chapel service. I was amazed when I heard Scripture reader read, "When my father and my mother forsake me, then the LORD will take me up." Later that afternoon, I attended the daily student prayer meeting. One student (who knew nothing of my situation) said he felt led to read, "When my father and my mother forsake me, then the LORD will take me up."

Not Hagar—not me—not you. Whatever you are going through today, you're not alone!

God Put It Here

Whoever can be trusted with very little can also be trusted with much,
and whoever is dishonest with very little will also be dishonest with much.
So if you have not been trustworthy in handling worldly wealth, who will

trust you with true riches? And if you have not been trustworthy with someone else's property, who will give you property of your own?
Luke 16:10–12

It was my first pastorate. As people were coming to Christ, I endeavored to lead them into a disciplined life for the glory of God. At an appropriate time, I urged some of these newer Christians to break free from their addiction to tobacco.

Mr. Mitchell was one of our attenders. He was outspoken about his belief in Jesus but was careless in his personal habits. I hadn't spoken to him about his tobacco use, but apparently he knew what I was teaching some of the other believers. One day, he approached me and said, "Pastor Shaver, I know God put tobacco here. It's a gift to be used. So my smoking is okay."

I was shocked at his rationale. Then I began to think of my experience way back when I was a teen. Back then, we were allowed to do agricultural work in Connecticut before we were sixteen. This was at a time in my life before any of my family had come to know Jesus. I took a summer job picking tobacco. Cigar-wrapper tobacco raised under hot and humid muslin tenting was a big industry. I followed the correct procedure for picking the leaves— sitting in the rows between the tobacco stalks and only picking the lowest leaves on both right and left. As I picked, tobacco juice got into the several warts I had on my hands. Within a few days, the warts dropped off, and my skin was clear.

At the end of the tobacco-leaf harvest, farmers went back into the fields and harvested the stalks. These were cut into two-foot lengths and sold to homeowners to put on their lawns. The powerful poisons in the stalks (especially nicotine) killed unwanted grubs and insects in the lawn, and as the stalk deteriorated, the lawns were fertilized.

So I went back to Mr. Mitchell and said, "The purpose of God putting tobacco here was not to make it into cigarettes to smoke. It was to remove warts from our bodies, kill grubs and insects, and fertilize our lawns. If you decide to put that in your mouth, that is your choice."

I was powerfully reminded that just because something is available does not mean I should use it in any way I want. *I can decide* to use something in destructive ways and falsely claim that God has blessed it—or I can use it for good.

Jesus taught a parable in Luke 16 of a manager wasting his boss's possessions. The cunning manager foresaw his imminent firing and cut deals with the master's debtors to curry their favor. Jesus spoke of his shrewdness and said children of light ought to deal with their wealth in such a way that they will be welcomed into eternal dwellings. Then Jesus taught a principle that applies to Mr. Mitchell and to us: "Whoever can be trusted with very little can also be trusted with much, and whoever is dishonest with very little will also be dishonest with much" (Luke 16:10).

Thus, the mere presence of tobacco, your weekly paycheck, your environment, your skills, another person's spouse, your neighbor's lawnmower, the years of your life—all must be managed in a way that glorifies God and does good for humanity. In other words, we have to make wise decisions about all the opportunities in front of us. And if we can be trusted with the little issues, we can be trusted with much. Will you use God's gifts wisely?

Jesus Is Coming Back . . . So?

Look, he is coming in the clouds, and every eye will see him,
even those who pierced him; and all peoples on earth will mourn
because of him. So shall it be! Amen.
Revelation 1:7

But the day of the Lord will come like a thief. The heavens will
disappear with a roar; the elements will be destroyed by fire,
and the earth and everything done in it will be laid bare.
2 Peter 3:10

Yes, I believe that the Jesus who was born in the manger is coming back to earth again as a mighty King. I preach that.

I get the impression that some who hear me preach that conclude, "I'll sit back and wait." Or, when they hear me preach on faithfulness, stewardship, and service, they think, "How does that fit? You just told us last week that Jesus is coming back."

The same Peter who said the day of the Lord would come like a thief also said, "You ought to live holy and godly lives as you look forward to the day of God and speed its coming" (2 Peter 3:11–12).

In 1 Peter 4:7–11, he writes:

> The end of all things is near. Therefore be alert and of sober mind so that you may pray. Above all, love each other deeply, because love covers

over a multitude of sins. Offer hospitality to one another without grumbling. Each of you should use whatever gift you have received to serve others, as faithful stewards of God's grace in its various forms. If anyone speaks, they should do so as one who speaks the very words of God. If anyone serves, they should do so with the strength God provides, so that in all things God may be praised through Jesus Christ.

If I were a layperson and I knew Jesus was coming back, I would live by the above words from 1 Peter. My day might include early Bible study and prayer, breakfast, a prayer with my family, and encouragement to my children as they left for school. At my job, I would work well to make us successful. I might speak some words of witness to one, pray for another, express concern to another whose family member was sick. Back at home, I would give support and encouragement to my spouse and children. I might make a call to a recent church visitor I had befriended, or I might make a hospital visit to one of our church members.

Jesus is coming back. So I would live for him here and now, day by day, moment by moment, like Peter said—love deeply, offer hospitality, and serve others. And I would be ready.

The Four Signs of a Dynamic Catholic

Make every effort to live in peace with everyone and to be holy;
without holiness no one will see the Lord.
Hebrews 12:14

In Matthew Kelly's book by the above title, he says:
- "The Four Signs of a Dynamic Catholic are:
  1. Prayer
  2. Study
  3. Generosity
  4. Evangelization" (18).
- "Transforming people one at a time is at the heart of God's plan for the world" (36).
- Kelly writes that he encountered one idea that turned his life upside down: "God calls you to holiness, and everything that happens in your

life, every triumph, trial, and tragedy is an opportunity to grow in holiness" (77).

- Kelly uses another phrase to explain the quest for holiness: "the quest to become the best version of yourself" (78).[120]

Webs and Grasshoppers

For it is by grace you have been saved, through faith—and this is not from yourselves, it is the gift of God—not by works, so that no one can boast.
Ephesians 2:8–9

Many times, when I walk through my garden, I run into a single strand of a web. I don't know if it is left over from a web that was destroyed, or if it is a spider getting ready to build a new one. Regardless, it stops me in my tracks, and I frantically try to pull it off and make sure the spider isn't still attached to it.

One day, God said to me, *"How do people react when they walk through your strands? Do they try to pull them off? With what are you weaving those single strands? Do you lace them with gossip or jealousy or envy? Or, when they encounter a strand, is there so much love and grace that they are enveloped and drawn to you? What kind of webs are you weaving and leaving? Rachel, if you spend time in the garden of your soul, you will weave webs of grace and mercy that will draw others to me."*

Until that point, I understood everything God had told me. But then I got stumped on the grasshoppers. I lay there for a long time, but I couldn't figure out the meaning of the grasshoppers. The answer came to me a few days later when my brother-in-law, Charlie, told me that while he was in my garden, he had thrown a grasshopper into the spider's web. The spider rushed down and captured the grasshopper, wrapping and spinning it up to eat later. The grasshopper hung there, hopelessly ensnared in the web, waiting to die at the spider's discretion. Suddenly, Charlie was struck with the thought that this was not fair, so he took a small twig and disengaged the grasshopper, pulled

---

120. Previously shared in *The Good News: The Chic Shaver Center for Evangelism Newsletter* (June 2014).

off the web, and set it free. As soon as I heard this, I knew the meaning of the grasshopper.

I was the grasshopper. At one point, I was ensnared in the web of sin, but Jesus came along and tenderly plucked me out of Satan's web and set me free. The grasshopper experienced grace that day. I experience God's grace, and he is calling me to spend more time in the garden of my soul.

I knew that God was calling me to be vulnerable enough to put this lesson on paper and share it with someone. Then he asked me to commit to spend more time with him in the garden of my soul. In sharing this parable with you today, I am giving you permission to hold me accountable—to ask me if I am spending time in the garden of my soul.

And I extend this invitation to you. This week, spend some time with God in the garden of your soul.

Rachel Rowley

In the Garden of Your Soul

In the morning, LORD, you hear my voice; in the morning I
lay my requests before you and wait expectantly.
Psalm 5:3

If you have visited my home, you have probably seen a large garden spider. It is black and yellow, and it spun a web between an evergreen tree and a lilac bush. The nucleus of the web was about three feet wide, and it had anchors at the corners that went out about six feet. The spider had caught several grasshoppers, and it was a large, fat, happy spider. After I observed the spider for about ten days, I had a unique and somewhat disturbing experience. It was a Thursday at 3:00 a.m. when I awoke to the most unusual presence of God. For an hour, God spoke to me in a parable about the spider, its web, and the grasshopper.

I love to walk out into my yard in the morning with a hot cup of cinnamon hazelnut coffee and watch God's creations. Until I moved into this house, I was pretty much deathly afraid of spiders. They still don't make my top-ten list, but I am learning to look at them through different eyes. I watch them spin their webs—those intricate tapestries, each an original design. My first thought about the webs is how much work they involve. Those spiders spin their webs and catch their dinner and then, by morning, a strong wind or a branch has moved and destroyed the web, or some spiders deconstruct their own webs on purpose. So they spin another web—another original design—and the story repeats itself. To be honest, I get tired just thinking about how hard they work, how their work only lasts a day or so, and then how they have to start over.

That's what I was thinking about when God interrupted my thoughts and said, *"The spiders don't think of it as work; it doesn't make them tired to do what they were created to do. Rachel, when you have a passion for someone, does it make you tired when you invest time in them? Does it weary you to cook a meal for them? Is it in vain when you have them in your home?"*

"No, not at all."

"Why?"

"Because I love them. Because I have been blessed and want to share that blessing with others."

God continued, *"Rachel, if you spend time in the garden of your soul, I will teach you how to create webs that don't leave you feeling tired or weary. Your webs will glisten like the dew because they will flow from a heart of love."*

Yes, Lord. I need to spend more time in the garden of my soul.

Rachel Rowley

Disobedience Brings Disaster

Therefore the LORD's anger burns against his people; his hand is raised and he strikes them down. The mountains shake, and the dead bodies are like refuse in the streets. Yet for all this, his anger is not turned away, his hand is still upraised.
Isaiah 5:25

As two scared freshmen, we tried to get acquainted. Jim had a lot going for him—he pulled top marks in high school, and in a few weeks, he became a leader on the freshman football team.

However, his lifestyle was not as disciplined as his mental or physical practices. He was "mighty to drink wine" (Isaiah 5:22, KJV), and when com-

302

bined with his card playing, his drinking would "continue until night" (5:11, KJV). He simply called it "moderate drinking." He bragged of his sexual exploits, anticipating the "new morality" by ten years. He was among "them that call evil good, and good evil" (5:20, KJV). When I accepted Christ, his response was ridicule, for he regarded "not the work of the LORD" (5:12, KJV).

I watched as his body, worn down by long nights, soon crumbled. During exam week, he awoke one morning unable to get out of bed—he had rheumatic fever. It caused him to miss a year of school. His heart was damaged by the illness—the football star couldn't climb a flight of stairs. By age thirty-three, he was dead. While there are other sources of personal tragedy than one's own sin, personal disobedience always brings personal disaster (5:25).[121]

It Seemed Like Such a Little Thing

Then Pharaoh's daughter went down to the Nile to bathe, and her
attendants were walking along the riverbank. She saw the basket among
the reeds and sent her female slave to get it. She opened it and saw
the baby. He was crying, and she felt sorry for him.
"This is one of the Hebrew babies," she said.
Exodus 2:5–6

In Pharaoh's mind, extermination of all baby boys was the only solution to his problem with the Hebrews. The Hebrews had come to Egypt when Joseph brought his family there to save them from famine in Israel. A previous pharaoh who had appointed Joseph his prime minister was sympathetic to Joseph's family. Now there was a new king who feared the Hebrews' fast population growth.

The new pharaoh urged the Hebrew midwives to kill the baby boys at birth. However, the midwives maneuvered around his command and would not do it. Then Pharaoh issued an order: "Every Hebrew boy that is born you must throw into the Nile, but let every girl live" (Exodus 1:22).

One day, Pharaoh's daughter went down to the Nile to bathe and saw a basket floating among the reeds. She sent her slave girl to get it. When Pha-

---

121. Previously published in *Come Ye Apart* March–April–May 1971 (Kansas City, MO: WordAction Publishing Co.), 83. Used by permission.

raoh's daughter opened the basket and saw a crying Hebrew baby, she felt pity and decided to spare him.

This was a gracious act of compassion by Pharaoh's daughter. It is always a great thing when anyone spares another human's life. However, since the Hebrew population was exploding, and Pharaoh had made his extermination orders public, we may assume that hundreds of baby boys were being thrown into the river. Thus, in the overall life of the nation, it must have seemed like such a small thing—one baby spared.

The baby was floating in the basket because after hiding him for three months, his mother determined she could hide him no longer. She prepared a papyrus basket, waterproofed it with tar and pitch, and put it among the reeds in the river with the baby inside. The baby's sister stood at a distance to watch what happened to him.

Once Pharaoh's daughter discovered the baby in the basket, the baby's sister approached her and asked if she wanted a Hebrew woman to nurse the baby. When Pharaoh's daughter said yes, the sister recruited their mother. To add to the surprising turn of events, Pharaoh's daughter paid the mother to take care of him. When the child was older, his mother took him to Pharaoh's daughter, and she named him Moses (Exodus 2:1–10).

Then Moses became an adult. And what happened next?

- God said, "I will be with you" (Exodus 3:12).
- Moses became the leader of the Hebrews.
- He confronted Pharaoh, called on him to release his people, and stood for God during the ten great judgments against Egypt.
- He led Israel out of Egypt and across the Red Sea, where Pharaoh's pursuing army drowned.
- He received God's Ten Commandments on Mount Sinai for his people and the world.
- He led Israel across the wilderness to the promised land.
- He brought them to the Jordan River and prepared them to enter the promised land.
- At age 120, after commissioning Joshua to lead Israel in the promised land, Moses was promoted into the Lord's presence (Deuteronomy 34:7–12).

At first, it seemed like such a little thing that a princess took a few minutes to retrieve a basket from the river. But once God used the situation to shape the life of his people, we see the end result. There is a song that says, "Little is much when God is in it." What do you suppose God might do in your life with something that seems like such a little thing?

Brought Out to Bring In

*But he brought us out from there to bring us in and give us the land
he promised on oath to our ancestors. The LORD commanded us to
obey all these decrees and to fear the LORD our God, so that we
might always prosper and be kept alive, as is the case today.
And if we are careful to obey all this law before the LORD our God,
as he has commanded us, that will be our righteousness.*
Deuteronomy 6:23–25

Life is filled with situations where you're brought out in order to be brought in.

I had to be brought out of my law school plan in order to be brought in to seminary. God had called me to ministry.

I had to be brought out of my relationship with a certain girlfriend in order to be brought in to my relationship with Nancy, who became my wife.

You'll probably agree that this pattern is part of your life too.

Israel had to be brought out of slavery in order to be brought into the promised land. From leeks, onions, and garlic to a land flowing with milk and honey; from being whipped by cruel taskmasters to winning great battles like Jericho; from making bricks in the hot sun to possessing their own personal property. By "bringing them out" to "bring them in," God did for Israel what they couldn't do for themselves. To accomplish this, God performed miracles—he unleashed plagues in Egypt; parted the Red Sea; led Israel through the wilderness by a pillar of cloud and a pillar of fire; provided them manna for breakfast and quail for supper. This new land would bring them prosperity as long as they obeyed the God who gave it to them. As a matter of fact, their obedience to the Lord would be their righteousness.

And for us in the new era under Jesus Christ, the principle remains. Peter preached, "Repent, then, and turn to God, so that your sins may be wiped out, that times of refreshing may come from the Lord" (Acts 3:19). We've been brought out of our sins and brought into a refreshing relationship with God. Jesus said to Paul, "I am sending you to them to open their eyes and turn them from darkness to light, and from the power of Satan to God, so that they may receive forgiveness of sins and a place among those who are sanctified by faith in me" (Acts 26:17–18). We've been brought out from darkness to be brought into the light. We've been brought out from the power of Satan to be brought in to God—and even more, to be brought into sanctification by faith in Jesus.

Is this bringing out in order to bring in at work in your spiritual life?

What Does the Voice of the Spirit Sound Like?

While Peter was still thinking about the vision, the Spirit said to him,
"Simon, three men are looking for you."
Acts 10:19

During a particularly challenging time in my life, I received this note from a former student and coworker: "I hope and pray both you and Nancy are well. I've been thinking of you the last couple weeks, for a number of reasons, and I thought I had better act on those thoughts (just like you taught us) and reach out."

Earl Lee taught me, "If an idea just won't go away, I tend to consider it divine leadership." Earl Lee was a godly, balanced, Christian man who kept moving forward in powerful ministry and influence. The New Testament, particularly the book of Acts, is filled with many references to divine leadership—these encounters can be dramatic, such as a vision or an audible divine voice. Note in today's scripture that Peter was still thinking about the dramatic vision God had given him when he heard the Spirit speak. When Peter was thinking about the vision, was it like my friend thinking about me and encouraging me, even though no one had told him I was going through a challenging time? Both of these scenarios sound like Earl Lee's notion of the idea that won't go away.

Sometimes we receive an impression that may be what some Christians call the prompting of the Holy Spirit. Admittedly, we must observe some guidelines and cautions when it comes to determining whether an impression *is* from the Spirit—otherwise, a person can go off the deep end. (These cautions will be discussed later.)

Early in the summer, we were urged to make an appointment with an outstanding doctor who specialized in a condition we were treating. When we called the doctor's office for an appointment, we learned that the earliest opening was December 9. However, the scheduler told us that we could call periodically to see if a cancellation opened up an earlier appointment.

A few months later, on August 4, I had the impression that I should call the office and ask whether there had been any cancellations (it was the only time I had done so). Amazingly, the doctor had just had one. The scheduler asked if we could be there at 8:30 the next morning. So we were able to go in for the much-needed specialist appointment four months earlier than originally scheduled.

Someone once said, "The divine voice is not often expressed in audible words; it is made known as a heart consciousness." Oh, Lord, make my heart and mind sensitive to your leadership in whatever form you give it!

From Atheism to Christ

No one can come to me unless the Father who sent me draws them,
and I will raise them up at the last day.
John 6:44

Angela had been a faithful attender at the local church, but her husband, Steffen, was not interested in church. As a matter of fact, he claimed to be an atheist. Eventually, as their marriage deteriorated and they seemed to be going separate ways, Steffen agreed to do marriage counseling with Angela's pastor. Over the course of their counseling sessions, he agreed to go to church, give it a chance, and rethink his position.

"I want to come to church," Steffen said, "but I'm not sure I'll ever believe."

Even so, Steffen started reading the Bible, Mark Cahill's *One Heartbeat Away—Your Journey into Eternity*, and Lee Strobel's *The Case for Christ*. As he attended church services, Steffen's attitude began to soften. He even joined Angela in attending the spring revival services.

One Wednesday, the pastor invited Steffen to lunch. I joined them, and during our meal, I was able to share with Steffen my journey from agnosticism to faith. Eventually, Steffen came to realize that he didn't need to have every question answered before making a decision. He also realized he didn't have to be perfect immediately.

Soon, Steffen was convinced he was ready. Finally, in the pastor's office, Steffen prayed to receive Christ. He immediately felt relieved, like the weight of the world was off his shoulders. He knew that someone was with him; that someone he could rely upon was listening. Indeed, he felt that Christ had entered his heart.

When he told Angela what happened, she was surprised and joyful. That closing night of the revival services, they came to the altar together. Others gathered around them, and Steffen felt their support. He said, "I knew I'd done the right thing. This is for real—Jesus is real."

Today, thirty-five years after his conversion, I talked to Steffen on the phone. He told me that his marriage has done a 180-degree turnaround from when he and Angela first started counseling—now their marriage is as close to perfect as possible.

Steffen has done five *Basic Bible Studies for New and Growing Christians* with people from his church and has read Matthew, Mark, Luke, and Acts. He's put in new shrubbery and landscaping for the church. He and Angela have begun tithing because they've realized that the money is all God's in the first place. He has been witnessing to a friend.

His pastor says that Steffen now has the biggest smile and is usually the last one out the door of any church service. Imagine—from atheism to Christ. And the last one out of the church, no less![122]

A Seeking Savior and One Bible Verse

For the Son of Man came to seek and to save the lost.
Luke 19:10

But seek first his kingdom and his righteousness,
and all these things will be given to you as well.
Matthew 6:33

Jesus is a seeking Savior!

---

122. Previously published in *The Good News: The Chic Shaver Center for Evangelism Newsletter* (June 2009).

My father did not have the blessing of growing up in a Christian home or going to church. When he was a young man, he often saw a billboard near his hometown with the Bible verse, "Matthew 6:33—Seek first the kingdom of God and his righteousness, and all these things shall be added to you" (NKJV). He wondered about these words for many years. Thus, before my dad started following Jesus, he knew *one* Bible verse—and it wasn't John 3:16! It was Matthew 6:33.

In the spring of 1972, at the invitation of a neighbor named Mike, my dad entered a church for the first time. At the time, my father was lost, broken, and living in sin. An evangelist was preaching that Sunday. My dad says it felt like the speaker had followed him around his whole life and was preaching *right at* him that day. Do you know what passage the evangelist preached from that first Sunday my dad went to church? Matthew 6:33—the one verse my dad knew! Jesus was seeking my dad!

At the end of that first service, my father met Jesus at the altar. His sins were forgiven. He was a healed man. His shame and disgrace were transformed by the mercy and grace of God. I had a new dad!

Jesus is a seeking Savior!

Dr. Scott Rainey
Global Director of Sunday School & Discipleship Ministries International
Church of the Nazarene
Co-director of the Chic Shaver Center for Evangelism[123]

I've Never Had a Bad Day

Rejoice always, pray continually, give thanks in all circumstances;
for this is God's will for you in Christ Jesus.
1 Thessalonians 5:16–18

There is something about followers of Christ—especially Spirit-filled and sanctified Christians—that enables them to live victoriously despite life's difficulties. They do not give thanks *for* all circumstances, but are empowered to

---

123. Previously published in *The Good News: The Chic Shaver Center for Evangelism Newsletter* (June 2020).

give thanks *in* all circumstances. I do not claim that all Christians live in that victory—but some do, and that life is available to all.

I have seen this victorious living in my son, Paul. (You can read more about him in devotionals #20 and #21 in this book.) A husband and father of four, he has undergone several cancer surgeries: doctors removed a melanoma from his shoulder when he was a young adult; a basal-cell carcinoma from his chest when he was in his thirties; a basal-cell carcinoma near his ear and down his jawline in his late forties; and a very aggressive basal-cell carcinoma in his neck in his early fifties. The last surgery included the removal of his voice box and much of his neck.

Paul's fourth cancer surgery took thirteen hours and was the most serious of them all. With additional surgery, he was eventually able to speak in a low, halting voice. When we spent some time with him about six months after his surgery, we were bursting with questions for him. He gave us the following responses:

"My field is narrowed, so I carefully pick my words."

"From the time the doctor said 'cancer' and 'the voice box might need to be removed,' I had this peace, and I felt that was what I had to do. I felt I could handle it."

When we asked him about the bulk in his neck due to it being rebuilt with his chest muscle, he said, "I had wished there was not so much bulk, and now it seems like such a little thing."

To the questions for which he had no answer, he repeatedly said, "God still knows my name."

And then he wept.

By the time of our family vacation a few months later, something in his throat had malfunctioned, and Paul lost what weak voice he'd had. He was facing another surgery. Yet somehow he could see hope beyond every difficulty. His sister Miriam asked him, "How do you feel after four cancer surgeries, the loss of your voice box and now your voice, and all that's happened to you?"

Because he could not speak, he wrote his answer: "I've never had a bad day."

If you pressed him, Paul would say, "I lost my voice box, but I'm still alive."

Joyful always; praying continually; giving thanks *in* all circumstances.

Living under the Bargain

When Jesus heard this, he said to him, "You still lack one thing. Sell everything you have and give to the poor, and you will have treasure in heaven. Then come, follow me." When he heard this, he became very sad, because he was very wealthy.
Luke 18:22–23

Peter said to him, "We have left all we had to follow you!" "Truly I tell you," Jesus said to them, "no one who has left home or wife or brothers or sisters or parents or children for the sake of the kingdom of God will fail to receive many times as much in this age, and in the age to come eternal life."
Luke 18:28–30

The frosting on the cake was a big deal when I was a kid. Our family suppers regularly included meat, potatoes, and vegetables, compliments of my mom, who was a good cook. After we had cleaned our plates, there was almost always great dessert—a homemade pie or cake. My favorite was the white cake with thick chocolate icing. I regularly cut the icing off, ate the cake first, then finally ate the pure icing, savoring every mouthful. I'm not sure where it came from, but I'd developed this little philosophy: *save the best for last.*

I carried that philosophy into adult life. However, I am now living in an age of instant gratification. Some people today would no doubt eat their frosting before eating one bit of meat or vegetable. But I believe my philosophy works well—it has enabled me to make choices with the long range in view.

A wealthy ruler approached Jesus and asked him, "What must I do to inherit eternal life?" (Luke 18:20).

Jesus responded by listing five of the Ten Commandments. When the ruler claimed to have kept them all, Jesus countered, "You still lack one thing. Sell everything you have and give to the poor, and you will have treasure in heaven. Then come, follow me" (18:22).

What was the ruler's response? He became "very sad." Should we assume that Jesus asks all Christians to sell all their possessions and give them to the poor? Probably not, though over time Christians have learned to give special help to the poor. In this encounter, Jesus touched the most sensitive spot in the young ruler's life and his dearest love—his wealth—and asked him to surrender even that. Likewise, Christ will also probe us to surrender our dearest love for our good and his glory.

Then Christ gives the ruler another instruction: "Come, follow me." With these words, Jesus asked the young ruler to surrender not just his wealth, but his whole life.

Picking up on what was happening, other people then asked Jesus, "Who then can be saved?" (18:26)

Christ assured them that with God, salvation is possible. Peter then asserted, "We have left all we had to follow you!" (18:28).

Jesus then responded that each of his followers, whatever their sacrifice, will receive back "many times as much in this age, and in the age to come eternal life" (18:30). Wow! What a bargain—for the long run.

I hesitate to use the term "bargain" when it comes to following Christ. I can honestly say that my life is a daily, personal, ongoing, joyous, love-filled, peace-producing fellowship with Christ; and this two-way relationship is so rich that it is a joy to worship him, serve him, and obey him. Thus, the notion of reward rarely comes to my mind. Shouldn't this be true for all of us?

My son, Paul, frequently says of his life, "I'm living under the blessing." I suppose we can add, "I'm living under the bargain." Even though we must be sure that our motives are pure, Jesus assures us that he is saving the best for last.

The Importance of *If*

If my people, who are called by my name, will humble themselves
and pray and seek my face and turn from their wicked ways, then I will
hear from heaven, and I will forgive their sin and will heal their land.
2 Chronicles 7:14

Imagine that I promise my oldest daughter that on the day of her sixteenth birthday, I will drive her down to the Department of Motor Vehicles to take her driving test and obtain her license. Then, one week before her birthday, she comes down with spinal meningitis and, for two solid weeks, she is hospitalized in critical condition.

I miss the promised date because, in my love for her, there is no way I'm hauling my daughter out of that hospital bed to force her to take her driving test. No one will accuse me of being a promise-breaker for delaying the test—

there has been a monumental change in the surrounding conditions. Thus, my character of love dictates the change in date. And a few months later, my daughter is a happy, licensed driver.

God has an unchanging, holy character. As James 1:17 proclaims, God "does not change like shifting shadows." God told Solomon that even when he stopped the rain or sent locusts or plagues in holy judgment, he would change his action *if* his people would do the following:

- Humble themselves
- Pray
- Seek his face
- Turn from their wicked ways

How could this change occur? By a major change in the people's condition—that is, a change in their attitude and posture toward the Lord.

Because God is holy, he must judge sin. As Romans 6:23 warns, "The wages of sin is death." But when the unholy human condition is transformed by prayers and repentance into forgiveness and holy living, God acts differently: he will "forgive their sin and will heal their land."

For all we know of a holy God, remember the importance of the *if*!

The Lord almighty proclaimed through his prophet Jeremiah, "Jerusalem will become a heap of rubble" (Jeremiah 26:18). And then what happened? Jeremiah 26:19 says, "Did not Hezekiah fear the LORD and seek his favor? And did not the LORD relent, so that he did not bring the disaster he pronounced against them?" What changed here? Someone prayed.

Pay close attention when you see the word "if" in Scripture (emphases mine):

- "*If* we confess our sins, he is faithful and just and will forgive us our sins and purify us from all unrighteousness" (1 John 1:9).
- "But *if* we walk in the light, as he is in the light, we have fellowship with one another, and the blood of Jesus, his Son, purifies from all sin" (1 John 1:7).
- "But now he has reconciled you by Christ's physical body through death to present you holy in his sight, without blemish and free from accusation—*if* you continue in your faith, established and firm, and do not move from the hope held out in the gospel" (Colossians 1:22–23). Yes! *If*!

The Power of a Sentence

Dear friend, do not imitate what is evil but what is good.
Anyone who does what is good is from God.
3 John 1:11

It's amazing what can result from a sentence or two—especially when it comes to giving someone advice. More important than the words themselves is the action they prompt. Of course, the people listening to the words must consider, decide, and act for themselves. Still, there is a certain power and influence in the original words.

The serpent said to Eve in the garden of Eden, "Did God really say, 'You must not eat from any tree in the garden'?" (Genesis 3:1). Though his words were a question, they implied that Eve should eat as she saw fit. Eve, and then Adam, disobeyed God's direct command by eating the forbidden fruit. They then became ashamed, hid from God, and brought a curse upon themselves and the whole earth.

Concerned about his political power, King Herod spoke a few sentences to wise men who sought the newborn king of the Jews: "Go and search carefully for the child. As soon as you find him, report to me, so that I too may go and worship him" (Matthew 2:8). The wise men found the child in Bethlehem but, after being warned in a dream, they did not return to King Herod (2:12). This is an example of refusing words of suggestion because they will result in evil.

Lydia, a wealthy businesswoman, had just opened her heart to the message of Christ when she uttered a sentence to Paul and his team: "If you consider me a believer in the Lord . . . come and stay at my house" (Acts 16:15). They agreed, and godly fellowship blossomed. Lydia became a strong leader for Jesus.

Paul encouraged his young friend and partner Timothy with the following words: "But you, man of God, flee from all this [evil], and pursue righteousness, godliness, faith, love, endurance and gentleness" (1 Timothy 6:11). Timothy pursued and took hold of eternal life. Now, two of Paul's letters to him have become part of our Holy Bible.

It started with a simple sentence. Phil said to me, "You ought to invite Scott to come to seminary." So I phoned Scott and invited him to attend the seminary. I also offered him an evangelism scholarship and a chance to assist me in my responsibilities at my local church. He attended, served, and flourished.

After graduating, Scott took a position as minister of evangelism in a strong church. Next, he served as lead pastor of another church for eight years. During his tenure, the church's attendance grew from four hundred to seven hundred.

Then Scott, his wife, and his daughters heard God's call to leave the USA and become missionaries. Scott became a field strategy coordinator and oversaw the planting of new churches in eight different countries.

Eventually, the leaders of his denomination called him to become international director for Sunday school and discipleship for all the denomination's churches worldwide.

I know many people and godly influences have formed Scott, but still, I am so glad for that single sentence from Phil: "You ought to invite Scott to come to seminary."

And then there is John's advice to his friend Gaius: "Dear friend, do not imitate what is evil but what is good. Anyone who does good is from God" (3 John 1:11).

What's a sentence someone said to you recently? What sentence have you said to someone else? What will happen in the future as a result?

Carry Another's Burden

Carry each other's burdens, and in this way you
will fulfill the law of Christ.
Galatians 6:2

Let us not become weary in doing good, for at the proper time
we will reap a harvest if we do not give up.
Galatians 6:9

Harry Rich's legacy is a powerful and distinguished life of ministry—from planting a church right out of college; to serving as a missionary to Haiti for fourteen years; to pastoring two other churches; to serving as his church's district superintendent in Quebec; to setting up French-speaking ministries in Rwanda and the Congo. In war, after 6,500 believers were martyred, Harry

Rich built schools, started a theological school, and planted forty-three churches in the refugee camps. Now retired, he lives in Waynesburg, Pennsylvania.

In Waynesburg, Harry assisted a couple in his local church who had mobility challenges—he built a ramp to their front door to make access easier. After her husband's death, the wife moved into an assisted-living apartment. When she was hospitalized, apartment management moved her to a different unit. Somehow, in the move, her food and kitchen utensils were lost. Harry had been serving at the assisted-living facility by holding regular Sunday afternoon services. As he did so, he sensed he must help his friend.

At first, Harry planned to go to the store to buy silverware and food for her. However, this was during the 2020 national shutdown for the coronavirus pandemic. Harry decided instead that he had enough of what she needed in his own house. He took some of his utensils and food to her.

I heard this story from Harry's son Dwight, who, along with wife, Carolyn, has served as a missionary in Ecuador for the past thirty-five years. Harry Rich—what a life. What a legacy of carrying others' burdens and never wearying in doing good. Harry is ninety-two years old—older than any resident of the assisted-living apartments where he served.

I am constantly amazed by the hundreds of Christ followers who live their lives with such faithfulness. You, too, can be part of this heroic crowd.

God Really Changes People

He replied, "Whether he is a sinner or not, I don't know.
One thing I do know. I was blind but now I see!"
John 9:25

The following testimony was shared in a Boise, Idaho, revival service on October 31, 2010:

Nearly three years ago, my life was consumed by drugs and alcohol. I was in an abusive relationship, had quit college several times, was constantly late for or missing work, and was barely hanging onto life. I was alone. In a moment of desperation, I went to a church near my home and asked the minister to pray with me for freedom from my addiction. That night I went home and felt the same, so I went on living my life as I had been before that day. I continued to live that horrible life, not knowing God had heard my prayer. Six months later, I got arrested. That was the first event of many that brought me back to God. The state told me I had to go to AA and counseling or else go to jail. I was scared.

Then God put a man in my life (who is now my husband) who held my hand and went to more than fifty AA meetings with me until I was comfortable enough to go on my own.

Then, through those meetings, God put a woman in my life who taught me how to love and forgive myself and pray every day.

Then God put another person in my life who encouraged me to quit smoking, and another who got me thinking about going back to school.

When Andrew and I decided to get married, we wanted to do so in a church. Then God put a pastor in my life who was patient and understanding, and who is helping me understand the word of God. God has continued to work in my life in more ways than I can count. By the grace of God, I have not had a drink or a drug since April 22, 2008. And I haven't had a cigarette since March 19, 2009. I turned my life over to Christ on August 27, 2010.

So maybe God didn't answer my prayer the way I thought he was going to—but he answered it exactly how he needed for me to get better. Then he continued to put people in my life who helped keep me that way.

Now I hope someday I can inspire someone by sharing my story and helping them to know God the way so many others have helped me. I know my past isn't pretty, but it brought me to where I am today, and for that I am grateful.

Trish Thomas[124]

AUGUST 31   **243**

Our Amazing Advantage

What may be known about God is plain to them,
because God has made it plain to them.
Romans 1:19

124. Previously published in *The Good News: The Chic Shaver Center for Evangelism Newsletter* (March 2011).

Regardless of personality, history, or background, when most people think about evangelism, their initial response is usually fear, anxiety, lack of confidence, and stress.

However, Scripture gives us an edge that prepares the way for disciples in their evangelistic work. This spiritual edge is what Wesleyans call "prevenient grace," which softens a pre-Christian's heart with an awareness of the divine. In Romans 5:8 (KJV), Paul writes, "While we were yet sinners, Christ died for us." In Romans 1:19–23, he reminds us that all creation is aware of God's presence. According to Paul, this awareness of God exists even in the darkest and most sinful places. Additionally, in John 6:44, Jesus reminds us that no one can come to the Father unless the Father who sent Jesus draws them.

Personally, before coming to faith, I experienced this keen awareness of God and eternity. I felt it as I mourned the loss of my brother, who had died at only nineteen years old. While living through this difficult time, I realized that I had a choice about how I would spend eternity—I knew that I needed to respond to God. I had a desire to move toward God. Additionally, I remember that during times of crisis, I would "happen" to hear a minister on the radio or see a church sign that reminded me of eternity. Each time, my soul was drawn to the thought of God. These were moments of prevenient grace!

I praise God for his prevenient grace that prepared me for a moment in 1976 when a young man asked me if I would make it to heaven. In the moments that followed, on a forty-minute drive from Virginia Beach to Williamsburg, Virginia, all these instances of God's prevenient grace raced to the forefront of my memory. In that pivotal moment, that young Christian took a risk and reached out to me. It became apparent to me that from the time of my birth, God's Spirit had been preparing my soul for that encounter. As I drove, those memories of God's fingerprints in my life from childhood became more real every mile. Upon arriving home, the investment of the Spirit and the risk taken by a young Christian all culminated in a moment of faith that changed my life forever.

I believe God is faithful to do his work in the following ways:

- He gave us his Word.
- He sent us his Son.
- He gave us his Holy Spirit.
- In this moment, his prevenient grace is active in the hearts and lives of every pre-Christian, preparing them for encounters with witnesses.
- Jesus asks us to go make disciples.

How encouraging it is to know that God's prevenient grace goes before us. Go share your faith and reap the harvest knowing that God has gone before us and goes with us!

Mark Bane
Director of Evangelism and New Church Development
USA/Canada Region
Church of the Nazarene[125]

Facts from the Rescue Mission

For I was hungry and you gave me something to eat, I was thirsty and
you gave me something to drink, I was a stranger and you invited me in,
I needed clothes and you clothed me, I was sick and you looked after me,
I was in prison and you came to visit me.
Matthew 25:35–36

In America, there is no greater group of outcasts than the individuals who make up the homeless population. Consider the following statistics:

- 90–95 percent of homeless men and 60 percent of homeless women are substance abusers.
- The average age of a homeless adult is thirty-five.
- More than 60 percent of the homeless are women and children.
- More than half of homeless adults were introduced to alcohol or drugs before the age of twelve
- Most of the homeless were physically and/or sexually abused as children.

Every day, the Sunday Breakfast Mission provides more than eight hundred meals to hungry men, women, and children. Some nights, more than three hundred men, women, and children are under our roof. Almost two hundred men and women have graduated from our eighteen-month disciple-

---

125. Previously published in *The Good News: The Chic Shaver Center for Evangelism Newsletter* (December 2019).

ship program. But we find our greatest joy in the nearly ten thousand people who have committed their lives to Christ in the last fourteen years.

Rev. Tom Laymon, Sr.

Director, Sunday Breakfast Mission

Wilmington, Delaware[126]

Not Too Old

So here I am today, eighty-five years old! I am still as strong today
as the day Moses sent me out; I'm just as vigorous to go out
to battle now as I was then.
Joshua 14:10–11

Mark is a young husband, father, and part-time pastoral staff member at his church. Just five years ago, he and his wife did not even attend church. Everything changed when, one day in a chance encounter at the local Applebee's, a man in his seventies invited them to a service.

Enoch is a young contractor who has built or remodeled a dozen churches over the past several years. He devotes his "secular" career to serving churches. As a young adult, Enoch dropped out of church. When he returned, a man discipled him using *Basic Bible Studies for New and Growing Christians*. The man, who was in his seventies, later stood up as best man at Enoch's wedding.

After his wife died far too young, Terry made a decision to follow Christ for the first time in his life. He reached out to his former sixth-grade teacher, who was now retired and—you guessed it—in his seventies. This retired teacher led Terry to the Lord and then led him through *Basic Bible Studies for New and Growing Christians*.

What do these three young men have in common? You already know—the same retired schoolteacher with no ministerial credentials played the role of soul winner and shepherd in each of their lives. Do we have to be young in order to win young people? Don't suggest that to my dad, John P. Sher-

---

126. Previously published in *The Good News: The Chic Shaver Center for Evangelism Newsletter* (June 2017).

wood—he doesn't know any better. I pray God will help us raise up an army just as oblivious as John.

Dr. Scott Sherwood
District Superintendent, Northwest Illinois District
Church of the Nazarene[127]

Did You Leave Jesus in the Parking Lot?

Obey them not only to win their favor when their eye is on you,
but as slaves of Christ, doing the will of God from your heart.
Serve wholeheartedly, as if you were serving the Lord, not people.
Ephesians 6:6–7

Keith Miller had gone to seminary, served on two church boards, and taught Sunday school. One day, a coworker who had been in the same office with Keith for over a year said, "Keith, I didn't know you were a Christian." Keith realized that, although he had accepted Christ, he left Christ in the parking lot when he walked into his workplace.

The words of today's scripture were directed to slaves—let's deal with that. There were sixty million slaves in the Roman Empire. Some were doctors or teachers; others were common laborers. The influence of Christianity eventually freed the slaves, but at this stage in history, the most immediate issue was how to function in the workplace. We can learn from this passage when we read it in terms of workers and bosses: Workers, do your work well—not just when the boss is watching you—as if you were working for Christ, not your boss. God's will is for you to do your work well. Let your relationships with authority figures show Christ. Surround that troublesome person with love and prayer.

Do your work as unto the Lord; show that piece of work to the Lord. The assembly-line worker who incorrectly installed the air-conditioning hose in my car must have known. As water dripped on my wife's feet and soaked

---

127. Previously published in *The Good News: The Chic Shaver Center for Evangelism Newsletter* (March 2018).

the car's floor, I was forced to go to the dealership again and again to get the problem fixed. The installer's poor work robbed me of my time.

Pray for coworkers on your way to the coffee machine or drinking fountain. Pray that God will cause them to ask you the right question so you may share Christ's good news.

Bosses, you are responsible for how you treat your workers. Remember, the Lord is above you, and he doesn't play favorites (6:9).

When it comes to unpleasant work conditions, you may not always be able to escape them, but you can conquer them. As to authority, obey as the servant of Christ. As to work, show it to God. As for those under you, don't take advantage.

In India, C. T. Venugopal brought Christ into his work for the government railroad. Eventually, he became a top authority figure at the railroad. He told his coworkers, "I'm a Christian, but I want you to help me be a better one." He asked them to tell him when he fell short.

Meanwhile, there was tension between India and Pakistan. India's approach had been to give Pakistan one record for every record Pakistan gave them. But Brother Venu, as he was called, gave Pakistan all the records, with no strings attached.

Upon receiving the records from Venu, the Muslims in Pakistan said, "We can't let the Hindus be better than us." So they gave India more records.

When Venu revealed that Pakistan owed India 2,200,000 rupees in the deal, someone said, "Check it."

Another said, "If Mr. Venu says so, it's so."

His reputation and Christian character preceded him.

Let this serve as a reminder: Don't leave Jesus in the parking lot.

The Hand of the Lord Was on Me

Because the hand of the LORD my God was on me,
I took courage and gathered leaders from Israel to go up with me.
Ezra 7:28

When I was a boy, the best words I ever heard from my dad were, "Son, I'm proud of you." In those words, I found the courage to move ahead to the next challenge in life. Strangely, the words made me feel like his hand was on my shoulder, as if to say, *Good job*, or, *Well done*; as if to say, *You can make it*, or, *I'll give you direction*; as if to say, *Here is the way into the unknown.*

Ezra, too, felt an unseen hand on his shoulder—the hand of the Lord. The Lord had moved the heart of Cyrus, king of Persia, to decree the rebuilding of the temple in Jerusalem and grant permission for exiles to return (Ezra 1:2–4). Now, King Artaxerxes commissioned Ezra to take silver, gold, temple articles, and people to supply the temple and teach God's law. After a four-month journey, Ezra arrived in Jerusalem. Throughout his mission, Ezra repeatedly sensed God's hand as he provided Ezra with the following: all that Ezra asked (7:6); a safe journey (7:9); the courage to gather leaders (7:28); capable leaders (8:18); protection on the road (8:22); protection from bandits (8:31).

I wrote the following entry in my devotional journal: *To live in your loving and powerful presence is my great joy. Often, I say, "Keep your hand on me." I do not wish to diminish the great joy of your full presence; it is my shortcut way of saying, "Lord, be with me in a certain endeavor. Your hand on me speaks of steadiness, strength, uplift, encouragement, guidance."*

The Lord would like to put his hand on *you*.

Just One Dollar

The very spring of our actions is the love of Christ.
2 Corinthians 5:14, PHILLIPS

*Our sole defence, our only weapon, is a life of integrity, whether we meet
with honour or dishonour, praise or blame. Called "impostors" we must be
true, called "nobodies" we must be in the public eye. Never far from death,
yet here we are alive, always "going through it" yet never "going under."*
2 Corinthians 6:7–9, PHILLIPS

It was almost Christmas, and our finances were limited. We would buy some gifts for our three children, but Nancy and I agreed to spend just one dollar on each other.

I had entered into full-time evangelism, which meant traveling to a different city and church every week. Often, I had no idea how much a given church would pay me. As an expression of my full surrender to God, I never set a minimum.

As a Christian, I know there are times when I must fight for the rights of others. But for me, as a spokesman for God, I believed that if *I* must fight for my rights, God may just let me do it. However, I also believed that if I surrendered my rights in order to be the servant of all, then the God who called me would have to fight for me. I really believe the words of John 12:25: "Anyone who loves their life will lose it, while anyone who hates their life in this world will keep it for eternal life."

Just before our financially strapped Christmas, I traveled a long distance to a small church for a revival meeting. I threw myself into the meeting, and there was real revival. As I left the church on the final night, the pastor handed me a check that I later saw amounted to less than my actual expenses for the week. I thanked him. Early in my ministry, I committed to being thankful for every offering given to me, no matter how small. At no time during the week had I made any comment about my personal financial needs.

As I walked to my car, a lady who had received spiritual help during the week stopped me. She pressed a piece of paper into my hand and told me to look in the back of my car. In the back of the car, I found a sack of groceries, a box of vegetables, a box wrapped in Christmas paper that said, "To Nancy, from Chic," and a wrapped box labeled, "To Chic, from Nancy." When we opened the boxes later, we discovered that Nancy's box "from" me contained two beautiful dresses, and my box "from" her contained an expensive topical Bible that I had wanted but couldn't afford. When I unfolded the piece of paper this woman had given me, I found a personal check made out for an amount that was two-thirds of the amount the church had paid me.

"Just one dollar." That's all I would spend on Nancy for Christmas, and all Nancy would spend on me. No one at the church knew about this. Yet "our sole defense, our only weapon, is a life of integrity." And, "We are always 'going through it' yet never 'going under.'"

A Godly Employer

Paul, a prisoner of Christ Jesus, and Timothy our brother,

To Philemon our dear friend and fellow worker—
also to Apphia our sister and Archippus our fellow soldier—
and to the church that meets in your home.
Philemon 1:1–2

I pray that your partnership with us in the faith may
be effective in deepening your understanding of every
good thing we share for the sake of Christ.
Philemon 1:6

His business wasn't large, but it was his own. And from that gas station enterprise, Clyde let his light shine for Jesus.

Like Philemon of old, Clyde's lifestyle could be characterized by the two phrases: "the church that meets in your home" (1:2), and "your partnership with us in the faith" (1:6). Philemon so loved Christ that he unselfishly gave up his beautiful home for worship each Lord's Day.

While Clyde didn't have organized church services in his home, he and his glowing wife opened their home to God's people in hospitality after many a church service. Some of the prayer that happened in that home hallowed the place as if it had been a church.

Clyde's ministry could also be described by the phrase "the church that meets in your gas station." When he first closed his station on Sundays, people said he was foolish; but Clyde was happy to obey God. Incidentally, his net profits were greater in six days with God than they had been in seven without God.

"Partnership in the faith"—Clyde embodied that too. He *radiated* for Jesus; he told people about Christ; he even got the family of one of his employees into church.

When it comes to a Philemon or a Clyde, the Pauls of every age rejoice in their faithfulness. Oh, Lord, increase their number.[128]

What if They Wanted Peanut Butter Sandwiches?

---

128. Previously published in *Come Ye Apart* October–November–December 1964 (Kansas City, MO: Nazarene Publishing House), 75. Used by permission. (This publication became *Reflecting God.*)

*Late in the afternoon the Twelve came to him and said, "Send the crowd
away so they can go to the surrounding villages and countryside and find
food and lodging, because we are in a remote place here." He replied, "You
give them something to eat." They answered, "We have only five loaves of
bread and two fish—unless we go and buy food for all this crowd." (About
five thousand men were there.) But he said to his disciples, "Have them sit
down in groups of about fifty each." The disciples did so, and everyone sat
down. Taking the five loaves and the two fish and looking up to heaven,
he gave thanks and broke them. Then he gave them to the disciples to
distribute to the people. They all ate and were satisfied, and the disciples
picked up twelve basketfuls of broken pieces that were left over.*
Luke 9:12–17

A very sharp layman was working with his pastor on a lay witness weekend.
Somehow they began discussing the miracle of the feeding of the five thousand. (Remember, five thousand *men* could mean something more like ten
or fifteen thousand *people* when we account for women and children.) By his
divine power, Jesus treated all of them to fish sandwiches.

At this point in the discussion, the layman blurted out, "What if they
wanted peanut butter sandwiches?"

He said it in jest, but his words describe many people's attitude toward Jesus's gracious work. Their small personal desires take precedence over God's
actions, and they miss some of the greatest blessings God wants to pour into
their lives. Open up your heart to this story.

Let's examine some of the messages we see in this scriptural account:
1. The disciples said, "Send the crowd away . . ." (Let the people do the
   best they can.)
2. He said, "You give them something to eat." (You take responsibility for
   the crowd.)
3. They said, "We have only five loaves . . . and two fish." (Our resources
   are so limited—this is impossible!)
4. He said, "Have them sit down. . . ." (*I've* got the answer. You watch!)
5. "The disciples did so." (This was the disciples' best move—they *obeyed*
   Jesus. And they did so without knowing all the details yet.)
6. He took the bread and fish and, "looking up to heaven," he gave thanks.
   (He showed them the only answer was by God's power.)
7. He gave the food "to the disciples to distribute to the people." (How
   good to finally get in line with God's will.)

8. "They all ate and were satisfied, and the disciples picked up twelve basketfuls" of leftovers. (As one preacher said, "No shortage, no wastage, no garbage.")

In this story, we see the difference between the disciples' way and Christ's way. Have you come to a place where you've realized that Christ's way is best? "All ate and were satisfied," and it was so abundant a blessing that there were even leftovers.

Ah! Rest!

For if Joshua had given them rest, God would not have spoken later about another day. There remains, then, a Sabbath-rest for the people of God; for anyone who enters God's rest also rests from their works, just as God did from his. Let us, therefore, make every effort to enter that rest, so that no one will perish by following their example of disobedience.
Hebrews 4:8–11

When I see Dan right after he gets off work, I see fatigue. The packages he lifts can weigh up to 75 pounds, and he will handle 1,200 packages in his shift. UPS delivers about 160,000 packages from his particular warehouse in a twenty-four-hour period. When Dan gets home, the sweetest thing he can experience is rest. Ah! Rest!

The Word of God offers rest for the people of God. In Hebrews 4:1–11, we read of four kinds of rest: creation rest, Sabbath rest, Canaan rest, and divine rest. The first three are illustrations and models for divine rest.

Israel's two greatest breakthroughs had been the crossing of the Red Sea and the crossing of the Jordan River. Their destination, the promised land, was to be their home. Soon after crossing the Red Sea, they were close to entering the promised land. But in that critical moment, they chose doubt over faith—they rejected the report of two faithful spies who urged them to enter the land. Because of their disobedience, they wandered in the wilderness for forty years until finally, Joshua led them in.

God brought Israel out of Egypt so he could take them into the promised land. Many Bible scholars believe that being freed from Egyptian slavery symbolizes salvation, and entering the land of blessing symbolizes sanctification. While Joshua gave the people rest from wilderness wandering, there still remains another rest for the people of God today—a divine rest; a Sabbath rest. This is so important that God urges us, "make every effort to enter that rest" (4:11).

How many Christians today, though, having truly accepted Christ and followed him in some measure, find themselves struggling, restless, uneasy, burdened?

Let a lesson from history help us. A. B. Earle was a Baptist evangelist whose ministry spanned from 1830 to 1880 in the United States, Canada, and the British Isles. He traveled 325,000 miles though the USA and Canada, preached 19,780 sermons, and saw 150,000 profess conversion in his meetings. Though Earle loved the work of ministry, he reported that he "long felt an inward unrest, a void in my soul that was not filled. . . . If I had peace, I feared it would not continue, and it did not." Meanwhile, his Christian life was up and down—now happy, then unhappy. He said, "The rest in Jesus for which I longed was still unfound." One sin that became especially troubling to him was his determination to have his own way. He realized that, "before I could be filled with the fullness of Christ's love, I must be emptied of self." During a meeting in Cape Cod, after years of prayer, seeking, and rededication, Earle gave the following testimony: "I was in my room alone, pleading for the fullness of Christ's love, when all at once a sweet heavenly peace filled all the vacuum in my soul, leaving no longing, no unrest, no dissatisfied feeling in my bosom. . . . Then for the first time in my life, I had the rest which is more than peace. . . . This change occurred about five o'clock, on the second day of November 1863. . . . A heaven of peace and rest fills my soul. Day and night the Savior seems by me."[129]

A. B. Earle went on in his ministry with new strength and greater victories. His personal life was marked by internal peace and rest. He even authored a book titled *The Rest of Faith*. No wonder!

Ah! Rest! Know that you too can experience it.

---

129. James Gilchrist Lawson, *Deeper Experiences of Famous Christians* (Anderson, IN: Warner Press, 1911), 301–09.

Back in Charge

*I pray that out of his glorious riches he may strengthen you
with power through his Spirit in your inner being.*
Ephesians 3:16

While Andy and Heather were facing challenges in their first church assignment, Heather sent me the following note:

Needless to say, much change has happened in our lives and has served to distract me from our ultimate goal here—to get this church alive again. However, since hearing your messages, I have realized that, although I was truly sanctified several years ago, I have since shoved Christ off the throne of my heart and hopped on, ready to reign myself. I began to feel the results of doing so: depression, anxiety, hopelessness, and a true feeling of defeat about the church before it has even begun!

Your messages were straight from the Holy Spirit into my heart and mind, and I have asked the Lord Jesus to reign supreme in my heart once more. I have begun praying and reading my Bible, and while I still don't know how the Lord is going to breathe life into this church or how we're going to get everything done that needs to be done, I do know for sure he is back in charge, as he should be, and we are straining once more to hear his direction. I am once again on fire for the Lord, and excited about what he's going to do in this ministry.

Let us be sure that the Lord Jesus reigns supreme in our hearts![130]

Under Pressure

*Your name will no longer be Jacob, but Israel, because you have
struggled with God and with humans and have overcome.*
Genesis 32:28

---

130. Previously published in *The Good News: The Chic Shaver Center for Evangelism Newsletter* (June 2006).

Have you ever felt the pressure?

Jacob did.

Sneaky; dishonest; deceptive. Born grasping his twin brother's heel, he is named Jacob, which means "heel grasper," or figuratively, "deceiver" (Genesis 25:26). As a young adult, he sells his famished and careless brother, Esau, a bowl of beans in exchange for Esau's birthright. This birthright includes the biggest portion of the inheritance from their father. Later, when their father Isaac is old and blind, Jacob and his mother trick him into giving Esau's blessing to Jacob.

When Esau learns of this, he angrily exclaims, "Isn't he rightly named Jacob? This is the second time he has taken advantage of me: He took my birthright, and now he's taken my blessing!" (Genesis 27:36). In his rage, Esau threatens to murder Jacob. Upon hearing this, Jacob flees.

To this point, though Isaac had pronounced blessings on Jacob, there is no indication that Jacob has a personal relationship with God. Under the pressure of his brother's threats, Jacob stops for the night at Bethel. There, God reveals himself to Jacob, telling him, "I am with you." For the first time, Jacob has a relationship with the almighty God.

Jacob arrives in Paddan Aram and gains two wives by working fourteen years for his uncle, Laban. Eventually, Laban's treatment of Jacob and his family becomes so harsh that Jacob determines to take his wives, children, and flocks back home. Laban pursues Jacob, but finally, they reach an agreement.

Now, as he nears his home country, Jacob has to face the brother who has threatened to murder him. All night at Peniel, Jacob wrestles with God, determined to receive the Lord's blessing. In the end, God touches the deepest part of his heart and changes his name from "Jacob" to "Israel," meaning, "he struggles with God." This change of name signifies a change in character.

After this divine encounter, Israel and Esau reunite in forgiveness and love. Jacob becomes the spiritual leader of his family and the father of the twelve tribes of Israel.

Israel's two great experiences with God are symbolic of our spiritual journey today. First, you accept Christ and enter into a relationship with God. Later, God probes to the deepest levels of your heart and reveals a self-centeredness that requires cleansing and full surrender. As in Jacob's story, the pressure of circumstances often brings us to that place.

Yes, pressure! And in our day!

As a young man, Dick Fields went to work at Nazarene Publishing House. He was a follower of Christ, but part of his job was difficult and put pressure on him. Back then, the huge printing presses pulled the paper through the press by means of a fabric. Sometimes the fabric tore. Dick would have to crawl under the press, lie on his back in dirt and debris, and sew the fabric together while oil dripped onto his body. He said, "I don't want to do this the rest of my life!" Then he paused. Dick prayed, "Lord, if you want me to do this the rest of my life, I will."

Later, Dick said, "I believe that's when God sanctified me."

Dick went on to work fifty-four years for Nazarene Publishing House (which became The Foundry Publishing in 2018). He eventually rose to become the production manager. His work contributed to the provision of Christian literature for millions of people. Under pressure, under the presses, under the oil, his full surrender to God brought a sanctifying presence to his character. At his funeral, Dick Fields was described using the following words:

1. Contagious warmth
2. Dignity, attentiveness, loyalty
3. Long-lasting obedience
4. A former pastor said, "In twenty-three years, I've never seen Dick waver from Christlikeness."
5. Another person testified, "God gave us Dick Fields so you could know what God was like."

Will you allow the pressures you face to drive you to seek God until he changes your name; your character; your heart; your plans; your future?

Jesus Was Tired

Jacob's well was there, and Jesus, tired as he was from the journey,
sat down by the well. It was about noon.
John 4:6

Probably the greatest president in the history of the United States was Abraham Lincoln. We have the following reports about Lincoln in the midst of the Civil War: "Lincoln slept scarcely at all night after night as he tried to locate divisions and follow the fast-moving tide of battle."[131] "Lincoln saw a Union

---

131. Benjamin Thomas, *Abraham Lincoln* (New York: Alfred A. Knopf, 1952), 336.

army badly beaten, a general's reputation shattered, Washington menaced by the enemy."[132]

On May 6, 1863, the White House received word that the Army of the Potomac had been badly beaten in the Battle of Chancellorsville. A newspaper reporter who was in the White House at the time observed that "the president's face turned ashen; he had never appeared so broken and dispirited. Head bent, hands tightly clasped behind his back, he paced his office, groaning, 'My God! My God! What will the country say? What *will* the country say?'"[133]

Yes, even the best and greatest among us experience their very human moments—their moments of pressure and anxiety, when their minds and bodies are deeply affected. Jesus Christ, the world's Savior and Lord, experienced these moments too.

In John 4, as Jesus is traveling (probably walking) from Judea to Galilee, he crosses through Samaria, which is unfriendly territory for Jews. At the town of Sychar, tired from his journey, he sits down by a well. So simple, so natural—the mighty Jesus Christ is tired, so he sits. The biblical writers are careful to point out that Jesus is both fully human and fully God. Hebrews 4:14–15 tells us, "Since we have a great high priest who has ascended into heaven, Jesus the Son of God, let us hold firmly to the faith we profess. For we do not have a high priest who is unable to empathize with our weaknesses, but we have one who has been tempted in every way, just as we are—yet he did not sin."

It's important to understand some of the pains and limitations Jesus experiences. In Matthew 13:57, he is dishonored by his own town. In Matthew 26:38–40, he feels great sorrow as he faces death on the cross and is troubled at the lack of support from his disciples. In Luke 4:1–2, the devil tempts him while he is experiencing hunger due to fasting. In Luke 19:45, he becomes angry at the commerce in the temple. In John 11:35, he weeps over the death of a dear friend. In all of these moments, we sense his humanity and his understanding of us. He has been tired, dishonored, sorrowful, troubled, tempted, hungry, angry—the same experiences we have every day

Even as he is weary and sitting by a well, Jesus still exerts his influence on others. He meets a thirsty, sinful Samaritan woman and gives her living water. She goes back into her city, announcing that she has found the Messi-

---

132. Thomas, *Abraham Lincoln*, 338.
133. Thomas, *Abraham Lincoln*, 369–70.

ah. Other Samaritans come out from the city, become believers, and exclaim, "This man really is the Savior of the world" (John 4:42).

Likewise, can't we, though we're tired and tried in many ways, still exert our spiritual influence on the world around us? Yes, we can—because of our relationship with the Savior of the world.

How Far Can God Trust You?

Who then is the faithful and wise servant, whom the master has put in charge of the servants in his household to give their food at the proper time? It will be good for that servant whose master finds him doing so when he returns. Truly I tell you, he will put him in charge of all his possessions.
Matthew 24:45–47

Jesus told us to "be ready because the Son of Man will come at an hour when you do not expect him" (Matthew 24:44). Thus, full faithfulness to your God-given task is the only guarantee of your readiness to meet Christ. Beyond that, faithfulness in little responsibilities is the doorway to bigger responsibilities in the future.

Ed was a faithful member of his local church. His pastor, impressed with both his godliness and his talent, predicted he would eventually be a vice president of U.S. Steel. Sure enough, his company offered him a big promotion and a pay raise. However, the young church plant to which Ed had committed himself desperately needed him, so he declined the promotion for the sake of the kingdom. As a result, his church became stronger.

Later, U.S. Steel asked Ed to manage a plant in Italy where he would have 3,500 workers under him. The executives felt it was time to appoint a manager with Christian values—especially since many managers with lesser values had not done well. Ed's denomination had also established a church in the city where Ed would be serving. What sort of spiritual impact would it make on 3,500 workers to see their Christian manager serving God in the local church?

Though they had never missed a service, Ed and his wife, Evelyn, completed the sale of their house, packed their luggage, and prepared for their flight to Italy while their local church held its revival services.

That Sunday morning, Evelyn came to me in tears. Their son and his wife were not serving the Lord and had not responded to God in the morning service. I urged Evelyn to be patient with the Lord.

Sure enough, at that night's service, Ed and Evelyn's son and daughter-in-law found the Lord. What a beautiful farewell gift for them.

Ed and Evelyn had been faithful in a little thing, and God was entrusting them with bigger things. The theme of Matthew 24:47—"he will put him in charge of all his possessions"—is repeated elsewhere in Scripture:

- Matthew 25:21—"You have been faithful with a few things; I will put you in charge of many things."
- Luke 16:10—"Whoever can be trusted with very little can also be trusted with much."
- Luke 19:17—"Because you have been trustworthy in a very small matter, take charge of ten cities."

Do you get the point? As the Lord said to me one day, "If I can trust you with a little thing today, I can trust you with a bigger thing tomorrow." How far can God trust you?

Take the Next Step

*Let us not become weary in doing good, for at the proper time
we will reap a harvest if we do not give up.*
Galatians 6:9

Jimmy Carter was the president of the United States, the shah of Iran had been forced out of his position, and many Iranians were angry at the U.S. government. A mob of young Iranians stormed the U.S. Embassy in Tehran and captured all the American diplomatic personnel. Soon, word came to Earl and Hazel Lee, pastors of a powerful church in Pasadena, California, that their son, Gary, was among the prisoners. But they had no communication with Gary. Hazel did not know if her son was alive or dead, tortured or safe, hungry or fed. She felt distress, anxiety, and numbness.

It was a Sunday morning. What should she do? As she prayed, she heard the Lord's voice say, "Take the next step." For Hazel, that meant doing what she would normally do on a Sunday morning—finish her Sunday school lesson; go to the church building; teach her class; worship and honor God. She may have felt numb, and she didn't know the future, but she could take the next step.

For months that stretched into a year, Earl and Hazel still didn't know what had happened to Gary. But they continued to lean on God and to "take the next step." The local TV station took interest in Earl and Hazel's situation and assigned anchor Janine Tartaglia to cover the story. Janine thought that, in order to report the story thoroughly, she should attend their church to see how they held up under pressure in a public setting. As she heard Dr. Lee preach, she sensed God speaking to her heart. Janine Tartaglia accepted Jesus as her Savior and Lord.

Four hundred and forty-four days after the storming of the Embassy, when President Ronald Reagan took office, all of the American diplomatic staff who had been taken captive were released. Within a few days, Gary was home. Earl and Hazel rejoiced and thanked God.

Not every day in our relationship with God will be a spectacular high. But as Oswald Chambers wrote, "We have to live in the grey day according to what we saw on the mount."[134]

By the way, the dark days that brought Janine Tartaglia and the Lees together has produced even more fruit. That young convert grew, and today Janine Tartaglia Metcalfe is a powerful preacher, teacher, and minister of the gospel—all because someone took "the next step."

Replace Falsehood with Encouragement

Do not let any unwholesome talk come out of your mouths,
but only what is helpful for building others up according to their needs,
that it may benefit those who listen.
Ephesians 4:29

Words! How important are they? How much power do we give them? What is your world saying to you? Are they angry, judgmental words about you not

---

134. Oswald Chambers, *My Utmost for His Highest* (Toronto: McClelland and Steward Limited, 1935), 107.

measuring up? Do you believe them? Do they keep you from becoming all that God meant for you to become? Do they keep you stuck with no fertile soil in which to grow?

When do you say "no" and take your power back? How do you teach people that you want to be treated with value and respect?

On the other hand, perhaps your world is filled with positive affirmations. Perhaps someone is patiently encouraging you and teaching you how to play the game of life until you hit a home run. Perhaps you're enveloped in the unconditional love and grace of our Father above, where it's okay to try new things, and it's okay to make mistakes. If so, you are blessed, and someone out there needs to hear those life-giving words.

Once, on our daughter's birthday, instead of flowers, we gave her verbal and written bouquets which filled her heart for days. What words are you speaking into your world?

Nancy Shaver[135]

He Cared to Climb

A man was there by the name of Zacchaeus; he was a chief tax collector and was wealthy. He wanted to see who Jesus was, but because he was short he could not see over the crowd. So he ran ahead and climbed a sycamore-fig tree to see him, since Jesus was coming that way.
Luke 19:2–4

He was a big-time tax collector, so most people didn't like him. He probably worked for the Roman government, and in Israel, that was unpopular. Beyond the required Roman tax, tax collectors would gouge out as many extra fees for themselves as they could. For this reason, they were *really* unpopular. They were also regarded as sinners (Luke 19:7).

You have to give Zacchaeus credit. Despite the way others felt about him, he did not let any damage to his self-image stop him from checking out the most important person in the world. "He wanted to see who Jesus was"—he

---

135. Previously published in *Come Ye Apart* September–October–November 2001 (Kansas City, MO: WordAction Publishing Co.), 81. Used by permission. (This publication became *Reflecting God*.)

had a good, wholesome curiosity. Moreover, he took action—he ran ahead and, since he was short, he climbed a tree.

Apparently, Jesus saw something special in Zacchaeus—a receptive heart—and picked him out of the crowd. Jesus invited himself to Zacchaeus's house for dinner. "Zach"—let me nickname him—was smart enough to seize an opportunity to get closer to Jesus. Of course, when other people saw him getting closer to the Savior, they began to mutter and criticize.

Zach must have deeply repented—meaning he was sorry for his sins, and sorry enough to turn from them. He declared that he would give half of his possessions to the poor and repay anyone he had cheated four times over (19:8)—this is called restitution. God can forgive you for all your sins, but inevitably, some of those sins involve wronging others. It is appropriate to go back to those you have hurt and make things right. When you do so, the recipients of your restitution will know you have truly gotten right with God.

When he met Zach, Jesus was passing through Jericho on his way to Jerusalem to die on the cross for the sins of the world. In a miniature expression of what he would soon provide for the whole world, Jesus said, "Salvation has come to this house" (19:9). Because of his response to Jesus, Zach and his whole family were blessed. By responding to Jesus as he did, Zach became a son of Abraham in the best sense of the term.

Then, Jesus states his larger mission: "For the Son of Man came to seek and to save the lost" (19:10). New Testament scholar and Bible translator Dr. Ralph Earle said that this was the key verse of the Gospel of Luke. How wonderful if we respond to this offer; how wonderful if we join with Jesus as he brings the lost to himself.

My own mother accepted Christ as her Savior and Lord when she was forty-nine years old. What a difference he made in her! Among the many changes in her life was one that traced back to her childhood.

My mom was raised in poverty in upstate New York. When she was in sixth grade, her class was going to take a trip to New York City. She went to her schoolteacher and asked for five dollars as a loan to help pay for the trip. In 1919, that was a lot of money. Now, as a new Christian, my mom realized that she had never repaid the loan. She made periodic trips to upstate New York to visit family, so on one of those trips, she went to see her former schoolteacher and repaid the five-dollar loan—forty-six years later. This was restitution, and people believed that Vera Shaver had the real thing.

Let the story of Zacchaeus and Jesus be a model for you:

- Regardless of your position in life, don't let anyone or anything keep you from seeking Jesus.

- Follow your spiritual curiosity with action; do what is necessary to connect with Jesus.
- Know that Jesus sees something special in you. Respond to the next step he invites you to take.
- Turn completely from your sins and make things right with those you have wronged.
- Jesus wants to seek and save—trust him to save you. Tell others how they can know the Christ you've come to know.

Thank you, Zacchaeus, for caring to climb. Realizing how much Jesus seeks us made the climb worth it.

A Servant by God's Grace

I became a servant of this gospel by the gift of God's grace
given me through the working of his power.
Ephesians 3:7

Saul had business to do with the God he had never met. His trip to destroy those worthless Christians was brought to an abrupt halt by a blinding light who confronted him, made him vulnerable, and changed him forever. He was now one of "them," and God graciously sent Ananias to be a healing servant to him.

Paul, as he was now known, had a great internal drive and passion to make up for his past and for lost time. He had been chosen to reveal the great mystery of God's love to everyone. He had been a successful sinner, and now he was a successful saint. He created a pattern of serving that is impossible without spiritual power to propel it.

Are we connected to that power so that we can serve where we've been placed? Are we amazed and humbled when God uses ordinary people like us to build bridges of love so grace can walk across? May it be so.

Nancy Shaver[136]

---

136. Previously published in *Come Ye Apart* September–October–November 1998 (Kansas City, MO: Nazarene Publishing House), 92. Used by permission. (This publication became *Reflecting God*.)

A Man Called Peter

As the deer pants for streams of water, so my soul pants for you, my God.
Psalm 42:1

A Man Called Peter is the name of a book (and, later, a movie based on the book) written by Catherine Marshall to tell the story of her famous preacher husband, Peter Marshall. A Scottish immigrant to America, Peter attended seminary and eventually became pastor of the historic New York Avenue Presbyterian Church in Washington, DC. He then was appointed chaplain of the United States Senate. He died prematurely at age forty-six.

Peter testified to feeling a "tap on the shoulder." He explained it this way: "The 'tap on the shoulder' is the almighty power of God acting without help or hindrance upon an elect fallen sinner so as to produce a new creature, and to lead him into a particular work which God has for him."[137]

There was a different man called Peter in my life. He was a couple years ahead of me in our high school in Manchester, Connecticut. He was student body president; a straight-A student when he tried; and, though he had been disabled since childhood, he played varsity goalie on the soccer team. Likewise, at Dartmouth, he was president of his fraternity, played varsity soccer, and was part of Green Key, the highest honorary organization in the school. But eventually, Peter developed a drinking problem so severe that he left college.

I attended Dartmouth too, and there, I began to feel a hunger for God. I didn't know how to find him, and no one seemed to be able to tell me—so I went to chapel. To my shock, Peter showed up in chapel too. He had been readmitted to college after more than a year's absence. When we saw each other, he told me, "Chic, I'm different than I used to be because I found the Lord." He was the first person I met who talked like God was real.

A few weeks later, Peter came to my dormitory and told me the greatest before-and-after story I'd ever heard. Before, he had been sleeping in the back of his car and was in trouble with the police in six different states. But then he met God personally through Jesus; was forgiven of all his sins; was

---

137. Dr. Peter Marshall, *Mr. Jones, Meet the Master: Sermons and Prayers of Peter Marshall* (Westwood, NJ: Fleming H. Revell Company, 1950), 31.

immediately delivered from alcohol; and experienced great joy and peace. Peter invited me to a nearby church, where Christ became real to me and gave me new life. As I grew spiritually, Peter taught me how to pray and read the Bible, and helped me through my struggles.

We both eventually ended up in Kansas City for seminary. When I arrived in Kansas City, the only person I knew was Peter, who had become superintendent of the Kansas City Rescue Mission. He gave me a place to sleep, and we often went out together, preaching as a team. Peter's favorite scripture was Psalm 42:1—and indeed, he has embodied that image of panting after God. When Nancy and I got married, he signed our marriage certificate as a witness—and added Philippians 4:19.

Peter married a wonderful woman named Mary, and they had four children whom he lovingly spoke to me about countless times. Peter went through a time of spiritual struggle, but we kept in contact. He came back strong for the Lord and taught Sunday school, trained pastors-to-be, and was influential in his local church. He shines with the presence of God and firmly promotes the sanctifying work of the Holy Spirit. In Mary's last years, he cared for her with great love.

During the COVID-19 pandemic, Peter contracted the virus, which led to pneumonia. He was on oxygen and in the hospital for seven weeks. Finally, one Sunday, he phoned to report that he'd been released from the hospital—it was one of the most joyous days of my life. Though he was still weak, he asked how he could pray for me.

Peter is one of the godliest people I know, and I am a Christian today because of his testimony. This is why I talk about "a man called Peter."

Two Angels

Do you not know that we will judge angels?
1 Corinthians 6:3

Are not all angels ministering spirits sent to
serve those who will inherit salvation?
Hebrews 1:14

Hebrews 1:14 describes angels as "ministering spirits sent forth to minister for those who will inherit salvation" (NKJV).

I believe that these are the "certain" angels we shall one day judge: "Do you not know that we will judge angels?" (1 Corinthians 6:3).

Once, when the Kansas City Rescue Mission averaged ninety people per nightly service, a scheduled church group failed to show up to conduct the service. That meant that one of us who lived in the Mission needed to preach. So I picked up my hymnal and Bible and went forward.

The congregation was entirely men, and one man kept disrupting the singing. I overlooked this. But before I read the scripture for the sermon, he continued with his disturbance. I asked him to "please be still and honor the Lord's Word." Still, he continued. After three more efforts to quiet the man, I went down and told him he should leave the meeting.

He was a big man. I helped him stand up and led him to the door. On the sidewalk, he grabbed both of my wrists and twisted them. Pain shot through my arm, and my knees buckled. Just then, a green two-passenger car pulled up to the curb next to us.

Two giant men filled the vehicle. They wore large cowboy hats, and a high-powered rifle stood vertically between them. Both of them looked straight ahead, not looking at the two of us on the sidewalk.

With no visible movement from the men in the car, the window on the passenger side lowered a bit. The man in the passenger seat, still looking straight ahead, opened his mouth and said three words: "Let him go."

The man instantly let go of me and walked away. I went back inside the Mission and completed the service. I never saw that green car with the two large men in cowboy hats again. But through the years, I have often thought about them and have concluded they were angels.

One year after this, the man who twisted my wrists came back and asked me to drive him to his sister's house, which I did. He was tired of his sinful lifestyle. I dropped him off with a smile, a handshake, and a prayer. I hope to see him in heaven. We both remember this episode and how it made us feel. Is it possible that one angel was watching out for him and the other angel was watching out for me? Each of us is well qualified to judge how these angels conducted themselves.

Peter Gunas

(This is the man who brought Chic Shaver to Christ)

What Seed Are You Sowing?

*I [Paul] planted the seed, Apollos watered it, but God has been
making it grow. So neither the one who plants nor the one who
waters is anything, but only God, who makes things grow.
The one who plants and the one who waters have one purpose,
and they will each be rewarded according to their own labor. For we
are co-workers in God's service; you are God's field, God's building.*
1 Corinthians 3:6–9

*Do not be deceived: God cannot be mocked. A man reaps what he sows.
Whoever sows to please their flesh, from the flesh will reap destruction;
whoever sows to please the Spirit, from the Spirit will reap eternal life.
Let us not become weary in doing good, for at the proper time
we will reap a harvest if we do not give up.*
Galatians 6:7–9

His English and Welsh accents intrigued Nancy and me. We were thrilled that the Heap missionary family had decided to rent the missionary home across from the sanctuary of the first church we pastored. Samuel and Gladys Heap had three children: Christiana, sixteen; Steven, thirteen; and Philip, eight.

We were amazed at how this family functioned. We knew the parents had sowed seeds of godliness, holiness, and love in their children. The parents left the children for weeks at a time to travel the U.S. and report what was happening on the mission field in deputation services. Christiana ran the home, cooked the meals, paid the bills, sent the boys to school, and did her own schooling by correspondence. The children never missed Sunday school or a church service, and Christiana paid the tithe. The parents told us the children could function this way because they had learned faith and dependability in the mission field.

The years passed, and Samuel and Gladys were both promoted to heaven. Christiana became a pastor's wife, and they had a rich ministry in churches. Steven and his wife, Brenda, became missionaries to Brazil and settled there after they retired. Philip is a pastor in the Washington, DC, area, has his own international congregation, and regularly ministers to other Hispanic congregations in the area. What great harvest Samuel and Gladys have reaped in the lives of their children.

Rev. and Mrs. Heap spent their missionary ministry in Colombia and Peru. From 1940 to 1954, their Colombia years saw the death of their first son; their beating by a mob; and physical and financial hardships. When they moved to their Peru assignment, they left behind a small congregation in Colombia. Fast-forward to an encounter in the line of a McDonald's in Indianapolis, where their son Steven was waiting to order:

> The couple in front of me were talking in Spanish and trying to decide what to order. They noticed my nametag and asked if I knew Don Samuel e Doña Gladys Heap. When I responded that they were my parents, I received an enormous hug that should have gone to my parents. They proceeded to tell me that the woman's grandparents had come to faith in Christ because of my parents' faithful witness. I asked them what they did in Colombia. Their answer should not have amazed me, based on the promises of God's Word—one plants, another waters, and the Lord gives the increase—but I was surprised when they told me they were pastors of a church in Cali, Colombia.

This was more fruit from seed planted by the Heaps from 1940 to 1954. I want to plant a lot of seed for Jesus's cause. What seed are you intending to plant for the rest of your life?

Husband and Wife Love

Husbands, love your wives, just as Christ loved the church and gave himself up for her to make her holy, cleansing her by the washing with water through the word, and to present her to himself as a radiant church, without stain or wrinkle or any other blemish, but holy and blameless.
Ephesians 5:25–27

However, each one of you also must love his wife as he loves himself, and the wife must respect her husband.
Ephesians 5:33

Love her like Christ loved the church and gave himself up for her. That means a sacrificial love; a holiness-producing love. I go to great lengths to care for her, help her, encourage her, and support her. I treat her in a way that will not coarsen her, degrade her, or belittle her but will enable her, grow her, produce a holy heart and life, and make her more like Christ.

"Make her holy . . ." The New King James says, "that he might sanctify and cleanse her." The American Standard Version renders it, "sanctify it, having cleansed it."

Paul is using the husband-wife relationship as an analogy for Christ's love for the church and his sacrifice to sanctify her and make her holy. He is using Christ's love and sacrifice for the church to teach husbands and wives how to love each other.

In my wedding vows to Nancy, I promised to "love, comfort, honor, and keep her, in sickness and in health; and forsaking all others, keep myself only unto her, so long as we both live." I pledged I would have and hold her "for better—for worse, for richer—for poorer, in sickness and in health, to love and cherish 'til death us do part."

Nancy's present health is affected by Alzheimer's. Somehow, in the midst of all the extra care, the Lord is empowering us to have a beautiful love for each other. Nancy leaves lots of notes for me beside the chair where I read my Bible every morning. Here is the note I found on March 15, 2020:

> *Thank you for our wonderful trip to Paul's and to revival—God really blessed, and many people got closer to God.*
>
> *You are amazing—to do all the work you do and take care of me too!*
>
> *I am so happy and still in love with you—my dapper guy!!*
>
> *XXOO*
>
> *Love always,*
>
> *Nan*

Because God helps you, you can love your spouse throughout your marriage—not just barely, but powerfully.

Your Living Sacrifice

Therefore, I urge you, brothers and sisters, in view of God's mercy,
to offer your bodies as a living sacrifice, holy and pleasing to God—
this is your true and proper worship.
Romans 12:1

Dottie watched him at work. Henry was principal of the public school, and she noticed that he was sweet under hostile questioning in public meetings with parents and citizens. Dottie was so impressed that she gave her life to the same Christ Henry served. Here was a man on the job as a living sacrifice.

Not a dead sacrifice, as in the Old Testament—but a living sacrifice. Paul urges that since God has given us mercy so freely and fully, the least we can do is offer our bodies back to God as a sacrifice. It is a call to Christian brothers and sisters.

Have you ever felt that God has called you to offer something back to him? Our God doesn't just deserve "some things"—he calls for all. Not just hands or feet or voice or strength or heart or mind . . . give him your whole body. It is a once-for-all sacrifice, a decisive moment.

A living sacrifice results in a dynamic, continuing action in which we are all his—yet alive, vibrant, and constantly making choices and living life to please God.

It was a June night in North Carolina when Linda surrendered her whole Christian life back to God. He accepted her surrender and bestowed his sanctifying fullness to her yielded heart. Her husband was amazed and said, "You're so happy."

Linda attended all the church services that special week. She said, "I've been doing more praying since Thursday night than I have in the last four years. And you know that jerk at work? Well, I've stopped complaining about him." She even assured me that she would handle her future finances faithfully before the Lord. She was enjoying and accepting God's "good, pleasing and perfect will" (12:2) as his living sacrifice.

Don't Let the World Squeeze You

Don't the world around you squeeze you into its own mould,
but let God re-mould your minds from within, so that you may
prove in practice that the plan of God for you is good, meets all his
demands and moves toward the goal of true maturity.
Romans 12:2, PHILLIPS

I was getting an MRI. Just before they slid me inside the machine, the technician said, "Do you have claustrophobia?"

I said, "No."

But after it was over, I realized that I should have said yes. The upper arch of the tube was almost touching my nose—I felt very squeezed.

Of course, in Romans, when Paul warned the Christians that the world would squeeze their minds, it meant something much more subtle. The world (the forces that live without God) can't stand for you to live for God—your difference convicts them. The world wants to conform your mind. But God wants to transform your mind.

At a church banquet, medical doctor Denny Kinlaw, son of the minister Dr. Dennis Kinlaw, testified to the world's squeezing power:

> When I was seven, my mother prayed with me to receive Christ. I have some very precious memories after that, of Jesus being very real to me. But when I began to approach that great chasm of inferiority that we call adolescence—when my Adam's apple was entirely too big and my muscles weren't nearly big enough—I began to be more conscious of me than of him. . . .
>
> Finally, I got into the university. I decided, *Ah, now I'm with people who are open and free.* I was shocked to find they were neither open nor free. . . . They wanted to impose on me a view of reality that neither fit what I had learned in my family nor what I had learned on my own.
>
> I began again to open my life to God, and he came back to the center. I decided that I wanted my life to be his wholly.
>
> Then I began my hospital internship and residency. I found I could work thirty-six hours without a break, without sleep, just like the other guys could. But I had no time for God. I also discovered that when I didn't talk to God, he didn't talk to me. He moved to the margin of my life again.
>
> When he moved to the margin, the hole that was left didn't stay empty. The place he occupied filled with appetites and passions. Slowly I discovered they were there and were controlling me. I began to feel sorry for myself. I looked at these other doctors with their private planes and summer homes and winter homes and places at the beach and big automobiles and luxurious living, and I thought, *Just let me get out in suburbia, and I'll make me some money and have a chance to enjoy some of those things.* Slowly, it began to dawn on me that those appetites controlled

me. I realized that, barring a miracle, I was already preprogrammed for disaster.[138]

Be very wise. Don't let the world squeeze you!

Transformed by the Renewing of Your Mind

Be transformed by the renewing of your mind. Then you will be able to test and approve what God's will is—his good, pleasing and perfect will.
Romans 12:2

Consider your mind raw material—what you put into it determines the finished product. Whereas offering your body to God as a living sacrifice was an event in a given moment, the renewing of your mind is an ongoing process. You will choose mental input that stagnates, corrupts, pollutes, degrades—*or* that edifies, grows, expands, renews. You decide!

One of the best decisions I ever made was to begin each day with the Bible and prayer. We can facilitate positive transformation with worship, Christian fellowship, reading spiritual material, and sharing our faith. Philippians 4:8 tells us to concentrate on what is true, noble, right, pure, lovely, admirable, excellent, and praiseworthy. Scan my life, Lord, and alert me to any change in my spiritual temperature.

Medical doctor Denny Kinlaw describes his renewal:

Six weeks later, the other surgeon's hand slipped, and I was given plenty of time for God. Three of us were operating on a girl who was a drug addict. When another surgeon's . . . instrument penetrated my glove and cut into the flesh of my hand . . . I contracted hepatitis of the worst kind.

Those next months were a time of great pain and despondency. . . . the Lord came back to the center of my life. And when he came back, he set me free. . . .

I asked him to heal me, and he did, but not in the way I expected. I thought he would heal me in such a way that I would have a guarantee

---

138. Dennis Kinlaw, *Preaching in the Spirit* (Grand Rapids: Francis Asbury Press, 1985), 56–57.

of tomorrow. . . . But that didn't happen. . . . He said, "I didn't give the apostle Paul a guarantee of tomorrow; why should I give you one?"

. . . That experience transformed my way of living. I don't take each day for granted anymore. I don't take my wife, my children, or my work for granted anymore. I take every one of them as a special gift from him, a gift of his grace. There are some mornings as I ride to work in Lexington that I watch the sun rise and find my cheeks wet with liquid gratitude for the new day. . . . You know, it's not a bad way to live.[139]

The rich fruit of such renewal is this: "you will be able to test and approve what God's will is—his good, pleasing and perfect will" (Romans 12:2).

A Good Samaritan Deed

But a Samaritan, as he traveled, came where the man was;
and when he saw him, he took pity on him.
Luke 10:33

The Samaritan took a chunk of his life and gave it away to save another. While most of us will not go to the cross and give our entire life away to save another, most of us will give a "chunk" of our life.

The Samaritan gave the injured man the following (Luke 10:34–35):

- Medical provision: "bandaged his wounds"
- Transportation provision: "put the man on his own donkey"
- Lodging provision: "brought him to an inn"
- Financial provision: "took out two denarii"
- Follow-up provision: "I will reimburse you"

Note that the Samaritan left the injured man with the innkeeper for a time while he attended to his personal business. (For most of us, this makes it more realistic for us to follow the Good Samaritan's example.) Then, he returns for further mercy and service. This Samaritan becomes forever famous for the "love your neighbor as yourself" principle that Jesus taught.

Though it is not presented as a directly Christian story, a farmer performed a Good Samaritan deed by stopping his work to save a life. His name

---

139. Kinlaw, *Preaching in the Spirit*, 57–58.

was Fleming, and he was a poor Scottish farmer. One day, while trying to eke out a living for his family, he heard a cry for help coming from nearby quicksand. He dropped his tools and ran to the emergency.

There, mired to his waist in black muck, was a terrified boy, screaming and struggling to free himself. Farmer Fleming saved the lad from what could have been a slow and terrifying death. The next day, a fancy carriage pulled up to the Scotsman's sparse surroundings. An elegantly dressed nobleman stepped out and introduced himself as the father of the boy Farmer Fleming had saved.

"I want to repay you," said the nobleman. "You saved my son's life."

"No, I can't accept payment for what I did," the Scottish farmer replied, waving off the offer.

At that moment, the farmer's own son came to the door of the family hovel. "Is that your son?" the nobleman asked.

"Yes," the farmer replied proudly.

"I'll make you a deal. Let me take him and give him a good education. If the lad is anything like his father, he'll grow to be a man you can be proud of."

And that he did. In time, Farmer Fleming's son graduated from St. Mary's Hospital Medical School in London and went on to become known throughout the world as the noted Sir Alexander Fleming, the discoverer of penicillin. Years afterward, the nobleman's son was stricken with pneumonia, and penicillin saved him.

The name of the nobleman was Lord Randolph Churchill. His son was Sir Winston Churchill, who was prime minister of England during World War II and, many would say, leader of the free world in the battle with Nazi Germany.

Look around! Who needs God's touch through you? You never know whom you might be saving!

Your Life a River

"Let anyone who is thirsty come to me and drink. Whoever believes in me,
as Scripture has said, rivers of living water will flow from within them."
By this he meant the Spirit, whom those who believed in him
were later to receive.
John 7:37–39

Your life is to be a river, a channel. Every river must have a source to feed it—whether a powerful spring, major snow melt, or rain. Spiritually, your source is coming to Jesus Christ and drinking. If it's like physical life, this does not mean just a one-time drink—it means frequent drinking. This water flowing from within is the work of the Spirit.

When we are filled with the Spirit, we must not fall into the trap of assuming we are a reservoir and the source is in us. No, we are a river. You maintain fullness by regular, consistent drinking of Jesus Christ. He will keep you full.

Myron Augsburger, a leader in the Mennonite Church, has said that you cannot keep Spirit-filled unless you are a person of prayer. If any blockage occurs in your river—sin, for example—deal with its removal at once.

So, keep regular contact with your source, Jesus Christ. Your life is a river, not a reservoir. Your banks can be full. And the extra blessing is that at the end of most rivers is a rich harvest.

Give Love and Give the Gospel

Or do you not know that wrongdoers will not inherit the kingdom of
God? Do not be deceived: Neither the sexually immoral nor idolaters nor
adulterers nor men who have sex with men nor thieves nor the greedy nor
drunkards nor slanderers nor swindlers will inherit the kingdom of God.
1 Corinthians 6:9–10

Stay calm. There has been a lot of recent discussion and debate about the spirituality of people practicing the homosexual lifestyle. Allow me to share some personal experience.

I've dealt personally with hundreds and hundreds of people in my sixty-five years of Christian life and ministry. I have been close to and dear friends with people who were currently involved in immorality, adultery, or homosexual practice.

One of these friends, a professional in his field, made an appointment with me for lunch. With many tears, he shared with me over an hour that he had been sexually involved with a number of men. Why did he ask to talk to me? Because he knew I loved him.

I was preaching for a week in one of America's large cities, and the pastor was introducing me to his staff. He said something like this as he spoke of his associate pastor and wife: "Jim was previously involved in homosexual behavior. But he found Jesus Christ and was changed and delivered. Today he is an ordained minister of the church. Madeline was a former prostitute. She has been transformed by Jesus Christ. They are happily married, and this is Celeste, their beautiful little girl."

In an unexpected phone call, Monica told me her story, which went something like this: "Years ago, in a camp meeting, I heard you preach a sermon called, People, Sex, and God. My lesbian partner was sitting next to me. At the end of the message, she turned to me and said, 'I think I've taken advantage of you, and we need to go our separate ways.' Sometime later, I met a wonderful man, and we fell in love. We have a happy marriage and just celebrated our twenty-sixth anniversary. I thought I should call you and give this report."

All people I was close to and loved—all of whom found or are seeking joyous new life in Jesus Christ.

After the apostle Paul names some of the Corinthians' sins, he adds, "And that is what some of you were. But you were washed, you were sanctified [set apart], you were justified in the name of the Lord Jesus Christ and by the Spirit of our God" (1 Corinthians 6:11). They were forgiven, changed, and became part of the church.

No wonder I say, "Give love and give the gospel."

A Required Power Level

They devoted themselves to the apostles' teaching and to fellowship,
to the breaking of bread and to prayer.
Acts 2:42

Every day they continued to meet together in the temple courts.
They broke bread in their homes and ate together with glad and sincere
hearts, praising God and enjoying the favor of all the people.
And the Lord added to their number daily those who were being saved.
Acts 2:46–47

He was possibly the best-known person in America, at least by sight—Francis Asbury, whom Wesley sent to preach the gospel in America.[140] From 1771 until 1816, Asbury traveled by horse and carriage to towns and cities telling of Jesus. Along with Washington, Jefferson, Adams, and Lincoln, he was identified as one of sixty-six Americans who are considered essential to the development of America as a nation. By 1813, one out of every eight Americans was attending Methodist camp meetings each year.[141]

One of the secrets of camp meetings was their week of concentrated preaching and teaching which led to the sort of spiritual breakthroughs that did not usually occur in a single worship service. This is similar to the intensity described in our Acts passage—concentrated meeting together and great spiritual breakthroughs.

Dr. Richard Taylor said that there is a required power level for every level of an achievement. The power of an idling jet is enough to propel a kiddie car, but not enough to shake a giant plane from its inertia. Many churches keep their engines running all year and have a measure of power, but not quite enough to accomplish things that need desperately to be done. Some Christians will only be sanctified when they are exposed to a sustained, cumulative spiritual thrust.

Many teens attend their regular church Sunday by Sunday, but when they go off for a week of teen camp, they come back transformed. The retreat, the camp meeting, and the revival fulfill the need for concentrated worship.

In a Florida Methodist revival I was part of, I saw the results of this concentration. Eighty-six people attended the Saturday witness seminar. Church services Sunday through Wednesday saw an attendance total of 1,221, and 112 people sought God at the altar. Here is the pastor's report:

> This year of 2006 will be our year of personal evangelism. Dr. Shaver has preached powerful sermons, given incredible insights, teaching us the "best-ever approach" to clearly bringing a true knowledge of Jesus Christ with the assurance of salvation. We encourage everyone to enter into Dr.

---

140. Darius Salter, *America's Bishop: The Life of Francis Asbury* (Nappanee, IN: Francis Asbury Press, 2003), 294.

141. Salter, *America's Bishop*, 9.

Shaver's *Basic Bible Studies* to make sure of your personal faith. We are right now developing plans through our new home fellowships to use this study guide, as well as other materials Dr. Shaver has shared with us. This truly is a day of new beginnings. Maybe the openness to this revival will encourage many other Methodists to return to their Wesleyan roots. In one study, Dr. Shaver quoted John Wesley's message to his ministers: "We have no other business but to save souls." Are you saved? Do you know it for sure? What a joy to know that you know that you know you are a child of God.[142]

Seek events that provide the spiritual concentration that leads to your personal victory, including your entire sanctification.

Give Him a Little Room

By contrast, the fruit of the Spirit is love, joy, peace, patience,
kindness, generosity, faithfulness, gentleness, and self-control.
There is no law against such things.
Galatians 5:22–23, NRSV

Love is patient, love is kind. It does not envy,
it does not boast, it is not proud.
1 Corinthians 13:4

On time! Oh yes, I would get to work on time. I had to drive narrow residential streets with a twenty-five-mile-per-hour speed limit and little opportunity to pass another car. The car in front of me began to slow—twenty, fifteen, ten, then five miles per hour. The man driving kept peering out the passenger side window. What was he looking for? Finally, he stopped dead in the street with no signal. Oblivious to all other drivers, he finally found what he was looking for—a garage sale.

For some time now, I had been enjoying the Spirit-filled life. Don't get me wrong—I had my challenges. But I considered one of my biggest weaknesses

---

142. Previously published in *The Good News: The Chic Shaver Center for Evangelism Newsletter* (March 2006).

to be my tendency to impatience. I was on a mission for God and had much to do—no roadblocks, please.

I stopped my car dead behind the car of the garage-sale seeker. What else could I do? I didn't yell at him; I didn't honk my horn; and, for some reason, my impatience hadn't even registered yet.

Then I heard that voice: *"Give him a little room!"*

Yes, that's it: "Give him a little room!" It was like those words opened a new chapter for me. Whatever my mission, all my life, I will encounter and talk to people who are living their *own* lives with their *own* interests, challenges, cares, hopes, and burdens. The Spirit of God and love both tell me to give them a little room.

It's been years since I heard that voice that day. The other driver finally pulled to the side, let me pass, and I made it to work on time. But far more importantly, I learned a lesson from the Spirit that day. At least a hundred times in the years since, under irritations and obstacles, those words have come back to me. And a hundred times, I've been able to "give him a little room." How grateful I am that the Spirit who fully invades our hearts at sanctification speaks and guides and grows us into greater Christlikeness—even in areas of weakness.

Give him a little room!

Spirit-Led: Rob and Barbara

Brothers and sisters, choose seven men from among you
who are known to be full of the Spirit and wisdom.
We will turn this responsibility over to them.
Acts 6:3

This proposal pleased the whole group. They chose Stephen, a man full
of faith and of the Holy Spirit; also Philip, Procorus, Nicanor, Timon,
Parmenas, and Nicolas from Antioch, a convert to Judaism.
Acts 6:5

The Spirit told Philip, "Go to that chariot and stay near it."
Acts 8:29

It started with a party—a chili cook-off sponsored by the Sunday school class. Lenny invited his relatives Rob and Barbara to it. There, Rob and Barbara experienced food, fellowship, and fun. They said it was a blast.

Barbara's background was Catholic and Rob's Protestant, but they had not been attending church anywhere. They had been saying they needed to find a church. After the chili cook-off, a follow-up phone call invited them to Sunday school and worship. They came.

Rob and Barbara had been married for three years. They had four daughters from previous marriages. Rob was the manager of a plumbing supply store, and Barbara was a project manager for institutional research at Barton County Community College.

Though they initially thought adult Sunday school was stupid, they were impressed with the friendliness and the follow-up welcome card they received. They found that the worship service was comfortable. And so they began attending regularly.

Eventually, some people in the class who'd built relationships with Rob and Barbara asked if they could meet with them, get to know them better, and share what the church believed. Rob and Barbara were open to it.

One day in February, by the Spirit opening doors, friends from the church shared the gospel with Rob and Barbara and challenged them to receive Christ into their lives. That night, they did.

Rob describes the change, saying, "I was taught to always win—baseball, football, basketball. I was almost the patriarch of the eleven children in my family. I was on a pedestal. It was a lot of pressure, and I didn't like it. When I prayed, I felt emotional release."

"His shoulders lifted," Barbara affirms. "The weight went off him. He's been different ever since."

Rob continues, "Now I can pray. It means something—I have a conversation with Jesus. My life has changed. People at work notice I'm different."

Barbara describes her spiritual response to the gospel this way: "I didn't change much at first. I was a little afraid. Then, as I watched Rob, I began growing. At first, I thought I was good; then I knew I wasn't as good as I thought. I was hiding. Now I'm doing more than going through the motions. As we're studying the *Basic Bible Studies for New and Growing Christians*, I feel like I'm eating the Word. It nourishes me. As Rob and I do our Bible studies, we're getting to know each other better, and we are closer. It's helping me heal. Jesus is now front and center. He has to steer my ship."

How do conversions like this happen? In Acts, the layman Philip was Spirit-filled and Spirit-led. When the Spirit led him to the chariot, he led the

Ethiopian to Christ. Jesus had promised his followers that when they were filled with the Holy Spirit, they would be empowered to witness (Acts 1:8).

More than two thousand years later, the people who talked to Rob and Barbara on that February day were filled with and led by the Holy Spirit, too. You too can be Spirit-filled and Spirit-led. Remember, at the end of that leadership, there will be another Rob and Barbara.

Love, Truth, and Peace

These are the things you are to do: Speak the truth to each other,
and render true and sound judgment in your courts.
Zechariah 8:16

Are you a truth-seeker? Do you ask the question, "Did I lie today?" If you have, are you strong enough to admit it? People who lie are cowards. I know this because I used to be one.

People didn't have to like me, but rejection so painful that I was willing to lie to myself in order to avoid it. I discovered that when I lied to myself, it was impossible to tell the truth. I was my own worst enemy. Then I found a safe place to be real, to heal, and to claim God's power in my personal life. Truth is a requirement for all change—for salvation, healing, and growth.

Shame is a great block to the truth. Some secrets that lie buried inside damage us and drain our energy. Just once, find one safe person to share your secret with and be on your way to freedom.

Truth hammers away at my reality until I open the door. Do I reject guidance unless it comes in a form I approve of? When I bow and surrender, when I take a risk for God, I always find peace and love, even if I fall on my face.

The most Jesus asks of me is to love the Lord my God with all my heart, soul, strength, and mind, *and* to love my neighbor as I love myself. Can I do that without speaking the truth?

Nancy Shaver[143]

---

143. Previously published in *Come Ye Apart* September–October–November 2001 (Kansas City, MO: WordAction Publishing Co.), 80. Used by permission. (This publication became *Reflecting God*.)

In the Morning, Lord

In the morning, LORD, you hear my voice;
in the morning I lay my requests before you.
Psalm 5:3

I dared not leave my room to face people or problems until I first faced the Lord. The college atmosphere in which I lived was that challenging.

Early in my Christian journey, I developed a daily devotional life. Since we read about living a continuous life in the Spirit, it seemed appropriate to lay out a structure for a devotional practice that would support that life.

Let me share a pattern that has worked for me. Take away whatever will help you develop your own special time with the Lord:

- I chose a specific time for every day. For me, it was mornings. If you are not a morning person, choose a time in the day when you can give God an alert mind. Don't give him just the leftovers of your energy.
- I get a cup of coffee, go to a favorite chair, and sit for a while with this attitude: *Lord, what do you wish to say to me today?* Sometimes he speaks a clear word to me; many times, I simply sense there is openness between us.
- I read one page from a daily devotional book, guided by the date. Books I've used include *My Utmost for His Highest*, by Oswald Chambers; *Take Time to Be Holy*, by Samuel Logan Brengle; *This Day with the Master*, by Dennis Kinlaw; and *Streams in the Desert*, by Lettie Cowman.
- I read from *The One Year Bible*, which includes two Old Testament chapters, a psalm, three verses from Proverbs, and a New Testament passage for every day. By daily reading, I go through the whole Bible in a year. I mark key scriptures with a highlighter as I go.
- I journal in a cheap spiral notebook. In my journaling, I cite a key scripture I've just read, then write a mixture of conversations with the Lord, diary entries, and plans for the day. Often I review answered prayers from a previous day's journal entry.
- Then I go to my favorite prayer room—a big office in my basement. I put a detailed prayer list in front of me and keep paper and a pen handy to note inspiration or divine leadership. I pray pacing the floor because

I'm more alert pacing than kneeling. During this time, I experience real communion with the Lord and give him much praise.

At a time when I was tempted to become slack in my devotional time, the Lord reminded me that, since he had come all the way to earth and died for me, it meant a great deal to him that I would spend time with him daily. For more than sixty years, I have been meeting him faithfully in the morning, and I've missed that meeting very few times.

Make a decision about your regular devotional time with the Lord—the reward is tremendous.

Loving Pastors

Don't let anyone look down on you because you are young,
but set an example for the believers in speech,
in conduct, in love, in faith and in purity.
1 Timothy 4:12

Co-pastors Ben and Kelly were young when they started pastoring their Maryland church. Now they have invested more than thirty-one years in their vibrant, joyful congregation. I was a guest in their home for a week of revival services, and they were such examples of godly speech and Christlike love that my spirit was uplifted. While there is much talk about the failings of some pastors, I am impressed by the huge number of loving pastors I have encountered in nearly a thousand revivals. In one week, here's what I saw in Ben and Kelly:

- They thoroughly prepared their church for revival week.
- They put me in a comfortable room with my own bathroom.
- Ben carried my heavy luggage to my room.
- Kelly fed me delicious meals.
- Ben sent out numerous texts to invite people to the services.
- Ben had built relationships with a group of teenage boys from single-parent homes by playing basketball with them. He was a father figure to them.
- Kelly had the basketball boys over for supper one day, and they were all in church that night.

- Ben had started a wood-splitting business and employed the basketball boys in order to help them develop a work ethic and earn income.
- Every night, at the end of each service, Ben and Kelly were at the altar praying with or counseling people who were seeking God.
- On the day I left to drive 1,100 miles to my next assignment, Ben and Kelly rose at 5:00 a.m. to help me load my car and pray with me.
- They checked on me with calls and texts to ensure I arrived home safely.

When I looked back on the week, I felt tremendously loved. Yes, there are so many loving pastors out there.

Certain—the Almighty

❖

From Jesus Christ, who is the faithful witness, the firstborn from the dead, and the ruler of the kings of the earth.
Revelation 1:5

The Roman Empire had stretched its powerful tentacles around Christ's churches, and Revelation 1 paints a dramatic scene for us. In this chapter, John and other concerned disciples receive a powerful word from a throne—but it is Christ's throne, not Caesar's (1:4). Christ is "the ruler of the kings of the earth" (1:5).

Whatever uncertainties we encounter in life, we can be certain of this in Christ: All our *past* sins have been forgiven (1:5); our *present* task is to serve God as "a kingdom and priests" (1:6); our *future* is to welcome him when he comes in the clouds (1:7).

To encourage his servants to triumph, John sends them "grace and peace" (1:4). So, when a company bonus is far less than expected and vacation plans have to be canceled; when a person we thought we could count on walks out; when a cyclone or earthquake or tornado strikes the land and people die—it's then that we need someone. There is still one who will have the final word, who is yet to come, who has strength for our day.

John, suffering but steadfast, received the message while he was "on the island of Patmos" (1:9). As one preacher said, "John was *on* Patmos; Patmos was not on him."

Samuel and Gladys Heap were godly, guided missionaries to South and Central America. I lived across the street from them during their furlough. Years passed, and they began to experience health problems. I phoned Mrs. Heap one day and asked, "Sister Heap, how are you doing under the circumstances?"

She shot back quickly and forcefully, "Oh, Brother Shaver, I'm not under the circumstances. I'm on top of them."

What an extraordinary level of victory! It's because she knew "the Alpha and the Omega . . . who is, and who was, and who is to come, the Almighty" (1:8).[144]

He Is Able

The one of the elders said to me, "Do not weep!
See, the Lion of the tribe of Judah, the Root of David, has triumphed.
He is able to open the scroll and its seven seals.
Revelation 5:5

A while back, Nancy and I visited a lawyer to prepare our last will and testament. Within the will's pages is a plan to dispose of all our earthly possessions so there will be no confusion. The original copy of the will is sealed in a lockbox at a local bank, and only one is worthy to open it. The named executor will use the hidden key to unseal the lockbox, open the will, and carry out our wishes.

Revelation 5 tells of a similar document—a seven-sealed scroll. It is a deed of promise, a covenant, and John weeps because no one is worthy to open it.

Suddenly, heaven speaks: "The Lion of the tribe of Judah . . . *is able* to open the scroll and its seven seals" (5:5). This leads to the coming of the kingdom.

Four creatures, twenty-four elders, thousands of angels, and every living creature begin to praise him. He is worthy because . . .

- He gave all: "with your blood" (5:9)

---

144. Previously published in *Standard* August 2009 (Kansas City, MO: WordAction Publishing Co.), 4. Used by permission.

- He reached out to all: "every tribe and language and people and nation" (5:9)
- He made all: "kingdom and priests to serve our God" (5:10)
- He will appoint us to rule over all: "they will reign on the earth" (5:10)

The Lamb is worthy because he purchased people for God with his blood.

As I write this, I just received a phone call from Janell, who came to our church as a young adult. Several people from our church visited her and shared Christ with her, and she received the Savior. She said to me, "He brought me back into a relationship with him. Now my life is different."

Yes, we should be among the ones praising God, because the one able to open the sealed scroll is also able to meet the needs of our individual lives. And he is reaching people of all cities: "every tribe and language and people and nation."[145]

Truly Just

They were seared by the intense heat and they cursed
the name of God, who had control over these plagues,
but they refused to repent and glorify him.
Revelation 16:9

Revelation 16 portrays the horrible consequences of sin. God's laws are the same for all of us, and disobedience reaps terrible results. In this chapter, these results are represented by the seven bowls of God's wrath.

Some think that God sends people to hell. The truth is that God tries to stop us from being eternally lost, but he allows us to go there if we insist—it is our choice.

To me, someone who chooses to go to hell is like an angry young man who bursts into his friends' apartment, threatening to jump out of the sixth-floor window to his death. His first friend pleads, "Don't do it!" He rushes past him.

---

145. Previously published in *Standard* August 2009 (Kansas City, MO: WordAction Publishing Co.), 4. Used by permission.

A second friend, with arms outstretched, assures him that he will help him solve his problems—if only he will talk. The young man continues toward the window.

A third friend tries to physically block him, but the young man shoves him aside and leaps.

On the way down, he yells, "Why didn't someone help me? Why didn't you stop me? I'm so mad at you for not saving me!"

Here is a person who has rushed past the Word of God; the call of the Father; the blood of Christ; the wooing of the Spirit; the witness of friends; the preaching of the gospel; the love of Christians; the worship of the church. This person is like those mentioned in verses 9 and 11: "They refused to repent."

Nevertheless, we must never give up hope for someone's salvation or stop praying for them. For instance, one day, Aaron knelt at an altar, wept, and prayed. I asked why he was broken, and he said, "I had given up on my dad, but God convicted me. I'm burdened for him again."

George Mueller, a man well known for his prayer life, prayed for the salvation of two friends for forty-eight years. It was not until after Mueller died that they both were saved.

We must not give up. God does not want "anyone to perish, but everyone to come to repentance" (2 Peter 3:9).[146]

Jesus Wins

Look, I am coming soon! Blessed is the one who keeps the words
of the prophecy written in this scroll.
Revelation 22:7

My wife, Nancy, had a difficult year. She journaled this: *If I had to give this year a title, I would call it "The Year of the Storms." The enemy came ripping and tearing, and Jesus comes to sew us back up again. . . . Don't tell God how big your storm is, tell the storm how big your God is.*

And in the end, she's won.

---

146. Previously published in *Standard* August 2009 (Kansas City, MO: WordAction Publishing Co.), 4. Used by permission.

In Revelation 22, we have a reaffirmation of the message of hope that resonates throughout the book. Three times in this chapter, Jesus repeats, "I am coming soon" (22:7, 12, 20). To all who are going through temptation, trial, and tribulation—hold on! Revelation is the book for those going through rough times.

This closing chapter also gives us the hope of heaven. Jesus assures us that all "who wash their robes" in the blood of Christ will "have the right to the tree of life" (22:14). No sin will be allowed in that place. It will only be for those who have had their character and conduct changed by Jesus.

Then, there is a surprise. After firmly stating that sin won't be allowed in heaven (22:15), the loving God, the gracious Christ, makes one more invitation: "Let the one who wishes take the free gift of the water of life" (22:17). Right until the end of the book, the end of the Bible, the end of the world as we know it, Christ is still pleading for everyone to receive salvation.

The message of Revelation is summed up in the story of a young man who had completed a study of the book and was pretty sure he knew it all. As he entered a classroom one evening, he saw an old man reading Revelation. Prepared to teach, he said, "Old man, do you understand it?" The man answered, "Yup. Jesus wins."

That's it! Jesus wins! And with him, we will too.[147]

Instead, Be Filled with the Spirit

Therefore do not be foolish, but understand what the Lord's will is.
Do not get drunk on wine, which leads to debauchery.
Instead, be filled with the Spirit.
Ephesians 5:17–18

He returned from a vacation with family members and drove straight to an alcohol rehabilitation facility for a three-week stay. Later, I asked him what made him drink.

---

147. Previously published in *Standard* August 2009 (Kansas City, MO: WordAction Publishing Co.), 4. Used by permission.

He said, "Socially, I felt like I didn't fit in. A few beers loosened me up. But as I went from place to place in an evening, I might drink twelve beers. What woke me up was that, when I drove home from Memorial Day drinking, I hit the post holding the canopy over my driveway."

The next week, after celebrating his birthday, he couldn't remember driving home, and he hit the same canopy post.

He had accepted Christ, but now he was serious about solving his drinking problem. He was shocked when a fellow rehab patient asked him if he planned to start using again—she already had an appointment with her drug dealer. But his attitude was, "I'm one and done."

It is true that the followers of Jesus drank wine. However, it was not the same as today's wine or other alcoholic beverages. The ratio of that day was three parts water to one part wine. The alcohol purified the water, and the water diluted the wine.[148] Furthermore, Scripture takes a strong stand against drunkenness. Romans 13:13: "Let us behave decently, as in the daytime, not in carousing and drunkenness." And Galatians 5:21 follows its statement on drunkenness with, "those who live like this will not inherit the kingdom of God."

I urge people to practice abstinence from all alcohol. Social drinkers often claim that it's no problem—they'll only have one drink. But one of the first affects of alcohol is the reduction of healthy inhibitions—which of course makes it easier to take a second and third drink. Scripture also urges us to consider our influence on others: "It is better not to eat meat or drink wine or to do anything else that will cause your brother or sister to fall" (Romans 14:21). For those who drink to release tension, Ephesians 5:18 provides a far better answer: "Instead, be filled with the Spirit."

When my friend finished rehab, he quit alcohol. He told me that, since that decision, his anxiety and stress have been reduced. He lost fifteen pounds and feels better physically. Rarely does he think about drinking again. Overall, he is more constructive in his interactions with others. A friend observed, "He's now smiling. He's relaxed and so happy—more joyful."

Now, after two years of sobriety, he is back at the same vacation spot from which he'd driven to rehab two years earlier. He said he feels a closeness to the Holy Spirit.

At the time of this writing, an intoxicated woman was pulled from the water at a nearby beach, dead.

---

148. Robert H. Stein, "Wine Drinking in New Testament Times," *Christianity Today*, June 20, 1975, 9–16.

Do You Believe in Hell?

*The time came when the beggar died and the angels carried him to
Abraham's side. The rich man also died and was buried. In Hades, where
he was in torment, he looked up and saw Abraham far away, with Lazarus
by his side. So he called to him, "Father Abraham, have pity on me and
send Lazarus to dip the tip of his finger in water and cool my tongue,
because I am in agony in this fire."*
Luke 16:22–24

Many people would tell you, "I don't believe in hell!" Yet many of them, in a
moment of anger or in an attempt to emphasize a statement, will refer to hell.
For example, if a person is offended by how he's addressed, he might counter
with, "Who the h*** do you think you are, speaking to me like that?"

Let's think about this for a moment. Would you attempt to emphasize a
statement by invoking a place or idea that did not even exist? Subconsciously,
is it possible that the person using the word "hell" really does believe it exists?

Consider what Scripture says about hell:

- Luke records Jesus speaking about the selfish rich man who is tormented in hell (Luke 16:22–24).
- Matthew records Jesus saying, "Depart from me, you who are cursed,
  into the eternal fire prepared for the devil and his angels" (25:41). Note
  the original purpose of the eternal fire: "prepared for the devil and his
  angels."
- Peter writes, "For if God did not spare angels when they sinned, but sent
  them to hell, putting them in chains of darkness to be held for judgment; if he did not spare the ancient world when he brought the flood
  on its ungodly people, but protected Noah, a preacher of righteousness,
  and seven others; if he condemned the cities of Sodom and Gomorrah
  by burning them to ashes, and made them an example of what is going
  to happen to the ungodly; and if he rescued Lot, a righteous man, who
  was distressed by the depraved conduct of the lawless (for that righteous man, living among them day after day, was tormented in his righteous soul by the lawless deeds he saw and heard)—if this is so, then
  the Lord knows how to rescue the godly from trials and to hold the

unrighteous for punishment on the day of judgment" (2 Peter 2:4–9). Note God's concern to rescue godly people.

- In his vision in Revelation, John records the following words: "He said to me, 'It is done. I am the Alpha and the Omega, the Beginning and the End. To the thirsty I will give water without cost from the spring of the water of life. Those who are victorious will inherit all this, and I will be their God and they will be my children. But the cowardly, the unbelieving, the vile, the murderers, the sexually immoral, those who practice magic arts, the idolaters and all liars—they will be consigned to the fiery lake of burning sulfur. This is the second death'" (21:6–8).

With all these strong statements about hell, let us remember why God sent Jesus Christ to this earth and to each heart:

- Luke 19:10 says, "For the Son of Man came to seek and to save the lost."
- John 3:17–18 says, "For God did not send his Son into the world to condemn the world, but to save the world through him. Whoever believes in him is not condemned, but whoever does not believe stands condemned already because they have not believed in the name of God's one and only Son."
- Revelation 3:19–20 records Jesus: "So be earnest and repent. Here I am! I stand at the door and knock. If anyone hears my voice and opens the door, I will come in and eat with that person, and they with me."

Jesus Christ makes every effort to save you and me and those around us from a broken, sin-controlled life here and in hell thereafter. What a reason to reach out to others with the love of God and the saving power of Jesus Christ.

The Cost of the Truth

*But even if he does not [save us], we want you to know, Your Majesty, that
we will not serve your gods or worship the image of gold you have set up.*
Daniel 3:18

It's easier for me to follow a "do" rather than a "don't," and that's what these three young men did. They worshiped the living God with all their hearts, souls, and minds, so there wasn't anything left for false gods. They were so committed to the truth that no matter what happened, they would not surrender their faith or bow and worship any other god—and certainly not one made of cold, lifeless gold. Even the threat of death did not shake them.

They were not willing to pretend to worship an idol to protect themselves. They didn't have a pity party, plead with God, or say, "This isn't fair! Look how faithful we've been—how could you let this happen?" When things weren't going their way, they didn't run away. They didn't try to control something they didn't have any power over. They just trusted that, in life or in death, "Thy will be done."

I can write these things because that's what I would have been tempted to do. I can be bad at listening. I can keep busy when I don't want to hear the truth about the next assignment. Yet in my struggles, God is there, coaching me on. He opens the way for me to stand up with courage and learn that I can do this—I can trust him.

Is God whispering truth to you today? Will you allow yourself to hear and obey?

Nancy Shaver[149]

A Letter from Prison

And because of my chains, most of the brothers and sisters have become confident in the Lord and dare all the more to proclaim the gospel without fear.
Philippians 1:14

What did preaching and witnessing get the apostle Paul? Time in prison, among other things. Unfairly accused; unfairly tried; unfairly jailed; now in chains and closely guarded—it seemed life could not get worse. Please note the attitude of this fully dedicated, wholly sanctified, Spirit-possessed follower of Christ. He writes from prison to the church he founded in Philippi:

- "I eagerly expect and hope that I will in no way be ashamed, but will have sufficient courage so that now as always Christ will be exalted in my body, whether by life or death" (Philippians 1:20).

149. Previously published in *Come Ye Apart* September–October–November 2001 (Kansas City, MO: WordAction Publishing Co.), 77. Used by permission. (This publication became *Reflecting God*.)

- "I have learned to be content whatever the circumstances" (4:11).
- "I can do all this through him who gives me strength" (4:13).
- "My God will meet all your needs according to the riches of his glory in Christ Jesus" (4:19).
- "Do not be anxious about anything, but in every situation, by prayer and petition, with thanksgiving, present your requests to God. And the peace of God, which transcends all understanding, will guard your hearts and your minds in Christ Jesus" (4:6–7).

Even today we get letters from prison. David attended a week of revival services in a little Illinois church. He was facing legal trouble and, seeking the Lord night after night, peeled away layers of sin. Weeks later he received his prison sentence. Here's what he wrote to us from his cell:

> I was recommended by the court and promised to go to boot camp (IIP), which is a four-month program, but the Capitol of Illinois denied me. So I'm stuck doing two years of a four-year sentence. My God is faithful and has a plan. The day after I found out, although I was crushed, I remained faithful, and something magical happened. My new cellmate, who had been observing me read my Bible and pray diligently in spite of everything, engaged in a conversation with me. I felt this overwhelming feeling to do it, and although I was scared and nervous (never having done anything like this before), I did it.
>
> I simply asked Bradley S. Peters, "Would you like to be saved?"
>
> To my amazement, with this soft puppy-dog look in this hardened young man's eyes, he said, "Yes."
>
> So, on June 30, in the X-house in Hillsboro, Illinois, DOC, on our knees right there on that filthy cell floor with our hands folded, I led Bradley in a prayer of salvation, and he accepted Christ. On that filthy floor he became as clean as bleach. He was the first person I've led to Jesus, and it was one of the most powerful things I've been part of. (Glory be to God!)
>
> It's hard to imagine that the dangerous, drug-dealing, drug-addicted, violent, evil, life-destroying shell of a man I used to be is now doing great work for Jesus Christ. You and I both know I was saved and set free from my addictions prior to my incarceration. I could utilize this place to up my street IQ and status and become more evil than I was. But, by the grace of God and my Savior, Jesus Christ, I have turned this place into a long Bible camp.

Paul couldn't get away from his guard—but, on the other hand, the guard couldn't get away from him. David couldn't get away from his cellmate—but his cellmate also couldn't get away from him. In both cases it could be said, "What has happened to me has actually served to advance the gospel" (1:12).

How are you allowing God to use your circumstances?

The Father and Jesus Are Working, Part 1

In his defense Jesus said to them, "My Father is always at his work
to this very day, and I too am working."
John 5:17

Would my mom and dad give me an appropriate present for my high school graduation? My dad gave me a fine watch for eighth-grade graduation, but high school—that was a lot bigger. Little did I know how much thinking, planning, paying, and working was going on behind the scenes. While I worried, he worked. I soon learned that my gift was a ten-thousand-mile, thirty-day trip across the United States with two high school teachers and fourteen students, camping most nights. To this day I remember Yellowstone, Glacier, Grand Canyon, the Badlands, Crater Lake, the Redwoods, Mount Shasta, and more. My dad was working it all out, and it was very good.

In a statement that seems strange at first glance, Jesus says, "My Father is always at his work . . . and I too am working." On the Sabbath, Jesus healed a man who'd been disabled for thirty-eight years. Jewish leaders subsequently began persecuting him for his "working" on the Sabbath. Jesus responded to them with the statement about his and his Father's work.

Make no mistake, Jesus was a faithful adherent to Sabbath worship. However, he had been expanding the meaning of Sabbath to include emergency works and deeds of love and compassion. The Father is at his work. His work includes love, mercy, compassion, caring, healing, saving, cleansing. There was a spiritual realm of work that went beyond what Jewish leaders understood.

This principle goes beyond Sabbath. In all the issues of your life, or big affairs of the nation or world, whether we see it or not, the Father is always working, and so is Christ. The Father and Son are dealing with individual people and working in the affairs of nations, for our good and his glory.

This working shows up in individual lives. In John 4:49–50, a royal official begged Jesus to heal his son, who was close to death. Jesus answered, "Go, your son will live."

As the official was returning home, his servants met him to report that his son had recovered. The official asked when this had happened, and the servants said, "'Yesterday, at one in the afternoon, the fever left him.' Then the father realized that this was the exact time at which Jesus had said to him, 'Your son will live.' So he and his whole household believed." (John 4:52–53). Many experiences like this divine timing are evidence that the Father and Son are working behind the scenes.

Sometimes we are troubled because of the presence of evil circumstances. Dr. Orval Nease went through a distressing and painful experience. He read in his Bible, "And we know that all things work together for good to them that love God" (Romans 8:28, KJV). The statement was troubling in the light of his experience. Dr. Nease was a student of Greek, the original language of the New Testament. So he opened his Greek New Testament to Romans 8:28 and read, "And we know that in all things God works for the good of those who love him, who have been called according to his purpose." Dr. Nease suddenly realized that God could take all things, even what the devil may send, and work it into a pattern for good. What relief! And note God's purpose in 8:29: that we would "be conformed to the image of his Son."

The Father and Jesus Are Working, Part 2

In his defense Jesus said to them, "My Father is always
at his work to this very day, and I too am working."
John 5:17

After Jesus tells the criticizing leaders that both he and the Father are working, he goes into longer, rich discussion about the intimate relationship of the Father and Son (John 5:19–30). Among the projects the Father and Son are working on is a time "when all who are in their graves will hear his voice and come out—those who have done what is good will rise to live, and those who have done what is evil will rise to be condemned" (5:28–29). Though the Father and Son are both working on this end-time plan, there is one limiting factor: "But about that day or hour no one knows, not even the angels in heaven, nor the Son, but only the Father" (Matthew 24:36).

Catherine Marshall battled severe illness. She saw trouble. Her husband, Peter Marshall, chaplain of the United States Senate from 1947 until 1949, died at age forty-six. After Peter was taken to the hospital by ambulance,

Catherine, at home with their young son, sank to the floor and pondered how to pray. She said, "Suddenly there was the feeling of being surrounded by the love of God the Father—enveloped in it, cradled with infinite gentleness. Awe swept through me, followed by the conviction that it was not necessary to *ask* for anything. All I had to do was to commit Peter and me and our future to this great love.[150]

She discovered that God could make even troubles ultimately work for good. After Peter died, with time and God's grace, Catherine wrote *A Man Called Peter* (which was later adapted into a film) and another book about her own spiritual journey, *Beyond Our Selves*. As a result, millions have been brought closer to God. The Father and the Son have been working.

In our troubled, seemingly out-of-control world, the Father has been working to this very day. The Son has been working. And in your own life, the Father and Son are working.

Come Back from Behind

This priceless treasure we hold, so to speak, in a common earthenware jar—to show that the splendid power of it belongs to God and not to us. We are handicapped on all sides, but we are never frustrated; we are puzzled, but never in despair. We are persecuted, but we never have to stand it alone: we may be knocked down but we are never knocked out! Every day we experience something of the death of the Lord Jesus, so that we may also know the power of the life of Jesus in these bodies of ours.
2 Corinthians 4:7–10, PHILLIPS

Patrick Mahomes and the Kansas City Chiefs did it again. For the third game in a row, they rallied from being ten or more points behind and won in the end. They won the 2020 Super Bowl in Miami with three touchdowns in the last eight minutes—the final score was 31–20. It's exciting to see your team come back from behind to claim the victory!

In a far more significant way, you are the recipient Jesus's promise of come-back-from-behind victory. Note that you hold your spiritual treasure

---

150. Catherine Marshall, *Beyond Our Selves* (New York: McGraw Hill Book Company, 1961), 24–25.

in a common earthenware jar—a "jar of clay," in other translations. It's good to remember that the amazing grace of God acknowledges that we are in limited human bodies. But our limitations provide all the more opportunity to highlight God's power.

Note that the great, godly, spiritually powerful apostle Paul admits his own limitations: he has been disabled, puzzled, persecuted, even knocked down. But each limit is followed by a comeback—despite it all, we are not frustrated, not in despair, never knocked out. Yes, the power of the life of Jesus is flowing through you. John put it this way: "The one who is in you is greater than the one who is in the world" (1 John 4:4).

So whatever pressure you may be undergoing today—health problems, financial struggles, relational conflict, unanswered prayers, criticism, resistance, fatigue, discouragement, you fill in the blank—remember the end of Paul's statement. There is always a response, a return, an answer, a comeback from behind. Why? As John writes, "Greater is he [Christ] that is in you, than he [Satan] that is in the world" (1 John 4:4, KJV).

Later in his second letter to the Corinthians, Paul reinforces this truth: "The very spring of our actions is the love of Christ. . . . Our sole defence, our only weapon, is a life of integrity. . . . Never far from death, yet here we are alive, always 'going through it' yet never 'going under'" (2 Corinthians 5:14; 6:7, 9, PHILLIPS).

Keep in Step with the Spirit

Those who belong to Christ Jesus have crucified the flesh with its passions and desires. Since we live by the Spirit, let us keep in step with the Spirit.
Galatians 5:24–25

Dr. David's frank testimony highlights the need to continually live in the fullness of the sanctifying Spirit. It stresses the importance of spiritual renewal whenever we stray from that ongoing commitment and life in the Spirit.

During college, David asked Jesus into his heart, started going to church, and prayed God would lead him to a good Christian woman. Now, for more than twenty-four years, his wife, Fay, has been the joy of his life.

Dr. David describes what happened next:

I struggled spiritually for twenty years. I have taught Sunday school for the past ten years and have been on the church board several different times in the past fifteen years. I only knew the first work of grace until seven years ago, when I was filled with the Holy Spirit. My business almost collapsed, and I was physically and emotionally exhausted. I finally fell on my knees before God and surrendered everything to him. Something happened that day that I may never really be able to explain. I knew I'd always felt that I had to earn God's acceptance and love. I was never good enough, even though I had read the Bible several times and even taught a Sunday school class. I felt God putting his arms around me that day, and I felt love unlike any I had ever felt. Within several months, I had led several people to the Lord.

But then spiritual struggles ensued. Dr. David continues:

I was very busy, too busy, and I knew my prayer life was suffering. Little by little I climbed back onto the throne. Not one person has been saved in nearly two years. Two months ago, I developed pneumonia and was very sick. My blood work resembled that of lymphoma. God was getting my attention.

And more recently, Dr. David says:

This brings me to the present. After listening to your messages, I knew I wanted God back in control of my life. I prayed Sunday night after services. I had the best night's sleep before performing surgery that I have had since I was initially sanctified. I had twelve hours of surgery on my schedule the next day. I remember asking God to specifically help me find something. When I checked with the C-arm, I was in perfect position although I could not see it with my eyes. I felt God directing my hands just like he did when I followed him closely before.

There is nothing on earth that compares with walking close to the Lord and doing his will in bringing lost sinners home.[151]

Take a moment to review your life with the Lord. If you need to seek the Holy Spirit's renewal, do so.

You Intended to Harm Me, But God . . .

---

151. Previously published in *The Good News: The Chic Shaver Center for Evangelism Newsletter* (December 2007).

You intended to harm me, but God intended it for good to
accomplish what is now being done, the saving of many lives.
Genesis 50:20

No question about it—Joseph had been a brat! He had continually irritated his eleven brothers and his father. But there's also no question that his brothers' solution to their irritation was dead wrong. When their father Israel sent Joseph to check on his brothers and their grazing flocks, the brothers captured him, threw him in a pit, and sold him to Midianite merchants. The merchants, in turn, sold Joseph to an Egyptian named Potiphar, the captain of the guard under Pharaoh.

Though Potiphar initially trusted him, Joseph was falsely accused of misconduct, then unjustly imprisoned. However, as Scripture tells us, "While Joseph was there in prison, the LORD was with him" (Genesis 39:20–21).

Even as he was in prison, Joseph eventually became the only one who was able to interpret Pharaoh's dreams. Pharaoh subsequently released him from prison and appointed him prime minister. In this position, Joseph stored up surplus grain in times of plenty and prepared the country for famine.

When famine eventually came, it reached all the way to his father Israel and his eleven brothers. The brothers came to Joseph, the prime minister overseeing food distribution, seeking help. But with the passage of time, they didn't recognize him. When they finally realized who they had been talking to, they begged him for mercy and even offered to become his slaves. Then Joseph said, "You intended to harm me, but God intended it for . . . the saving of many lives" (Genesis 50:20). Joseph forgave his brothers and provided for their physical needs.

From the days of Genesis even to the present, God still has a way of turning the evil of others into good for those who follow him. I saw it in my first pastorate. A small independent church that had been established only five weeks earlier asked me to be their pastor. A local businessman had gathered the group, and they met in his remodeled horse shed. The local businessman agreed that we could develop it as a Church of the Nazarene, and we paid him a very nominal rent. Once the church was somewhat established and my wife and I were neck-deep in commitment, the businessman suddenly told us that we must buy the property—the church, two houses, a little Sunday school building, and four acres—in a short period of time. Otherwise, he would sell it out from under us to another denomination. At the same time, we learned that every person he had gathered to attend the church owed him money. Not good!

We had about forty people in the congregation at that time. Our church board gathered to discuss the offer (or threat). One board member said, "I think he got us involved here just to sell off his property."

I was so convinced that God had led us to pastor the church that I responded, "You may be right. He may have meant it for evil, but God meant it for good." We voted to buy the property.

After that, the church grew, we built a beautiful sanctuary and education unit on the acreage, and we saw many people find Christ. Out of that church came an outstanding prison chaplain; a singer who became part of a traveling gospel quartet; a lady who earned her ministerial credentials; a college church pastor; a district superintendent; outstanding, godly lay people; and many more.

It will be true for you who have yielded all to Jesus and are living a Spirit-filled and Spirit-led life: people may intend to harm you, but God intends it for good. We can even save many lives through it. What a God!

Did Not Inquire of the Lord

The Israelites sampled their provisions but did not inquire of the LORD.
Joshua 9:14

Israel's military had been mopping up the opposition. God led them to victory at Jericho, where the walls came tumbling down. After dealing with disobedience at Ai, Israel launched a second attack with divine direction, and achieved a major victory.

As news of Israel's military success spread, the citizens of nearby Gibeon decided they must resort to deception to protect themselves. They sent a delegation to Israel whose donkeys were loaded with worn-out sacks and whose people wore patched sandals and old clothes. Their bread was dry and moldy. They pretended to have come from a distant country, and asked for a peace treaty.

As Scripture says, "The Israelites sampled their provisions but did not inquire of the LORD." Instead, they accepted the delegation's story and made a peace treaty with them. Three days later, they discovered they had been duped. Serious problems followed—Joshua 9 will tell you more.

For those of us who follow the Lord today, it is important to inquire of the Lord about life's major decisions. These include:

- What type of education you'll receive
- Whether to be single or whom to marry
- Where to live
- What sort of work or career you will pursue
- Which church you will attend

There are five ways to know the will of God:

- The Word of God (the Bible)
- The leadership of the Spirit in prayer
- Opened and closed doors
- Advice of mature Christian friends
- Sanctified reason

Israel thought the circumstances (the open door) proved that Gibeon was far away, so they made the decision to draw up a peace treaty. If they had only asked the Lord first.

Kathy told me she invited a homeless woman to come live with her, just assuming it was the compassionate thing to do—she didn't ask the Lord's direction. Before long, she had to ask the woman to leave.

Charles told me he'd decided to purchase a weekend house at the beach because he consistently took his family there for weekends. He didn't seek the Lord's direction. The end result, he realized, was that he consistently took his children out of church, and now they were far from God.

On the other hand, Nancy and I sensed a need to move to a different house. We prayed about it consistently. One day in prayer, I heard the Lord say, *"Now is the time to move."* We did, and in multiple ways, our new home became the source of multiple blessings.

Please inquire of the Lord.

What Can You Do When You're Eighty-Five?

"Now then, just as the LORD promised, he has kept me alive for forty-five years since the time he said this to Moses, while Israel moved about in the wilderness. So here I am today, eighty-five years old! I am still as strong today as the day Moses sent me out; I'm just as vigorous to go out to battle

now as I was then. Now give me this hill country that the LORD promised
me that day. You yourself heard then that the Anakites were there and
their cities were large and fortified, but, the LORD helping me,
I will drive them out just as he said." Then Joshua blessed Caleb
son of Jephunneh and gave him Hebron as his inheritance.
Joshua 14:10–13

Eighty-five years old and ready to go out to battle again—God had given Caleb a promise, and now he pressed Joshua so he could claim it. In turn, Joshua gave Caleb Hebron as his inheritance.

Forty-five years earlier, Caleb and Joshua had been the only two faithful spies out of twelve when they scouted the promised land. Meanwhile, Israel's people were in the wilderness waiting to enter that land.

Ten spies came back and said, "We can't enter the land."

But Caleb and Joshua said, "With God, we can."

In the end, Israel believed the ten and wandered in the wilderness for forty years. Finally, with Joshua as their new leader, they had entered the land and had been clearing out the enemy and claiming territory for five years. And now Caleb, at age eighty-five, claimed another promise and received Hebron as his inheritance.

Dr. Paul Rees and Dr. Edward Lawlor were both preaching with power when they were in their seventies, maybe eighties. When he was almost eighty, Ernie Loganbill took two weeks to carve me a walking stick. He has carved sticks for people like Mother Teresa and Senator Bob Dole—and mine was number 283.

Caleb claimed a promise and received his inheritance at age eighty-five. You too can do the same whether you're eighty-five, older, or younger.

I have been thinking of some of the promises Jesus and his followers made. Here are a few:

- "But seek first his kingdom and his righteousness, and all these things [food and clothes] will be given to you as well" (Matthew 6:33).
- "For everyone who asks receives; the one who seeks finds; and to the one who knocks, the door will be opened" (Matthew 7:8).
- "I am the bread of life. Whoever comes to me will never go hungry, and whoever believes in me will never be thirsty" (John 6:35).
- "I have come that they may have life, and have it to the full" (John 10:10).
- "My sheep listen to my voice; I know them, and they follow [present tense—keep following] me. I give them eternal life, and they shall never perish" (John 10:27–28).

- "You may ask me for anything in my name, and I will do it" (John 14:14).
- "Do not be anxious about anything, but in every situation, by prayer and petition, with thanksgiving, present your requests to God. And the peace of God, which transcends all understanding, will guard your hearts and your minds in Christ Jesus" (Philippians 4:6–7).
- "There remains, then, a Sabbath-rest for the people of God; for anyone who enters God's rest also rests from their works, just as God did from his" (Hebrews 4:9–10).
- "May God himself, the God of peace, sanctify you through and through. May your whole spirit, soul and body be kept blameless at the coming of our Lord Jesus Christ. The one who calls you is faithful, and he will do it" (1 Thessalonians 5:23–24).

Last night at 7:00 p.m., I began to pray for a need. I cited a promise in Jesus's name, very simply and without drama. By 8:30 p.m., the answer was in my hand. Like Caleb, I'm eighty-five years old.

Eighty-five, or older, or younger—what can you do? Claim your promises; possess your inheritance.

God Is Not Shut Down

Now I am about to go the way of all the earth. You know with all your heart and soul that not one of all the good promises the Lord your God gave you has failed. Every promise has been fulfilled; not one has failed.
Joshua 23:14

As I write this in 2020, society is shut down. Because of the COVID-19 pandemic, nations around the world have closed stores, factories, schools, shops, sports complexes, and more. But whatever happens next in our world, we know God is not shut down.

Joshua was at the end of his physical life. He had led Israel across the Jordan and into the promised land, and he'd led them in conquest of the land for twenty-five to thirty years. He reminded them that God fulfilled every promise he had made to Israel. Then Joshua got specific and lists the victories, the fulfilled promises:

- He led Abraham to Canaan.
- He used Moses and Aaron to lead Israel out of Egypt.
- He opened the Red Sea for Israel and drowned the pursuing Egyptian army.
- He gave Israel victory over Amorite kings east of the Jordan.
- He brought Israel across the Jordan and gave them Jericho.
- He gave Israel victory over numerous inhabitants of the land.

The Lord summed it up: "I gave you a land on which you did not toil and cities you did not build" (Joshua 24:13). In other words, despite all challenges, God was not shut down.

Think about your life for a moment; think of promises made and promises kept. Here are a few from my life, all of which God has kept:
- "If we confess our sins, he is faithful and just and will forgive us our sins and purify us from all unrighteousness" (1 John 1:9). He did!
- "Here I am! I stand at the door and knock. If anyone hears my voice and opens the door, I will come in and eat with that person, and they with me" (Revelation 3:20). He did!
- "May God himself, the God of peace, sanctify you through and through. May your whole spirit, soul and body be kept blameless at the coming of our Lord Jesus Christ. The one who calls you is faithful, and he will do it" (1 Thessalonians 5:23–24). He did! And he does!
- "And my God will meet all your needs according to the riches of his glory in Christ Jesus" (Philippians 4:19). He did! He does!
- "When my father and my mother forsake me, then the LORD will take care of me" (Psalm 27:10, NKJV). He did!
- "I will instruct you and teach you in the way you should go; I will guide you with my eye" (Psalm 32:8, NKJV). He does!
- "For the Lord himself will come down from heaven, with a loud command, with the voice of the archangel and with the trumpet call of God, and the dead in Christ will rise first. After that, we who are still alive and are left will be caught up together with them in the clouds to meet the Lord in the air. And so we will be with the Lord forever" (1 Thessalonians 4:16–17). He will!

No matter what, God is not shut down!

The Gift of God

You have not kept the command the LORD your God gave you;
if you had, he would have established your kingdom over Israel for all time.
But now your kingdom will not endure; the LORD has sought out a man
after his own heart and appointed him ruler of his people,
because you have not kept the LORD's command.
1 Samuel 13:13–14

Saul was an exceptional man. He was tall and handsome, and God chose and anointed him to be the first king of Israel (9:2, 16). "God changed Saul's heart," and "the Spirit of God came powerfully upon him" (10:9–10). At first, Saul was reluctant to the point that, at his public introduction as king, he hid himself among the equipment (10:22). His military skill, empowered by God, was such that his first campaign resulted in a total rout of the threatening Ammonite camp (11:11). Saul was thirty when he became king, and he reigned for forty-two years (13:1).

God had given him an amazing gift—kingship over Israel, God's chosen possession. Yet, somewhere along the way, a pattern began to emerge with Saul. He would do *part* of what God commanded, but not *all*—in other words, he was only partially obedient (13:8–10; 15:9–10). Above all else, his life revolved around preserving his rule.

Over time, Saul became an obsessed, jealous, bitter, murderous man who lashed out at those who wished to do him good. In the end, after being wounded in battle, Saul committed suicide (31:4). The divine conclusion was this: "You have not kept the command the LORD your God gave you" (13:13).

What went so wrong? Though God had blessed Saul with natural gifts— most of all, the great gift of ruling Israel—he failed to follow Proverbs 4:23: "Above all else, guard your heart, for everything you do flows from it." Saul's problem was that he shifted one priority: He came to value the gift of God as greater than the God who gave it.

I am sure every one of us will face this issue. Think of all the possible gifts God may give you—health, education, work, loved ones, house, bank account, possessions, skills, influence, power—and be careful. Guard your heart. God is greater than any gift he gives you. While many of the gifts will be temporary, God is forever. Check your relationship with God today in the light of any gift he has given you.

Peace for the Dividing Wall of Hostility

*For he himself is our peace, who has made the two groups one
and has destroyed the barrier, the dividing wall of hostility.*
Ephesians 2:14

The rift between Jews and Gentiles was huge; for years, they had been hostile toward each other. And now, Jesus Christ shows up. He sets aside the law of the Jews and instead brings the Jew and Gentile to himself; he makes them both right with God through his death on the cross. He gives them both access to the Father by the Holy Spirit. He creates one new humanity out of the two, and finally, there is peace (Ephesians 2:14–18).

In today's society, too, there is so much that angers people. A dividing wall of hostility exists between them. In an effort to illustrate how to break down the wall of hostility between people, let me tell you the story of Kathy and Carolee.

Kathy had tried for years to help her brother Dave. Countless times, she appealed to him and to authorities who could help him. Dave was addicted to pain pills as well as alcohol, and he was angry and violent. It was so bad that Kathy started sleeping upside-down from her usual position on her bed. Fearing her brother might shoot her through the bedroom window, she said, "Better my feet than my head."

One day, in a rage, Dave beat his neighbor to death, stole a gun, and drove to the mall. He shot and killed a young lady in her car and a young man in his car, and eventually, police officers killed Dave. Later, the police arrived at Carolee's house to tell her that Dave had killed her thirty-three-year-old daughter, Leslie.

The next day, Kathy stood in front of her local church with her pastor and family members by her side to express her heartbreak and sorrow to the community. While local TV news broadcast the footage across the city, Carolee watched. How easy it would be for Carolee to be bitter and to rage against Kathy for what her brother had done to Leslie. She could easily say, "I don't want to see her, talk to her, or have anything to do with her"—a dividing wall of hostility. But instead, as Kathy stood before the TV cameras that day, speaking of Dave's condition and offering her condolences, apologies, and tears, Carolee knew she had to meet Kathy.

Three months later, Carolee met Kathy in the pastor's office and explained that she'd already forgiven Dave. The two women hugged. Later, they went together to the site of the shooting. There, they hugged, cried, and expressed and received forgiveness.

God began to work through the tragedy. Soon, Kathy and Carolee were telling their story together to TV news and church groups. Kathy began studying and leading groups in grief recovery. They both had articles published in *Chicken Soup for the Soul*.

Carolee said, "Though my heart was broken, I have new friends, old friendships are deeper, I have become more loving and caring, my family has a tighter bond, and I have grown in my relationship with God."

If you visited their Sunday school class, you would see **Kathy and Carolee** sitting side by side as dear friends. All of this is possible because both women have a relationship with Jesus Christ—he is their peace, destroying any wall of hostility and bringing the two together. He can do this in your world too.

God's Love Can Be Forfeited

Those who cling to worthless idols turn away from God's love for them.
Jonah 2:8

Would you consider people to be our most precious commodity; our most important asset; our most valuable treasure? If so, why would they trade themselves for a meaningless existence on drugs and alcohol, exchanging their precious birthright for a mess of pottage or sugarcoated sin? We're too valuable to live without finding our purpose for being here; we're too valuable to live below the level God intended.

For years, I carried baggage from my childhood that kept me hidden from view. I lived my life through my family until the pain from broken dreams demanded that I take time to deal with my past. The healers in the body of Christ allowed me to be honest; and in that safety, I opened the wounds to let light and love make a beautiful scar. I traded the idol of shame and fear for a relationship with the real God, who gives me the courage, boldness, confidence, and trust to simply be myself and serve him wherever I am.

Don't be afraid to trade your worthless idol for the real thing.

Nancy Shaver[152]

Wait on the Lord

Yet the LORD longs to be gracious to you; therefore he will
rise up to show you compassion. For the LORD is a God of justice.
Blessed are all who wait for him!
Isaiah 30:18

On one occasion, while he was eating with them, he gave them this
command: "Do not leave Jerusalem, but wait for the gift my Father
promised, which you have heard me speak about. For John baptized with
water, but in a few days you will be baptized with the Holy Spirit."
Acts 1:4–5

I want you to know I am pulling for you. You have now read numerous devotionals about sanctification and being filled with the Holy Spirit. Perhaps you have been praying for God to do this gracious work in you but do not yet have assurance that he has. I urge you to wait on the Lord. The early disciples prayed for forty days in intense prayer (Acts 1:14; 2:1) until they were filled with the Spirit (2:4).

Dr. Wes Tracy wrote about the importance of taking significant time before the Lord as you wait for him to answer this prayer for you. Here are several of his insights:

- There is much to do to prepare the convert's heart for sanctification. For one thing, even the rejoicing convert usually does not have an accurate image of how deeply ingrained sin is in his very being.
- During the time between conversion and sanctification, God faithfully reveals the person's need for sanctifying grace and creates in the heart a longing for Christ. This takes time. During the Wesleyan revival the

---

152. Previously published in *Come Ye Apart* July–August–September 1964 (Kansas City, MO: Nazarene Publishing House), 94. Used by permission. (This publication became *Reflecting God*.)

typical amount of time that the convert spent seeking sanctifying grace was five years. Those early Wesleyans provide a helpful model. They were *quick* to *seek* sanctifying grace but *slow* to *profess* it.

- Wesley coached them to "fret not," "repine not," nor "murmur against God because you are not yet sanctified," nor should one spend time "uselessly tormenting yourself because the time has not fully come." Instead, Wesley advised them to "calmly and quietly wait for it, knowing that it will come."

My own pursuit of entire sanctification took time. My conversion was clear-cut, and my early days of Christianity showed evidence of a changed life. But about five months into my Christian life, I began to sense ugly tempers arising from the basement of my soul. I learned of a deeper Christian life called sanctification. I began to seek God daily for that blessing. After five months, God answered. God was using that time to probe the deeper levels of my heart and prepare me for full reception of the Spirit. So my heart joins you in waiting and seeking. As Wesley said, "He will speak the second time, 'Be thou clean.'"[153]

Dr. Bresee's Testimony

Therefore Jesus also suffered outside the city gate in order to sanctify the people by his own blood.
Hebrews 13:12, NRSV

Dr. Phineas Bresee is considered the founder of the Church of the Nazarene. In 1884, he experienced a dramatic work of the Holy Spirit. He described the result in his own words:

It felt like fire on my lips, and the burning sensation did not leave them for several days. While all of this of itself would be nothing, there came with it into my heart and being, a transformed condition of life and blessing and unction and glory, which I had never known before. I felt that my need was supplied. I was always very reticent in reference to my own personal experi-

---

153. Information from Wesley Tracy, "Entire Sanctification and Uncertain Trumpets," *Herald of Holiness* October 1990 (Kansas City, MO: Nazarene Publishing House), 6–7. Used by permission. (This publication became *Holiness Today.*)

ence. I have never gotten over it, and I have said very little relative to this; but there came into my ministry a new element of spiritual life and power. People began to come into the blessing of full salvation; there were more persons converted; and the last year of my ministry in that church was more consecutively successful, being crowned by an almost constant revival. When the third year came to a close, the church had been nearly doubled in membership, and in every way built up.

Dr. William Greathouse, in his outstanding book *Wholeness in Christ,* quotes John Wesley:

"But what is the faith whereby we are sanctified . . . ?" . . . To this confidence, that God is both able and willing to sanctify us now, there needs to be added one thing more, a divine evidence and conviction that he doeth it. . . . If you seek it by faith, you may expect it as you are; and if as you are, then expect it now! . . . Expect it by faith, expect it as you are, and expect it now!

Join with those praying for this holiness truth to sweep our world![154]

A Spiritual Battle

*For the flesh desires what is contrary to the Spirit,
and the Spirit what is contrary to the flesh. They are in conflict
with each other, so that you are not to do whatever you want.*
Galatians 5:17[155]

What a predicament! If you are even halfway serious about following Jesus Christ, this struggle has got to shred your soul. The words above were written to Christians in Galatia, but many today who belong to Jesus Christ still experience a battle between the Holy Spirit and remaining self-centeredness.

In his letter to the Ephesian Christians, Paul affirms that they *used* to live in transgressions and sins, but now they are saved from that lifestyle by the grace of Jesus Christ (2:1–2, 5). But then he drops a clue. Behind the commission of sins, there is an internal force prompting those actions: "gratifying the

---

154. Previously published in *The Good News: The Chic Shaver Center for Evangelism Newsletter* (December 2008).

155. It may be helpful to know that the 1984 version of the NIV used the term "sinful nature" instead of "flesh."

cravings of our flesh and following its desires and thoughts" (Ephesians 2:3). Behind the sins, cravings; behind the cravings, the sinful nature—or what we might call self-centeredness.

The Galatians faced the same issue. The law could not resolve this problem. There is a subtraction and an addition involved:

Subtraction: "Those who belong to Christ Jesus have crucified the flesh with its passions and desires" (Galatians 5:24). "Crucified" sounds like death.

Addition: "Since we live by the Spirit, let us keep in step with the Spirit" (5:25). This is obviously an ongoing relationship, but to live this relationship, you must enter it—to live the marriage, you must have the wedding. And, once you're in it, how dynamic that relationship is: "*Keep* in *step* with the Spirit."

It's true—from the moment you accept Christ and begin to follow him, you are "born of the Spirit" (John 3:8) and have the Holy Spirit (Romans 8:9). But you may not be "filled with the Spirit."

The minute you walk into your living room and flip the light switch, light moves naturally to every corner of the room. You do not have to stand on a chair, reach up to your bulbs, and point the light to the floor and far end of the room.

However, a careful inspection of the room reveals shadows—furniture blocks the beams of light. For the light to *fill* the room, you will have to move the furniture out as in a thorough spring cleaning. So, it should be no surprise that in the spiritual realm, to be filled with the Spirit and walk in the Spirit, the sinful nature must first be crucified.

David had been faithfully attending his church for thirteen years. He had been converted, but he'd heard of a deeper Christian life called "sanctification." He thought he could work his way into it. Periodically, he would go to the front of his church and pray, but nothing happened. He concluded, "This is not for me."

However, in preparation for an intensive week of revival services, his church issued the challenge to pray for five others to find spiritual help. David ended up praying for himself. One night during revival, he felt that if he didn't take the step that night, he never would. He went forward, knelt, and was empowered to believe God for the answer. David recounted, "I felt so peaceful. The battle is over. So long, roller coaster."

Afterward, he sent the following email to his pastor: "I just want you to know you have a new church member, and it's me."

David began praying, reading the Bible, and keeping in step with the Spirit daily, exclaiming, "Why didn't I do this sooner?"

For Galatians, for David, for you and me—the battle can be won by the crucifixion of the sinful nature and the filling and leading of the Holy Spirit.

Today's Priority

That at the name of Jesus every knee should bow,
in heaven and on earth and under the earth.
Philippians 2:10

Offer yourselves to God as those who have been brought from death to life;
and offer every part of yourself to him as an instrument of righteousness.
Romans 6:13

The correct order of a Christian's priorities has long been debated. One order says, "God first; others second; myself third." Another says, "Christ, family, Christian service, work." I believe there is a more dynamic way to understand our daily priorities.

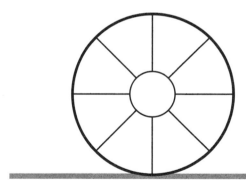

Like the center of a wheel, Christ is the controlling force for all of life's activities; every part of our lives is to be his instrument of righteousness. This is expressed in our family relationships; our Christian service or ministry; our work; and more. As you travel the road of life, in one moment, the family spoke of the wheel touches the ground because, at that time, your family needs the most attention. At another time, the finance spoke may hit the ground; at another, it may be the Christian service spoke or the work responsibility spoke.

Let me relate this to my own life. When I was traveling the country as a full-time evangelist, my son was having trouble in school. When I was invited to teach at our local seminary, one major factor in my decision to take the job was to give my son more attention. At that time, the family spoke of the wheel had special attention and application on my road of life.

When I was writing my final project for my doctoral degree, I pulled away from my regular work (teaching) to devote time to the project. I met my deadline, and the Lord spoke to me, saying, *"This will be published."* Sure enough, that project became *Living in the Power of the Spirit*, which in turn produced *Basic Bible Studies for the Spirit-filled and Sanctified Life*.

When I was pastoring, a couple named Roy and Nora were active in our church. Nora had just had both her legs amputated and was still hospitalized. It was Christmas morning, and our three kids were excited to open gifts. But I received a phone call informing me that Roy had just had a massive heart attack and was in the same hospital as Nora. I asked my children to wait a few hours for Christmas gifts so I could give comfort to this desperate couple. In that moment, Christian service, or ministry, became the predominant spoke.

Recently, after forty-five years of teaching my beloved Sunday school class, I had to step back to focus on completing this devotional book (the work spoke) and give more loving attention to my wife, who is battling Alzheimer's (the family spoke).

In all of these cases, Christ was at the center of these various priorities. At different times of life, our commitment to Christ will be expressed with different emphases. Which spoke is your priority today?

A Damaged Thumb

A man reaps what he sows. Whoever sows to please their flesh, from the flesh nature will reap destruction.
Galatians 6:7–8

The skin at the end of my thumbnails had split open. Winters in Kansas City can be very cold. Most of us heat our homes with natural gas, which is cheap but has a drying effect on a home's atmosphere. And of course, excessive dryness affects the skin.

I tried to treat my damaged thumb with lotion when I was home and gloves when I went out. This gave me a little relief, but most of the time I was still in pain. Eventually, the issue wasn't just my thumb—I discovered that everything my thumb touched was affected too. Buttoning buttons became a special challenge. Can you get a button through a tight buttonhole without your thumb?

I learned that the problem with the thumb created the problem with the buttons. It's an illustration of the law of cause and effect. This principle is also true in the spiritual realm: if you continue to harbor a sinful nature, every action that springs from that nature and everything you touch will be affected, even contaminated—it will even cause you to "reap destruction." The acts of the sinful nature will produce things like "sexual immorality, impurity and debauchery; idolatry and witchcraft; hatred, discord, jealousy, fits of rage, selfish ambition, dissensions, factions and envy; drunkenness, orgies, and the like" (Galatians 5:19–21). Thus, I conclude, it is really important to be set free from the sinful nature.

How Can I Come to the Temple?

Jesus answered them, "Destroy this temple, and I will raise it again in three days." They replied, "It has taken forty-six years to build this temple, and you are going to raise it in three days?" But the temple he had spoken of was his body. After he was raised from the dead, his disciples recalled what he had said.
John 2:19–22

Though more than four thousand people attended the 1989 Lausanne II Congress for World Evangelization in Manila, we had many small group meetings. During one small group meal, I asked the Chinese man next to me what he did. He told me he was a pastor and had just been released from prison. He planned to go back to China to preach and, after that, would be imprisoned again. He was so calm as he told me this—how come? My Chinese brother knew that, even in a prison cell, he could still worship and have a living relationship with Jesus Christ.

Today's scripture picks up right after Christ cleansed the temple by driving out the money changers. When the Jewish leaders challenged him, Jesus said, "Destroy this temple, and I will raise it again in three days." He was referring to his resurrection, implying that he himself would be the new temple of worship.

At another point in this devotional book, I described the importance of Christians meeting together for worship. I quoted Hebrews 10:25, which talks about "not giving up meeting together." I stand by all I wrote. Yet, at the time of this writing, many people are not gathering in large crowds due to the risk of spreading COVID-19. Some watch worship services via Facebook or Zoom with a few family members. Others are imprisoned by hostile governments. Yet, because they have a personal relationship with Jesus Christ, these people are still truly worshiping.

The old temple is gone; Christ is now our temple of worship. Even when we can't go to a building, we can still go to the temple, Jesus Christ. At the moment Jesus died on the cross, the curtain to the temple's Holy of Holies tore from top to bottom, powerfully symbolizing that we now have full access to the holy God and full cleansing from all sin (Matthew 27:51). He is the one we ask for forgiveness of our sins; he is the connection between heaven and earth. When the Pharisees criticized Jesus for his actions on the Sabbath, he replied, "I tell you that something greater than the temple is here" (Matthew 12:6).

In describing the Holy City, Jerusalem, coming down from heaven, John reported, "I did not see a temple in the city, because the Lord God Almighty and the Lamb are its temple" (Revelation 21:22). The Lamb is Christ.

This present, personal relationship with our temple, Jesus Christ, is made possible by the ministry of the Holy Spirit. Jesus explained this to his disciples thus: "But when he, the Spirit of truth, comes, he will guide you into all the truth. He will not speak on his own; he will speak only what he hears, and he will tell you what is yet to come. He will glorify me because it is from me that he will receive what he will make known to you. All that belongs to the Father is mine. That is why I said the Spirit will receive from me what he will make known to you" (John 16:13–15).

Pastor Chen, a major speaker at the Lausanne Congress, had spent eighteen years in Chinese prison camps. Yet, as an evangelist, he keeps going back. During those eighteen years, the prison guards did all they could to humiliate and harass Pastor Chen. They gave him the job of cleaning the prison's cesspool of human waste. Normally, the guards did not like for Pastor Chen to be alone, but when he was working in the cesspool, the guards didn't want to be close to him. Then Pastor Chen could pray out loud, sing, and quote Scripture without harassment. Pastor Chen said, "I looked forward to my time in the human waste cesspool. I could sing a favorite hymn." Here are some of the words from the hymn Pastor Chen liked to sing while cleaning the cesspool:

> I come to the garden alone,
> While the dew is still on the roses;
> And the voice I hear,
> Falling on my ear,
> The Son of God discloses.
> And he walks with me,
> And he talks with me,
> And he tells me I am his own.
> And the joy we share as we tarry there,
> None other has ever known.[156]

It is all possible because Jesus Christ is our true temple—our haven in which we can worship the almighty God.

Food Distribution: Men Full of the Spirit

❖

> *Their widows were being overlooked in the daily distribution of food. So the Twelve gathered all the disciples together and said, "It would not be right for us to neglect the ministry of the word of God in order to wait on tables. Brothers and sisters, choose seven men from among you who are known to be full of the Sprit and wisdom. We will turn this responsibility over to them and will give our attention to prayer and the ministry of the word."*
> *Acts 6:1–4*

The widows in the church needed food—however, the preachers couldn't do everything. Instead, they determined to choose seven laymen to organize, administer, and serve the food. The church had grown since the outpouring of the Spirit at Pentecost five years earlier—they numbered in the thousands around Jerusalem. They had many who had accepted the Savior and been

---

156. C. Austin Miles, "In the Garden," 1912, *Sing to the Lord: Hymnal* (Kansas City, MO: Lillenas Publishing Company, 1993), #606.

born of the Spirit, but the ones they chose for this task had to be men of exceptional spiritual strength. The apostles instructed the church to choose only those "who are known to be full of the Spirit and wisdom" (Acts 6:3).

When he was nineteen, Robert Nicholas migrated from Ontario, Canada, to find work in Chicago. He'd learned hard work on his family farm in Canada, and he'd learned the way of salvation from the Methodist Church. When he arrived in Chicago, he began working in a local hardware store and faithfully tithed on his weekly wages. Soon, he became active in Sunday school and evangelism in the Methodist church he attended. He made new friends. One lovely young woman became his wife.

Within five years, Robert had established his own hardware business in nearby Oak Park. He built his store into one of the largest hardware, house-furnishing, and appliance businesses in Illinois. He was influential in developing the Lake Marion business district, which eventually became the commercial center of the city.

But Robert's heart was not satisfied. Though his business was growing and he was happy with his wife and three young children, he still felt like something was lacking. One day, he received word from his sister in Saskatchewan that she needed him. While Robert was visiting her, he drove across the plains to visit another family member. As he drove, the wind became so severe that he turned his car around and went back to his sister's house. When Robert arrived back at his sister's house, she introduced him to an evangelist who had come for a brief visit and was holding local services.

The evangelist asked him, "Mr. Nicholas, have you given your life completely to God?"[157]

Immediately, Robert fell to his knees and prayed to be completely consecrated to the Lord. He promised the evangelist that he would attend the evening service.

When the altar call was given, Robert Nicholas went forward. He later testified: *I yielded my life without reservation to God. Finally as I prayed, I began to praise God; then the Holy Spirit filled my heart until I could not contain the joy. . . . I arose from the altar of prayer a new man, and my life, notwithstanding my failures and shortcomings, has never been the same since that meeting with God. Over the years there has been tremendous pressure of business and large responsibility in the community and church, and these very pressures might have drawn*

---

157. V. Raymond Edman, *They Found the Secret* (Grand Rapids: Zondervan, 1960), 101.

me away from the Savior but for the fact that there was always the knowledge of the indwelling Spirit who had come to abide in my heart.[158]

When Robert arrived back home, his wife was in the basement doing laundry. As soon as he came down the stairs, she knew something was different—her first words to him were, "Rob, what has happened to you?"[159]

He testified and wept, and he and his wife knelt together, and she surrendered all to Jesus and was also filled with the Spirit.

Soon, Robert Nicholas sold his hardware store. For ten years, he was president of a building and loan association. Then he became a trustee of both Moody Bible College and Wheaton College, served his church, and contributed to enterprises in Oak Park.

He had been a man like the people described in 1 Thessalonians 3:10: "We pray most earnestly that we may see you again and supply what is lacking in your faith." But after being filled with the Holy Spirit, he became like the people described in 2 Timothy 2:21: "Those who cleanse themselves from the latter will be instruments for special purposes, made holy, useful to the Master and prepared to do any good work."

Why do so many Christians lack such joy and overflowing praise? According to Robert Nicholas, "There must be a full surrender of life to the Savior to have the fullness of the Holy Spirit."[160]

Oh, Lord, might we surrender! Might we experience the fullness of the Spirit!

I Believe

*But you will receive power when the Holy Spirit comes on you;
and you will be my witnesses in Jerusalem, and in all Judea and Samaria,
and to the ends of the earth.*
Acts 1:8

---

158. Edman, *They Found the Secret*, 102.
159. Edman, *They Found the Secret*, 103.
160. Edman, *They Found the Secret*, 104.

For the last ten years, the Spirit of God has repeatedly impressed four great issues upon my heart: witness, evangelism, revival, and holiness. I believe in all four.

Witness: It is the privilege and responsibility of each Christian to share with others what Christ has done in their life (Acts 1:8).

Evangelism: Since the biblical meaning of the term "evangelize" is "to tell good news," we must share the facts of the gospel and seek to persuade people to accept Christ, as Peter in Acts 2:38 and Paul in 2 Corinthians 5:11, 20.

Revival: Since it is human nature to need renewal in all realms of life (physical, mental, social, and spiritual), it is the church's responsibility to promote revivals—a concentrated series of gospel meetings that call people to make a commitment. Additionally, we are to pray for widespread revival—a great spiritual movement that will sweep large numbers of people into the kingdom, as in Acts 4:4 and the Hebrides Revival in Scotland (1949–52).

Holiness: Since there is a deeper level of Christian life beyond the new birth, we must endeavor to lead people into the Spirit-filled and Spirit-led life (Galatians 5:25). This life begins with entire sanctification (1 Thessalonians 5:23–24; 1 Peter 1:2) and grows in grace to a life of rich fulfillment and adventure for God (2 Peter 3:18).

I believe! Do you?[161]

Sensitive to the Holy Spirit

Since we live by the Spirit, let us keep in step with the Spirit.
Galatians 5:25

As I write these words in 2020, the world is in a great battle with COVID-19. For weeks and months now, we've been reminded repeatedly to wash our hands, to keep our distance from others, and to wear masks in public.

In a recent conversation with a resident of an assisted-living facility, he told me, "We are not to leave our rooms. All meals are delivered to our door. Even our mail is brought to us."

---

161. Previously published in *The Good News: The Chic Shaver Center for Evangelism Newsletter* (December 2017).

Leaders, scientists, medical personnel, and ordinary people are doing all they know to defeat this virus. Many are praying and seeking the intervention of the almighty God.

Recently, as I was speaking with an acquaintance, he remarked, "We are so keenly aware of what we are to do—like washing our hands and keeping our distance from others. What would it be like if we were as sensitive to the Holy Spirit?"

At first, I was jarred by his words. But then I began thinking about what the Bible teaches about the Holy Spirit. The Spirit has many tasks, but one of the greatest is to represent Jesus. Jesus said, "When the Advocate comes, whom I will send to you from the Father—the Spirit of truth who goes out from the Father—he will testify about me" (John 15:26).

Jesus also said, "But when he, the Spirit of truth, comes, he will guide you into all truth. He will not speak on his own; he will speak only what he hears, and he will tell you what is yet to come. He will glorify me because it is from me that he will receive what he will make known to you" (John 16:13–14).

Notice that Jesus said the Spirit "will guide you." The New Testament is filled with reports of the Spirit speaking to, directing, and guiding Christians. For us, the challenge is to be sensitive enough to hear and obey.

Here are some insights:

- Galatians 5:18: "But if you are led by the Spirit, you are not under the law."
- Ephesians 4:30: "And do not grieve the Holy Spirit of God, with whom you were sealed for the day of redemption."
- 1 Thessalonians 5:19: "Do not quench the Spirit."
- Romans 8:4: "In order that the righteous requirement of the law might be fully met in us, who do not live according to the flesh but according to the Spirit."
- Acts 9:31: "Living in the fear of the Lord and encouraged by the Holy Spirit, [the church] increased in numbers."
- Acts 20:22: Paul reports, "And now, compelled by the Spirit, I am going to Jerusalem, not knowing what will happen to me there."
- Acts 8:29: "The Spirit told Philip, 'Go to that chariot and stay near it.'"

Please note earlier descriptions of Paul and Philip's spiritual states:

- Acts 13:9: "Then Saul, who was also called Paul, filled with the Holy Spirit, looked straight at Elymas."
- Acts 6:3, 5: "Brothers and sisters, choose seven men from among you who are known to be full of the Spirit and wisdom. This proposal

pleased the whole group. They chose Stephen, a man full of faith and of the Holy Spirit; also Philip . . ."

Oh, Lord, fill me with your Holy Spirit. Lead me by your Spirit. Make me so sensitive to the Spirit that I will not miss your direction.

I Haven't Lost My Temper

Love is patient, love is kind. It does not envy, it does not boast,
it is not proud. It does not dishonor others, it is not self-seeking,
it is not easily angered, it keeps no record of wrongs.
1 Corinthians 13:4–5

I met Lou in Ohio when he came to me in tears after a Saturday seminar.

"I've been seeking to be sanctified for ten years," he told me. "Can you help me?" So I counseled Lou.

On Sunday, he went to the altar and gave clear testimony that God had sanctified him. On Monday, I asked him if he'd seen any difference in his life since his sanctification.

He responded, "I haven't lost my temper, I helped my wife, and I keep telling her I love her."

On Wednesday night, as the revival services were ending, Lou told me, "I haven't lost my temper since Saturday. I'm a hundred percent certain. I know where I'm going—to heaven!"[162]

How Good Can You Be?

May your whole spirit, soul and body be kept blameless
at the coming of our Lord Jesus Christ.
1 Thessalonians 5:23

---

162. *The Good News: The Chic Shaver Center for Evangelism Newsletter* (June 2014).

Back when our kids were still at home, one Sunday morning we were getting ready to leave for church and Sunday school. Since we served coffee and donuts before class started, my wife, Nancy, and I regularly carried our giant-sized coffee pot to church and back each week. That day, while our three children were at the far end of the house getting dressed, I said to Nancy, "We're going to leave the coffee pot at church today because the church asked to use it tonight for an evening reception."

Later, after Sunday school and morning service, we were driving home, and everybody was happy. The girls were in the backseat with Nancy. Our son, Paul, who was about nine years old, was up in the front with me. He looked at me with a big smile and said, "I helped you out today, Dad. While you were greeting people after service, I put the coffee pot in the trunk for you."

Frustrated, I shot back, "Why did you do that? I wanted to leave it at church."

Do you think I should have punished my son? He did the wrong thing, after all—he brought the coffee pot home when I wanted to leave it behind.

I'm sure you would vote against punishing him because of course he didn't know I had wanted to leave it at church, and he had acted out of a loving motive—he was trying to help.

How good can you be?

Paul wasn't faultless, but he was blameless—we make a distinction between those words in the English language. So don't set an impossible standard for yourself. God didn't promise "faultless." Instead, he promised to keep you "blameless"—to purify your heart motives so that you desire to love him and please him at all times.

The Continuous Habit of the Soul

Therefore, I urge you, brothers and sisters, in view of God's mercy,
to offer your bodies as a living sacrifice, holy and pleasing to God—
this is your true and proper worship. Do not conform to the pattern of
this world, but be transformed by the renewing of your mind.
Romans 12:1–2

Even after my dramatic, life-changing conversion, I found that resentment, irritability, and a judgmental spirit were still lurking in my heart. For months I prayed and sought the cleansing, purifying, sanctifying work of the Spirit. Then, during one Sunday night service, God's Spirit sanctified me. It was a clear, definite, and real experience—I sensed purification and was filled with an overwhelming love that spilled over to the next day.

My tasks that next day included working in my family's business by clearing out motel rooms after guest checkouts. Storage space was at a premium, and we were in a rush. I took an extra rollaway bed from one room and attempted to slide it into the only available storage space. But pieces of the metal frame got caught on the stored bed frames on either side—it just wouldn't slide into place. This irritated me so much that I *slammed* the rollaway against the other stored beds.

Of course, that didn't solve my problem, but more importantly, I was aghast at my irritated outburst. I had just been sanctified the night before—didn't sanctification take care of this?

Afterward, I spent months thinking, reading, and praying about this problem. I began to think about habits I'd developed in my twenty-one years of life. We understand the power of physical habits such as tobacco addiction. What about emotional habits? I came from a door-slamming family, and for years, I had acted out of a hot temper. There was major evidence of a positive change in my life after my sanctification experience—could it be God had truly cleansed my heart, but I still had deeply ingrained emotional and mental habits that needed to be reprogrammed?

I found help in studying the life of Hudson Taylor, the great missionary who founded the China Inland Mission. Taylor had a clear-cut conversion, and later, an undeniable sanctification experience. Yet, years later, under the great pressure of his growing ministry, he became out-of-sorts and fretful. He then took a friend's wise advice and renewed his sanctified relationship with Christ.

Later, Taylor wrote, "Do not let us change the Savior's words. It is not 'whosoever has drunk' but 'whosoever drinketh' (John 4:14, KJV). It is not of one isolated draught he speaks, or even many, but of the *continuous habit of the soul*" (emphasis mine).[163]

---

163. Quoted in Charles "Chic" Shaver, *Basic Bible Studies for the Spirit-Filled and Sanctified Life*, Lesson 6 (Kansas City, MO: Beacon Hill Press of Kansas City, 2009).

I needed a reprogramming of mental and emotional habits. I need to drink of Christ's grace moment by moment, even in the midst of life's irritating challenges.

In Romans 12:1–2, Paul challenged the Christians to make a once-for-all surrender: "Offer your bodies as a living sacrifice . . . to God." But note that he also instructed, "be transformed by the renewing of your mind," implying a continuing process.

And so I seek new habits—a continuous habit of soul. What about you?

A Really Big Mistake, Part 1

Therefore, as God's chosen people, holy and dearly loved, clothe yourselves with compassion, kindness, humility, gentleness and patience. Bear with each other and forgive one another if any of you has a grievance against someone. Forgive as the Lord forgave you. And over all these virtues put on love, which binds them all together in perfect unity.
Colossians 3:12–14

I made a big mistake—I mean a *really* big mistake! I received word that an esteemed, godly leader of our international church had passed away. At one time, he had been our family's beloved pastor. When I checked to see whether the report was true, a knowledgeable source confirmed, "Yes, he died yesterday."

My heart went out to his wife, who was a wonderful, loving, godly woman. I bought a card and wrote a note in it expressing my sympathy and describing some of the beautiful memories I had of his life. That day, I mailed the card.

That night, I received a phone call from a coworker—she had learned from several others that this leader had in fact *not* died. Another international leader had died, and somehow names got confused—the initial report had been incorrect.

My esteemed friend had not passed away, and I had just sent his wife a sympathy card. I was so embarrassed. I knew I would have to phone his wife and apologize. I was uneasy about doing this—what shock and sorrow would I create in her! But still, I knew I must call.

So I made the call to this godly woman I had known for years. She told me how happy she was to hear my voice. Immediately, I confessed to her, "I've made a big mistake." I explained the false report and my sympathy card. As I apologized, I suggested perhaps she could find some encouragement in the memories I detailed in my note.

In the warmest, most understanding tone, she said, "Chic, don't you worry about this one bit. I understand." She said she and her husband appreciated my family and me, and she expressed her gratitude for my ministry and influence.

"And don't let the devil beat you up over this," she added.

I was so relieved, encouraged, and warmed by her loving acceptance. I said, "You have always been at the top of my admiration list—but you just got even *higher* on that list!"

A Really Big Mistake, Part 2

Therefore, as God's chosen people, holy and dearly loved, clothe yourselves with compassion, kindness, humility, gentleness and patience. Bear with each other and forgive one another if any of you has a grievance against someone. Forgive as the Lord forgave you. And over all these virtues put on love, which binds them all together in perfect unity.
Colossians 3:12–14

I thought back over what I had done in sending the sympathy card. In writing the card, I had been acting out of love, compassion, and concern. Though I was embarrassed by the mistake, the phone call to admit my blunder was evidence of honesty and integrity. I was in error, was mistaken in my understanding, and did a troubling thing. However, my motive was love and concern; I was trying to comfort and encourage my friend's wife. This was a mistake—not a sin. I was reminded that, while sanctification gives you a pure heart and fills you with love, it does not promise perfect understanding or perfect communication skills.

When I finished the phone call with my friend's wife, I sat back. I felt greatly relieved—even loved. I realized I had just talked to a great leader who had shown me compassion, kindness, gentleness, and patience. She had just forgiven someone against whom she could have held a grievance—she had forgiven like Jesus. And, on top of it all, she expressed love. Her behavior embodied Paul's instructions to the Colossians (3:12–14).

I know this woman to be a sanctified, Spirit-filled believer, and what she showed me was the expression of the truly sanctified. May we have more like her!

A Clear, Direct Witness

This is how we know that we live in him and he in us:
He has given us of his Spirit.
1 John 4:13

The one who calls you is faithful, and he will do it.
1 Thessalonians 5:24

On October 29, 1789, John Wesley wrote the following to a woman named Betsy: "Have you received a clear, direct witness that you [were] saved from inbred sin? At what time? In what manner? And do you find it as clear as it was at first? Do you feel an increase?"

Even today, people are having clear experiences of entire sanctification. Here is the testimony of a lady named Nancy:

In my previous years I was—I thought—saved and sanctified. I believed you needed to go to the altar two times—once to be saved, and the second time to be sanctified. It seemed it didn't last.

On Sunday evening, the sermon was on sanctification—just what I needed and wanted. During the altar call, I went forward to receive this wonderful experience. It was so easy. He forgave me of all my sin, and I knew I was a ready candidate. Just as the scripture reads in 1 Thessalonians 5:23, he sanctified me through and through on Sunday night, October 19.

I can't explain the joy and peace I have in my heart! I have been basking in his Spirit ever since and have a burning desire to tell everyone I can about my experience so they can have it too!

Praise his name!

In another letter in 1790, Wesley writes of "how impossible it is to retain pure love without growing therein."

So to Nicks and Nancys everywhere, we urge you to find a "clear and direct witness" to God's sanctifying fullness. Once God has graciously bestowed that grace, be sure to *keep growing.*[164]

When Leaders Change and Lessons Are Learned

After the death of Moses the servant of the LORD, the LORD said to Joshua son of Nun, Moses' aide: "Moses my servant is dead. Now then, you and all these people, get ready to cross the Jordan River into the land I am about to give to them—to the Israelites. I will give you every place where you set your foot, as I promised Moses. No one will be able to stand against you all the days of your life. As I was with Moses, so I will be with you; I will never leave you nor forsake you. Be strong and courageous, because you will lead these people to inherit the land I swore to their ancestors to give them.
Joshua 1:1–3, 5–6

It was a huge, heartbreaking loss—Moses, Israel's leader for forty years, and the most spiritually powerful person they had ever known, was dead. The thirty days of mourning for him were appropriate (Deuteronomy 34:8).

But Moses's death could not paralyze Israel. God had called them; they were on a mission, and fulfillment was near.

Our passage begins with the phrase, "The LORD said to Joshua" (Joshua 1:1). How many times the Lord had spoke—we serve a God who speaks. It is our privilege to hear him. Of course, we must be intentional in developing our spiritual hearing. It is especially important to hear God's direction in times of leadership change.

Joshua was to be Israel's new leader. This was not a shock; God had been preparing Joshua for this, and so had Moses. Even at the time of Moses's death, Scripture emphasizes this: "Now Joshua son of Nun was filled with the spirit of wisdom because Moses had laid his hands on him" (Deuteronomy 34:9). And because of the new leader's preparation, "the Israelites listened to him and did what the LORD had commanded Moses" (34:9). It was wise to prepare the succeeding leader.

---

164. Previously published in *The Good News: The Chic Shaver Center for Evangelism Newsletter* (March 2009).

God then commanded, "Now then, you and all these people, get ready to cross the Jordan River" (Joshua 1:2). Whatever part God had, Israel also had a part. The book of Numbers reports that there were 600,000 fighting men among them. Accounting for women and children, we must be talking of over 1.5 million people—plus livestock and spoils of their victories. Joshua used his chain of command and ordered his officers to go through the land to tell the people to get ready (1:10–11). Having working structure in place to handle a change in leaders was key.

But, above all, this is the Lord's doing: "I will give you every place where you set your foot" (1:3). I remember one of my denomination's most effective leaders saying, "It was one of the most Spirit-led decisions I ever made."

God says, "I will do it." We honor the Lord and give him the glory. We remember he is primary; and we are secondary. We must cooperate with him and act for him. He provides the place; we must step into it. How often has God already prepared the way for us but we do not possess what is to be our privilege? It is available—possess it!

Knowing that this move presents a tremendous challenge, God commands his people, "Be strong and courageous" (1:6), giving them the encouragement they need.

God is big on keeping promises and remembering history. Note that he says here, "the land I swore to their ancestors to give them" (1:6). Often, God names these ancestors—Abraham, Isaac, and Jacob. These references evoke much history, many promises, and God's long-range plan. Even after Jesus came to earth, these issues were still playing out. Christ issued the following warning to rebellious people of his day: "When you see Abraham, Isaac and Jacob and all the prophets in the kingdom of God, but you yourselves thrown out" (Luke 13:28). Keeping God as the Lord is the most essential issue in seasons of leadership change.

Observing such leadership changes blesses those of us who watch it happen. To this day, we possess spiritual land that has been shaped and built by our spiritual predecessors. I think of the teachers in my life and the lessons they taught me:

1. Peter: God is real
2. Ralph and Bernice : How to pray with seekers
3. Earl and Hazel: Divine leadership
4. Gordon: How to make disciples who will make disciples who will make disciples
5. Ralph: The dependability of God's Word
6. Mendell and Gertrude: Hospitality

7. Rees: How to pray through circumstances

8. Scott: Strong leadership

And there are so many more.

I am having the time of my life as I walk out and over the promised land of my life, setting my feet on blessed territories that were shaped by so many others whom I can never repay. And I have other possibilities open to me because I live in the age of Jesus Christ: "For no one can lay any foundation other than the one already laid, which is Jesus Christ" (1 Corinthians 3:11). Praise God!

These possibilities are open to you too. What promised land will you possess this week?

A Hero under a Villain

So Elijah went to present himself to Ahab. Now the famine was severe in Samaria, and Ahab had summoned Obadiah, his palace administrator. (Obadiah was a devout believer in the LORD. While Jezebel was killing off the LORD's prophets, Obadiah had taken a hundred prophets and hidden them in two caves, fifty in each, and had supplied them with food and water.)
1 Kings 18:2–4

You could hardly imagine a more ungodly, villainous king than Ahab (1 Kings 16:33). Obadiah worked under this evil king as his palace manager. The text notes that "Obadiah was a *devout believer* in the LORD"—and indeed, we see that Obadiah demonstrated that belief in his actions. But the evil Ahab had the power; the righteous Obadiah was his servant. Did Obadiah believe he could ever have a godly influence on the king?

Despite his fear of being killed, Obadiah arranged a meeting between Ahab and the prophet Elijah. This meeting led to a contest between the prophets of Baal and Elijah's God—which in turn led to God showing his power by fire and the destruction of the 450 evil prophets of Baal. I'm glad Obadiah didn't quit, despair, or decide he couldn't have a godly influence.

It was a perilous time in the United States: 100,000 people had marched in Washington, DC, to protest the Vietnam War, and President Nixon was to address a joint session of Congress. At the time, I was in DC preaching in a local church for a week. The chief recorder of debate for the U.S. Senate happened to be a member of that local church, and he got me a seat in the joint session. I do not remember the president's words, but I've never forgotten what the chief recorder later said: "I've seen such evil in the cloak room of the Senate. Sometimes I wish I could just go back to my native Wyoming. But then I think, *What will happen to our government if the godly people leave?*"

Whether under an evil king or in the midst of evil in the Senate, godly people will still make their impact. Where do you find yourself today? Do not miss your opportunity to make a godly impact! Even under a villain, you can be a hero.

Is There Anything Else?

Therefore, I urge you, brothers and sisters, in view of God's mercy,
to offer your bodies as a living sacrifice, holy and pleasing to God—
this is your true and proper worship.
Romans 12:1

Over the years I've met people who have surrendered all to God and received the Spirit's sanctifying fullness. Here is Kathy's story:

For a lot of years, I ignored the God who was with me—no prayers, no Bible reading, no church. I just slip-slid through life.

In July 2000, my husband, Gary, received a cancer diagnosis with a prognosis of only months to live, and by February 2001, he was gone. My days of slip-sliding were over. God now had my attention—God and grief. They were with me everywhere and in all things I was doing.

I was invited to join a small group Bible study by my Sunday school teacher, Dr. Chic Shaver. I started the study on the book of John and quickly hit a roadblock—a big one—in my spiritual journey. It didn't have to do with the material; it had to do with the teacher. I had been careful not to let any man, not even my husband, be an authority figure in my life after the abuse I received from my father. Dr. Shaver was becoming an authority figure, for he expected me to be present, prepared, and participatory. I was reaching a spiritual crisis point as I recognized that God also expected more of me, and he was the authority figure! Something had to give.

I moved into another study with Dr. Shaver—a much more intensive and introspective study—called Living in the Power of the Spirit. *It was all about moving into and maintaining a deep personal relationship with the Holy Spirit—something called sanctification. I learned, during the many weeks of intensive study, prayer, and group discussion, that God wanted the very best—his best—for me, and that was to be achieved by willingly relinquishing power over all areas of my life and handing it over to him. Slowly, I arrived at a place of understanding that my heavenly Father would never harm me, and I could trust his authority over me. In fact, it was something I desired! All that was left were the details. I remember asking at the altar, "Is there anything else you want me to give you?" I continued asking that question until God's silence and my deep peace assured me there was nothing else.*

I experienced entire sanctification as a one-time, spiritual-crisis-point decision and continue to experience it as an ongoing decision to live my life as God wants me to. The great thing about it all is that with the intimate, loving communion we have, it's also the way I want to live!

I could never have dreamed where God would take me and the ways he'd love me and lead me to serve. My life in him is an adventure with divine appointments strewn along the way. I'm just so blessed to belong to him!

Besides Him, There Is No Other, Part 1

You were shown these things so that you might know that the Lord *is God; besides him, there is no other.*
Deuteronomy 4:35

God wrapped my heart around a series of verses in Scripture. Join me in exploring this series of biblical reports. As you read, may God shape your heart as he did mine.

As Moses was receiving the Ten Commandments on Mount Sinai—commandments that included, "You shall have no other gods before me," and, "You shall not make for yourself an image in the form of anything in heaven above or on the earth below" (Exodus 20:3–4)—Israel was making and worshiping a golden calf at the bottom of that same mountain.

God spoke, and Moses responded:

"I have seen these people," the LORD said to Moses, "and they are a stiff-necked people. Now leave me alone so that my anger may burn against them and that I may destroy them. Then I will make you into a great nation."

But Moses sought the favor of the LORD his God. "LORD," he said, "why should your anger burn against your people, whom you brought out of Egypt with great power and a mighty hand? Why should the Egyptians say, 'It was with evil intent that he brought them out, to kill them in the mountains and to wipe them off the face of the earth'? Turn from your fierce anger; relent and do not bring disaster on your people. Remember your servants Abraham, Isaac and Israel, to whom you swore by your own self: 'I will make your descendants as numerous as the stars in the sky and I will give your descendants all this land I promised them, and it will be their inheritance forever.'" Then the Lord relented and did not bring on his people the disaster he had threatened. (Exodus 32:9–14)

Moses then interceded for the people:

The next day Moses said to the people, "You have committed a great sin. But now I will go up to the LORD; perhaps I can make atonement for your sin."

So Moses went back to the LORD and said, "Oh, what a great sin these people have committed! They have made themselves gods of gold. But now, please forgive their sin—but if not, then blot me out of the book you have written." (Exodus 32:30–32)

Finally, God told Moses to go on to the promised land:

The LORD would speak to Moses face to face, as one speaks to a friend. Then Moses would return to the camp, but his young aide Joshua son of Nun did not leave the tent.

Moses said to the LORD, "You have been telling me, 'Lead these people,' but you have not let me know whom you will send with me. You have said, 'I know you by name and you have found favor with me.' If you are pleased with me, teach me your ways so I may know you and continue to find favor with you. Remember that this nation is your people."

The LORD replied, "My Presence will go with you, and I will give you rest."

Then Moses said to him, "If your Presence does not go with us, do not send us up from here." (Exodus 33:11–15)

I'm impressed by the following elements of the story:

- Moses appealed to God's honor and his reputation in Egypt (32:12).
- Moses appealed to God's promises to Israel's spiritual fathers (32:13).
- God relented in response to Moses's prayer (32:14).
- Moses was so burdened for his people that he was willing to risk being blotted out of God's book (32:32).
- God's presence would go with Moses to the promised land (33:14).

Besides Him, There Is No Other, Part 2

*You were shown these things so that you might know that
the LORD is God; besides him there is no other.*
Deuteronomy 4:35

Moses brings water from the rock to the Israelites but not the right way:

"Take the staff, and you and your brother Aaron gather the assembly together. Speak to that rock before their eyes and it will pour out its water. You will bring water out of the rock for the community so they and their livestock can drink."

So Moses took the staff from the LORD's presence, just as he commanded him. He and Aaron gathered the assembly together in front of the rock and Moses said to them, "Listen, you rebels, must we bring you water out of this rock?" Then Moses raised his arm and struck the rock twice with his staff. Water gushed out, and the community and their livestock drank.

But the LORD said to Moses and Aaron, "Because you did not trust in me enough to honor me as holy in the sight of the Israelites, you will not bring this community into the land I give them." (Numbers 20:8–12)

Israel arrived at the Jordan River, after forty years, soon to cross into the promised land. Moses and the Lord have a very personal conversation:

At that time I pleaded with the LORD: "Sovereign LORD, you have begun to show to your servant your greatness and your strong hand. For what god is there in heaven or on earth who can do the deeds and mighty works you do? Let me go over and see the good land beyond the Jordan—that fine hill country and Lebanon."

But because of you the LORD was angry with me and would not listen to me. "That is enough," the LORD said. "Do not speak to me anymore about this matter. Go up to the top of Pisgah and look west and north and south and east. Look at the land with your own eyes, since you are not going to cross this Jordan. But commission Joshua, and encourage and strengthen him, for he will lead this people across and will cause them to inherit the land that you will see." (Deuteronomy 3:23–28)

Moses makes an appeal to his people:

Ask now about the former days, long before your time, from the day God created human beings on the earth; ask from one end of the heavens to the other. Has anything so great as this ever happened, or has anything like it ever been heard of? Has any other people heard the voice of God speaking out of fire, as you have, and lived? Has any god ever tried to take for himself one nation out of another nation, by testings, by signs and wonders, by war, by a mighty hand and an outstretched arm, or by great and awesome deeds, like all the things the LORD your God did for you in Egypt before your very eyes?

You were shown these things so that you might know that the LORD is God; besides him there is no other. From heaven he made you hear his voice to discipline you. On earth he showed you his great fire, and you heard his words from out of the fire. Because he loved your ancestors and chose their descendants after them, he brought you out of Egypt by his Presence and his great strength, to drive out before you nations greater and stronger than you and to bring you into their land to give it to you for your inheritance, as it is today.

Acknowledge and take to heart this day that the LORD is God in heaven above and on the earth below. There is no other. Keep his decrees and commands, which I am giving you today, so that it may go well with you and your children after you and that you may live long in the land the LORD your God gives you for all time. (Deuteronomy 4:32–40)

I'm impressed by the following details of this story:

- In his anger with Israel, Moses disobeyed God's instructions, violating the holiness of God and losing the privilege of leading Israel into the promised land (Numbers 20:11–12).
- God permitted Moses to see the promised land but commissioned Joshua to lead the people into it (Deuteronomy 3:25–28).
- Moses recounted God's greatness and called Israel to obedience (Deuteronomy 4:35, 40).

The Lord is God; besides him, there is no other!

What "De-Masters" Sin?

For sin shall no longer be your master,
because you are not under the law, but under grace.
Romans 6:14

Grace reached me as a young teen while I was still serving my old master, sin. That master left me lost, alone, and fearful that I would be abandoned again and again by those I loved. I carried this fear as a heavy burden, and I was searching for a place to lay it down when I heard Jesus calling to me through his loving family: "Come to me, all you who are weary and burdened, and I will give you rest" (Matthew 11:28).

This was good news to me, for it gave me hope. With some fear in my heart, I knelt down and offered my sin-sick soul to God. Very gently, I opened the door and invited the Christ of the cross in. At that moment the great exchange was made, my burden slipped away, and Christ was home in my heart.

Sin is no longer my master because one day I chose Jesus, and each day he gives me the power to choose. I do not hear the voice of my old master, because Jesus loves the unlovable. He forgives the unforgivable. He finds the unfindable, and we find ourselves wrapped in the arms of God.

Nancy Shaver[165]

Set Free

You have been set free from sin and have become slaves to righteousness.
Romans 6:18

---

165. Previously published in *Come Ye Apart* July–August–September 1964 (Kansas City, MO: Nazarene Publishing House), 89. Used by permission. (This publication became *Reflecting God*.)

Patrick grew up as an atheist and believed that the Bible contradicted itself. After a challenging encounter, he began reading the Old Testament and finished it in 2003. That same year he got married. In 2008, he started reading the New Testament. In October 2009, Patrick viewed a website about hell. He was troubled to realize that eternity is never done.

On October 28, 2009, he got rid of his pornography, started praying, and intellectually began to believe in Jesus. On November 1, Patrick and his wife attended church for the first time. He began meeting with the pastor.

On November 28, while his son, Eric, was in the hospital, Patrick read Acts and prayed for Saul's (Paul's) vision. Patrick fell asleep and was startled to awake to a white light—Jesus stood in front of him. Patrick said, "Thank you."

Jesus said, *"Into discipleship I go."*

Patrick knew his first step was to be baptized. After his baptism, he began experiencing a deeper love for his wife. Eric, his son, commented, "You started becoming nice." Patrick now is planning to attend Bible school.

At camp meeting, after a sermon called "I Am Crucified with Christ," Patrick agonized at the altar over the deep self-centeredness that remained within him. A few nights later, Patrick prayed and experienced a deep assurance and that he was set free.[166]

"Be Perfect"—C. S. Lewis

There is no fear in love. But perfect love drives out fear, because fear has to do with punishment. The one who fears is not made perfect in love.
1 John 4:18

The following is an excerpt from C. S. Lewis's *Mere Christianity*:

[Christ] never talked vague, idealistic gas. When he said, "be perfect," he meant it. He means we must go in for the full treatment. It is hard, but the sort of compromise we are hankering after is harder—in fact, it is impossible. It may be hard for an egg to turn into a bird; it would be a jolly sight harder for it to learn to fly while remaining an egg. We are like eggs at present. And

---

166. Previously published in *The Good News: The Chic Shaver Center for Evangelism Newsletter* (September 2010).

you cannot go on indefinitely being just an ordinary egg. We must be hatched or go bad.

May I come back to what I said before? This is the whole of Christianity. There is nothing else. . . . The church exists for nothing else but to draw [people] into Christ, to make them little Christs. If they are not doing that, all the cathedrals, clergy, missions, services, even the Bible itself, are simply a waste of time. God became [human] for no other purpose.[167]

NOVEMBER 14   **318**

The Payoff for Ministry

*Let us not become weary in doing good, for at the proper time
we will reap a harvest if we do not give up.*
Galatians 6:9

"I just have to say thank you to you, Dr. Shaver."

I know I looked totally surprised when Christine greeted me that way at the East Ohio camp meeting. Then she told me her story.

Christine was ten years old when her mother took her to revival services at a church in Plattsburgh, New York. She went forward to pray, and God sanctified her young heart completely. After that, she begged her mom to take her to all the revival services. Every night, she sat in the first row of the balcony and looked over the edge to take in all that God was doing.

Now Christine is married to Neil, who has been called to the ministry. They are on their way to Niagara Falls, New York, where they will begin their first pastorate. At ten years old, Christine experienced God's grace—and now she and her husband are pastoring. What a payoff.

After that night's service at the East Ohio camp meeting, Kristi, another pastor's wife, looked at me with a big smile and said, "I was sanctified in your personal evangelism class in Kansas City."

"Did it make a difference?" I asked.

"Oh, yes," she replied. "I had never realized how selfish I had been."

Another payoff!

---

167. C. S. Lewis, *Mere Christianity* (New York: McMillan, 1952), 169–70.

Laura Fitzsimmons sent me a congratulatory note when I received an award. In her card, she reflected on the time in 1993 when she and her husband accepted Christ after I and several others shared the gospel with them. She wrote: "Just think—all those lives that have been changed because of your heart for the lost. Praise God that my family's path crossed yours! I'm writing to you from the third- and fourth-grade camp this week in Augusta, Kansas. I am cooking for three hundred people! Did you ever think I'd do something like this? I've come a long way from meeting you nearly fifteen years ago. Praise God—praise God. Thank you, my friend, for loving me."

Yet another payoff. Imagine the payoff that will come to your life.[168]

John and Sin

My dear children, I write this to you so that you will not sin.
But if anybody does sin, we have an advocate
with the Father—Jesus Christ, the Righteous One.
1 John 2:1

John had a big problem with the idea that true Christians (followers of Christ) go on sinning. Look at some of his key statements in 1 John 3:
- "Sin is lawlessness" (3:4).
- "He [Christ] appeared so that he might take away our sins" (3:5).
- "No one who lives in him keeps on sinning" (3:6).
- "The who does what is sinful is of the devil. . . . The reason the Son of God appeared was to destroy the devil's work" (3:8).
- "No one who is born of God [and still living] will continue to sin, because God's seed remains in them" (3:9).

Some basic definitions will help us:
- Sin (the sinful nature)—The sinful condition of the heart from which sinful actions spring. May also be called selfishness or self-centeredness.
- To sin—To willfully break the known law of God.

---

168. Previously published in *The Good News: The Chic Shaver Center for Evangelism Newsletter* (September 2008).

- Surprise sin—To break God's law in an unguarded moment, but not with deliberate, set purpose.
- Mistake—An act that falls short of God's perfect will but is unintentional and committed out of ignorance.

All of these need the cleansing blood of Christ. However, making a mistake does not carry the same weight as sinning. All sins need forgiveness. Self-centeredness, on the other hand, can't be forgiven—it needs to be cleansed.

Some of John's contemporaries had claimed to be without sin (1:8). John preached, "But if we walk in the light, as he is in the light, we have fellowship with one another, and the blood of Jesus, his Son, *purifies us from all sin*" (1:7). Note that the issue is not forgiveness, but purification or cleansing.

This is not to claim that the Christian can't sin. It is to claim that the Christian *need not* sin. In this case, it's not physically impossible for the person to sin; rather, it is morally out of the person's character. As an honest man cannot lie, so a Christian man cannot sin. Sinning is inconsistent with being a follower of Jesus Christ.

You might wonder, "What if I do sin after becoming a Christian?" In today's scripture, John says his whole purpose in writing is "so that you will not sin." However, he goes further: "But *if* anybody does sin, we have an advocate with the Father—Jesus Christ." Note that John says "if," not "when." *If* sin should occur, we should immediately confess to God through Jesus Christ for forgiveness, cleansing, and restoration.

When Curt and Jan came to Christ, it meant confessing and turning from their past sins. It meant receiving Jesus as forgiver of their sins (Savior) and leader of their lives (Lord). It meant immediate lifestyle changes, including deliverance from the use of both alcohol and tobacco.

It also meant restoration of their broken marriage. They looked at the marriages of other Christians and said, "That might work for us." Soon, Curt and Jan began to raise their children with a godly influence.

As they began faithfully attending church services, they realized that since God had blessed them with financial resources, it was only appropriate that they should tithe (give ten percent of their income back to God).

Eventually, Curt and Jan began bringing others to Christ. They came to understand that there was a deeper level of cleansing from remaining self-centeredness, and eventually, they experienced God's sanctification. They identified with Paul's claim in Galatians 2:20: "I have been crucified with Christ."

Jan put it this way: "We believed we could be victorious."

Isn't this the kind of Christianity you want too?

Rivers of Living Water Again

"Let anyone who is thirsty come to me and drink.
Whoever believes in me, as Scripture has said, rivers of living water
will flow from within them." By this he meant the Spirit,
whom those who believed in him were later to receive.
John 7:37–39

"Does it really say, rivers of living water?" she asked her pastor.

"Yes," he said, "it says *rivers*."

The word "rivers" implies an abundant supply. And many Christians are indeed experiencing "rivers." This life is by the Holy Spirit.

At the time of this writing (2020), most schools, businesses, and church buildings are closed. Many people are out of work. Thousands are dead.

Today, I received a note from a Christian laywoman that reads: "God is certainly moving and creating new ways to reach his people and drawing new ones to himself. What a wonderful time to be alive and witness his handiwork." I sense a river flowing.

V. Raymond Edman was a missionary, pastor, and president of Wheaton College. Impacted by the life of Hudson Taylor and others, he wrote about Taylor's notion of "the exchanged life:" "It is new life for old. It is rejoicing for weariness, and radiance for dreariness. It is triumph even through tears, and tenderness of heart instead of touchiness. It is lowliness of spirit instead of self-exaltation, and loveliness of life because of the presence of the altogether Lovely One."[169]

In *They Found the Secret*, Edman wrote of twenty Christians who discovered the deeper Christian life: "The pattern of their experiences is much the same. They had believed on the Savior, yet were burdened and bewildered, unfaithful and unfruitful. . . . Then they came to a crisis of utter heart surrender to the Savior, a meeting with him in the innermost depths of their spirit; and they found the Holy Spirit to be an unfailing fountain of life and refreshment."[170]

---

169. V. Raymond Edman, *They Found the Secret* (Grand Rapids: Zondervan, 1960), 7.
170. Edman, *They Found the Secret*, 9.

Hudson Taylor was founder of the China Inland Mission and a great missionary. Yet, at age thirty-seven, he poured out his heart to his mother in a letter. He wrote, "I never knew how bad a heart I had," and requested, "Pray that the Lord will keep me from sin, will sanctify me wholly, use me more largely in his service."[171]

John McCarthy, a fellow missionary, wrote to Taylor of his own experience: "To let my loving Savior work in me his will, my sanctification is what I would live for by his grace. Abiding, not striving or struggling; look off unto him; trusting him for present power; trusting him to subdue all inward corruption; resting in the love of an almighty Savior."[172]

As Taylor read the letter, his heart was moved. He said, "As I read, I saw it all. I looked to Jesus; and when I saw, oh how the joy flowed."[173]

A person who observed Taylor after this experience said, "He was a joyous man now, a bright, happy Christian. He had been a toiling, burdened one before, with latterly not much rest of soul. It was resting in Jesus now, and letting him do the work—which makes all the difference."[174]

Yes, Hudson Taylor drank—and rivers of living water flowed from him by the Spirit.

Sanctified by Faith in Me

I am sending you to them to open their eyes and turn them
from darkness to light, and from the power of Satan to God,
so that they may receive forgiveness of sins and a place
among those who are sanctified by faith in me.
Acts 26:17–18

In 1917, during World War I, British troops camped in the Egyptian desert. They were scared. Battles raged around them, and their friends were being killed.

---

171. Edman, *They Found the Secret*, 18.
172. Edman, *They Found the Secret*, 18.
173. Edman, *They Found the Secret*, 19.
174. Edman, *They Found the Secret*, 17.

Meanwhile, the chaplain moved among the troops. He counseled, encouraged, prayed, preached, taught, and performed funerals. He was not famous, but everyone who knew him knew he was a man of God—a man of faith.

One day, the chaplain got sick and experienced abdominal pain. But he delayed seeking medical attention because he felt the troops should come first. When he made it to the doctor, it was too late—appendicitis took his life. He was only forty-three.

His wife had been faithful. Whenever he preached or taught, she wrote down all he said, and in 1927, she published his first book. *My Utmost for His Highest*, by Oswald Chambers, is still in print today and is considered the most famous devotional book in the world. Now, more than a hundred years after his death, Oswald Chambers, through his faith, is still speaking (Hebrews 11:4).

Like the apostle Paul, Oswald Chambers was sent to open people's eyes, to turn them from darkness to light, from the power of Satan to God, "so that they may receive forgiveness of sins and a place among those who are sanctified by faith in [Christ]" (Acts 26:18). Furthermore, he did not stop at the forgiveness of sins, but took his audience deeper. In his book, he writes of sanctification on twenty-one different occasions; he also makes numerous other references to related truths.

After discussing the remission of sins, Chambers proclaimed, "Then there follows the second mighty work of grace—'an inheritance among them which are sanctified.'"[175] Chambers challenged people in his day and in ours:

When we pray to be sanctified, are we prepared to face the standard of these verses? . . . It will cost us an intense narrowing of all our interests on earth, and an immense broadening of all our interests in God. Sanctification means intense concentration on God's point of view. . . . Sanctification means being made one with Jesus so that the disposition that ruled him will rule us. . . . Are we prepared to say—Lord, make me as holy as You can make a sinner saved by grace?[176]

In another place, Chambers writes, "Sanctification is not my idea of what I want God to do for me; sanctification is God's idea of what he wants to do for me, and he has to get me into the attitude of mind and spirit where at any cost I will let him sanctify me wholly."[177]

---

175. Oswald Chambers, *My Utmost for His Highest* (Uhrichsville, OH: Barbour Publishing, 1963), January 10.

176. Chambers, *My Utmost*, February 8.

177. Chambers, *My Utmost*, August 14.

I'm willing! Are you?

How Much More

If you then, though you are evil, know how to give good gifts to
your children, how much more will your Father in heaven
give the Holy Spirit to those who ask him!
Luke 11:13

Nine months after he met Jesus Christ, Richard Halverson, former chaplain of the United States Senate, began reading Oswald Chambers's *My Utmost for His Highest*. From then on, Halverson consistently read this devotional book for the rest of his life. Of it he said, "No book except the Bible has influenced my walk with Christ at such deep and maturing levels."[178]

Oswald Chambers had accepted Christ as a child. As an adult, while teaching at Dunoon College, Chambers heard F. B. Meyer speak about the Holy Spirit. Afterward, he went to his room and prayed for the baptism of the Holy Spirit, but no answer seemed to come. For four years he struggled.

Then Luke 11:13 got hold of him. One day, in a public meeting, Chambers stood and claimed the gift of the Holy Spirit, citing Luke 11:13. He had no special vision, but days after he spoke at a meeting, forty people came forward. When his friend reminded him that he had claimed the Holy Spirit, and that Jesus said, "You shall receive power" from the Spirit, suddenly, in a flash, something happened inside of him. He was changed. He testified, "Love is the beginning, love is the middle, and love is the end. After he comes in, all you see is 'Jesus only, Jesus ever.'"[179] The impact of this work of the Spirit flows through Chambers's words in *My Utmost for His Highest*: "Jesus said, 'When he, the Spirit of truth, is come . . . he shall glorify me.' When I commit myself to the revelation made in the New Testament, I receive from God the gift of the Holy Spirit who begins to interpret to me what Jesus did; and does in me subjectively all that Jesus did for me objectively."[180]

178. Richard Halverson, "Introduction," Oswald Chambers, *My Utmost for His Highest* (Uhrichsville, OH: Barbour Publishing, 1963).

179. V. Raymond Edman, *They Found the Secret* (Grand Rapids: Zondervan, 1960), 47.

180. Chambers, *My Utmost*, November 29.

In another devotional, Chambers says, "We have slowly to form our walk and conversation on the line of the precepts of Jesus Christ as the Holy Spirit applies them to our circumstances. The Sermon on the Mount is not a set of rules and regulations: it is a statement of the life we will live when the Holy Spirit is getting his way with us."[181]

Elsewhere in the book, Oswald emphasizes again, "You will never get further until you are willing to do that one thing. The Holy Spirit will locate the one impregnable thing in you, but he cannot budge it unless you are willing to let him."[182]

How sensitive he was to the Holy Spirit. A simple headstone in the military cemetery in Cairo, Egypt, marks Chambers's grave. The following words are engraved on his headstone: "How much more will your heavenly Father give the Holy Spirit to those who ask him."[183]

The Glass Is Full

Do not get drunk on wine, which leads to debauchery.
Instead, be filled with the Spirit.
Ephesians 5:18

Imagine that I come to your front door with a water glass in my hand and ask for water. You know me well, so you say, "Of course. Come on in."

You lead me to your kitchen sink, and I turn on the faucet. The glass fills up—half-full, two-thirds full, completely full. I turn off the faucet.

But then, for some reason, I become tremendously excited. After placing the full glass on the counter, I begin to exclaim, "The glass is full! The glass is full!"

This event is so thrilling to me that I find one of your family members watching TV in the living room and report, "The glass is full!"

It doesn't seem right to limit the news, so I go out into your neighborhood. For a week, I tell everyone I meet, "The glass is full!"

---

181. Chambers, *My Utmost*, July 25.
182. Chambers, October 8.
183. Edman, *They Found the Secret*, 49.

Finally, I return to your home, your kitchen, your counter, my glass, still proclaiming, "The glass is full!"

But to my shock, I see that the glass is not full anymore. While I spent a week rejoicing over a single moment in the past when the glass was filled, the slow process of evaporation reduced the water level. The glass is no longer full!

Let's repeat this earlier scene. I'm back at your kitchen sink, filling another water glass, exactly the same as the first glass. The glass is filling up—half-full, two-thirds full, completely full. But then, instead of turning off the faucet, I let it keep flowing. Now the glass is full—and overflowing. No matter how much evaporation removes some of the water, the flowing faucet—the source—is always greater than the evaporation. I rejoice. The glass is full—and overflowing!

These glasses are like two kinds of Christians. Some come to God and are filled by the Holy Spirit but seem to put all their emphasis on a past point in time when they were filled. Meanwhile, they've evaporated.

Other Christians come to God, are filled with the Spirit, and *continue* to draw on divine resources. These believers not only filled but also overflowing. In other words, once the Spirit has filled you:

- Keep open; keep receiving from the source.
- Keep praying, obeying, and reading the Word.
- As 1 Thessalonians 5:19 says, "Do not quench the Spirit."
- As Ephesians 4:30 says, "Do not grieve the Holy Spirit of God."
- As Galatians 5:25 says, "Since we live by the Spirit, let us keep in step with the Spirit."
- As someone once said, "Keep under the spout where the glory comes out!"

Paul's words in Ephesians 5:18 are, "Be filled with the Spirit." Have you been filled? Have you evaporated? Have you kept filled? Are you overflowing? If you've been filled with the Spirit, if you continue living in the Spirit, and if you are overflowing, you will have enough for yourself and others as well. It's like the lady who approached her pastor excitedly, saying, "My cup overfloweth! My cup overfloweth! What should I do?"

He replied, "Go and slosh it on somebody!"

Filled full—and overflowing!

Overflow

Do not get drunk on wine, which leads to debauchery. Instead, be filled with the Spirit, speaking to one another with psalms, hymns, and songs from the Spirit. Sing and make music from your heart to the Lord, always giving thanks to God the Father for everything, in the name of our Lord Jesus Christ. Submit to one another out of reverence for Christ.
Ephesians 5:18–21

If you have a lake or pond on your property and water flows in but no water flows out, then you know that body of water will become stagnant and unhealthy. Likewise, in spiritual life, once a Christian is filled with the Spirit, there must be channels for spiritual overflow. According to our Ephesians passage, once a Christian is filled with the Spirit, there are three natural channels for that overflow: praise, thanksgiving, and submission.

A number of years ago, I was going through a difficult period in my life. I was not responding well to the stress—I complained to others about my heavy workload. I often griped about my sacrifice and low pay. I exalted myself over others because the home office did not appreciate the great worth of my work. Finally, I woke up. I realized that, instead of complaining, I should be praising; instead of griping, I should be giving thanks; instead of exalting myself, I should be submitting. Sure enough, as soon as I started praising, thanking, and submitting, channels of overflow opened in my soul.

After Paul mentions submission in 5:21, he goes all out on the topic:

- Wives, submit to your husbands (5:22).
- Husbands, love your wives, just as Christ loved the church (5:25).
- Children, obey (or submit to) your parents (6:1).

Wow, that's a lot of submission. How can we handle so many demands? In American culture, people don't handle such demands well. After getting off work, a guy who's been under pressure from his boss may walk into the house and yell to his wife, "Get me a beer!"

Paul has a far healthier response: "Do not get drunk on wine, which leads to debauchery. Instead, be filled with the Spirit" (5:18). "Be filled" refers to the present—*keep* filled with the Spirit. A testimony to this imperative is that New Testament Christians often received a fresh filling of the Spirit in the midst of high-pressure circumstances (Acts 4:31).

E. Stanley Jones was one of the spiritual giants of the Methodist church. He was converted to Christ as a young man. Later, after being filled with the Holy Spirit, he offered himself for missionary service. His first assignment was in India, where he was put in charge of a mission station with five hundred workers. He would be eligible for a furlough only after ten years of service. After awhile, Jones had a nervous breakdown. He tried taking a vacation, spending time in the mountains, and returning home to Baltimore. Still, after all this, he remained unhealed. But, out of a sense of duty, he returned to his mission assignment. In Lucknow, he attended revival services led by Tamil David. While Jones knelt at the back of the church, God asked him, *"Are you ready for the work to which I've called you?"*

Jones answered, "No, Lord, I'm done for. I've reached the end of my resources, and I can't go on."

God replied, *"If you'll turn that problem over to me and not worry about it, I'll take care of it."*

"Lord," he said, "I close the bargain right here."

Suddenly, Jones was flooded with energy, peace, power, and a sense of adequacy.[184] The man who had once been filled with the Spirit was filled afresh with the Spirit. From then on, he kept filled and entered the richest period of his ministry.

Christian friend, be filled with the Spirit, and keep filled with the Spirit. Overflow with praise, thanksgiving, and submission.

Love in Alzheimer's

Dear friends, let us love one another, for love comes from God.
Everyone who loves has been born of God and knows God.
1 John 4:7

Husbands, love your wives, just as Christ loved the church
and gave himself up for her to make her holy, cleansing her
by the washing with water through the word.
Ephesians 5:25–26

---

184. E. Stanley Jones, *A Song of Ascents* (Nashville: Abingdon Press, 1968), 89–90.

At the time of this writing, Nancy, my wife, has had Alzheimer's for nearly a decade. By now, her short-term memory is very short, and we regularly attend meetings of our local Alzheimer's association. There are vast differences among patients with this disease; thus, I do not claim that what I share is true for all patients and their caregivers.

Somehow, by prayer, God's grace, and our Christian faith, Nancy and I have experienced a special, loving and sharing relationship. Frequently, when I come to the breakfast table, I find a note she has left me the night before. Here is one I found recently:

> *To my handsome, dapper guy who takes care of me with love and tenderness.*
>
> *Thank you for the many ways you make me feel loved and cared for. Look forward to our travels. Thank God every day for our productive lives with the blessing and guidance of our heavenly Father. I love you more every day.*
>
> *Nan, your sweetheart*

So when Nancy announces that she can't find her phone and I know I will have to help search for it, I keep showing her love despite any frustration. And, because of the way she loves me back, it isn't hard to do.

Is there a challenging situation in your life that would be helped by a fresh dose of love?

Just Say Thank You

Rejoice always, pray continually, give thanks in all circumstances;
for this is God's will for you in Christ Jesus.
1 Thessalonians 5:16–18

She was distressed at how someone was treating her. As we talked, she recounted how, in the past, this person had changed for the better in an answer to prayer. As she recalled this, her face brightened, and she smiled. Together, we thanked God for past answers as we also asked for new ones.

Notice that Paul's instructions us are to pray and give thanks not *for* all circumstances but *in* all circumstances. Even in a present, difficult circumstance, you can sense something good in the middle of it. Beyond that, "we know that in all things God works for the good of those who love him" (Romans 8:28)—

and, as one man put it, "all things" includes "what even the devil sends." Giving thanks to God brings appropriate glory to God. Beyond that, thanking God for past answers to prayer builds faith to trust him for future answers.

And give thanks to people. In an age framed by an attitude of entitlement and, "What's in it for me?" how right it is to say "thank you." Saying thank you communicates that the other person is important, has contributed to my life, and is valued.

When Paul wrote to the Philippian church, he said, among other things, "Yet it was good of you to share in my troubles"; "You sent me aid more than once when I was in need"; and, "I am amply supplied, now that I have received from Epaphroditus the gifts you sent" (Philippians 4:14, 16, 18). How do you think the Philippians felt when they read that?

Just now, a thank-you letter sits in front of me. In part, it reads: "You have done all these outward things, but there are inward things as well. You have instilled confidence in me as a husband, father, pastor, and a leader. You have deeply influenced my spiritual journey with our Savior. Thank you."

How do you think I felt when I read that? How would you feel?

Now I must take a break from this to write some thank-you notes. Do you need to write one too?

Hidden with Christ in God

For you died, and your life is now hidden with Christ in God.
Colossians 3:3

I was afraid I had made a big mistake. There was no question that God sanctified me through and through (1 Thessalonians 5:23) that September night. One of the overwhelming realities of that experience was that the old Chic Shaver died. In place of my old self was inner purity, peace, and love beyond what I'd ever known—so great that I sang Charles Wesley's "Love Divine, All Loves Excelling" twenty times in the next twenty-four hours. The second verse especially spoke to me:

> *Breathe, O breathe thy loving Spirit*
> *Into every troubled breast!*
> *Let us all in thee inherit;*

Let us find that second rest.
Take away our bent to sinning;
Alpha and Omega be.
End of faith, as its Beginning,
Set our hearts at liberty.[185]

For months, I sought the fullness of the sanctifying Spirit as the cure to my internal sins and lack of spiritual power. And now—an answer!

But then came my mistake. It was subtle. I mistakenly assumed that, because God delivered me in that moment, I would have automatic victory in every future challenging situation I experienced. How wrong I was! I discovered I had to depend on Christ moment by moment and lean hard on God in every test of life. This was a dynamic, ongoing relationship! Filled with the Spirit, yes, but also:

- "Walk . . . according to the Spirit" (Romans 8:4, NKJV).
- "Do not grieve the Holy Spirit of God" (Ephesians 4:30).
- "Do not quench the Spirit" (1 Thessalonians 5:19).
- "Let us keep in step with the Spirit" (Galatians 5:25).

Or, as Everett Lewis Cattell so wisely put it, "Now the chief weapon of temptation used by the devil against the surrendered and holy heart is to try to draw the self out of its hidden place and, in some particular at least, get it to set up again in independence from God."[186]

Proved Faithful

Now it is required that those who have been given
a trust must prove faithful.
1 Corinthians 4:2

She was a schoolteacher by profession and a Sunday school teacher by God's calling. I never heard her teach a boring class—she prayed over her class members, called on them, sometimes wept as she taught, and often rejoiced. She lived in the joy of the sanctifying fullness of the Spirit. Oh yes, the fruit

---

185. Charles Wesley (words) and John Zundel (music), "Love Divine, All Loves Excelling," *Sing to the Lord: Hymnal* (Kansas City, MO: Lillenas Publishing Company, 1993), #507.
186. Everett Lewis Cattell, *The Spirit of Holiness* (Grand Rapids: Eerdmans, 1963).

of the Spirit includes not only love, joy, and peace but also faithfulness (Galatians 5:22).

When Jim and Anita moved out of state, they did not get settled in a church, and they began to drift spiritually. Sunday school teacher Ferne could not stand or accept this—she followed them with prayers, love, concern, and frequent communication. She kept it up until word came back that Jim and Anita had returned to God and to church.

When Ferne was concerned about one of the little girls in her public-school class, she decided to make a house call to meet the girl's parents. As she talked to the parents, she realized that part of what the home needed was spiritual life. She told her own story of being a rebellious twenty-some-year-old, realizing that her lifestyle wouldn't work, coming to know Jesus Christ, and finally seeing the pieces of her life fit together.

After the parents heard her story, they said, "Ferne Long, you've got what we need. We're coming to your church this Sunday."

Immediately, Ferne was in a dilemma. This was the weekend she'd be gone on vacation. She was certain that, if she told them she wouldn't be there, the young family wouldn't come to church. She knew that someone's life, future, and soul were at stake. So Ferne decided to postpone her vacation so she could sit with the new family in church that Sunday. Talk about faithfulness!

It was no surprise when, at the annual assembly of the sixty or so churches that made up the district, Ferne was honored as Outstanding Sunday School Teacher of the Year. That seems to fit with what most Christians would like to hear when they cross from this world to the next: "Well done, good and faithful servant! You have been faithful with a few things; I will put you in charge of many things. Come and share your master's happiness!" (Matthew 25:21).

Certainly you'll desire to be proved faithful too.

Freedom and Slavery

So if the Son sets you free, you will be free indeed.
John 8:36

A sneer creeps across his face as he makes a remark of the smart-aleck variety: "What do you mean you don't do that activity or go to those places? Doesn't your religion give you any freedom?" And he feels superior because he goes to places where you don't care to go.

Some of the Jews of Jesus's day had a superiority complex too. But neither the ancient Jews nor today's misguided critics come close to understanding what freedom means. Christians live the way they do out of desire, while sinners live under the cracking whip of their master, sin. Until the Son sets a person free, human nature is enslaved to sin.

Don't believe me? Ask Starr Daily. Starr was rotting in "the hole" (solitary confinement) of a prison, where he had bread and water for food and stones for a bed. Only hate for his guard and the warden kept him alive. Then, in his sleep one night, Starr was confronted by Jesus Christ, the man he had always tried to avoid. Christ penetrated to the depths of Starr's soul, and his love drew all the poison of sin out. When he awoke, the gray walls around him looked different. But it was Starr who was different—for the first time in his life, he had freedom within.

Offended

A person's wisdom yields patience; it is to one's glory to overlook an offense.
Proverbs 19:11

Offended! How easily people are offended. Some just seem to be waiting for an opportunity to be offended.

I was surprised by a report from my son, Paul, about a recent incident in his life. Here's some background first.

Paul has had multiple cancers throughout his body and multiple surgeries to address them. The most invasive surgery was to remove cancer in his neck, which also involved the removal of his voice box. Now, in order to talk, he must cover the hole in his neck that he breathes through and force air through his mouth to form words. Every so many words, he must pause, uncover the hole, and inhale. As a result, his voice has a husky, raspy sound. He does not complain about this, but he has been receiving treatments to improve his vocal quality.

Recently, Paul got into a conversation with a coach at a volleyball game Paul was officiating. (He does this with an electronic whistle.) The coach asked Paul, "How are you doing?"

Paul responded in his husky voice, and the coach commented, "It sounds like you've got it bad" (meaning a bad cold).

Paul simply said, "No."

But a little while later, the coach came back and offered Paul a cough drop.

As I heard Paul recounting this story, I wondered if he felt offended by the coach's misguided gesture. It was bad enough to have cancer, let alone lose his voice box—and now a man who didn't even know the facts was offering him cough drops for a cold he didn't have!

But Paul was not offended—actually, he was thankful. He thought it was great that, as a result of his recent treatments, his vocal quality had *moved up* to the level of a sore throat or a cold. This was an improvement! Paul was joyous and positive about it.

For a long time, Paul has been living under the blessing of God. God gave him tremendous peace when the doctors said they would have to remove his voice box. He looks at life from a different perspective than most. He lives in the following scriptures: "Rejoice in the Lord always" (Philippians 4:4); and, "Rejoice always, pray continually, give thanks in all circumstances; for this is God's will for you in Christ Jesus" (1 Thessalonians 5:16–18). He has learned that "Whoever would foster love covers over an offense" (Proverbs 17:9).

Consider what you've had to face in the last week. And remember that "it is to one's glory to overlook an offense."

Evil in Me, Part 1

Now if I do what I do not want to do, it is no longer I who do it,
but it is sin living in me that does it.
Romans 7:20

When I was young, my parents did not allow me free rein in every room of our house. But on one particular day, I was allowed into the living room, which contained many breakable objects. I was immediately attracted to a heavy glass ashtray (these were days before we'd allowed Jesus much control in our house).

I picked up the heavy ashtray and raised it over my head. My mother saw and sternly commanded, "Don't you throw that ashtray!"

In an instant, I fired it across the room. And I paid for it.

What made me do that? Paul had already figured it out. In Romans 7:9, he wrote, "Once I was alive apart from the law; but when the commandment came, *sin sprang to life* and I died." Apart from God and his grace, I'm amazed at how much evil I see in myself if I'm halfway honest. Besides systemic evil and the evil deeds of others, I have to contend with the evil within. And indeed, systemic evil is the result of the compilation and multiplication of the evil of many individual hearts.

Romans 7:19–20 tells us, "For I do not do the good I want to do, but *the evil* I do not want to do—this I keep on doing. Now if I do what I do not want to do, it is no longer I who do it, but it is *sin living in me* that does it." Considering some events across my lifetime confirms this truth.

While I was in high school, someone was kind enough to give me a summer job at his furniture store. Yet, the next year, when I read in the newspaper that my former boss was in financial distress, I took a strange delight in reporting the news to others. Did spreading that news make me feel superior to one who had been my superior? Was that my heart issue? Jesus said, "For it is from within, out of a person's heart, that evil thoughts come . . . envy, slander, arrogance and folly. All these evils come from inside and defile a person" (Mark 7:21–23).

As a young man, I felt I had developed some high standards. Honesty was a priority for me, and I became irritated with dishonesty in others. Still, when I was in a tight jam, I found myself lying to get out of it. I didn't appreciate what Paul had said: "You, therefore, have no excuse, you who pass judgment on someone else, for at whatever point you judge another, you are condemning yourself, because you who pass judgment do the same things" (Romans 2:1).

I began to feel religious stirrings inside me. When someone suggested to me that the way to God was through Jesus Christ, I bristled. I thought, *I'll get to God any way I want!* I tried—and it didn't work. In my self-centeredness, I did not yet understand Jesus's words: "I am the way and the truth and the life. No one comes to the Father except through me" (John 14:6).

Evil in Me, Part 2

Now if I do what I do not want to do, it is no longer I who do it,
but it is sin living in me that does it.
Romans 7:20

Unbelievably, as two young seminary students, we were invited to preach and give our testimonies in a weekend revival at a big church. Amazing things happened. Many sought God publicly, and the pastor's wife spoke of six couples who received spiritual help, saying, "I venture to say that every marriage will be saved."

Driving home, I said to myself, "My, didn't I give a good altar call!"

Immediately, the Holy Spirit said to my heart, *"I will not yield my glory to another"* (Isaiah 42:8). I was rebuked and forced to look into the depths of my heart.

A few days ago, I was telling my wife of more than sixty beautiful years about my dissatisfaction on some issue. She said, "You're scolding me." Her word seemed almost as powerful as the Spirit's. She was right; I was wrong. I asked her forgiveness, and I asked for the Lord's forgiveness, cleansing, and a renewed walk in the Spirit.

Oswald Chambers said,

> At the beginning of the human race, the conception was that Adam was to be master over everything but himself. He was to have dominion over the life on the earth and in the air and in the sea, but he was not to have dominion over himself—God was to have dominion over him. The temptation came on this line—"Disobey, and you will become as God." Man took dominion over himself and thereby lost his lordship over everything else. According to the Bible, the disposition of sin is my claim to my right to myself.[187]

We might also describe "my claim to my right to myself" as "sin living in me" (Romans 7:20). I have found only two answers for such a deep issue. We need forgiveness for what we've done in the past, but we must go deeper still.

I find the first answer in Paul's words in Galatians 2:20: "I have been *crucified with Christ* and I no longer live, but Christ lives in me. The life I

187. Oswald Chambers, *My Utmost for His Highest* (Toronto: McClelland and Steward Limited, 1935).

now live in the body, I live by faith in the Son of God, who loved me and gave himself for me."

Only a *crucifixion* of my ego—"my claim to my right to myself" or "the sin living in me"—is deep enough to address this issue. But once I am crucified with Christ, I will need the second answer, from Galatians 5:25: "Let us keep *in step* with the *Spirit.*" I need a moment-by-moment walk in the Spirit.

I Have Been Crucified with Christ

For through the law I died to the law so that I might live for God.
I have been crucified with Christ and I no longer live,
but Christ lives in me. The life I live in the body, I live by faith
in the Son of God, who loved me and gave himself for me.
Galatians 2:19–20

Spectacular catch—feet down within the line—touchdown. And then the victory dance—or, more accurately, the victory swagger. The player flaunts his success: "I faked you out; I beat you; I'm spectacular; I win, you lose." We've all seen it before—the exaltation of the "Big I."

What some athletes do with football, the apostle Paul (when he was still Saul) did with religion. A top Pharisee, utterly scrupulous, and ultra-religious, he could brag, "I was advancing in Judaism beyond many Jews of my own age" (Galatians 1:14). This was a very "Big I." Yet, in his best moments, Saul knew he had not kept the law of God successfully. As the apostle Paul, he finally concluded, "Through the law I died to the law." But that failure opened the door to something far better: "so that I might live for God" (2:19).

Have you ever reveled in the "Big I"?

- I aced that exam.
- I faked him out.
- I told her a thing or two.
- I busted him real good.
- I showed her.
- I told him where to get off.

The "Big I" is aggressive, pushy, obvious, and not very pretty. Paul knew his problem was greater than the law; it was the dominating force of the "Big

I." After his conversion to Christ, he discovered that, between life under sin and life under Christ's sovereignty, there is a no-man's land of life under shared control—and it doesn't work. So Paul took it to the cross: "I have been crucified with Christ" (2:20). The death of the "Big I" was the only answer—only then would Christ be able to live abundantly and fully through him. The crucifixion was a crisis capitulation. It had taken place in the past, but it was still in effect. It had not lost its power.

Jim, a ministerial student, sat across the desk from his professor. Though he'd accepted Christ, another mighty power still was at work in him. He confessed, "I love to make money. In my head I know I ought to surrender, but emotionally I'm tied to it. I pay my tithe, but I don't like to." The professor urged him to surrender his whole forgiven life back to God (consecrate); to ask for a full cleansing or crucifixion of his remaining self-centeredness (cleanse or crucify); and to reach out in faith and trust the Spirit to do it (claim). Jim's "Big I" was so controlled by money that he prayed, "O God, help me to be willing to be willing." He put his head down on the desk and wept. Over and over he said, "Okay, okay, okay," as he surrendered issue after issue. Suddenly, he looked up and told his professor, "The desire for money is gone!"

The professor asked, "Who controls you?"

"The Holy Spirit," Jim replied.

The professor instructed, "Write this down: On May 9, at 4:15 p.m., Jim died."

Jim continued to rejoice, saying, "The Holy Spirit is more exciting than money. I don't feel all tied up anymore."

No wonder Jim and Paul could both testify, "I have been crucified with Christ." Both became productive channels for the gospel.

A Brother in Christ

No longer as a slave, but better than a slave, as a dear brother.
He is very dear to me but even dearer to you, both as a fellow man
and as a brother in the Lord.
Philemon 1:16

Paul wrote these words about Onesimus, a recent convert who was returning to his former master, Philemon. What has more power to uplift the powerless ("better than a slave, as a dear brother") than the gospel story? What can do more in solving labor unrest and race riots than to bring both boss and worker, black and white, into a brotherhood by knowing Jesus Christ?

They called him the "angel in ebony"—the son of a king, he was captured by a warring African tribe, sold into slavery, and held for ransom. His daily beatings became so severe that the young man ran away. Afterward, he found work at a coffee plantation, and there, he found Christ. Soon, he called prayer "talking to my Father." He journeyed to America to find a man to tell him about the Holy Spirit. He lived so close to God that, on his first night in America, he led seventeen men to Christ. He had once been kidnapped, enslaved, and oppressed, but in the end, Sammy Morris was my brother in Christ.

God Sanctified Me!

May God himself, the God of peace, sanctify you through and through.
1 Thessalonians 5:23

No question about it—I knew God had saved me! On the night of November 20, my sins were forgiven; Christ entered the center of my life; God became real; love, joy, and peace became my major emotions. I continued a day-by-day, living relationship with Jesus. The Bible became an exciting book; I was receiving answers to prayer; by grace, I resisted old temptations. I was in church every time the doors were open. I was telling others what Jesus had done for me and bringing my friends to church.

Six months later, I was in crisis. Despite my continuing relationship with God and the blessings he'd given me, ugly tempers began to arise from the basement of my soul. Certain people, even Christian friends, rubbed me the wrong way. I knew that Christians should be loving, so I gritted my teeth, clenched my jaw, and said, "Make yourself love this person!" But I couldn't do it.

Bitterness, resentment, impatience, jealousy, and pride began rising up from deep within me. Along with that, I sensed a lack of spiritual power—though I was sharing my faith with many, few were being changed. I wondered, "Is this the best my Christianity can be?"

Then, some glimmers of light began to break through to me. I heard it in a sermon; read it in the Bible; heard it in a song; caught it in a personal testimony. I began to hear phrases like "entire sanctification"; "filled with the Spirit"; "purity of heart"; "crucified with Christ"; "the rest of faith"; "full cleansing." Daily, consistently, I prayed for God's answer to my struggle.

Then, in one Sunday night service, God spoke to my heart and prompted me to go to the altar for prayer. God asked me, "What have you been praying for all this time?"

I responded, "Lord, sanctify me."

Suddenly, what felt like an electric shock went all through my body and I was facedown on the floor. Though I was a completely healthy twenty-one-year-old, I felt so weak that I thought I was going to die. Then I realized, "That's exactly what's going to happen. The 'old Chic Shaver' is going to die."

Surrendering all of my forgiven life back to God and asking him to crucify the remaining core of self-centeredness, I attempted to reach out in faith and believe God for the answer. At the urging of Christian friends, I gathered all my faith and trusted God to sanctify me.

When I did so, the most amazing peace and joy flooded my heart. My strength suddenly returned. And oh, the love! I stood and testified God had just sanctified me through and through. Immediately, a man in the congregation rushed forward to seek God. There was spiritual power in the room. I went home singing Charles Wesley's "Love Divine, All Loves Excelling," and sang it repeatedly over the next twenty-four hours.

My self-centeredness had gone to the cross; God had sanctified me completely. The Spirit had filled me, and my Christian life rose to a whole new level. I still had many lessons to learn about the continual "walk in the Spirit"—and I'm still learning. But I had entered a land called "victory." I'm still living there and exploring new territory.

Entirely Sanctified and In Step with the Spirit

May God himself, the God of peace, sanctify you through and through.
1 Thessalonians 5:23

Let us keep in step with the Spirit.
Galatians 5:25

Many claim that the ministry of John Wesley in eighteenth-century England saved the nation from a revolution. With concern for the poor and the influence of the wealthy, his work reached all segments of society. Wesley was especially powerful because his preaching and teaching led people beyond conversion and into a deeper experience with God. This entire sanctification fully purified the believers' hearts from the sinful nature. But Wesley was careful to urge Christians that as a necessity for spiritual victory, they must remain in God's grace, continue in perfect love, and walk in the Spirit moment by moment. Two of his letters highlight these issues.

To Miss Cook, September 24, 1785:

And how soon may you be made a partaker of sanctification! And not only by a slow and insensible growth in grace, but by the power of the Highest overshadowing you, in a moment, in the twinkling of an eye, so as utterly to abolish sin, and to renew you in his whole image! If you are simple of heart, if you are willing to receive the heavenly gift, as a little child, without reasoning, why may you not receive it now? He is nigh that sanctifieth; He is with you; He is knocking at the door of your heart![188]

And to Adam Clarke, November 26, 1790: *"To retain the grace of God, is much more than to gain it: Hardly one in three does this. And this should be strongly and explicitly urged on all who have tasted of perfect love."*[189]

So seek him until you know he has entirely sanctified your heart. But do not be presumptuous—be diligent to draw on all divine resources and keep in a daily step with the Spirit. As Galatians 5:25 says, "Let us keep in step with the Spirit." If you do so, "your whole spirit, soul and body" will "be kept blameless at the coming of our Lord Jesus Christ. The one who calls you is faithful, and he will do it" (1 Thessalonians 5:23–24).

A Relevant Sanctification, Part 1

It is God's will that you should be sanctified.
1 Thessalonians 4:3a

---

188. John Wesley, *The Works of John Wesley* (Kansas City, MO: Nazarene Publishing House, n.d.), vol. XIII, 94.
189. Wesley, *Works*, 104.

Sanctification is relevant because of:

1. **The call of the Word of God**

   "It is God's will that you should be sanctified" (1 Thessalonians 4:3). "May God himself, the God of peace, sanctify you through and through" (1 Thessalonians 5:23).

2. **The need of people**

   There is still an alarming self-centeredness in the hearts of converted people, as well as a lack of spiritual power. This needs to be resolved by divine intervention.

3. **The sanctified heart is attractive**

   Sherwood Wirt, former editor of *Decision* magazine, testified to his experience of sanctification: "I don't know just how the love came in, but I know that all the bitterness I held against others . . . disappeared. Resentment—hostility—hurt feelings—you name it. They all dissolved. Evaporated. Went."

4. **People are seeking**

   In the twelve months from June 1, 2015, to May 31, 2016, in fourteen revivals from Florida to Michigan, and from Texas to Idaho, 146 people sought God publicly after sermons on sanctification.[190]

A Relevant Sanctification, Part 2

It is God's will that you should be sanctified.
1 Thessalonians 4:3a

Believers testify to the reality of the need for sanctification.

Isabel: A few days after she saw her friend accept Christ, Isabel testified, "When I started this class, I was afraid to present the gospel. Now that God has sanctified me, I'm not afraid anymore. I am confident, excited, and more alert to my opportunities."

Kathy: Slowly, I arrived at a place of understanding that my heavenly Father would never harm me and that I could trust his authority over me. In

---

190. Previously published in *The Good News: The Chic Shaver Center for Evangelism Newsletter* (September 2016).

fact, it was something I desired! All that was left were the details. I remember asking at the altar, "Is there anything else you want me to give you?" I continued asking that question until God's silence and my deep peace assured me there was nothing else. I experienced entire sanctification as a one-time spiritual-crisis-point decision, and continue to experience it as an ongoing decision to live my life as God wants me to. The great thing about it all is that with the intimate, loving communion we have, it's also the way I want to live!

Keith: How could I be a believer and follower of Christ if my natural instinct was to curse and grumble? So I started to look for what was missing. I searched for answers, but it seemed like I had all the bases covered: believe, tithe, serve—yet nothing in my nature changed. Then, near the end of July 2008, our church needed some custodial help while a few of the regulars were out. I remember thinking that was way below my status, but I begrudgingly volunteered to take a shift. During Sunday worship on July 27, 2008, I ran into the retired former head custodian. I jokingly told him I was going to take his old job and asked him, "How do you handle this?"

He told me that he considered his custodial job a ministry and that he was working for God: "If Christ can die on a cross for me, I can surely clean up a church for him."

His words hung in the air and surrounded me. And then it happened. I felt hot, cold, empty, and full inside all at the same time. I knew I needed to be a custodian. Problems became situations to help; situations became opportunities to do something; my chores became acts of service. I realized that God used a custodian to open my eyes and heart to his fullness. So when people ask me how I am "fixed with the Lord," I tell them I am filled with the Spirit, and I let God take charge of things.[191]

DECEMBER 5   **339**

A Relevant Sanctification, Part 3

It is God's will that you should be sanctified.
1 Thessalonians 4:3a

---

191. Previously published in *The Good News: The Chic Shaver Center for Evangelism Newsletter* (September 2016).

Christian philosopher Dallas Willard said that the only book that influenced him more than the Bible was James Gilchrist Lawson's *Deeper Experiences of Famous Christians*. This book is filled with the testimonies of those who have been sanctified and filled with the Spirit.

Matthew Kelly, in *Four Signs of a Dynamic Catholic*, calls Catholics to revival. He poses the question, "How is the best way to live?" He says the answer is to become the best version of oneself by dying to the lesser self so the best self can emerge in Christ. The pursuit of holiness is the pursuit of the best version of yourself.

The best-selling devotional book of all time is Oswald Chambers's *My Utmost for His Highest*. Around the world, Christians of all backgrounds are reading it. In the book, Chambers uses the word "sanctification" twenty-one times, and there are many more instances of related words. In the February 8 entry, he writes: "When we pray to be sanctified, are we prepared? . . . Sanctification means intense concentration on God's point of view. . . . Sanctification means being made one with Jesus so that the disposition that ruled him will rule us. . . . Are we prepared to say, 'Lord, make me as holy as you can make a sinner saved by grace?'" In the October 20 entry, he writes: "It is not a question of whether God is willing to sanctify me; is it *my* will? Am I willing to let God do in me all that has been made possible by the Atonement?"[192]

If the Word of God; the needs of people; the sanctified heart's attractiveness; seeking people; testifying people; as well as Sherwood Wirt, Dallas Willard, Matthew Kelly, and Oswald Chambers are all calling us—shouldn't we press on to experience God's sanctification personally and tell others the truth?[193]

Fear and Spiritual Power

He told them, "This is what is written: The Messiah will suffer and rise from the dead on the third day, and repentance for the forgiveness of sins will be preached in his name to all nations,

---

192. Oswald Chambers, *My Utmost for His Highest* (Toronto: McClelland and Steward Limited, 1935).

193. Previously published in *The Good News: The Chic Shaver Center for Evangelism Newsletter* (September 2016).

*beginning at Jerusalem. You are witnesses of these things. I am going
to send you what my Father has promised; but stay in the city
until you have been clothed with power from on high."*
Luke 24:46–49

They were followers of Christ, to an extent—but they fled and hid when the pressure was on. Then Jesus gave them the promise of power from on high—a reference to the Holy Spirit (Acts 1:4–5). And indeed, the Spirit descended on 120 Christ followers as they prayed (1:14 and 2:4). Peter, too, was filled with the Spirit—now the denier became the persuader, and three thousand people received Christ. John was filled with the Spirit and spoke God's word boldly (4:31). Stephen, full of the Spirit (7:55), saw heaven and Jesus, and forgave those who martyred him. The Spirit-filled layman, Philip (6:5), led by the Spirit (8:29), led the Ethiopian to Christ. And Dwight Moody, Charles Finney, Samuel Logan Brengle, and E. Stanley Jones all testified to being filled with the Spirit at a time after they had known Christ as Savior for a while. They all said that this relationship with the Spirit empowered their ministries.

Maybe this is for the clergy, the big guns. But what about ordinary people? Is fear subconsciously blocking us from witnessing (telling others what Jesus means to us)?

We had just concluded a twelve-week personal evangelism training class at a church in Houston. One participant in the class was Isabel—young, newly married, from Venezuela, and had been a Christian for a little more than two years. The class developed her skills to where she could confidently testify and share the gospel message. Shortly after, she shared the gospel, and the person accepted Christ. I must also tell you that during the same time as her evangelism training, Isabel was sanctified through and through (1 Thessalonians 5:23) and filled with the Holy Spirit. A few days after she saw her new friend accept Christ, she testified, "When I started this class, I was afraid to present the gospel. Now that God has sanctified me, I'm not afraid anymore. I am confident, excited, more alert to my opportunities."

By the power of the sanctifying Spirit, let us overcome our fears.[194]

194. Previously published in *The Good News: The Chic Shaver Center for Evangelism Newsletter* (June 2005).

The Magnetic Pull

Throw off your old sinful nature and your former way of life,
which is corrupted by lust and deception. Instead, let the Spirit
renew your thoughts and attitudes. Put on your new nature,
created to be like God—truly righteous and holy.
Ephesians 4:22–24, NLT

Did you ever play with magnets when you were a kid? I had both a horseshoe magnet and a single bar magnet. I could sprinkle iron filings on a piece of paper, hold the horseshoe magnet under the paper, and instantly, the magnetic pull grouped the iron filings into two distinct points around the poles of the magnet. Some iron filings had a hard time deciding which side to land on. However, if I put the single bar magnet under the paper, the iron filings grouped into a unified, single point around that one magnetic pole.

In the lives of many truly converted Christians, there are still two great poles—God and the self—that form two overlapping patterns of action. These people are partially self-centered and partially God-centered—in other words, they are "double-minded" (James 1:8).

The way Galatians 5:24 addresses this issue is radical: "Those who belong to Christ Jesus have *crucified* the flesh with its passions and desires." If the flesh is crucified, if the old self (self-centeredness) is thrown off, then a single remaining pole may control the heart and life: "your new nature, created to be like God—truly righteous and holy" (Ephesians 4:24, NLT).

Which pull are you feeling? Remember that you will not drift into a place of victory—you must decide. So, as Paul writes, "throw off your old sinful nature and . . . put on your new nature" (Ephesians 4:22, 24, NLT).[195]

The Second Work of Grace

---

195. Adapted from Everett Lewis Cattell, *The Spirit of Holiness* (Grand Rapids: Eerdmans, 1963), 24–28.

It is God's will that you should be sanctified.
1 Thessalonians 4:3a

"When should I expect God to sanctify me?" is a big question for many sincere Christians. The Thessalonians were real, true, good Christians. They were imitators of the Lord (1 Thessalonians 1:6) and models to all the believers in their area (1:7). Paul and other leaders instructed them "how to live in order to please God," and they were doing so (4:1). Yet Paul said to them, "It is God's will that you should be sanctified" (4:3)—which, among other things, would mean empowerment for sexual purity.

My friend Paul is a key example of that spiritual discovery. By the time he arrived at a Christian college, he was a nominal Christian. His lifestyle was one of sinning and repenting, sinning and repenting. Meanwhile, he saw Christians around him who were thriving spiritually. He noticed that God talked to them but not to him.

Paul questioned God about this, asking, "Why aren't you speaking to me?"

God answered, *"I've never stopped speaking to you. You have stopped listening to me. You can't hear me because of all the other stuff you're listening to."*

So Paul repented and experienced what he called his "adult conversion." Philippians 4:8 (which gives guidance for the Christian's thought life) became the filter that guided him. The result was that, at age nineteen, his spiritual growth was off the charts.

Now God was speaking to him. He was a criminal justice major, but God told him, *"I've got something better for your life."* Paul wondered how he would know if he were called to ministry. Within weeks, he received confirmation of his call, and his course was set.

Paul kept hearing people talk about sanctification. They spoke of a true conversion to Christ, but then a second, deeper experience with God—a second work of grace. He thought, *I was saved as a seven-year-old child, and now I've had an adult conversion. That must be the second work of grace.*

But there were problems. Paul had a judgmental spirit toward Christians who were less zealous than he. He went to a revival and heard the evangelist say that, to be sanctified, you have to walk in all the light God has given you. He later testified: "From my childhood acceptance of Christ at seven to age nineteen, I was in a sinning religion. I was not walking in light. My adult conversion was not my sanctification; it was my reclamation of a saved relationship. I'm saved, not sanctified. God showed me my judgmental spirit and my un-Christlike heart that needed cleansing. I went to the altar and poured out my heart. Nothing happened. I said, 'Have I been duped?'"

In that moment, a professor came to Paul and wisely counseled him. Paul prayed again, and his faith began to rise. He said, "Yes, I believe." A warm sensation coursed through his chest, his arms, and his feet.

Next, he heard God say, *"Paul, I am pleased with you."* He knew then that God had sanctified him.

Nearly everyone had left the sanctuary by the time he finished praying. Then the devil spoke: *"This is the greatest thing that has ever happened to you, and nobody cares."*

But God wasn't finished. He said, *"It doesn't matter what others say about you. I'm pleased with you."* And the warm sensation flowed through his body again.

The next day, Paul went to a professor of whom he had been critical and apologized. "I was wrong," he said. "I was sanctified last night." After this, they became best friends.

Paul's life trajectory moved to a new level. Today, he is a powerful minister of the gospel and one of the godliest men I know.

Man, She Sure Is Slow!

A man must not say when he is tempted, "God is tempting me."
For God has no dealings with evil, and does not himself tempt anyone. No,
a man's temptation is due to the pull of his own inward desires,
which can be enormously attractive. His own desire takes hold of him,
and that produces sin. And sin in the long run means death—
make no mistake about that, brothers of mine!
James 1:13–16, PHILLIPS

Yes, he said it—an evangelist, waiting for his breakfast in the pastor's home, said of the pastor's wife, "Man, she sure is slow!"

The pastor later told me, "That irritated me." Yet when I proceeded to ask the pastor if he held a grudge, tried to retaliate, or carried a chip on his shoulder toward the evangelist, he said no.

The pastor's irritation was normal for even a sanctified man. It was his *continuing* Christian reaction and attitude afterward that demonstrated his sanctification.

How should we treat the problem of temptation? First, we must distinguish between temptation and sin. James 1:14–15 (PHILLIPS) says, "A man's temptation is due to the pull of his own inward desires, which can be enormously attractive. His own desire takes hold of him, and that produces sin. And sin in the long run means death." James seems to be saying that our inward desires exert temptation on our will. If, on the other hand, our inward desires *control* or direct our will, that means we commit sins.

It is easier to distinguish between temptation and sin when we're dealing with outward acts rather than inward desires (sins of the spirit). Impatience, jealousy, arrogance, resentfulness, and irritability (1 Corinthians 13) are examples of inward sins. If, in a moment of pressure or trial, a sanctified Christian experiences a *momentary feeling* of impatience or irritability, does that mean that he is no longer sanctified? No. That momentary feeling is not yet sin, for the following reasons:

1. For temptation to be real, there must be a real "pull of . . . inward desires" (PHILLIPS).
2. High-pressure circumstances will produce inward frustration in even the holiest of people, and this is normal. Dr. Richard Taylor says that even in sanctified people, there is normal, combative reaction to circumstances they do not like. The pastor's reaction to the criticism of his wife is an example of this.
3. Perhaps Romans 8:7—"The carnal mind is enmity against God: for it is not subject to the law of God, neither indeed can be" (KJV)—provides us with a distinction between the carnal and the human. In the midst of inner agitation or desire, ask, "Is this subject to the law of God?" The carnal is not subject to the law of God; the human is.
4. A fleeting wrong desire or feeling is not sin as long as the will only says, "I will respond in the moment of frustration by the law of love." As the saying goes, "You can't keep the birds from flying over your head, but you can keep them from making a nest in your hair."[196]

---

196. Charles "Chic" Shaver, *Keeping Spiritual Victory* (Kansas City, MO: Beacon Hill Press of Kansas City, 1972), 13–16.

There's Peace

Peace I leave with you; my peace I give you.
John 14:27

In a Sunday morning revival service in Illinois, Jack took his wife's hand and came to the altar in tears. He came back to Christ.

Here's Jack's story:

I made excuses every week as to why I couldn't go to church. Then, two weeks ago Saturday, I set down my last beer. I needed to be a good example for my thirteen grandchildren.

On Sunday, a strong-headed man walked into church. I had become spiritually stagnant. I had not picked up a Bible in a year. This proud, foolish man came to the altar with weak knees. He [Christ] took all the burdens I had. He took me out of the rough and put me on the Rock.

That night, I had the first peaceful sleep I'd had in a long time. There were no problems on my mind.

The next day, I didn't argue with my wife over payday or how to spend the money. We had been arguing all the time.

This is how Jack summed up his experience with Jesus that Sunday morning: "I never had such a load lifted."

His wife summed it up this way: "There's peace around our house."[197]

Christmas: Fearful or Faithful

Do not be afraid. I bring you good news that will cause great joy.
Luke 2:10

In my eighty-five years of life, I can't remember a time when national or international affairs have been more dysfunctional then they are now. Jesus Christ

---

197. Previously published in *The Good News: The Chic Shaver Center for Evangelism Newsletter* (June 2014).

prophesied, "On the earth, nations will be in anguish and perplexity at the roaring and tossing of the sea. People will faint from terror, apprehensive of what is coming on the world" (Luke 21:25–26). Anguish, perplexity, terror, and apprehension all speak of a fear-filled world. Recently, it became apparent to me that two predominant types of fear appear in Scripture.

The first is fear of the Lord and his divine overtures. There is the healthy fear or reverence for the Lord that Scripture describes (Proverbs 9:10). And then there is the fear that, if I let God get too close to me, he'll interfere with the way I've been living. An example of the latter is the rich young ruler who turned away from Jesus because he feared Jesus's claim on his wealth and his life (Matthew 19:21–22). Conversely, the well-known Christmas story tells of an angelic messenger from God reporting the birth of Jesus Christ. And what did the angel say to the shepherds? Simply, "Do not be afraid. I bring you good news that will cause great joy" (Luke 2:10). We also read that when God came close to Moses, "Moses hid his face, because he was afraid to look at God" (Exodus 3:6).

Beyond fear of the Lord, the second type of fear we see in Scripture is fear resulting from pressures in our personal life and society. God powerfully speaks to that. As the psalmist wrote, "The LORD is my light and my salvation—whom shall I fear?" (Psalm 27:1). Likewise, in Psalm 56:3, we read, "When I am afraid, I put my trust in you." And Hebrews 13:6 says, "The Lord is my helper; I will not be afraid." Amazing! The God we are often afraid to approach wants to be close to us and help us with our fears.

In 2014, I wrote in our Christmas newsletter about our son (Paul)'s thirteen-hour cancer surgery that removed his voice box and much of his neck. We were able to report that, in prayer before the surgery, the peace of God had descended on me in Mississippi; on Nancy in Kansas; and on Paul in Indiana (Philippians 4:6–7).

Since that thirteen-hour surgery, Paul has had four reconstructive surgeries. All the while, Paul has been working his full-time job plus two part-time jobs. During a visit with Paul, Nancy peppered him with questions about his condition, his feelings, and his future. Repeatedly, he answered, "God knows my name." Even if Paul could not give detailed answers about the future, he had confidence in the God who personally knows him by name.

On another occasion, our daughters questioned Paul about how he was handling such an invasive surgery, the loss of his voice box, and the follow-up surgeries. He answered simply, "I've never had a bad day." Courageous! Strong! Joyful!

"He knows my name," and, "I've never had a bad day." By his answers, we see that Paul is not fearful but faithful toward a prayer-hearing, personal, helping, loving God.

In light of our troubled world this Christmas, let us be faithful to the message, "Do not be afraid. I bring you good news that will cause great joy."[198]

Full Sanctification

*I am sending you to them to open their eyes and turn them from
darkness to light, and from the power of Satan to God,
so that they may receive forgiveness of sins and a place
among those who are sanctified by faith in me.*
Acts 26:17–18

John Wesley wrote the following to Reverend Freeborn Garrettson in 1785: "The more explicitly and strongly you press all believers to aspire after full sanctification, as attainable now by simple faith, the more the whole work of God will prosper."

An Alabama layperson wrote this to me after a week of revival services in the local church: "You have made so much sense out of things I have struggled with. I feel the power of God's love more than ever. . . . I pray for that sanctification more now because you have helped me desire that."

After special services, an Ohio pastor sent me a note that read: "Thank you for . . . messages that led to a high percentage of the . . . church people moving up spiritually. . . . Your emphasis on personal evangelism will result in many people being added to the kingdom. In my twenty-three years of pastoring I have never witnessed so many pray for sanctification."

I urge all Christians to press on to full sanctification.[199]

---

198. Previously published in *The Good News: The Chic Shaver Center for Evangelism Newsletter* (December 2015).

199. Previously published in *The Good News: The Chic Shaver Center for Evangelism Newsletter* (March 2008).

Self, Part 1

Love your neighbor as yourself.
Matthew 19:19b

"He is no fool who gives what he cannot keep to gain what he cannot lose"[200] are the dramatic words Jim Elliot wrote when he was twenty-two years old. He was one of five men who would give their lives as martyrs for the salvation of Huaorani tribe of Ecuador—like Jesus Christ gave his life for the salvation of the world. Jim Elliot had one self to live and give for Christ.

Jesus Christ had a serious conversation with a wealthy man who was trying to attain eternal life. They discussed the commandments, then Jesus spoke the famous words, "Love your neighbor as yourself." Of course, Jesus's main concern was to root out the man's selfishness and move him to love others. However, in doing so, Jesus acknowledged that there is a legitimate love for self.

Your self is a gift from God. Jesus wants you to have self-value, self-esteem, self-respect, self-awareness, self-concern, self-care, self-control, and more. That is legitimate love for yourself.

Your self is the vehicle God works through. When God sanctifies you and fills you with his Spirit, he does not obliterate your self—you will always be a self.

Rather, when God sanctifies you, he cleanses and purifies your self. God roots out your selfishness or self-centeredness. There are other terms for self-centeredness—the flesh, the sinful nature, the old Adam, Adamic nature, the carnal nature, the carnal mind, and others. You must understand you can be a self without being self-centered. Often, I will preach, "You know your sins are forgiven; you've come to know Christ; you are born again; but you are still battling a core of self-centeredness in your personality. God has an answer for you."

One of the most vivid expressions of this truth is the apostle Paul's testimony: "I have been crucified with Christ and I no longer live, but Christ lives in me. The life I now live in the body, I live by faith in the Son of God, who loved me and gave himself for me" (Galatians 2:20).

---

200. Elisabeth Elliot, *Shadow of the Almighty* (New York: Harper and Brothers, 1958), 247.

In the original Greek text, the "I" that has been crucified is the word "ego." We understand what it means when someone says, "Man, he's got a big ego." It means the person is overly impressed with himself, considers himself above others, and has to have a lot of praise. That is a self that is selfish—the kind that needs to be crucified, put to death.

When Christ comes to live in that person's life, the person still dwells in a physical body which in itself is not sinful. After crucifixion, this self lives in a new way: "I live by faith in the Son of God." He lives more abundantly than before. Christ is on the throne of his life, whereas before, the self was on the throne.

Self, Part 2

Love your neighbor as yourself.
Matthew 19:19b

Scripture teaches, "Encourage the young men to be self-controlled" (Titus 2:6), but discourages *self-seeking*: "[Love] does not dishonor others, it is not self-seeking, it is not easily angered" (1 Corinthians 13:5).

We are warned not to "harbor bitter envy and selfish ambition in [our] hearts" (James 3:14). Instead, Scripture invites us to live a life full of delicious fruit: "But the fruit of the Spirit is love, joy, peace, forbearance, kindness, goodness, faithfulness, gentleness and self-control" (Galatians 5:22–23).

All Christians are asked to take their selfishness to the cross and allow God's Holy Spirit to cleanse, unify, and sanctify their whole personality. The self must know its master.

What are people like when they allow God to crucify their selfishness and launch their *selves* out to love and serve him? To find out, let's read more from Jim Elliot:

> In my own experience I have found that the most extravagant dreams of boyhood have not surpassed the great experience of being in the will of God, and I believe that nothing could be better. That is not to say that I do not want other things, and other ways of living, and other places to see, but in my right mind I know that my hopes and plans for myself could not be any better than He has arranged and fulfilled them. Thus

may we all find it, and know the truth of the Word that says, "He will be our guide even until death."[201]

Later, he writes of "one treasure, a single eye, and single master."[202]

Further, he writes, "God, I pray thee, light these idle sticks of my life and may I burn for thee. Consume my life, my God, for it is thine. I seek not a long life but a full one, like you, Lord Jesus."[203]

These are the words of a God-controlled and blessed "self."

My Christmas Wish for You

But the angel said to them, "Do not be afraid. I bring you good news that will cause great joy for all the people. Today in the town of David a Savior has been born to you; he is the Messiah, the Lord."
Luke 2:10–11

If Jesus came to your house and knocked upon your door
Would you rush to let him in and be excited to the core?
Would your heart skip a beat as he stepped inside the door?
Would you thank him and praise him, and then you'd sing some more?
To know he saved you, then forgave you, and peace came all day long
So now you share his love and grace and forgiveness for the wrong
You pray for those who need him to have a heavenly point of view
To live their life with love and grace with a heart that beats brand new
We thank him and praise him for all our earthly days
To know that he is with us and blesses all our ways
It pays to serve Jesus—it pays every day—it pays every step of the way
Though the pathway to glory may sometimes be drear
I will trust him each step of the way.

Nancy Shaver[204]

---

201. Elisabeth Elliot, *Shadow of the Almighty* (New York: Harper and Brothers, 1958), 196.
202. Elliot, *Shadow*, 247.
203. Elliot, *Shadow*.
204. Previously published in the Shaver Christmas letter, 2017.

Hit the Target

❖

Night and day we pray most earnestly that we may see you
again and supply what is lacking in your faith.
1 Thessalonians 3:10

It is God's will that you should be sanctified.
1 Thessalonians 4:3a

Anyone who rejects this instruction does not reject a
human being but God, the very God who gives you his Holy Spirit.
1 Thessalonians 4:8

Keith is the director of student accounting at the University of Kansas Medical Center, where he manages the student loan and tuition funds—75 to 110 million dollars per year. He and his wife, Laura, also have an income tax service they run out of their home. Keith and Laura have been married since 1986, have an adult son, Andy, and are members of their church. Here is Keith's story in his own words:

I became a follower of Christ as a heavenly work of God and an earthly work of Pastor Chic Shaver. That night, I knew something had happened, but since nothing looked different, I started seeking assurances that whatever it was that was supposed to have happened actually did. My values, habits, and willingness to serve completely changed. These changes served as proof for me that it had happened—I was changed.

This seemed fine, and I accepted it for a number of years. I was so busy doing church and community activities I hadn't noticed that something may have been missing—until one day, when my dear wife, Laura, and I were circling a parking lot searching for a space at a local shopping center. When I finally found one, I began to park my vehicle when I noticed a wheelchair symbol painted on the asphalt. I backed up and began to curse and grumble about the inconvenience when Laura said, "Well, that's a fine Christian attitude."

It was right then that I knew something was missing. How could I be a believer and follower of Christ if my natural instinct was to curse and grumble? So I started to look for what was missing. I searched for answers, but it seemed like I had all the bases covered: believe, tithe, serve—yet nothing in my nature changed. It was like trying to hit a moving target when I didn't even know how to aim!

I remember telling God I was ready to know what to do, but I think it was more of a demand than a prayer: "God, what are you waiting for? Let's get on with this!"

It took awhile, but I noticed that many of my church friends always seemed to be kind and patient when something went wrong. They reached out with empathy rather than blame. They offered assistance or support as needed. And they always prayed.

That all seemed to make sense to me, but I made only a cursory attempt to figure it out. As you might expect, nothing really changed.

Then, near the end of July 2008, our church needed some custodial help while a few of the regulars were out. I remember thinking that was way below my status, but I begrudgingly volunteered to take a shift. During Sunday worship on July 27, 2008, I ran into the retired former head custodian. I jokingly told him I was going to take his old job and asked him, "How do you handle this?"

He told me he considered his custodial job to be a ministry, and that he was working for God: "If Christ can die on a cross for me, I can surely clean up a church for him."

His words hung in the air and surrounded me when I heard them. And then it happened. I felt hot, cold, empty, and full inside all at the same time. I knew that I needed to be a custodian. I spoke to one of the pastors about it, and he said, "This is a real answer to prayer."

I went from volunteer to permanent custodian and have been at it ever since. My service at church was easy and fulfilling. At the same time, problems became situations to help; situations became opportunities to do something; my chores became acts of service. People began to appreciate and count on my help at church, and most problems disappeared when I had a positive approach.

I realized God had used a custodian to open my eyes and heart to his fullness. I no longer have to be in control or follow the Keith Plan—not only in church, but in all areas. It's a real joy to wait on God to take charge of a problem and then follow his lead.

So, when people ask me how I am "fixed with the Lord," I tell them I am filled with the Spirit, and I let God take charge of things. Then I gratefully accept when he solicits my help.

I never did hit that moving target. It hit me.

Evangelism and Human Need

*For if the Gentiles have shared in the Jews' spiritual blessings, they owe
it to the Jews to share with them their material blessings. So after I have
completed this task and have made sure that they have received this
contribution, I will go to Spain and visit you on the way.*
Romans 15:27–28

Doris's words spilled out. She and her daughter Sylvia had been serving at
the rescue mission, and there, they had met Fidel. He once worked at a local
restaurant and lived in a room there. But at age forty-six, diabetes took its
toll, and one of Fidel's legs had to be amputated. With that, he lost his job and
his housing. That day, Doris asked if our Sunday school class could join with
others to raise the $4,400 to buy a prosthetic leg for Fidel.

Our class, which aims to bring people into relationship with Christ and
help them grow as his disciples, had just finished giving our Christmas offering. Above their regular giving, class members raised more than $2,600 for
the education of children in Peru, Bangladesh, and Ethiopia. Would they be
able to give again?

Later that week, when Doris and Sylvia told Fidel that the class had already raised $674 for his leg, Fidel wept and said, "Thank you, thank you."

Paul, on his evangelistic journey to Spain through Rome, took joy in
meeting Jerusalem's physical needs with loving service. Likewise, our Sunday
school class, on its journey of evangelism and discipleship, took joy in meeting
Fidel's need. Today, Doris, Sylvia, Fidel, the rescue mission nurse, and the
members of our class are all overflowing with thanks to God.[205]

Sent to Save the World

---

205. Previously published in *Reflecting God* June–July–August 2010 (Kansas City, MO:
WordAction Publishing Co.), 17. Used by permission.

For God did not send his Son into the world to condemn the world,
but to save the world through him.
John 3:17

My parents rarely went to church, but they thought I should go to Sunday school. The neighbor girl went to Sunday school, so my mom dropped the two of us off at church, and the neighbor picked us up after Sunday school. The next week, the two mothers would reverse roles. Some Sundays one mother would do both—drop us off and pick us up.

One Sunday, as we came out of Sunday school, no mother was present to pick us up. The little girl, who was six, considered herself quite mature. She announced, "I know the way home. We'll just walk." I was only five, and I had no idea of the way home.

Our homes were two miles directly east of the church. She took my hand and began walking south on Main Street, into the heart of the city. Meanwhile, my mother began to wonder why it was taking so long for me to get home. She called the neighbor and asked, "Did you pick the kids up yet?"

"No," the neighbor replied, "I thought you were picking them up."

My mom immediately went to the police station to report two missing children. As my frantic mother stood in the station filing her report, she looked out the window and saw two little children walking down Main Street. She rushed out, called to us, hurried over, and hugged us. She did not condemn us but loved us and held us. She saved us. Within twenty minutes, everyone was safely home and rejoicing.

In God's book, there is no mystery about his plan for you, me, or the world: "For God did not send his Son into the world to condemn the world, but to save the world through him." Do you get it? God sent his Son to save the world.

Isaiah, Jeremiah, and the other Old Testament prophets preached. The law thundered down from the mountain; judgment fell when people rebelled. The sin-damaged and sin-warped world convulsed to throw great waves or mighty winds; humanity, who had left God out, did evil to one another, demonstrating the awfulness of sin. John the Baptist spoke up. Great Christ followers like Peter and Paul emerged to lead the way. God used every possible element he could to alert us, awaken us, put up detour signs, stop us from driving off the cliff, and point us to Christ. He is the way, the truth, and the life (John 14:6). Christ is trying to save the world, and he is God's plan to do it. God does not have a back-up or alternate plan—this is it. "There is no other name under heaven . . . by which we must be saved" (Acts 4:12)—only Jesus Christ.

Christ came in humility, grew to maturity, and began to preach and teach. He healed the blind and the lame; he cast out demons; he raised the dead; he taught us to love, to care, to forgive, to serve. He died on the cross for the forgiveness of our sins and was raised from the dead. He is now praying for us at the right hand of the throne of God in heaven, and he is coming back to earth.

Now, he asks us to do the following:

- Turn from our damaging and damning sins
- Open our hearts and lives to him
- Receive him as the forgiver of all our sins
- Follow him as the leader of our lives
- Yield our whole life to him
- Be filled and sanctified by his Holy Spirit
- Revel in a life of meaning, abundance, joy, significance, love, and fulfillment
- Tell others the way
- Bring people with us into his glorious heaven

People may pledge themselves to sin and condemnation, but God is doing everything he can to bring people to the one saving Christ. Once more: "For God did not send his Son into the world to condemn the world, but to save the world through him."

If you wonder why, here's the answer: "For God so loved the world that he gave his one and only Son, that whoever believes in him shall not perish but have eternal life" (John 3:16).

The Presence of God

And I will ask the Father, and he will give you another advocate to help you and be with you forever—the Spirit of truth. . . . On that day you will realize that I am in my Father, and you are in me, and I am in you.
John 14:16–20

As revealed in many Old Testament passages, the presence of God came to his people in awesome and even frightening ways. For instance, when the ark of the covenant was brought into Solomon's temple, this happened: "When the priests withdrew from the Holy Place, the cloud filled the temple of the

LORD. And the priests could not perform their service because of the cloud, for the glory of the LORD filled his temple" (1 Kings 8:10–11).

God came in a less threatening way when Jesus came to earth. Even then, there was no shortage of the glory of the Lord. Ordinary shepherds experienced it firsthand: "An angel of the Lord appeared to them, and the glory of the Lord shone around them, and they were terrified. But the angel said to them, 'Do not be afraid. I bring you good news. . . . A Savior has been born to you. . . . You will find a baby wrapped in cloths and lying in a manger'" (Luke 2:9–12). A baby—they could handle that.

When the baby grew to adulthood, we saw the loving and powerful ministry of Jesus Christ. He spent a lot of time trying to help his disciples understand God the Father. As he was preparing to leave the earth, he said to Philip, "Don't you believe that I am in the Father, and that the Father is in me?" (John 14:10).

Then Jesus promised he would not leave the disciples as orphans. He promised to send an advocate, the Spirit of truth, to be with them forever: "On that day you will realize that I am in my Father, and you are in me, and I am in you" (14:20). When the Holy Spirit, the Advocate, takes possession of your heart, the Father and the Son are there too. The Father, Son, and Spirit—the presence of God—lives *in* you.

No wonder Jesus said, "Anyone who loves me will obey my teaching" (14:23). How natural that the indwelling presence of Father, Son, and Holy Spirit results in a life of obedience.

Christmas, the Wicked, and the Good

When Herod realized that he had been outwitted by the Magi,
he was furious, and he gave orders to kill all the boys in Bethlehem
and its vicinity who were two years old and under, in accordance
with the time he had learned from the Magi.
Matthew 2:16

The first Christmas included an unusual combination of wicked and good. Matthew 2:11–12 tells the story of wise men who came to Jesus Christ: "On coming to the house, they saw the child with his mother Mary, and they bowed down and worshiped him. Then they opened their treasures and presented him with gifts of gold, frankincense and myrrh. And having been warned in a dream not to go back to Herod, they returned to their country by another route."

But then there was a wicked response to this joyous birth. Matthew 2:16 records, "When Herod realized that he had been outwitted by the Magi, he was furious, and he gave orders to kill all the boys in Bethlehem and its vicinity who were two years old and under."

This battle goes on today—even this Christmas, in our world. I saw it in Newport, Oregon, during revival services. We experienced an unusual moving of the Holy Spirit, and numbers of people came forward to pray. A woman named Gail was one of them. Gail had an active imagination. She created places in her mind where she could go to pray. If she had thoughts she shouldn't have, she sequestered them in "the dungeon" of her mind. The problem is that, after a while, the dungeon can get full of bitterness, slights, hurts, pain, and resentment. During the Monday night service she told me, "Last night I gave him the dungeon and he cleaned it out. I slept the soundest I have in a long time. I am more free today."

I know Gail is only one person in a big and troubled world, but week by week, in special services presenting the good news of Christ, and by the ministry and witness by many Christians, people are being changed. Adding them all up makes a huge difference.

Today King Herod is dead and dishonored, while Jesus, the Savior, is alive forevermore and worshiped by millions. And Gail is free—and so are many like her.

Despite the difficulties you may face, remember this Christmas that Jesus will have the last word.[206]

Christmas . . . as "Fulfilled"

So was fulfilled what was said through the prophets,
that he would be called a Nazarene.
Matthew 2:23

---

206. Previously published in *The Good News: The Chic Shaver Center for Evangelism Newsletter* (December 2008).

Isn't it intriguing how often the word "fulfilled" is part of the Christmas story? Here are a few examples:

- Matthew 1:22–23—"All this took place to *fulfill* what the Lord had said through the prophet: 'The virgin will conceive and give birth to a son.'"
- 2:15—"And so was *fulfilled* what the Lord had said through the prophet: 'Out of Egypt I called my son.'"
- 2:17–18—"Then what was said through the prophet Jeremiah was *fulfilled*: 'A voice is heard in Ramah, weeping and great mourning.'"
- 2:23—"He went and lived in a town called Nazareth. So was *fulfilled* what was said through the prophets, that he would be called a Nazarene."

These instances are evidence of the reality of Jesus's birth and life, the truth of Scripture, the trustworthiness of God, and the authority of the biblical message. Yet I am looking for another of Jesus's *fulfillments*:

- 24:44—"So you also must be ready, because the Son of Man will come at an hour when you do not expect him."

We are fulfilled when we have made Christ the center of our lives. This Christmas, may you enjoy all the benefits of the first fulfilled promises and be ready for the one that is yet to come.[207]

A Baby in a Manger: The King in His Glory

So Christ was sacrificed once to take away the sins of many;
and he will appear a second time, not to bear sin,
but to bring salvation to those who are waiting for him.
Hebrews 9:28

If the first Christmas was the baby in the manger, could this Christmas be the King in his glory?

In regular Bible reading, I've been impacted by a number of proclamations about Christ's return. See below for some of these verses:

---

207. Previously published in *The Good News: The Chic Shaver Center for Evangelism Newsletter* (December 2010).

- Hebrews 9:27–28—"Just as people are destined to die once, and after that to face judgment, so Christ was sacrificed once to take away the sins of many; and he will appear a second time, not to bear sin, but to bring salvation to those who are waiting for him."
- Titus 2:11–14—"For the grace of God has appeared that offers salvation to all people. It teaches us to say 'No' to ungodliness and worldly passions, and to live self-controlled, upright and godly lives in this present age, while we wait for the blessed hope—the appearing of the glory of our great God and Savior, Jesus Christ, who gave himself for us to redeem us from all wickedness and to purify for himself a people that are his very own, eager to do what is good."
- 2 Thessalonians 1:7–10a—"[God will] give relief to you who are troubled, and to us as well. This will happen when the Lord Jesus is revealed from heaven in blazing fire with his powerful angels. He will punish those who do not know God and do not obey the gospel of our Lord Jesus. They will be punished with everlasting destruction and shut out from the presence of the Lord and from the glory of his might on the day he comes to be glorified in his holy people and to be marveled at among all those who have believed."

For further study, read 2 Timothy 4:1–2, 1 Thessalonians 4:16–17, and 2 Peter 3:9–13.

I'm ready![208]

Happy Birthday, Jesus!

*Then they opened their treasures and presented him with
gifts of gold, frankincense and myrrh.*
Matthew 2:11

From the east, the wise men followed Jesus's star and came to worship him, bearing expensive gifts. Since then, the world has given relatively little to Jesus—but look at what he has given to the world:

---

208. Previously published in *The Good News: The Chic Shaver Center for Evangelism Newsletter* (December 2016).

- "She will give birth to a son, and you are to give him the name Jesus, because he will save his people from their sins" (Matthew 1:21).
- "Today in the town of David a Savior has been born to you; he is the Messiah, the Lord. . . . 'Glory to God in the highest heaven, and on earth peace on those on whom his favor rests'" (Luke 2:11, 14).
- Jesus: "I have come that they may have life, and have it to the full" (John 10:10).
- Jesus: "My Father's house has many rooms . . . I am going there to prepare a place for you" (John 14:2)
- Jesus: "You may ask for anything in my name, and I will do it" (John 14:14).
- Jesus: "Peace I leave with you; my peace I give you" (John 14:27).
- Jesus: "Whoever drinks the water I give them will never thirst" (John 4:14).
- John: "For God so loved the world that he gave his one and only Son, that whoever believes in him shall not perish but have eternal life" (John 3:16).

It was his birthday, but he has turned out to be the biggest giver of gifts. I've seen him give some of these gifts, such as eternal life, and life to the full. I saw these gifts come to Bill, Keith, Laura, Dennis, Frank, Peggy, Rachel, Paul, and Miriam.

How Can It Be?

Be reconciled to God. God made him who had no sin to be sin for us,
so that in him we might become the righteousness of God.
2 Corinthians 5:20–21

I always wondered: How can it be that another could take on the cost and responsibility of my sin? I had no problem with the truth that "all have sinned and fall short of the glory of God" (Romans 3:23). I saw that in my own life and in the world around me. And in light of the total holiness of God, I realized that "the wages of sin is death" (Romans 6:23). I mean, what else would you expect? But I found it far harder to accept how another could assume the cost and responsibility of *my* sin.

My son, Paul, was sixteen or seventeen, and I was taking a Sunday afternoon nap. As I slept, Paul sneaked out of the house, took my car without my permission, and picked up his buddy. Contrary to my urging to keep Sunday holy, they took in a pro basketball game. On the way home, Paul ran a yellow light as it was turning red and collided with another car.

Upon arriving home, he sheepishly said, "Dad, I wrecked the car, but I'll pay for it." At the time, we had liability insurance but not collision coverage. The other car and passenger injuries were paid for, but we'd have to shell out big bucks for our car's repairs.

If I remember correctly after all these years, I think my son paid five dollars toward the car repairs. I assumed all the other costs, legal negotiations, paperwork, and insurance discussions. I took on all the cost and responsibility of my boy's sin so he could go free, move forward, and become an influence for good in the lives of others.

If I can absorb the consequences of my son's sins, then I understand (and rejoice) that Christ would take my sin upon himself and so change me that I could, in him, become the righteousness of God.

DECEMBER 25 **359**

He Had a Dream

But after he had considered this, an angel of the Lord appeared to him in a dream and said, "Joseph son of David, do not be afraid to take Mary home as your wife, because what is conceived in her is from the Holy Spirit."
Matthew 1:20

Embarrassed by his fiancée's pregnancy, he did not know what to do—especially since he knew he was not the father. Then he had a dream, and an angel of the Lord spoke to him: "Joseph son of David, do not be afraid to take Mary home as your wife, because what is conceived in her is from the Holy Spirit. She will give birth to a son, and you are to give him the name Jesus, because he will save his people from their sins" (Matthew 1:20–21).

Do you know how long Joseph had to wait to see the dream of Jesus saving people from sins come true? You and I get to see what Joseph didn't.

A few days ago, at an Ohio church, I saw Samantha weeping and praying. She told me, "I had a boulder on me—now I feel light as a feather. I'm one hundred percent for the Lord!" The boulder-bearing Jesus saved her from her sins.

This Christmas, I have some dreams—personal dreams, family dreams, big-world dreams. My biggest dream is that the forgiving, freeing Jesus will bring a major spiritual movement that produces witness, evangelism, revival, and holiness across the churches and our tattered world.

I'm sure you have dreams this Christmas too. May your biggest and best dreams come true. Joseph's did![209]

He Will Turn the Lights On

The true light that gives light to everyone was coming into the world.
John 1:9

Yet to all who did receive him, to those who believed in his name,
he gave the right to become children of God.
John 1:12

It was a college ritual—if you joined certain fraternities, you'd have to endure a period of initiation. The most dreaded event was the brothers taking you for "a ride." One night, my roommate, Al, rushed to our dorm door and locked it. He shouted, "They're coming!"

It was no use; they came in through the fire escape. They tied our hands, put pillowcases over our heads, and shoved us into a car. They drove, making many turns along the way, then stopped. Finally, they removed the pillowcases from our heads, took us out of the car, then drove off.

We were in a large, open field in the pitch-black dark, and I recognized nothing. I was uneasy.

Thankfully, Al spoke up: "I know where we are. I've been here before."

Whew! A little glimmer of hope. At the end of the field, we started down a crunchy gravel road. As we passed each farmhouse, watchdogs barked and ran toward us. Every time, we heard the snap of a restraining chain.

---

209. Previously published in *The Good News: The Chic Shaver Center for Evangelism Newsletter* (December 2009).

Eventually, there was a little more light. Soon we saw the lights of our town. Before long, we were back in our room, and the bright lights were on.

Jesus Christ is the lights-on Savior. In John's Gospel, the word "light" is used twenty-one times. In John 8:12, Jesus is "the light of the world;" in John 1:9, Jesus "gives light to everyone." That includes you.

If you've ever been in a dark place in your life, you might feel like you don't know what to do. It might be a big decision; the death of a loved one; poor health; financial pressure; a broken relationship; joblessness; an uncertain future; the state of society; separation from God. For all these dark places, he offers the greatest light-producing event of your life: "To all who did receive him, to those who believed in his name, he gave the right to become children of God" (John 1:12).

I had known Jesus only a few days when we sang "O Little Town of Bethlehem" in the college chapel service. The lyrics spoke to me as never before:

> Yet in thy dark streets shineth
> The everlasting Light
> The hopes and fears of all the years
> Are met in thee tonight

And then,

> O holy Child of Bethlehem
> Descend on us, we pray
> Cast out our sin, and enter in
> Be born in us today[210]

Christ will turn the lights on for you.

A Picture toward Sanctification

The person without the Spirit does not accept the things that come from the Spirit of God but considers them foolishness, and cannot understand them because they are discerned only through the Spirit.
1 Corinthians 2:14

---

210. Phillips Brooks (words) and Lewis H. Redner (music), "O Little Town of Bethlehem," *Sing to the Lord: Hymnal* (Kansas City, MO: Lillenas Publishing Company, 1993), #169.

*Brothers and sisters, I could not address you as people who live
by the Spirit but as people who are still worldly—mere infants in Christ.
I gave you milk, not solid food, for you were not yet ready for it.
Indeed, you are still not ready. You are still worldly.
For since there is jealousy and quarreling among you,
are you not worldly? Are you not acting like mere humans?*
1 Corinthians 3:1–3

We're going to look at some images to understand the stages of Christian life and how to move into the sanctified life. In today's scriptures, Paul is addressing the Christians in the Corinthian church. The circles below represent the three groups of people he describes, as well as the lives of people today:

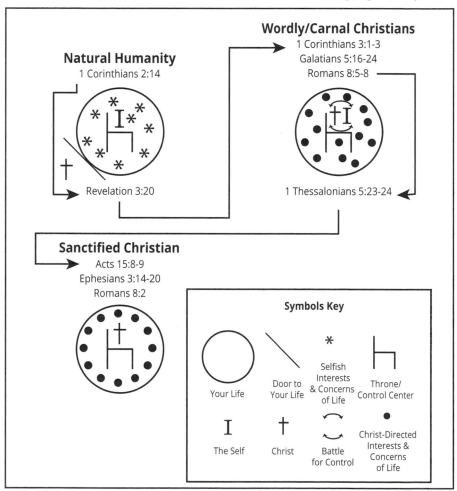

Natural Humanity
1 Corinthians 2:14
Revelation 3:20

Wordly/Carnal Christians
1 Corinthians 3:1-3
Galatians 5:16-24
Romans 8:5-8
1 Thessalonians 5:23-24

Sanctified Christian
Acts 15:8-9
Ephesians 3:14-20
Romans 8:2

Symbols Key

○ Your Life

╲ Door to Your Life

* Selfish Interests & Concerns of Life

⊓ Throne/Control Center

I The Self

† Christ

↶↷ Battle for Control

● Christ-Directed Interests & Concerns of Life

The natural human does not accept what comes from the Spirit. Rather, they live by their own natural human resources. The circle represents life; the throne is the seat of control in a person's life. The big "I" on the throne is self-centeredness. The asterisks (interests of life) are expressions of the core control—the big "I." They are meant to look like distorted circles, and they could be financial life, social life, work life, home life, religious life, and more. In one person's life, the biggest outward expression of sin could be party animal; in another's, it could be worship of money. Sinful expressions will be different for different people. The cross represents Christ knocking at the door of the heart. After resistance, finally this person says yes to Christ and invites him into their heart, as in Revelation 3:20.

A new life begins. Christ moves to the throne—the center of control. The interests of life become more balanced. Yet, after a while, this Christian discovers an internal battle. The big "I" doesn't want to give up control, and a battle for control erupts. This battle is explained in Galatians 5:16–24 and Romans 8:5–8. There may be internal manifestations of jealousy or outward quarrels. This is a worldly, or carnal, Christian.

This troubled Christian senses that there must be something better. After hearing that God can sanctify a person through and through, this person seeks God. When the person trusts the God of 1 Thessalonians 5:23–24, Christ takes full control of the throne, and the self-centered big "I" is cast out. God's keeping power maintains this Christian. Built on 1 Thessalonians 5:23–24, Acts 15:8–9, Ephesians 3:14–20, Romans 8:2 and 4, this is the spiritual—or sanctified—Christian.

Which circle most represents your present life? Which circle is most like the life you would like to have?

Chad's Distress

But I see another law at work in me, waging war against the law of my mind and making me a prisoner of the law of sin at work within me.
Romans 7:23

What is it like to be sanctified, filled with the Spirit? How does it happen? Here is how it happened to a young man named Chad, in his own words:

At age twenty-four, I graduated with my Doctor of Pharmacy degree and started my first job as a pharmacist in my hometown. I had a shiny new car, was making decent money, and had a beautiful girlfriend. I attended church as regularly as I could, but it was more of an obligation than anything. Overall, things couldn't have been better. I was as close as I had ever been to living the American dream; however, something big was missing from my life, as I would soon realize.

As my relationship with my girlfriend (now my wife), Celia, became more serious, we began to have deeper conversations about religion. We discovered that our viewpoints were a little different: I was a Baptist, and she was a Nazarene. If I'm totally honest, I had never heard of Nazarenes before, so I immediately saw my viewpoint as superior to hers due to the popularity of my denomination. I believed wholeheartedly that once a person had been saved by God, there was nothing that could change that—not even my lifestyle. In my everyday life, I professed to be a Christian; yet, looking back, I see that my thoughts, behaviors, and actions were not very different from those of the non-Christians around me. I didn't see this as a big deal, because, "We're all human after all!" There was apparent sin in my life, but I was under the impression that there was nothing I could do about it, so I continued along without much thought. However, I came to realize that Celia thought differently: she believed that we are called to live a life that is holy and pleasing to God and that, by the help of the Spirit of God, we can live above willful sin in our lives.

Needless to say, this disagreement quickly became a point of contention in our relationship. That's when I realized that I could solve this problem. Being scientifically-minded, I would research the Bible and gather as much "evidence" as possible to support my viewpoint, then present it to Celia in an indisputable way. I knew for a fact that I was right; I just needed to show her the "proof." Once I did, she would not only be impressed, but the disagreement between us would be resolved. However, when I set out to unearth this "evidence," I soon found something entirely different than what I was looking for.

In my searching, I discovered some recurring themes that I had never noticed before. I came across scriptures such as the following:

- Mark 13:13—"But the one who stands firm to the end will be saved."
- John 15:6—"If you do not remain in me, you are like a branch that is thrown away and withers; such branches are picked up, thrown into the fire and burned."

- Colossians 1:22–23—"You [are] holy in his sight, without blemish and free from accusation . . . IF you continue in your faith, established and firm, and do not move from the hope held out in the gospel."
- Hebrews 10:26—"If we deliberately keep on sinning after we have received the knowledge of the truth, no sacrifice for sins is left."
- 1 John 3:6—"No one who lives in him keeps on sinning."

I could go on and on, but suffice it to say that I became greatly overwhelmed by this clear overarching theme. For years I had only read the Scriptures in bits and pieces, but once I began to delve deeper, I found that this theme of continuing, remaining, and living without sin spanned the entire Bible. It became immediately evident to me that God does not intend for us to continue sinning after we are saved—and that there is much more to this Christian walk than being saved and then waiting on heaven. My original mission had backfired. Instead of finding proof that I was right, I began to see that I was wrong—and I sure dreaded having to admit that to Celia!

After this, I began to feel God's clear call to holiness and a deeper relationship with him. Not coincidentally, I realized during this time that my life needed "cleaning up." I wasn't too awful in the world's view—I didn't abuse drugs or drink alcohol or hurt people. But I struggled with anger, pride, and selfishness, among other things. With this revelation from God, things began to change in my life. I began to get excited about the things of God because for the first time, I realized the importance of a relationship with him. I decided that I would begin to really live for God and hold up my end of this relationship! These were exciting days! However, I soon grew frustrated and annoyed because my efforts would fail. The old saying, "You don't know how bad you are until you try to be good," rang true for me. It seemed that no matter how hard I tried to change my ways, my thoughts, my behaviors, my habits, I couldn't do it with any consistency. I related quite well to Paul's words in Romans 7:18b–19, where he says, "For I have the desire to do what is good, but I cannot carry it out. I do not do the good I want to do, but the evil I do not want to do—this I keep on doing." I failed again and again and again.[211]

---

211. Previously published in *The Good News: The Chic Shaver Center for Evangelism Newsletter* (September 2018).

God's Deliverance

It is God's will that you should be sanctified.
1 Thessalonians 4:3a

because through Christ Jesus the law of the Spirit who gives life
has set you free from the law of sin and death.
Romans 8:2

Chad continues:

Day after day, I grew more and more discontented and angry, until one day, I finally reached a breaking point. I hit my knees in prayer and began to sob uncontrollably. I told God how frustrated I was and how I wanted to live for him, but no matter how hard I tried, I couldn't. I had simply decided that this holy life I had read about was not something I could achieve; it was obviously an impossible mandate, and, in my futile attempts, my heart was broken.

I'll never forget what happened next. It was at this point I heard the Lord whisper to my heart, "No, you can't do it—but I can."

Suddenly, I was overcome with his presence and realized in a moment what I was missing; I was trying to do it all in my strength. I couldn't change myself; I needed him to change me! And so, in that moment, I prayed for more of him. I admitted that I had tried with what strength I could muster, but it wasn't enough—I needed his Spirit to help me. I had reached the end of me, and that's right where I found him waiting. I surrendered my life and my will to the Lord that day—it's a moment that I'll never forget and always treasure.

Later, I would learn that this "surrender" goes by various names: entire sanctification, baptism of the Spirit, second work of grace, etc. But regardless of what you call it, I know this: from that moment on, I have been a totally different man. Something powerful happened to me, and, ever since then, I have hungered for the Lord in ways I never had before. I have communed with him daily and uninterruptedly, and my life was finally "cleaned up"—not by trying harder, but by surrendering to him daily and allowing his Spirit to have his way in my life. The things I struggled with back then just aren't an issue anymore. I'm still walking as closely as I can to him as I'm led by the Spirit, and it's made all the difference in the world in my life. I can definitely reflect back on that moment of crisis when I gave myself fully to God; how-

ever, I also have come to realize that holiness is very much a daily process. It's vital that we reach a moment of surrender—but we must continue to stay surrendered every single day of our lives. I can say wholeheartedly through this experience that the only way to true, lasting spiritual victory is through God's purification of our hearts through sanctification—and he is faithful to do it if we cooperate with his love and grace.

Months later, this desire to go deeper with God began to culminate into a call to ministry. I began to realize how all of this had come together in a way that only God can orchestrate. I had questions for God, obviously, but he has been faithful to answer every one along the way. When I asked him how I was supposed to be a pastor when I had just graduated from pharmacy school, God sent me a retired minister and former pharmacist who was in town for just a few months at just the right time. When I realized I couldn't just quit my job as a pharmacist due to my student loans, God introduced me to a bivocational pastor. I began to realize for the first time that I could be a pharmacist and a pastor, so I continued my pursuit. While I was wrestling with the costs of seminary on top of my pharmacy school loans, God introduced me to another pastor who told me about a program called Course of Study, which would lead me toward ordination in a more cost-effective way than seminary. All along the way, God has answered my questions and doubts.

I'm now an ordained elder in the church, and I currently serve as a bivocational young adult pastor at a church in middle Georgia. I do not know what God has in store for me in the future, but I do know he is already there. His grace is truly sufficient, and, for that, I'm most thankful! To God be the glory![212]

How to Be Sanctified

May God himself, the God of peace, sanctify you through and through. May your whole spirit, soul and body be kept blameless at the coming of our Lord Jesus Christ. The one who calls you is faithful, and he will do it.
1 Thessalonians 5:23–24

---

212. Previously published in *The Good News: The Chic Shaver Center for Evangelism Newsletter* (September 2018).

He was totally joyful! His pastor had asked him to assume a major assignment in his local church—the kind that would take great dedication and very hard work. Now he was not only joyful, but excited—he had to tell somebody.

A while back, Keith, who had been growing in his Christian life, went deeper with the Lord, and God sanctified him through and through. In coming to this place in life, he was experiencing God's great purpose for his life—as one person put it, he was living as "the best version of himself." Above all else, as you seek to be sanctified, remember that this new level of life will give you great joy and fulfillment.

As we have moved through weeks of devotional thoughts, we have discovered that there are a number of biblical terms to describe the deeper Christian life:

- The rest of faith (Hebrews 4:9–11)
- Crucified with Christ (Galatians 2:20)
- Sanctified through and through (1 Thessalonians 5:23)
- Filled with the Holy Spirit (Acts 1:8; 13:9)
- Christ to settle down and be at home in your heart (Ephesians 3:17)

Other terms describe aspects of this life:

- Rivers of living water (John 7:38)
- That they may have life, and have it to the full (John 10:10)

Perhaps you have been longing to enter and enjoy this deeper life. You have wondered what you have to do in order for God to do this work in you. You'll find a number of steps below. Please understand that these steps are not taken in a mechanical way, but rather, are elements of a deep heart-searching for God.

- Concern: You have a deepening concern for God to bring you into this life of victory and fullness. You are praying (Acts 1:12–14; Luke 11:9–10, 13).
- Consecration: You must already be a Christian. You are now offering your whole forgiven life to God 100 percent, to be used by him as he pleases (Romans 6:13; 12:1–2).
- Cleansing: You are asking God to cleanse you, to purify you from any remaining selfishness or self-centeredness (1 John 1:7; Acts 15:8–9; James 4:8).
- Claiming: Claiming the promises of God, you reach out in faith and trust God to sanctify you through and through (Acts 26:18; Galatians 3:14; 1 Thessalonians 5:23–24 [especially lean on verse 24]).

If you sincerely follow these steps in a real time before the Lord, God will sanctify you and fill you with the Holy Spirit. Remember 1 Thessalonians

5:23–24: "May God himself, the God of peace, sanctify you through and through. . . . The one who calls you is faithful, and *he will do it.*" God may search your heart very deeply as you pray like this.

That was true for Cheri. She attended a Tuesday night class I held for the spouses of seminary students. She approached me after class one evening and said she wished I'd given an altar call after the previous week's class because she had been so convicted. As she drove home with another seminary spouse that night, she never heard a word the woman said. She felt she was in another world.

When she got to her apartment, her husband greeted her, but she said, "Honey, I can't talk. I have business to tend to."

In tears, she went to the back bedroom. She shut herself in and prayed into the night. It seemed like the Holy Spirit reached down deep into her heart and pulled up an issue before her. She struggled over the issue, and finally said, "Okay, okay, okay, I give it to you."

Then the Spirit reached into her heart again and brought up another issue. This went on and on until she felt he had pulled out every unclean thing. But the Spirit reached down again and pulled up another issue: *"Cheri, you resent your own husband. I've called him to preach, and I expected you to follow him. Yet you have resented him because, to follow the call, you had to leave your beautiful home and move to a small apartment; you had to leave lucrative jobs and take more ordinary jobs; you had to leave old friends and start with new. You've resented him. It's not right."*

Finally, she said to the Lord, "Okay, I give it to you." And God accepted and sanctified her.

At the next class, she told me, "Oh, Professor Shaver, this week has been so wonderful. I feel so free. The burden is gone—I'm free."

She was totally joyous—yes, she was free. God had removed her resentment and self-centeredness. He had done a miracle in her. He had sanctified her through and through.

Do not fear God's searching you while you pray. The result will be very good, and may even result in your sanctification.

A Time to Pray

Sanctify them by the truth; your word is truth.
John 17:17

I pray that out of his glorious riches he may strengthen you with
power through his Spirit in your inner being, so that Christ may
dwell in your hearts through faith. And I pray that you, being rooted
and established in love, may have power, together with all the Lord's holy
people, to grasp how wide and long and high and deep is the love of Christ,
and to know this love that surpasses knowledge—
that you may be filled to the measure of all the fullness of God.
Ephesians 3:16–19

When they heard this, they raised their voices together in prayer to God.
Acts 4:24a

After they prayed, the place where they were meeting was shaken. And
they were all filled with the Holy Spirit and spoke the word of God boldly.
Acts 4:31

Do not get drunk on wine, which leads to debauchery.
Instead, be filled with the Spirit.
Ephesians 5:18

In light of all you have read and thought about as you've read through this book, perhaps it's time for *you* to pray . . .

- To be sanctified
- To be filled with the Holy Spirit
- To receive a fresh infilling of the Spirit
- To reestablish a continuous life of the Spirit's fullness

Or is it time to thank God that he has done all this for you already? Let's pray!

Scripture Index

OLD TESTAMENT

19:2–4	Sept. 15	2:46–47	Sept. 27
19:10	Aug. 24	3:6	Mar. 29
21:14–15	Mar. 8	3:19	Jan.6, May 17
22:31–32	May 16	4:13	Apr. 23
24:46–49	Dec. 6	4:12	Feb. 20
24:49	May 31	4:20	July 5
		4:24	Dec. 31

John

1:9	Dec. 26	4:31	Apr. 23, Dec. 31
1:12	Dec. 26	5:32	July 17
2:19–22	Oct. 27	6:1–4	Oct. 28
3:3	Feb. 22	6:3	Sept. 29
3:17	Dec. 18	6:5	Apr. 11, Sept. 29
4:6	Sept. 11	7:35	June 8
4:15	Mar. 11	7:55, 59–8:1	May 28
4:34	Feb. 16	7:59–60	Apr. 11
5:17	Oct. 11, Oct. 12	8:18–19	Apr. 30, July 14
5:31–32	Apr. 19	8:27	July 15
6:40	July 31	8:29	Apr. 30, July 14, Sept. 29
6:44	Aug. 23	9:5	Jan. 26
7:37–39	Sept. 25, Nov. 16	9:26–27	Mar. 15
7:38–39	Aug. 11	9:27	Jan. 5
8:12	May 15	10:15	Aug. 2
8:3	Feb. 9	10:19	Aug. 22
8:34	Nov. 25	11:23	Apr. 25
8:44	July 6	11:24	June 20
9.25	Aug. 30	11:25–26	Jan. 5
12:2–3	Mar. 18	16:14	Jan. 26
12:25–26	Jan. 29	16:25–26, 29–30	Jan. 19
14:12	July 7, July 8	18:2–3	June 26
14:16–17	June 5	20:24	June 18
14:16–20	Dec. 19	26:17–18	Nov. 17, Dec. 12
14:21	Feb. 13	26:18	Jan. 6
14:27	Dec. 10		

Romans

15:9–10	May 14	1:4	Apr. 4
15:16	June 23, June 24	1:16	Mar. 9, Aug. 8
16:7	Mar. 3	1:19	Aug. 31
16:13	June 12	2:1	Feb. 2
17:17	Dec. 31	5:3–5	Apr. 16
20:17–18	Apr. 9	5:5	Apr. 22, June 15
		5:15	June 27

Acts

1:4–5	Oct. 22	6:13	Oct. 25
1:8	Feb. 11, Oct. 29	6:14	Nov. 11
2:4	July 24	6:18	Nov. 12
2:14	July 24	7:20	Nov. 27, Nov. 28
2:17	May 20	7:23	Dec. 28
2:19–22	Oct. 27	8:1	Jan. 7
2:37	July 24	8:2	May 22, May 23, July 20, Dec. 29
2:38–39	Jan. 10	8:4	May 24, July 20, July 21
2:42	Sept. 27	8:28–29	July 25

1 Thessalonians

3:10	Dec. 16
4:3	May 12, Dec. 3, 4, 5, 8, 16, 29
4:8	Dec. 16
5:16–18	Aug. 25, Nov. 22
5:23	Nov. 1, Dec. 1, Dec. 2
5:23–24	Dec. 30
5:24	June 7, Nov. 5

2 Thessalonians

1 Timothy

4:12	May 4, Oct. 2

2 Timothy

1:9	May 4
2:20–21	July 23
4:7–8	Apr. 13

Titus

Philemon

1:1–2	Sept. 6
1:6	Sept. 6
1:16	Nov. 30

Hebrews

1:14	Sept. 18
4:8–11	Sept. 8
4:15	June 25
9:28	Dec. 22
10:10	June 30
10:14	June 30
10:23	Aug. 5
10:23–25	Feb. 19
10:35	Apr. 15
12:1–2	July 2
12:14	Aug. 16
13:5	June 11
13:12	Oct. 23

James

1:2–4	.July 13
1:13–16	Dec. 9

1 Peter

2:24–25	Apr. 2
4:7–10	Mar. 6

2 Peter

3:9	June 9
3:10	Aug. 15
3:11–12	June 9
3:18	Feb. 22, Feb. 23

1 John

1:7	Apr. 20, July 29
2:1	Jan. 27, Mar. 12, Nov. 15
3:16–17	May 19
4:4	Jan. 1
4:7	.Mar. 1, Nov. 21
4:9	Apr. 22
4:11	Apr. 22
4:13	Nov. 5
4:18	Feb. 4, Nov. 13
5:13	June 6

2 John

3 John

1:11	Aug. 28

Jude

Revelation

1:5	Oct. 3
1:7	Aug. 15
2:10	Mar. 22
3:19–20	Feb. 25
3:20	Feb. 24
3:21	Jan. 8, Apr. 10
5:5	Oct. 4
11:15	Feb. 10
16:9	Oct. 5
20:12, 15	May 21
21:1	Mar. 28
21:2	Mar. 5
21:3–4	Mar. 28
21:7	Mar. 5, Apr. 14
22:7	Oct. 6